Book 1
1853–1895

Marriages
of
Gloucester
County,
Virginia

Frances Haywood

HERITAGE BOOKS
2016

HERITAGE BOOKS

AN IMPRINT OF HERITAGE BOOKS, INC.

Books, CDs, and more—Worldwide

For our listing of thousands of titles see our website
at
www.HeritageBooks.com

Published 2016 by
HERITAGE BOOKS, INC.
Publishing Division
5810 Ruatan Street
Berwyn Heights, Md. 20740

International Standard Book Numbers
Paperbound: 978-1-55613-717-4
Clothbound: 978-0-7884-6369-3

BOOK 1
Marriages of Gloucester County
Virginia

To make my book as accurate as possible I
spent about eighteen months copying Book 1
of The Marriages of Gloucester County, Va.
It is almost word for word. I have made no
changes.

The book is located in the Clerks Office of
Gloucester County, Va. The Court House
Building is located near the northern border
of the county on State Route 17.

This book covers the years from 1853 to 1895.

Frances Haywood
Frances Haywood

Gloucester County, Virginia is a rural community located in the Tidewater bely of Virginia along the Atlantic seaboard. Take your left hand, open it palm up, spread your fingers, and it will look like a map of Gloucester County. It is one of the counties that make up the Middle Peninsula. It is Bounded on the south by the York River, on the north by the Piankatank River, on the east by the Mobjack Bay, and on the west by the Pororotank Creek. It covers 223 square miles.

It is never severely hot or cold here. It has almost perfect farmlands. Some of the land called "marl", is found in some sections. Marl is a loose crumbly, earthy deposit (as sand, silt, or clay), that contains a substantial amount of calcium carbonate and is used especially as a fertilizer for soils deficient in lime. This makes excellant farm land. "Marlfield", one of the more interesting plantation houses was named because of that soil. Cedar trees were plentiful here. They were used to make furniture, fence posts, fishing gear, etc. Fishing, crabbing, and farming has always been the main source of making a living in Gloucester. At one time, tobacco and silk were grown here. The silk worms were fed leaves from the mulberry trees.
These crops are no longer grown.

At one time, York County and Mathews County were a part of Gloucester. About 1642 York County was named and Gloucester, a happy land, was born. It is believed to have been named for the Duke of Gloucester, son of King Charles. Some say it was named for Gloucestershire, a county in England. The motto for Gloucester and Mathews Counties today is "Fertile Farms on Smiling Waters".

There were four parrishes to begin with: Ware, Peasley, Petsworth, and Kingston. In 1781 Kingston became a part of Mathews.

Walter Reed, the man who is credited with discovering the cause of yellow fever was born in Gloucester County. His birthplace is in the Belroi area and is on the historical list.

Seawell's Ordinary dates back to the 18th century and today there is a restaurant in the building.

Rosewell, early 18th century, seat of the Page families was the largest and finest of the colonial mansions. The Page family helped build Gloucester from the beginning to the present. The mansion burned in 1916. The walls still stand. It was here that Thomas Jefferson wrote the Declaration when he was visiting. Many tourists visit the site.

In 1667 a fort was built with a wall ten feet high and ten feet thick. It had eight great guns and a court of guards.

In 1707 Tyndall's Point became Gloucestertowne.

When the Revolutionary War ended, 1781, British soldiers occupied Gloucester Point.

During the years 1860-1865 John M. Gregory was judge of the court.

The Cooke family was the oldest and most prominent of the early settlers.

On present day Main Street is the Botetourt Hotel. Now it houses office buildings. The building is over 200 yrs. old. Other stores of honorable standing are J. H. Martin, W. C. Tucker, and L. H. Vaughan. The Gloucester Gazette was an unusually good country paper. It is now the Gloucester Mathews Gazette Journal, serving the two counties.

The Confederate monument, located in the center of the court circle, has the names of 132 men who lost their lived in the War Between the States.

Powatan was the King or Emporer of the
Indians in Gloucester. He rules 30 tribes,
8,000 square acres of land, and 8,000
subjects. 2,400 of these were fighting men.
John Smith was taken prisoner by Powatan in
in Gloucester. Powatan's daughter saved
Smith's life by placing her body over his to
protect him from blows that would have
killed him. In 1608 Capt. John Smith sent
Dutch workers to build a house of wood with a
mare chimney for Powatan. This chimney still
stands today on the banks of the York River.
Many people come to the area and visit this
historical site.

In 1608 the earliest map of Virginia by
an English settler was made. The first map
maker was Robert Tyndall. One of the four
locations on this map was designated as
Tyndall's Point, now known as Gloucester
Point. The first land grant was applied for
by Hugh Gwynn in 1635. He was denied. The
second was made by Robert Throchmorton in
1639. The third was by George Memefie in
1639. Col. Augustine Warner received a land
patent of 600 acres located on the Severn
River called Austin's Desire, now Warner
Hall. Col. Warner was to become great grand-
father to George Washington. Warner Hall was
the first house built in 1642.

To mention a few of the historical places
in the county, I will start with Abingdon
Episcopal Church and Ware Episcopal Church.
These churches were started 1692-1715.
Record keeping began around 1677. Long
Bridge Ordinary and the Botetourt Building
were built in 1750. Gloucester Court was
built in 1776. Cappahosic was an Indian
village. The community still goes by that
name and a post office carried the name, too.
It has been discontinued.

The Debtor's prison was built in 1810. During the War Between the States it was used as an arsenal.

Burgh Westra was built in 1855. Holly Knoll, 1855, was built overlooking the York River. Lands End was built in 1776 for John Sinclair, a captain who achieved fame in the Revolutionary War. Little England, dating from the 18th century is a small community in eastern Gloucester county that still keeps the name. Little England was the home of the Perrin family and served as a hospital in the War Between the States.

The Protestant Church was established in 1785.

In 1896, the Roane building was built on the Court Green and was used for a clerks office and local court building. A new building was built in 1956. Today the Roane building is an office for the local judge.

War of 1812 - Points along the York River were protected by the British Fleet. The 4th Regiment of Artillery of the Virginia militia, Sgt, James Baytop's Company under command of Capt. William A. Rogers went to Capt. John Sinclair's in Robins Neck as the enemy vessels were there.

In 1863 large Federal forces ransacked Gloucester county and carried off horses, farm animals, and poultry. They burned every barn and grist mill in the county.

Gloucester's most distinguished soldier in the Civil War was Gen. William Booth Taliaferro. The most distinguished Naval officer was Capt. Thomas Jefferson Page.

In 1865 William H. Ashe bought the Yorktown-Gloucester ferry franchise to run the first ferry between the two counties across the York River. The first ferry was named Cornwallis.

1865-1870. Gloucester was under Federal Rule.
Education came in 1675. Henry Peasley bequeathed 600 acres of land for the education of children of Abingdon and Ware Parishes forever. In 1991 a new school was built and named for him.
Today, most of the people in lower Gloucester County, known as Guinea, make their living from the surrounding waters. Although fishing has died out with the older generation, crabbing and clamming are abundant.Farming is still carried out in the upper parts of the county.
Route 17, which goes through the entire length of the county has shopping centers and businesses all the way.
All in all, we are still a rural community. We are getting a water line and sewage systems are being put in. Private wells and the old fashiones outhouses are a thing of the past. Gloucester County is one of the garden spots of the world. Come and visit.
This information was taken from a book written by Clementine Rhodes Bowman. It is titled, Gloucester County, Virginia, A History. It was printed in the United States of America by McClure Printing Co, Inc. of Verona, Va. 1982. The Library of Congress Catalog Card Number is 82-81290.

Geo. W. Jenkins, ae 23y, farmer, s/o
Edmund & Mapy Jenkins; Susan Howard, ae 22y,
d/o Thomas & Martha Howard; Aug ? 1853 by
Rev. W. S. Hawkins.

Philip H. Dutton, ae 26y, farmer, s/o
Henry Dutton; Lucy Ann Mallory, ae 15y, of
King and Queen Co VA, d/o Edward Mallory;
Sept 22 1853 by Rev. Archer Bland.

Wm. T. Mouring, widower; Elizabeth Minor;
Oct 6 1853 by Rev. A. F. Scott.

James H. South, ae 21y 1m, carpenter;
Jane B. C. Mallory, ae 17y, d/o Edward T.
Mallory; Nov 24 1853 by Rev. A. F. Scott.

Elias Dungee, ae 23y, colored, laborer,
of Middlesex Co VA, parents unknown; Julia
Dungee, ae 21y, colored, d/o Mary Dungee;
Dec 18 1853 by Rev. Thomas M. Hundley.

William E. Gaines, ae 34y, doctor, of
Essex Co VA, s/o John & Matilda Gaines; Ann
B. Callis, ae 14y, d/o Lewis B. & Elizabeth
Callis; Dec 22 1853 by Rev. Archer Bland.

Elijah Jenkins; Mary Belvin, widow,
Dec 20 1853 by Rev. W. S. Hawkins.

Thomas Lewis; Lavinia Bray; Dec 21 1853
by Rev. W. S. Hawkins.

Samuel B. Chapman, ae 26y, clerk, s/o
Henry & Sarah C. Bristow Chapman; Harriet B.
Davis, ae 16y, d/o Warner O. & Elizabeth C.
Bridges Davis; Dec 22 1853 by Rev. Archer
Bland.

John Perrin Belvin, ae 19y, waterman, s/o
John & Maria Belvin; Mary Walker, ae 16y,
d/o John & Polly Walker; Jan 16 1854 by Rev.
W. S. Hawkins.

Vincent Jenkins Jr, ae 22y, farmer, s/o
Vincent & Dier Jenkins; Georgianna Hogg, ae
18y, d/o Warner & Susan Hogg; Jan 20 1854 by
Rev. W. S. Hawkins.

Rev. John Bailey, ae 39y, minister of the
gospel at M. E. Church South, of ENGLAND,
s/o William & Ann Bailey; Elizabeth Lee
Robins, ae 22y, d/o Joseph H. & Catharine C.
Robins; Dec 20 1853 by Rev. J. H. Davis.

William Norton, ae 24y; Catharine Bristow
Norton, ae 22y; Jan 12 1854 by Rev. Wm. E.
Davis.

James Soles, ae 35y, widower, farmer, s/o
James & Lucy Bristow Soles; Harriet Didlake,
ae 37y, widow, d/o Benjamin & Harriet Miller
Didlake; Mar 18 1854 by Rev. Archer Bland.

Brley Coats, ae 44y, widower, farmer, s/o
John S. & Jane Horseley Coats; Lucy Coats,
ae 44y, widow, d/o John & Mary Puller Coats;
Feb 19 1854 by Rev. Archer Bland.

John M. West, ae 23y, s/o Isaac & Harriet
Roane West; Harriet A. Newcomb, ae 24y, of
King and Queen Co VA, d/o John & Lucy Roane
Newcomb; Apr 1 1854 by Rev. Archer Bland.

Uriah Wroten, ae 39y, widower, farmer, of
Dorchester Co MD, s/o Steavon & Elizabeth
Willey Wroten; Mary Ann Lawson, ae 33y,
widow, d/o James & Eleanor Rilee Lawson;
Apr 8 1854 by Rev. Archer Bland.

James H. Newcomb, ae 29y, farmer, of King
and Queen Co VA, s/o William & Nancy Groom
Newcomb; Hester F. Bowden, ae 19y, d/o John
& Sarah Roane Bowden; June 15 1854 by Rev.
Archer Bland at New Hope Meeting House.

Spencer Roane, ae 21y, farmer, s/o Chas.
Roane Jr. & Mary Dutton; Susan J. Adams, ae
17y, of King and Queen Co VA, d/o William F.
& Lucy Deagle Adams; Apr 12 1854 by Rev.
Archer Bland at Wm. F. Adams'.

Alfred Huckstep, ae 36y, widower, farmer,
of King William Co VA, s/o James S. &
Elizabeth Jackson Huckstep; Elizabeth A.
Easter, ae 23y, d/o William & Sary Bristow
Easter; Apr 22 1854 by Rev. Archer Bland at
John F. Bristow's.

Paulin A. Blackburn, ae 23y, farmer, of
Middlesex Co VA, s/o Paulin A. & Ann S.
Blackburn; Betty Ann Burke, ae 26y, of
Caroline Co VA, d/o John M. & Sophia F.
Burke; Apr 20 1854 by Rev. R. A. Christian.

Thomas r a Wise, ae 34y, widower, oysterman, of Mathews Co VA, s/o John & Sarah
Wise; Diana Barbary Green, ae 40y, widow, of
York VA, d/o Robert & Diana Shroud; June 3
1854 by Rev. W. S. Hawkins at Wm. Dudley's.

James M. Carmines, ae 21y, oysterman, s/o
Smith R. & Elizabeth M. Carmines; Margaret
Ann Fosque, ae 19y, of Accomac Co VA, d/o
Nathaniel & Margaret Ann Fosque; June 7 1854
by Rev. W. S. Hawkins at Jane Croswell's.

John Cary Robins, ae 22y, farmer, s/o Wm.
& Elizabeth C. Robins; Fanny W. Thurston, ae
23y, d/o Chas. B. & Fanny P. Thurston; June
21 1854 by Rev. W. S. Hawkins at Benjamin
Seawell's.

Thomas Rich Kemp, ae 23y, oyster, s/o
Peter B. & Sarah Kemp; Elizabeth Seawell, ae
21y, d/o Benja. & Elizabeth Seawell; July 18
1854 by Rev. W. S. Hawkins at Benja.
Seawell's.

James K. Horseley, ae 25y, widower, farm,
s/o Kilingham & Eliza Tonlin Horseley;
Martha A. Hibble, ae 26y, d/o Lewis & Elizabeth Martin Hibble; July 13 1854 by Rev.
Archer Bland at John Watkins'.

Jesse H. Bloodsworth, ae 28y, waterman,
of Somerset MD, s/o Nathan & Margaret
Bloodsworth; Ann H. Stubblefield, ae 18y,
d/o Henry & Susan Stubblefield; Aug 8 1854
by Rev. Jas. Baytop at Thomas W. Campbell's.

James H. Brown, ae 25y, farm, s/o John F.
& Mary A. Brown; Lucy Ann Didlake, ae 21y,
d/o Philip & Mary Ann Didlake; Sept 27 1854
by Rev. Jas. Baytop at Mrs. Frances Care's.

Henry C. Palmer, ae 54y, widower, farm,
of Northumberland Co VA, s/o David & Nancy
Condiff Palmer; Mary Moby Duval, ae 39y, of
Tarboro N. C, d/o Francis & Elizabeth S.
Curtis Duval; Oct 4 1854 by Rev. Thos. B.
Evans.

Robert H. Dutton, ae 27y, farm, s/o
Lorenzo & Frances F. Chapman Dutton; Mary
Ann Purcell, ae 15y, d/o Jos. & Eliza Thrift
Purcell; Oct 4 1854 by Rev. Archer Bland at
Salem.

William B. Guthrie, ae 23y, farm, s/o
Major & Martha Guthrie, of King and Queen Co
VA; Susan Elizabeth Graves, ae 22y, d/o John
& Frances Graves; Dec 20 1854 by Rev. William
A. Robinson at Timberneck.

James H. Bentley, ae 25y, widower, ship
carpenter, s/o Jas. H. & Mary Bentley;
Harriet Gayle, ae 25y, of Mathews Co Va, d/o
Zelotes & Eliza Gayle; Sept 18 1855 by Rev.
P. A. Peterson at Zelotes Gayle's.

Benjamin King, ae 26y, free person of color, blacksmith, s/o Benjm. Brooken & Ruthy King; ---, ae 17y, free person of color, d/o Elija & Dinah Hayes; Sept 16 1855 by Rev. P. A. Peterson at Elizabeth Howard's.

William Hogg, ae 45y, widower, oysterman, s/o Daniel & Catharine Hogg; Mildred Reynolds, ae 36y, widow, d/o John & Milsey Hogg; Oct 3 1855 by Rev. W. S. Hawkins at Mrs. Oliver's.

Robert Hill, ae 27y, ditcher, of King and Queen Co VA, s/o Robert & Virginia Hill; Elizabeth Robinson, ae 17y, d/o Louisa Robinson, father unknown; Sept 6 1855 by Rev. W. S. Hawkins.

John Harvey, ae 35y, widower, oysterman, s/o Smith & Frances Harvey; Susan Robins, ae 21y, d/o Jesse & Chitty Robins; Aug 26 1855 by Rev. W. S. Hawkins at Thos. Kemp's.

John Walden, ae 51y, widower, farmer, lived in King and Queen Co VA, s/o Wm. & Catharine Wiatt Walden; Louisa J. Booker, ae 30y, d/o Louis C. & Polly Ware Booker; June 28 1855 by Rev. Archer Bland at Overton Kemp's.

Lewis T. Booker, ae 30y, farmer, s/o Lewis C. & Polly Ware Booker; Lucy F. Fary, ae 19y, d/o Thomas & Sarah Row Fary; Aug 22 1855 by Rev. Archer Bland at Thos. Hogg's.

James F. Mersereau, ae 22y, engaged in oyster business, of Staten Island N. Y, s/o David N. V. S. & Emma Mersereau; Emiline Lucas, ae 23y, d/o Hill & Lucy Lucas; Nov 8 1855 by Rev. P. A. Peterson at Lucy Lucas'.

James C. Graves, ae 25y, engaged in oyster business, lived in Norfolk VA, s/o John & Frances T. Graves; Susan C. Davis, ae 19y, of Mathews Co VA, d/o James & Mary B. Davis; Nov 14 1855 by Rev. P. A. Peterson at Matilda Croswell's.

Edward Hart, ae 33y, mechanic, of New York City N. Y, s/o James & Isabella Hart; Elizabeth Catharine Hall, ae 20y, d/o Lorenzo & Catharine Hall; Dec 26 1854 by Rev. W. S. Hawkins at John White's.

James Daniel White, ae 33y, mechanic, s/o
Richard & Elizabeth White; Charlotte
Elizabeth Wallington, ae 23y, of Nashville,
Tenn, d/o Sterling & Elizabeth Wallington;
Jan 2 1855 by Rev. W. S. Hawkins at John
White's.

John Wm. Puller, ae 21y, farmer, s/o
Lawrence & Mary Puller; Emily Simcoe, ae
28y, d/o Henry & Ann Simcoe; Jan 4 1855 by
Rev. W. S. Hawkins at William White's.

Levi Thomas, ae 27y, wood cutter, s/o
Levi & Elizabeth Thomas; Sarah Ann Thomas,
ae 21y, d/o Jesse & Nancy Thomas; Jan 18
1855 by Rev. W. S. Hawkins at Jesse Thomas'.

Wm. Revel Heywood, ae 22y, oysterman, s/o
James C. & Mary Heywood; Virginia Elizabeth
Hobday, ae 21y, d/o William & Ann Hobday;
Jan 18 1855 by Rev. W. S. Hawkins at Wm.
Hobday's.

James H. Marchant, ae 23y, merchant, of
Mathews Co VA, s/o Thomas & Mary Marchant;
Lucy A. Dobson, ae 21y, d/o Edward & Lucy C.
Dobson; Jan 22 1855 by Rev. A. F. Scott.

William Bayse, ae 26y, merchant, of
Northumberland Co VA, s/o William & Harriet
Bayse; E. Johnston, ae 22y, d/o Lewis F. &
Ann Johnston; Feb 1 1855 by Rev. A. F. Scott.

Geo. E. Shackelford, ae 21y, saddle and
harness maker, s/o Wm. & Eliza Shackelford;
Martha A. Martin, ae 21y, lived with Wm. R.
Stubbs, d/o John & Maria D. Martin; Mar 22
1855 by Rev. P. A. Peterson at Wm. R. Stubbs.

Joseph Coleman Tilledge, ae 31y, widower,
oysterman, s/o John & Mary Ann Tilledge;
Georgianna Belvin, ae 14y, of York Co VA,
d/o John & Ann Belvin; Feb 22 1855 by Rev.
W. S. Hawkins at Thomas Oliver's.

William Olison Finis, ae 23y, seaman, s/o
of Westmoreland Co VA, s/o Wm. & Catharine
N. Finis; Sarah Williams, ae 22y, d/o Thos.
C. & Joanna Williams; Mar 21 1855 by Rev. W.
S. Hawkins at Elizabeth Ambrose's.

Edward T. Beverage, ae 21y, waterman, s/o
Wm. & Elizabeth Beverage; Virginia Walden,
ae 25y, of Middlesex Co Va, d/o Robert &
Nancy Walden; Mar 21 1855 by Rev. A. F.
Scott.

William Denton, ae 22y, waterman, of
ENGLAND, lived Gloucester Co VA, s/o James &
Sarah Denton; Susan Ann Edwards, ae 38y, d/o
John & Sarah West; Dec 11 1855 by Rev. W. S.
Hawkins at Mrs. Edwards'.

James Mattox, ae 21y, waterman, s/o John
& Matilda Mattox; Mary E. Woodland, ae 19y,
d/o Wm. & Mary Woodland; Dec 25 1855 by Rev.
Wm. A. Robinson at Abberdeen.

W. H. Martin, ae 20y, coach maker, s/o
John & Mary Martin; Mary M. Kemp, ae 17y,
d/o Wm. & Mary Kemp; Jan 7 1855 by Rev. P.
A. Peterson at Wm. R. Stubbs.

John L. Blake, ae 35y, widower, farmer,
of Middlesex Co VA, s/o W. C. & S. P. Blake;
Matilda E. Johnston, ae 30y, d/o John &
Nancy Johnston; Apr 16 1855 by Rev. A. F.
Scott.

John S. Brown, ae 23y, overseer (farmer),
s/o John S. & Mary A. Brown; Martha A.
Pitts, ae 24y, of King and Queen Co VA, d/o
Benjm. & Catharine Pitts; Aug 7 1855 by Rev.
P. A. Peterson at Sam'l P. Enos'.

Robert P. Bagby, ae 50y, widower, land
and pension agent, of King and Queen Co VA,
lived City of Richmond VA, s/o Rich'd
& Susanna Jeffries Bagby; Mary F.
Cluverious, ae 35y, d/o Benjamin & Sally
Cluverious; Aug 20 1855 by Rev. A. F. Scott.

James H. Bently, ae 25y, widower, ship
carpenter, s/o James H. & Mary C. Bently;
Harriet Gayle, ae 25y, of Mathews Co VA, d/o
Zelotes & Eliza Gayle; Sept 18 1855 by Rev.
P. A. Peterson at Zelotes Gayle's.

Lewis Hogg, ae 38y, farmer, s/o Lewis &
Leah Hogg; Martha Ellen Hall, ae 22y, d/o
Wm. Polly Hall; Oct 25 1855 by Rev. W. S.
Hawkins at Mrs. Polly Hall's.

Thomas Sampson Oliver, ae 44y, widower,
farmer, s/o Wm. & Susan A. Oliver; Sarah
Turlington, ae 26y, widow, d/o Wm. & Susan
Brown; Nov 30 1855 by Rev. W. S. Hawkins at
William Brown's.

Eleaner Philpots, ae 23y, capt. of
vessel, s/o John Philpots; Rosa A. Sale, ae
19y, of Mathews Co VA, d/o John Sail; Jan 25
1855 by Rev. Wm. Eastwood.

Waid Stubblefield, ae 33y, merchant, s/o
Waid Stubblefield; Maria Leigh, ae 27y,
widow, d/o Dolly Hughes; July 3 1855 by Rev.
Wm. Eastwood at Charter Creek.
  Thomas F. A. Aherron, ae 31y, widower,
lived an Caffee's Land, Capt. of vessel, s/o
Thos. & Harriet Aherron; Harriet Aherron, ae
30y, lived at Thos. Hughes, d/o Frank &
Malvina Stubblefield; July 18 1855 by Rev.
Wm. Eastwood at Belomys Church.
  Edward Belvin, ae 24y, Capt. of vessel,
of York Co VA, s/o Thomas & Harriet Aherron;
Harriet Aherron, ae 19y, d/o Wm. & Harriet
Aherron; Oct 11 1855 by Rev. Wm. Eastwood at
Belomys Church.
  Elijah Easter, ae 21y, blacksmith, s/o
Wm. & Sarah Easter; Frances Heath, ae 21y,
d/o Joseph & Frances Heath; Dec 18 1855 by
Rev. W. E. Davis at Oak Lawn, Gloucester VA.
  Edward Williams, ae 47, widower,
farmer, of Middlesex Co VA, s/o Carter &
Mary Williams; Rebecca P. Guthrie, ae 39y,
of Surry Co VA, d/o Henry S. &. Sally
Guthrie; Dec 15 1855 by Rev. A. F. Scott.
  Thomas B. Montague, ae 38y, widower,
farmer, of Richmond VA, s/o Wm. & S. M.
Montague; M. A. B. Jones, ae 46y, widow, of
King William Co VA, d/o Joseph & Sarah A.
Pollard; Oct 28 1855 by Rev. A. F. Scott at
Marlfield, Gloucester Co VA.
  Cary West, ae 25y, oysterman, s/o Francis
& Rachel West; Ellen V. Cox, ae 17y, of
Hampton/Elizabeth City Co VA, d/o John &
Susan Cox; Dec 1 1856 by Rev. Wm. E. Wiatt
at Gloucester Court House VA.
  Robert C. Crew, ae 22y, painter, s/o John
& Miley A. Crew; Hester A. Proctor, ae 22y,
d/o James H. & Elizabeth Proctor; Sept 4
1856 by Rev. J. L. Garrett at Belomys Church.
  Robert T. Boss, ae 24y, farmer, of
Middlesex Co VA. s/o John J. & M. A. Boss;
Bettie G. Gibbs, ae 28y, d/o Mathew &
Elizabeth Gibbs; Dec 26 1855 by Rev. A. F.
Scott.
  John Willis, ae 23y, farmer, of King and
Queen Co Va, s/o John & Patsy Willis; Sarah
E. Harwood, ae 21y, d/o Christopher & Juliet
Harwood; Feb 27 1856 at Rev. Eastwood.

John A. Harwood, ae 50y, widower, farmer, s/o Horatio G. & Mary Harwood; Parke Pharley Clements, ae 23y, lived at Burley, d/o Robert G. & Jaza A. P. Clements; Dec 25 1855 by Rev. Wm. A. Robinson at Burley.

Theophilus Richardson, ae 20y, merchant, of New Kent Co VA, s/o John & Mary Richardson; Clarisa Hayes, ae 23y, d/o Joel & Margaret Hayes; Dec 6 1856 by Rev. P. A. Peterson at Woodville in Gloucester Co VA.

John A. Ward, ae 23y, seaman, of Somerset Co MD, s/o Wm. E. & Patsy Ward; Elizabeth J. Davis, ae 19y, d/o David & Frances Davis; Dec 27 1855 by Rev. H. Billups at John White's.

John W. Shackelford, ae 31y, widower, oysterman, s/o James & Mary Ann Shackelford; Matilda M. Travillian, ae 26y, d/o James & Mary Ann Travillian; Jan 25 1856 by Rev. J. L. Garrett at Mary Ann Travillian's.

Thomas W. Banks, ae 23y, farmer, s/o Wm. & Martha Banks, Margaret E. T. Baytop, ae 20y, d/o James & Lucy Baytop, Dec 25 1855 by Rev. Wm. Eastwood at James Baytop's Springfield.

James Henry Brown, ae 25y, widower, farmer, s/o John S. & Mary A. Brown; Ann Elizabeth Kiningham, ae 21y, d/o John & Nannie Kiningham; Jan 2 1856 by Rev. W. S. Hawkins at Wm. Hogg's.

John William Lillaston, ae 28y, waterman, of Accomac Co VA, s/o Elijah & Ann F. Lillaston; Lucy Jane Diggs, ae 24y, d/o Alexander & Frances Diggs; Jan 25 1856 by Rev. W. S. Hawkins at Alexander Diggs'.

Benjamin Michell Lewis, ae 27y, oysterman, s/o Wm. & Rebecca Lewis; Martha Allen Jenkins, ae 20y, d/o Harwood & Susan Jenkins; Jan 31 1856 by Rev. Wm. S. Hawkins at Mr. Lewis'.

Warner Washington Hern, ae 37y, widower, lumber getter, of Mathews Co VA; Elizabeth Tillege, ae 34y, widow, d/o Edmund & Fanny Tillege; Feb 17 1856 by Rev. Wm. S. Hawkins at Benja. Seawell's.

John Padgett, ae 25y, farmer, s/o John &
Mary Buckner Padgett; Maria Elliot, ae 19y,
d/o Richard & Mary Padgett Elliot; Feb 7
1856 by Rev. --- at Wm. Haynes.

William J. Massey, ae 20y, farmer, s/o
Robert Randel & Frances L. Kemp Massey; Mary
Elizabeth Bohannon, ae 20y, d/o John & Susan
Hall Bohannon; Feb 7 1856 by Rev. Archer
Bland at John Wilson's.

George D. Rilee, ae 26y, widower, black-
smith, s/o Thomas R. & Susan Lamberth Rilee;
Sarah A. Fary, ae 22y, d/o Thomas & Sarah
Row Fary; Mar 8 1856 by Rev. Archer Bland at
Thomas Fary's.

Richard Hall, ae 34y, waterman, s/o John
& Ann Hall; Rebecca Lewis, ae 68y, widow,
d/o William & Elizabeth Pippin James; Mar 4
1856 by Rev. W. S. Hawkins at Mrs. Lewis'.

Hoalder Croswell, ae 50y, widower,
farmer, s/o Wm. & Nancie Croswell; Mary
Blake, ae 35y, widow, d/o Sam & Milsey
Minor; Mar 15 1856 by Rev. W. S. Hawkins at
Mr. Pierce's.

William Purcell, ae 25y, oysterman, s/o
John & Eliza Purcel; Julia Seawell, ae 17y,
d/o Benjamin & Mary Seawell; Apr 7 1856 by
Rev. W. S. Hawkins at Benja. Seawell's.

John M. Rilee, ae 39y, shoemaker, s/o
Louis F. & Elizabeth Soles Rilee; Caroline
V. Foster, ae 19y, of Mathews Co VA, d/o
Augustin & Elizabeth Pew Foster; Apr 8 1856
by Rev. Archer Bland at John Walker's.

John W. Leigh, ae 24y, merchant, s/o
Caleb & Elizabeth C. Leigh; Emily Julia
Hughes, ae 20y, d/o Jasper C. & Frances A.
Hughes; Mar 25 1856 by Rev. P. A. Peterson
at Jasper Hughes'.

John F. Boswell, ae 26y, oyster and farm,
of King and Queen Co VA, s/o Wm. & Catharine
Boswell; Sarah A. Dunston, ae 27y, d/o
Dennis & Ann M. Dunston; Apr 3 1856 by Rev.
P. A. Peterson at Mrs. Ann Dunston's.

Wm. Yates Massey, ae 51y, widower,
farmer, s/o Robert Y. & Rebecca Massey;
Harriet A. Hackney, ae 49y, widow, d/o Wm.
& Susanna Foster; May 15 1856 by Rev. P. A.
Peterson at Lawrence S. Stubbs.

Lewis Hall, ae 21y, carpenter, s/o Lewis
& Catharine Hall; Martha Ann Enos, ae 23y,
d/o Francis & Catharine Enos; May 29 1856 by
Rev. P. A. Peterson at Susan Enos'.

Henry Burges, ae 25y, cord wainer, of
Lenington ENGLAND, s/o Robert & Sarah
Burges; Maria F. Ransone, ae 25y, d/o James
& Lucy Ransone; Apr 15 1856 by Rev. A. F.
Scott.

William D. Griffin, ae 23y, blacksmith,
s/o Henry & Martha Griffin; Mary A. Griffin,
ae 17y, d/o Thos. & Maria F. Griffin; May 6
1856 by Rev. P. A. Peterson at Maria F.
Griffin's.

William Benson King, ae 21y, oysterman,
s/o James & Susan King; Nancy Jenkins, ae
22y, d/o Margaret Jenkins, father unknown;
May 7 1856 by Rev. W. S. Hawkins at Peyton
Smith's.

Philip Gard Thomas, ae 32y, widower,
mechanic, of Portsmouth VA, s/o John & Susan
Thomas; Sarah Virginia Spaulding, ae 22y,
d/o John & Priscilla Spaulding; May 13 1856
by Rev. W. S. Hawkins at Wm. Freeman's.

John Belote, ae 33y, farmer, of Accomac
Co Va, s/o George & Elizabeth Heath Beloat;
Fanny Carr, ae 32y, d/o John & Mary Fuller
Carr; July 17 1856 by Rev. Archer Bland at
John Coats'.

William A. Stubblefield, ae 23y,
carpenter, s/o Simon & Martha Davis
Stubblefield; Sarah A. Corr, ae 25y, widow,
d/o Jesse & Sarah Padgett Fary; July 24
1856 by Rev. Archer Bland at Sarah Corr's.

John R. Cutchin, ae 22y, mariner, of Isle
of Wight Co VA, s/o Nathaniel & Lidia
Cutchin; Emiline M. Hobday, ae 19y, d/o Wm.
& Nancy Hobday; Sept 25 1856 by Rev. John R.
Wade.

James T. Croswell, ae 29y, widower,
tailor, s/o Holder Croswell; Sarah T.
Fleming, ae 19y, d/o James T. Fleming; Sept
25 1856 by Rev. Wm. E. Wiatt at Mrs. Ann
Robins'.

Lemuel Ambrose, ae 22y, farmer, s/o Wm.
Ambrose; Emily Lawson, ae 16y, d/o James &
Nelly Riley Lawson; Sept 23 1856 at Nelly
Lawson's. No Rev. listed.

John S. Brown, ae 24y, widower, farmer,
s/o John S. & Mary A. Brown; Rosia F.
Williamson, ae 17y, d/o James & Martha
Williamson; Nov 1 1856 by Rev. P. A.
Peterson at Elizabeth Pointer's.

Francis Rancies, ae 22y, farmer, of
Middlesex Co VA, s/o Dudley & Edna West
Rancies; Nancy Hodges, ae 25y, d/o Richard &
Ellen Hackney Hodges; Jan 3 1857 by Rev. W.
D. Howard at Sarah Bridges'.

John T. Brister, ae 50y, widower, farmer,
s/o Jno. & Lucy Bristow Brister; Nancy
Wiatt, ae 30y, widow, of Mathews Co VA, d/o
Jno. & Frances Hudgins Drisgall; June 23
1856 by Rev. W. D. Howard at Nancy Wiatt's.

John Blake, ae 28y, farmer, of Middlesex
Co Va, s/o Jno. & Joanna Lenge Blake; Mary
L. Bentley, ae 24y, d/o James H. & Mary E.
Bentley; Sept 11 1856 by Rev. Thomas C.
Howard.

John Richard Hogg, ae 21y, oysterman, s/o
Wm. & Patsy Hogg; Sarah Foxwell, ae 22y, d/o
Soloman & Nancy Ann Foxwell; Dec 3 1856 by
Rev. W. S. Hawkins at Nancy Ann Foxwell's.

Edward C. Dutton, ae 41y, widower,
farmer, s/o Henry & Elizabeth Dutton; Sarah
E. Kemp, ae 23y, d/o Gregory & Susan F. W.
Kemp; Sept 23 1856 by Rev. P. A. Peterson.

John Randolph Page, ae 28y, physician,
s/o Mann & Ann Jones Page; Delia Bryan, ae
22y, d/o John R. & Elizabeth Bryan; Oct 30
1856 by Rev. Chas. Mann, Rector of Ware and
Abingdon Parrishes at Eagle Point, residence
of the bride.

John Franklin Rowe, ae 23y, merchant, s/o
Sterling & Frances Rowe; Rachel Frances
Smith, ae ae 23y, d/o Armistead & Patsy Smith;
Dec 9 1856 by Rev. W. S. Hawkins.

Vincent Hogg, ae 25y, waterman, s/o
Vincent & Nancy Hogg; Martha Ann Lewis, ae
25y, d/o Henry & Charlotte Lewis; Dec 25
1856 by Rev. W. S. Hawkins at Fayette
Cluverious'.

Edward Fields, ae 27y, oystering, s/o
Jno. & Betsy Fields; Margaret Hogg, ae 17y,
d/o Jno. & Julia Hogg; Dec 30 1856 by Rev.
William E. Wiatt.

James Rob't Claytor, ae 20y, coach maker,
s/o John James & Elizabeth Claytor; Rebecca
Ann Adams, ae 20y, of Mathews Co VA, d/o
Geo. W. & Matilda M. Adams; Dec 25 1856 by
Rev. J. L. Garrett at Geo. W. Adams'.

Joseph Leah, ae 23y, waterman, of
PENNSYLVANIA, s/o Joseph & Adaline Leah;
Harriet Banks, ae 37y, widow, d/o James &
Elsy Powers; Nov 24 1856 by Rev. Wm.
Eastwood at John D. Foster's.

Richard Micure, ae 29y, overseer, of King
and Queen Co VA, s/o James & Nancy Micure;
Emoline Booker, ae 25y, Dec 1 1856 by Rev.
Wm. Eastwood at Salem Church.

Michael Hibble, ae 20y, farmer, s/o
Mathew & Letty Hibble; Emiline Booker, ae
17y, d/o Harry & Nancy Booker; Dec 23 1856
by Rev. Wm. Eastwood at Salem Church.

Augustine Dunston, ae 24y, farmer, s/o
Richard & Julia Dunston; Anna Dunston, ae
19y, d/o Willy & Harriet; Dec 24 1856 by
Rev. Wm. Eastwood at Joseph Lear's.

Benjamin Dudley, ae 25y, farmer, of King
and Queen Co VA, s/o Thos. & Patsy Dudley;
Sarah Gressitt, ae 22y, d/o John & Louisa
Gressitt; Dec 25 1856 (No Rev. listed) at
Rowland Fletcher's.

William R. Leavitt, ae 28y, merchant, s/o
Charles & Ann Leavitt; Henrietta Bridges, ae
18y, d/o Richard & Caroline Bridges; Jan 8
1857 by Rev. Wm. Eastwood at Rich'd Bridges'.

James W. Gibbs, ae 34y, farmer, s/o
Matthew & Elizabeth Gibbs; Julia A. Hughes,
ae 27y, widow, d/o Wm. & Ann Leavitt; Dec 18
1856 by Rev. A. F. Scott.

Andrew Carter Crittenden, ae 22y,
merchant, of King and Queen Co VA, s/o
Richard H. & Mary Crittenden; ---, ae 17y,
of King and Queen Co VA, d/o John & Mary
Summerson; Dec 25 1856 by Rev. A. F. Scott.

William J. Thrift, ae 26y, farmer, s/o
Jeremiah & Mary A. Thrift; Catharine E.
Jones, ae 22y, d/o Lewis & Elizabeth Dutton
Jones; Nov 25 1856 (No Rev. Listed) at Wm.
J. Thrift's.

Thomas Kelly, ae 21y, ditcher, waterman, farmer, s/o Allen & Courtney Dennis Kelly; Mary E. Dungy, ae 20y, d/o Henry & Nancy Dungy; Aug 18 1857 by Rev. Wm. G. Foster.

Aaron Spragg, ae 22y, waterman, of Ocean City N. J, s/o Charles & Julia Spragg; Charlotte Pippin, ae 15y, s/o Richard & Charlotte Pippin; July 27 1857 by Rev. W. S. Hawkins at Mrs. Pippin's.

John Edward Davis, ae 22y, mechanic, of Portsmouth VA, s/o David & Frances Davis; Elizabeth Frances Thomas, ae 19y, d/o Jesse & Nancie Thomas; Sept 17 1857 by Rev. W. S. Hawkins at Jesse Thomas'.

John R. Potter, ae 26y, farmer, of Middlesex Co VA, s/o John R. & Eliza Mathis Potter; Harriet J. Banks, ae 23y, d/o Jno. & Frances Mildred Hobday Banks; Feb 10 1857 by Rev. Archer Bland at Abraham Satterwhite's.

William Nelson Purcell, ae 40y, widower, farmer, s/o Wm. & Charity Purcell; Joanna Enos, ae 22y, d/o Francis & Catharine Enos; Mar 4 1857 by Rev. W. S. Hawkins at Mrs. Enos'.

John Green, ae 24y, oysterman, s/o Geo. & Nancie Green; Anna West, ae 19y, d/o Christopher & Nancie West; Mar 5 1857 by Rev. W. S. Hawkins at Benjamin Seawell's.

John Wm. Newton, ae 29y, waterman, s/o Jno. & Nannie Newton; Myra Ann Harris, ae 13y, d/o John & Elizabeth Harris; Mar 13 1857 by Rev. W. S. Hawkins at Mr. Jordan's.

Joseph West, ae 24y, oysterman, s/o Christopher & Frances West; Ann C. Deal, ae 34y, d/o Geo. & Susan Brown; Mar 26 1857 by Rev. W. G. Walker at Rev. Walker's.

Charles E. C. Booker, ae 21y, farmer, s/o James & Elizabeth Booker; Frances Dutton, ae 18y, d/o John W. & Sarah Ann Dutton; Feb 4 1857 by Rev. Wm. Eastwood at Locust Grove.

Thomas Freeman, ae 23y, s/o William & Catherine Freeman; Maria Curry, ae 14y, d/o Sowersby & Mary Curry; Feb 11 1857 by Rev. Wm. Eastwood at Sowersby Curry'.

Robert Dee Miller, ae 26y, farmer, s/o James & Mary Miller; Maria G. Thornton, ae 20y, d/o Francis & Harriet E. Thornton; Mar 12 1857 by Rev. A. F. Scott.

James Shackelford, ae 23y, oysterman,
s/o George & Elizabeth Shackelford; Ella
Adaline Walker, ae 21y, d/o Mead & Maria
Walker; Dec 21 1857 by Rev. W. S. Hawkins
at Mrs. Walker's.

William Smith, ae 23y, oysterman, s/o
Wm. & Dolly Smith; Mary Catharine Thompson,
ae 30y, widow, d/o Wm. & Elizabeth Ransone;
Dec 26 1857 by Rev. W. S. Hawkins at Mrs.
Thompson's.

Thomas Newton, ae 21y, oysterman, s/o
Thos. & Virginia Newton; Elizabeth Ann
Jenkins, ae 15y, d/o Edmund & Ann Jenkins;
Dec 31 1857 by Rev. W. S. Hawkins at Mr.
Belvin's.

James William Hogg, ae 22y, farmer, of
York Co VA, s/o Wm. & Sarah Hogg; Cornelia
Hayes Hogg, ae 19y, d/o Richard & Catharine
Hogg; Dec 29 1857 by Rev. W. S. Hawkins at
Mrs. Hogg's.

Christopher West, ae 30y, oysterman, s/o
Christopher & Fannie West; Winnie West, ae
24y, d/o Christopher & Jane West; Apr 10
1857 by Rev. W. G. Walker at Rev. Walker's.

William Bonawell, ae 22y, oysterman, of
Accomac Co VA, s/o Wm. & Elizabeth Bonawell;
Susan Jenkins, ae 16y, d/o Isaac & Dolly
Jenkins; May 15 1857 by Rev. W. G. Walker
at Rev. Walker's.

Smith Hall, ae 45y, farmer, s/o Jno. &
Nancy Hall; Sarah Rowe, ae 35y, widow, d/o
John & Mildred Hall; Dec 21 1857 by Rev.
W. G. Walker.

James Smith, ae 22y, oysterman, s/o
Anthony & Charlotte Ann Smith; Mary Jane
Hogg, ae 21y, d/o James & Rosa Hogg; Dec 23
1857 by Rev. W. G. Walker at Rev. Walker's.

Simon Green, ae 23y, oysterman, d/o Geo.
& Nancy Green; Susan Ann Oliver, ae 23y, d/o
Thos. & Catharine Oliver; Dec 25 1857 by
Rev. W. G. Walker at Rev. Walker's.

James Leigh, ae 21y, merchant, s/o Caleb
& Elizabeth Leigh; Fanny J. Harwood, ae 17y,
d/o John A. & Emiline Harwood; Dec 16 1857
by Rev. Wm. A. Robinson at Seth Pointer's.

George E. Richardson, ae 26y, farmer, of
James City Co VA, s/o Allmand & Sarah P.
Richardson; Lucy B. Lane, ae 19y, of Mathews
Co VA, d/o J. H. & Ann P. Lane; Mar 11 1857
by Rev. A. F. Scott.

John A. Bridges, ae 23y, farmer, s/o
Robertson & Ann R. Bridges; Florida S.
Stubblefield, ae 20y, d/o Thomas M. &
Elizabeth Stubblefield; Apr 30 1857 by Rev.
A. F. Scott.

John Baylor Foster, ae 29y, farmer, of
King and Queen Co VA, s/o James & Fanny
Douglas Foster; Lucy Ann Kemp, ae 38y,
widow, of King and Queen Co VA, d/o Sterling
& Ann Corr; May 19 1857 by Rev. John
Spencer.

Claiborne T. Roane, ae 27y, mechanic, s/o
Chas. & Mary B. Roane; Lucy F. Chapman, ae
21y, d/o Wm. & Frances Chapman; May 24 1857
by Rev. Jacob Shengh at Woods Cross Roads.

William H. Howlett, ae 26y, waterman, s/o
Henry & Sarah Howlett; Elizabeth Walden, ae
18y, d/o Robert & Frances Walden; June 10
1857 by Rev. Jacob Shengh at Thos. H.
Wilkins'.

William C. Fary, ae 49y, widower, farmer,
s/o Wm. & Frances Elizabeth Fary; Rosay Ann
E. Solds, ae 17y, d/o Wm. & Lucy Ann Solds;
July 4 1857 by Rev. Wm. Eastwood at Salem
Church.

Uriah Kelly, ae 27y, mechanic, s/o Jesse
(slave) & Mary Kelly; Mary West, ae 24y, d/o
John West & Sally Scoot; June 18 1857 by
Rev. Thomas C. Howard.

Benjamin Rowe, ae 50y, widower, farmer,
s/o Edward & Tabitha Rowe; Margaret A.
Glass, ae 31y, of Baltimore Md, d/o Andrew
& Sarah C. Glass; Sept 15 1857 by Rev. Sam'l
Walker.

Franklin Shackelford, ae 32y, widower,
merchant, s/o Wm. & Eliza Shackelford; Parke
F. Harwood, ae 25y, widow, d/o Ro. Y. &
Josey Clements; Sept 3 1857 by Rev. Jacob
Shengh at Burleigh, Gloucester Co VA.

Washington Robins, ae 26y, mechanic, s/o
Thos. & Elizabeth Robins; Nannie Thomas, ae
18y, d/o Jesse & Nancie Thomas; Nov 4 1857
by Rev. W. S. Hawkins.

Henry C. Shackelford, ae 35y, widower, harness maker, s/o Warner & Hannah Shackelford; Lilly Ann Wilkins, ae 37y, widow, d/o Richard & Elizabeth Coleman; Dec 15 1857 by Rev. Joshua L. Garrett at the bride's res.

Andrew J. Cottee, ae 22y, farmer, s/o Catharine Cottee; Catharine A. Adams, ae 18y, of Somerset Co MD, d/o Sam'l & Jane Adams; May 30 1857 by Rev. Stephen D. Howard at Capt. Sam'l Adams'.

Albert Norton, ae 27y, tailor, s/o Geo. & Eliza Norton; Betsy Hodges, ae 27y, d/o Richard & Ailsy Hodges, Dec 19 1857 by Rev. A. F. Scott.

Thomas J. Catlett, ae 29y, merchant, s/o Temple G. & Martha S. Catlett; Margaret A. Hackney, ae 21y, of King and Queen Co Va, d/o John G. & Elizabeth Hackney; Dec 17 1857 by Rev. James Baytop at Locust Grove.

Cyrus T. Fletcher, ae 33y, merchant, s/o Henry & Rebecca Fletcher; Mira A. Amory, ae 20y, d/o Dennis & Anna Amory; Dec 22 1857 by Rev. A. F. Scott.

Albert Dutton, ae 21y, mechanic, s/o John W. & Sary Ann Dutton; Mary Ann Fletcher, ae 16y, d/o Rowland & Frances Ann Dutton Fletcher; Dec 23 1857 by Rev. Wm. Eastwood at Rowland Fletcher's.

Cornelius R. Coats, ae 22y, farmer, s/o Belchy & Ann Riley Coats; Avery Riler Hosley, ae 25y, d/o Kilingham & Elizabeth Soussen Hosley; Jan 5 1858 by Rev. Archer Bland at James Soles'.

William T. Pointer, ae 24y, merchant, s/o Michael S. & A. B. Harwood Pointer; Fanny Dixon, ae 17y, d/o Anthony T. & Margaret West Dixon; Jan 7 1858 by Rev. Wm. A. Robinson at A. T. Dixon's.

James Norton, ae 25y, farmer, s/o Zacriah & Frances Norton; Frances Bristow, ae 21y, d/o Richard & Mary Proctor Bristow; Jan 13 1858 by Rev. Stephen D. Howard at Mary Bristow's.

Joseph H. Robins, ae 24y, oysterman, s/o Jesse & Mary Robins; Mary Rowe, ae 18y, d/o Joseph & Frances Rowe; Jan 15 1858 by Rev. W. G. Walker at Rev. Walker's.

Elijah Easter, ae 23y, widower, black-
smith, s/o Wm. & Sarah Easter; Virginia Ann
Drumon, ae 14y, d/o John Prosser & Hetty
Drumon; Jan 26 1858 by Rev. Jas. Bayton at
Edward Easter's.

William Shackelford, ae 31y, widower,
farm, s/o Wm. & Lucy D. Burn Shackelford;
Mary E. Nuttall, ae 20y, d/o Iverson & Lucy
D. Bristow Nuttall; Jan 28 1858 by Rev.
Stephen D. Howard at Lucy Nuttall's.

James Franklin Padgett, ae 30y, farm, of
King and Queen Co VA, s/o Fleming & Susan
Padgett; Martha Ann J. Fletcher, ae 27y, d/o
Wm. & Sarah Fletcher; Feb 20 1858 by Rev. J.
L. Garrett at Sarah R. Hall's.

Machen Jenkins, ae 30y, oyster, s/o Reed
& Nancy Jenkins; Dicey Jenkins, ae 23y, d/o
Winston & Priscilla Jenkins; Feb 27 1858 by
Rev. W. G. Walker at Rev. Walker's.

John T. Gwynn, ae 24y, farm and merchant,
of Freeport Gloucester Co VA, s/o Chas. R. &
Mary Gwynn; Mary Cary Thruston, ae 20y, d/o
Chas. Thruston; Dec 23 1857 by Rev. Chas.
Mann, Rector of Abingdon and Ware Parrishes.

Samuel Norman Hudgins, ae 23, waterman,
of Mathews Co VA, s/o John & Emily Hudgins;
Sarah Emma Parker, ae 19y, of Accomac Vo VA,
d/o Thos. & Mary Parker; Feb 2 1858 by Rev.
W. S. Hawkins at Capt. John Auld's.

Benjamin Hogg, ae 23, farm, s/o Warner &
Susan Hogg; Dolly Belvin, ae 23y, d/o Geo.
& Fannie Belvin; Feb 11 1858 by Rev. W. S.
Hawkins at Benja. Seawwell's.

Bailey Jenkins, ae 23y, farm, s/o Armistead & Rebecca Jenkins; Emily Frances West,
ae 19y, d/o Christopher & Ann West; Feb 18
1858 by Rev. W. S. Hawkins at Benja.
Seawell's.

Beverly Randolph Wellford, Jr, ae 29y 9m
21d, attorney-at-law- of Fredericksburg VA,
s/o Beverly Randolph & Mary Alexander Wellford; Susan Seddon Taliaferro, ae 28y 4m 4d,
of Belle Ville Gloucester Co VA, d/o Warner
Throckmorton & Leah Seddon Taliaferro; Mar
3 1858 by Rev. Chas. Mann at Belle Ville.

George Brewer, ae 28y, merchant, of Annapolis Md, s/o The Honorable Nickolas Brewer and wife; Lucy H. Tabb, ae 28y, of Toddsbury Gloucester Co VA, d/o Thomas & Eliza Tabb; Mar 4 1858 by Rev. Chas. Mann at The Exchange, residence of J. K. Dabney.

James M. Cruser, ae 32y, capt. or master of vessel, of Staten Island N. Y, s/o Cornelius C. & Susan Crockrene Cruser; ---, ae 22y, d/o Abram Satterwhite; Mar 18 1858 No Rev. listed at Abram Satterwhite's.

Zachariah Dews, ae 54y, widower, farmer, s/o John & Frances Dews; Mary Ann E. Wilkins, ae 39y, d/o Nathan & Ann Wilkins; Mar 21 1858 by Rev. J. L. Garrett.

John E. Turlington, ae 20y, waterman, of Accomac Co VA. s/o Edward & Sarah E. Turlington; ---, ae 16y, d/o Thos. S. & Lucy Ann Oliver; Apr 1 1858 by Rev. Jacob Shengh at Thos. Oliver's.

Thomas B. Blake, ae 29y, farmer, s/o Thos. & Elizabeth Blake; Eliza R. Coleman, ae 19y, d/o Carter & Elizabeth Coleman; Apr 15 1858 by Rev. Jacob Shengh at John Coleman's.

Robert Haywood, ae 24y, tailor, s/o Thos. & Eliza Haywood; Mary A. Shackelford, ae 20y, d/o Geo. & Elizabeth Shackelford; Apr 19 1858 by Rev. Jacob Shengh at John A. Shackelford's.

Henry S. Proctor, ae 27y, farmer, s/o Drenry & Elizabeth Proctor; Elizabeth F. Massey, ae 17y, d/o Chas. & Mary Massey; May 22 1858 by Rev. James Baytop at Clayborne Hudgins'.

John R. Willis, ae 26y, widower, farmer, of King and Queen Co VA, s/o John & Patsy Bowden Willis; Mary E. Hall, ae 22y, of King and Queen Co VA, d/o Thos. B. & Sarah E. Clarke Hall; June 3 1858 by Rev. Archer Bland at Sarah E. Hall's.

Henry Hansford Ambrose, ae 23y, oyster-man, s/o Michael & Elizabeth Ambrose; Margaret Callis, ae 18y, of Mathews Co VA, d/o Daniel & Nancy Callis; June 17 1858 by Rev. W. S. Hawkins at Wm. Lemmon's.

William Y. Massey, ae 22y, farmer, of
King and Queen Co VA, s/o B. Y. & Catharine
Massey; Martha Rowe, ae 22y, d/o Robert &
Caroline Rowe; July 18 1858 by Rev. Stephen
Howard at Robert Rowe's.

William H. Hunter, 34y, 9m 25d, farmer,
s/o James & Mary Williams Hunter; Angelina
Clements, ae 20y, 1m 4d, d/o Rob't Y. & Jaza
A. P. Clements; July 29 1858 by Rev. Jacob
Shengh at Rob'y Y. Clements'.

Charles Dennis, ae 22y, farmer, s/o Samson
Stubbs & Peggy Dennis; Eliza Dennis; Aug 12
1858 by Rev. S. D. Howard at Peggy Dennis'.
They are free persons of color.

William Slaughter, ae 22y, free person of
color, oysterman, s/o Jefferson & Elizabeth
Slaughter; Susan Rilee, ae 20y, free person
of color, d/o Richard & Polly Rilee; Sept 7
1858 by Rev. Joshua L. Garrett at Polly
Rilee's.

Christopher A. Williams, ae 27y, farmer,
s/o James & Polly Williams; Victoria A.
Williams, ae 17y, d/o Andrew & Palina
Williams; Sept 16 1858 by Rev. Joshua L.
Garrett at Andrew Williams.

William W. Crosswell, ae 21y, oysterman,
s/o Wm. & Matilda Crosswell; Mary Gibson, ae
21y, widow, d/o Benjamin & Mary Seawell;
Sept 30 1858 by Rev. Wm. E. Wiatt at Benja.
Seawell's.

Tazewell Thompson, ae 24y, farmer, of
Norfolk VA, s/o Wm. H. Thompson & wife;
Susan Lewis Byrd, ae 23y, d/o Samuel Powell
Byrd and his late wife, Catharine Byrd; Oct
2 1858 by Rev. A. F. Scott at Ware Church.

Joseph Jackman, ae 46y, widower, farmer,
s/o Sally Jackman; Mary Robinson, ae 51y,
widow, d/o Humphrey & Polly Casey; Oct 21
1858 by Rev. A. F. Scott.

James Washington Thomas, ae 28y, machanic,
s/o John & Mildred Thomas; Maria Jane
Walker, ae 17y, d/o Meade & Maria Walker;
Oct 28 1858 by Rev. W. S. Hawkins at Mrs.
Walker's.

Samuel Emerson, ae 23y, laborer, s/o Elijah & Sarah Jane Emweson; Mary Eliza Hall;
ae 21y, of Mathews Co VA, d/o Jas. & Warner
Hall; Jan 16 1881 by Elder R. Latimore.

Benjamin F. Blake, ae 28y, merchant, of
Mathews Co VA, s/o Wm. & Caroline Blake;
Martha A. Dutton, ae 20y, d/o Benja. &
Martha Dutton; Nov 2 1858 by Rev. S. D.
Howard at B. B. Dutton's.

Robert F. Lyall, ae 24y, blacksmith, s/o
Wm. & Rosa Lyall; Margaret H. Hall, ae 16y,
d/o John & Asenath Hall; Dec 23 1858 by Rev.
Joshua L. Garrettt at John A. Teagle's.

John Mathews Walker, ae 23y, carpenter,
s/o Wm. & Margaret Hibble Walker; Mary E.
Brooking, ae 17y, d/o Henry & Valinda Bland
Brooking; Dec 23 1858 by Rev. Archer Bland
at Henry Brooking's.

John W. Blake, ae 30y, farmer, s/o John &
Mary Drisgall Blake; Ann M. Howard, ae 23y,
d/o John & Susan Powers Howard; Dec 23 1858
by Rev. Stephen D. Howard at Nancy Powers'.

Jefferson Robins, ae 38y, widower,
oysterman, s/o James & Jedica Robins; Sarah
C. Ransone, ae 28y, d/o Thos. & Joice
Ransone; July 31 1858 by Rev. W. G. Walker's.

William J. Lial, ae 29y, carpenter, s/o
Wm. & Patsy Wiatt Lial; Adaline Rilee, ae
22y, d/o Thos. R. & Susan E. Lamberth Rilee;
Jan 4 1859 by Rev. Archer Bland at Thos. R.
Rilee's

Jeame R. Beers, ae 22y, waterman, of Long
Island, NEW YORK, s/o Jorge & Johana Satby
Beers; Leaura Warraton, ae 22y, of Accomac
Co VA, d/o John & Elizabeth Oliver Warrenton;
Jan 4 1859 by Rev. Archer Bland at John W.
Coleman's.

William Henry Jenkins, ae 25y, mechanic,
s/o Warner & Margaret Jenkins; Mary Jane
Brown, ae 19y, d/o Thos. & Mildred Brown;
Jan 27 1859 by Rev. W. S. Hawkins at Joseph
Shackelford's.

Seymour Brown, ae 23y, mariner, s/o Cary
& Elizabeth Brown; Sarah Jane Hogg, ae 18y,
d/o Geo. & Rachel Hogg; Feb 1 1859 by Rev. W.
S. Hawkins at Geo. Hogg's.

George D. Mathews, ae 26y, farmer, s/o
John G. & Elizabeth Padgett Mathews; Mary
Frances Dunston, ae 20y, d/o John & Lucy
Coats; Feb 2 1859 by Rev. Archer Bland at
Belcha Coats'.

John H. S. Leigh, ae 22y, medical profession, s/o Richard D. & Dorothy D. Leigh; Martha A. Harwood, ae 19y, d/o John A. & Emiline Harwood; Feb 10 1859 by Rev. Joshua L. Garrett at Seth Pointer's.

Elijah Morriss, ae 24y, oysterman, s/o Seth & Polly Morriss; Lucy Saunders, ae 19y, d/o Isaac Lancaster (slave) & Polly Saunders; Feb 10 1859 by Rev. Joshua L. Garrett on the Marlfield plantation.

John Morriss, oysterman, s/o Seth & Polly Morriss; Cathrine Sterges, d/o Thos. & Fannie Sterges; Feb 19 1859 by Rev. Joshua L. Garrett on the farm on W. S. Field's.

Atwood C. Chapman, ae 30y, farmer, lived Mathews Ct VA, s/o Thos. & Fannie Chapman; Courtney A. Blake, ae 23y, d/o Thos. & Mary P. Blake; Feb 23 1859 by Rev. Stephen D. Howard at Mary Blake's.

Charles M. Bohannon, ae 28y, farmer, of upper Gloucester Co, s/o Jno. & Susan Hall Bohannon; Sarah E. Wood, ae 18y, Middlesex Co VA, lived upper Gloucester Co VA, d/o Lewis L. & Mary Ann Bristow Wood; Feb 24 1859 by Rev. James C. Crittenden at Wm. Bristow's.

J. F. Powers, ae 22y, saddle and Harness maker, s/o Jno. & Nancy Powers; Mary C. Dutton, ae 19y, d/o James C. & Mary A. Dutton; Feb 24 1859 by Rev. A. F. Scott.

Jeams K. Dutton, ae 21y, farmer, s/o Jeams & Jane S. Booker Dutton; Doratha E. Jones, ae 22y, d/o Lewles & Elizabeth Dutton Jones; Mar 10 1859 by Rev. Archer Bland.

Smith Horseley, ae 25y, farmer, s/o John & Mary Riley Horseley; Elizabeth Horseley, ae 24y, d/o Kininham & Elizabeth Fendly Horseley; Mar 17 1859 by Rev. Archer Bland.

Thomas B. South, ae 33y, farmer, Middlesex Co VA, s/o Toddy & Polly South; M. A. Sears, ae 28y, widow, d/o Thos. C. & Nancy Edwards; Mar 29 1859 by Rev. A. F. Scott.

George W. Cox, ae 24y, blacksmith, of Essex Co VA, s/o Wm. & Mary W. Dunn Cox; Sarah F. Williams, ae 21y, d/o James & Mary Thruston Williams; Mar 31 1859 by Rev. W. W. Towill at W. H. Williams.

John W. West, ae 28y, widower, farmer, of
upper Gloucester Co VA, s/o Isaac & Harriet
Roane West; Martha A. Bohannon, ae 19y; of
upper Gloucester Co VA, d/o John & Susan
Hall Bohannon; Rev. James C. Crittenden at
New Hope Meeting House.

Alexander W. Hayes, ae 25y, sailor, s/o
--- & Mary Hayes; Frances Dennis, ae 24y,·'·/··
d/o Samson & Peggy Dennis; Apr 12 1859 by
Rev. Stephen D. Howard at Fanny Dennis'.

William Richerson, ae 18y, farmer, of
King and Queen Co VA, s/o Henry & Susan
Richerson; Mary F. Brushwood, ae 45y, of
King and Queen Co VA, d/o Elijah & Ann
Brushwood; May 19 1859 by Rev. Cyrus Doggett
at Salem Church.

James H. Butler, ae 23y, waterman, of
Richmond City VA, s/o Nathan & Susan Butler;
Elizabeth Townshend, ae 19y, d/o Kendall &
Elizabeth Townshend; Dec 22 1859 by Rev. Wm.
E. Wiatt at Kendall Townshend's.

Alexander Hogg, ae 29y, Liantiate Univ,
of York Co VA, lived at University of VA,
s/o Lewis & Elizabeth Hogg; E. B. Cooke, ae
24y, d/o John M. & Julia E. Cooke; Dec 29
1859 by Rev. Cyrus Doggett.

Achilles Rowe, ae 23y, waterman, s/o
Ralph & Mary Rowe; Emiline Thomas, ae 22y,
d/o Washington & Ann Thomas; Dec 8 1859 by
Rev. W. S. Hawkins at W. Thomas'.

Samuel R. Marshall, ae 21y, waterman, of
Accomac Co VA, s/o Washington & Susan
Marshall; Elizabeth Sparrow, ae 21y, d/o
Jacob & Delilah Sparrow; Jan 6 1860 by Rev.
Wm. E. Wiatt at Washington Marshall's.

Benjamin Hogg, ae 25y, widower, farmer,
s/o Warner & Susan Hogg; Georgianna Haywood,
ae 18y, d/o Wm. & Eliza Haywood; Jan 5 1860
By Rev. W. S. Hawkins at Warner Hogg's.

John Leamon, ae 21y 10m, free person of
color, sailor, s/o Mary Lemon & Sterling
Morris; Agnes Wilson, ae 24y, free person of
color, d/o Mary Wilson & Richard Easter; Feb
9 1860 by Rev. James Baytop at Harry House.

William Jenkins, ae 21y, farmer, s/o
Lewis & Sarah Jenkins; Elizabeth Belvin, ae
19y, d/o Sterling & Mary Belvin, now
Jenkins; Feb 16 1860 by Rev. Wm. E. Wiatt.

William J. J. Thrift, ae 28y, farmer, s/o
Jeremiah & Letty Thrift; Mary Frances
Thrift, ae 19y, d/o Thos. J. & Eliza Thrift;
Feb 22 1860 by Rev. Joshua L. Garrett at
Thomas J. Thrift's.

John Nye, ae 24y, waterman, of Staten Is.
New York, s/o Wm. & Sarah Reynolds Nye;
Maria C. Rilee, ae 24y, d/o Thos. R. &
Susan Lamberth Rilee; Feb 23 1860 by Rev.
Archer Bland.

John Thomas Anderton, ae 26y, waterman,
s/o James & Louisa Anderton; Sarah Margaret
Elliott, d/o Archer & Elizabeth Elliott; Mar
1 1860 by Rev. W. S. Hawkins.

William Belvin, ae 24y, oysterman, s/o
Geo. & Fanny Belvin; Lucy Smith, ae 19y, d/o
Stephen & Maria Smith; Mar 3 1860 by Rev. W.
S. Hawkins on the road.

Edward Wilcox, ae 22y, farmer, s/o Isaac
& Fanny Going Wilcox; Lucy Lyall, ae 23y,
d/o Wm. & Rosy Fary Lyall; Jan 5 1860 by
Rev. Archer Bland at Richard H. Walker's.

Edward F. Beverage, ae 26y, widower,
mariner, s/o Wm. & Elizabeth Bestpritch
Beverage; Edmonia H. Lucas, ae 24, d/o Hill
& Lucy P. Lewellin Lucas; Mar 7 1860 by Rev.
Joshua L. Garrett.

William Henry Ambrose, ae 21y, of King &
Queen Co VA, s/o Wm. & Lucy Pagget Ambrose;
Sarah Jane Trevillian, ae 28y, widow, d/o
Thos. & Mary Gresit Trevillian; Mar 8 1860
by Rev. Archer Bland at G. W. Cruser's.

Richard Charles Croswell, ae 22y, s/o
John & Ann Croswell; Ann Thomas Seawell, ae
19y, d/i Joseph & Sarah Seawell; Mar 22 1860
by Rev. W. S. Hawkins at Joseph Seawell's.

James Jenkins, ae 23y, oysterman, s/o
James & Charity Jenkins; Caroline West, ae
22y, d/o Ambrose & Hannah West; Mar 29 1860
by Rev. W. S. Hawkins at James Robins.

Miles Allmand, ae 65y, widower,
oysterman, s/o Oliver Parrott & Easter
Allmond; Ann Ellston Major, ae 59y, widow,
of King William Co VA, d/o Ellston & Sarah
Edwards; Apr 19 1860 by Rev. W. S. Hawkins,
Husband- Free Negro, Wife- Indian.

William Clements, ae 32v, widower,
engineer, of Mathews Co VA, s/o Jas. & Alsa
Clements; Elizabeth Pointer, ae 22v, d/o
Isaac & Asenath Pointer; Apr 26 1860 by Rev.
Wm. E. Wiatt at George Lark's.

Edward Harper, ae 35v, merchant, s/o
Rob't & Dorothy Harper; Elizabeth Shepherd,
ae 21v, d/o Geo. & mary Shepherd; June 10
1860 by Rev. Cyrus Doggett at New Upton.

Schuyler S. Padgett, ae 26v, farm, s/o
John & Polly Booker Padgett; ---, ae 22v,
d/o Wm. Fletcher & Sarah R. Buckner; June 14
1860 by Rev. Archer Bland at Jeams Padgett's.

Southall B. Shelton, ae 21v, tobacconist,
of Henrico Co VA, s/o Alexander & Sarah E.
Shelton; ---, ae 17v, of Middlesex Co VA,
d/o P. H. & Mary S. Fitzhugh; June 20 1860
by Rev. R. A. Christian.

Thomas J. Howlett, ae 24v, blacksmith,
s/o Henry & Sarah Kemp Howlett; Maria J.
Gressitt, ae 21v, d/o John M. & Ann W. White
Gressitt; June 28 1860 by Rev. Joshua L.
Garrett at Wm. H. Gressitt's.

William Cary Owens, ae 21v, waterman, s/o
Geo. & Nancy Owens; Elizabeth Ann Bonnywell,
ae 21v, d/o Wm. & Elizabeth Bonnywell; June
28 1860 by Rev. Wm. S. Hawkins at William
Bonnywell's.

William Kellum, ae 18v, farm, s/o Walter
& Rebecca Kellum; Elizabeth Hogg, ae 22v, d/o
Jas. & Roseana Hogg; June 28 1860 by Rev.
W. S. Hawkins at Mrs. West's.

Soloman Foxwell, ae 23v, oysterman and
waterman, s/o Soloman & Nancy Graves Foxwell; Sarah Hutson, ae 17v, of Accomac Co
VA, d/o Geo. Hutson & Lev: Stephens; Aug 7
1860 by Rev. Wm. E. Wiatt at Ryland
Oliver's.

David R. Grevis, ae 34v, merchant, of
Baltimore MD, s/o John & Maria Grevis;
Catharine F. Hall, ae 18v, d/o John N. &
Mary Ann Hall; Aug 29 1860 by Rev. Joshua L.
Garrett at Capt. John N. Hall's.

Christopher Rowe, ae 22v, waterman, s/o
John & Frances Hall Rowe; Elizabeth Ann Cox,
ae 21v, d/o John & Susan Callum Cox; Aug 26
1860 by Rev. Joshua L. Garrett at John W.
Jenkins' in Guinea.

James R. Coleman, ae 23y, oysterman, s/o
Carter & Lucinthia Puller Coleman; Emily J.
Williams, ae 18y, d/o Augustine & Elizabeth
Coleman Williams; Sept 5 1860 by Rev. Joshua
L. Garrett at Pigeon Hill, Gloucester Co VA.

Robert B. Pearce, ae 32y, farmer, s/o
Thos. & Brigget Coats Pearce; Ann E. Masey,
ae 22y, d/o James R. & Agnes Powers Masey;
Sept 13 1860 by Rev. Thomas C. Howard at Wm.
Y. Masey's.

Thomas Harris, ae 18y, mariner, s/o Rob't
& Mary Span Harris; Henrietta Savage, ae
16y, d/o Wm. Major & Sarah Turlington
Savage; Sept 19 1860 by Rev. Joshua L.
Garrett at Lorenzo Powell's residence.

William Webb, ae 21y, waterman, of
Northumberland Co VA, s/o Joseph & Catharine
Blendon Webb; Anna Foxwell, ae 15y, d/o
Soloman & Ann Graves Foxwell; Oct 31 1860 by
Rev. Wm. E. Wiatt at Ann Foxwell's.

John T. Lewis, ae 21y, farmer, of Middle-
sex Co VA, s/o John & Lucy Hall Lewis;
Eudorer Gibbs, ae 17y, d/o Frances Ann Gibbs
& Jorge W. Parmer; Nov 14 1960 by Rev.
Archer Bland at Vernendol Palmer's.

Charles W. West, ae 20y, waterman, s/o
Wm. & Courtney Brown West; Susan Ann Brown,
ae 19y, d/o Robert & Mary Smith Brown; Nov
20 1860 by Rev. Wm. E. Wiatt at Sadler's
Neck Meeting House.

Warner Smith, ae 51y, widower, farmer,
s/o Joseph Rowe & Betsy Smith; Sarah Cooly
Acra, ae 38y, widow, d/o Franklin & Nancy
Major; Dec 20 1860 by Rev. W. S. Hawkins at
Mr. Seawell's.

Lewis Thomas Brown, ae 25y, farmer, s/o
James & Susan Brown; Frances Savage, ae 17y,
d/o Major & Maria Savage; Dec 11 1860 by
Rev. W. S. Hawkins at Mr. Wiatt's.

Thomas J. Minor, ae 25y, carpenter, s/o
Thos. & Sarah West Minor; Mrs. Joanna
Purcell, ae 25y, widow, d/o Frank &
Catherine White Enos; Dec 25 1860 by Rev.
Wm. E. Wiatt at Wm. T. Minor's.

William Mattox, ae 19y, oystering, s/o
James & Matilda Mattox; Mary Herns, ae 32y,
widow, d/o Thos. & Ann Purcell; Oct 4 1860
by Rev. Cyrus Doggett at Belle Roy.

Timothy M. Allmond, ae 19y, waterman, s/o Wm. & Mary L. Wood Allmond; Mary F. M. Martin Puller, ae 27y, d/o Thos. & Mary S. Wright Puller; Jan 18 1861 by Rev. Archer Bland.

James R. Kemp, ae 23y, oysterman, of King and Queen Co VA, s/o Lucy A Corr & Robert D. Kemp; Lucy A. Carney, ae 19y, d/o Wm. S. & Elizabeth G. South Carney; Jan 12 1861 by Rev. Stephen D. Howard.at Mrs. E. Carney's.

William T. Dutton, ae 25y, carpenter, s/o Wm. H. & Lucy Dutton; Martha E. Dunston, ae 19y, d/o John H. & Mary Dunston; Jan 13 1861 by Rev. Stephen D. Howard at John Dunston's.

William C. Bristow, ae 46y, widower, overseer, s/o Lucy Bristow & --- Dunston; Sarah Jenkins, ae 37y, d/o --- & Margaret Jenkins; Jan 3 1861 by Rev. Wm. E. Wiatt at Edward J. Carney's.

Peter B.Hughes, ae 21y, farmer, s/o Wm. B. & Susan Stubblefield Hughes; Catharine M. Wallace, ae 20y, d/o John & Mary Hite Hill; Feb 7 1861 by Rev. Joshua L. Garrett at Pleasant Grove, Gloucester Co VA.

Enock Washington Walker, ae 22y, oysterman, s/o Meade & Maria Hudson Walker; Elizabeth Browne, ae 26y, d/o James & Susan More Browne; Mar 19 1861 by Rev. Joshua L. Garrett at Joseph H. Shackelford's.

Robert H. Gwynn, ae 34y, widower, mechanic, of Mathews Co VA, s/o Henry & Elizabeth Williams Gwynn; Adeline F. Bridges, ae 22y, d/o Roberson & Rosy Dutton Bridges; Apr 11 1861 by Rev. Stephen D. Howard at Chas. C. Duval's.

Ceasar Harris, ae 37ym free person of color, waterman, s/o Lizzie Peed, father unknown, of King and Queen Co VA; Sarah C. Cheaves, ae 21, free person of color, d/o Sampson Stubbs & Peggy Dennis; May 1 1861 by Rev. Stephen D. Howard.

James H. Ison, ae 21y, farmer, of King and Queen Co VA, lived James City Co VA, s/o Reuben & Nancy Walden Ison; Frances A. Corthran, ae 24y, of Essex Co VA, d/o Isaac & Maria Davis Corthran; May 7 1861 by Rev.J. C. Crittenden at Dunbar Edward's.

Richard Henry Blake, ae 23y, oysterman, of Mathews Co VA, s/o James & Elizabeth Hudgin Blake; Martha Amm Boswell, ae 21y, d/o Joseph & Eliza Douglas Boswell; May 16 1861 by Rev. Stephen D. Howard at Mary Bristow's.

Francis Williamson Smith, ae 23y, military, of Norfolk VA, s/o James Marsden & Ann Walke Williamson Smith; Anna Maria Deans, ae 21, of Rosewell, Gloucester Co VA, d/o Josiah S. & Mary Deans; Aug 7 1861 by Rev. Chas. Mann, Rector of Abingdon and Ware Parrishes, at Rosewell.

John William Blake, ae 30y, widower, farmer, s/o Thos. & Mary Drisgall Blake; Lucy Frances Chapman, ae 16y, d/o Richard & Caroline Jackman Chapman; Aug 28 1861 by Rev. Stephen D. Howard at Rich'd Chapman's.

William Wiliams, ae 20y, oysterman, s/o Peyton G. & Nancy Williams; Caroline B. Fosque, ae 19y, d/o John S. & Nancy Croswell Fosque; Oct 22 1861 by Rev. W. S. Hawkins at Wm. Hogg's.

Thomas Robins, ae 36y, oysterman, s/o Thos. & Elizabeth Rowe Robins; Indiana B. Ransone, ae 21y, d/o Thos. & Mary Freggs Ransone; Nov 9 1861 by rev. W. S. Hawkins at Benjamin Seawell's.

James Cox, ae 23y, farmer, of York Co VA, s/o John & Mary Cox; Elizabeth Smith, ae 21y, d/o John & Mary Smith; Nov 27 1861 by Rev. W. S. Hawkins at James Hogg's.

S. W. Carmichael, ae 31y, physician, of Fredericksburg VA, s/o Geo. F. & Mary C. Wellford Carmichael; Fannie Tucker Bryan, ae 24y, of Stafford Co VA, lived Gloucester Co VA, d/o John R. & Elizabeth Cotter Bryan; Dec 19 1861 by Rev. Chas. Mann, Rector of Abingdon Parrish at Eagle Point, home of the bride.

Richard H. Wallace, ae 17y, farmer, s/o Joseph & Lilly Ann Figg Wallace; Virginia Susan Jenkins, ae 17y, d/o Edward & Ann East Jenkins; Dec 26 1861 by Rev. Humphrey Billups at Edward Jenkins'.

Christain P. Hibble, ae 22y, of Lancaster Co PA, s/o Jacob & Catharine Bartholomew Hibble; Ann M. Enos, ae 15y, d/o George & Sarah A. E. Moore Enos; Dec 26 1861 by Rev. Joshua L. Garrett at Robert Walden's.

James Leigh, ae 25y, widower, farmer, s/o Caleb & Elizabeth Davis Leigh; Emily Jane Hayes, ae 18y, d/o Joel & Susan Stubblefield Hayes; Mar 13 1862 by Rev. Joshua L. Garrett at Col. Joel Hayes.

Edward Vernon Palmer, ae 21y, farmer, s/o Vernon & Elizabeth Gibbs Palmer; Jane Belle South, ae 22y, widow, of Mathews Co VA, d/o Edward & Lucy Ann Chapman Mallory; Mar 26 1862 by rev. J. C. Crittenden at Edward Mallory's.

William Washington Thompson, ae 22y, oysterman, s/o Peter & Susan Woodland Thompson; Margaret Seawell, ae 18y, d/o Benjamin & Mary Oliver Seawell; Mar 26 1862 by Rev. Wm. E. Wiatt at Providence Church.

William bristow, ae 55y, widower, farmer, free person of color, s/o Betsy Bristow, father unknown; Ann Elizabeth Hayes, ae 21y, free person of color, d/o Polly Hayes, father slave; Mar 8 1862 by Rev. Stephen D. Howard at Jacob's.

George Edwin Shackelford, widower, saddle and harness maker, s/o Wm.Shackelford; Missouri Ellen Medlicott, ae 19y 6m, d/o Sam'l R. & Elizabeth C. Medlicott.

John Purcell, ae 37y, widower, farmer, s/o Thos. & Ann Minor Purcell; Margaret Ann James, ae 22y, parents unknown; Jan 2 1862 by Rev. Joshua L. Garrett at John R. Walker's.

John J. Graves, ae 25y, oysterman, s/o Wm. I. & Eliza Elliott Graves; Elizabeth Fields, ae 14y, d/o John & Maria Hudgin Fields; Jan 2 1862 by Rev. Wm. E. Wiatt at Providence Meeting House.

William D. Jones, ae 28y, farmer, of New Kent Co VA, s/o C. R. & Delia Slater Jones; Virginia F. Broaddus, ae 24y, d/o Edwin & Eliza Montague Broaddus; Jan 9 1862 by Rev. A. F. Scott at Edwin Broaddus'.

John C. Woodland, ae 24y, mariner, s/o
John W. & Catharine C. Lewellan Woodland;
Lucy Jane Teagle, ae 20y, d/o Thos. &
Elizabeth Evans Teagle; Feb 6 1862 by Rev.
Joshua L. Garrett at Thos. Teagle's.

Edward A. DeBerry, ae 21y, farmer, of
Northampton Co N. C, s/o Henry & Frances A.
Bryan DeBerry; Sarah Margaret Rowe, ae 19y,
d/o Edward H. & Susan Hays Rowe; Jan 30 1862
by Rev. Joshua L. Garrett at Capt. E. H.
Rowe's.

Thomas Archer Shackelford, ae 45y, sailor
and fisherman, s/o Thos. Hogg & Franky
Shackelford; Ann West, ae 26y, d/o
Christopher & Fanny West; Feb 12 1862 by
Rev. W. S. Hawkins at Benja. Seawell's.

Algernon Willis, ae 41y, widower, farmer,
of King and Queen Co VA, s/o Wm. S. & Susan
Smither Willis; Elizabeth Smither, ae 41y,
widow, d/o Henry Crittenden & Catharine
Wedderbern, of King and Queen Co VA; Apr 23
1862 By Rev. A. F. Scott at H. Crittenden's.

Warner Hern, ae 40y, widower, carpenter,
of Mathews Co VA, free man of color, s/o
Adam & Miley Hern; Lizzie Ann Allmand, ae
27y, free woman of color, d/o Miles &
Courtney Allmand; June 12 1862.

Joseph Washington Eubank, ae 38y,
widower, carpenter, of Richmond VA, s/o
Hezekiah & Mary Ann Grimes Eubank; Edmonia
Braxton Insley, ae 21y, d/o Wm. H. & Edmonia
B. Thrift Insley; July 1 1862.

Lewis Morris, ae 25y, free person of
color, oysterman, s/o Tom Morris & Winney
Bluford; Ellen Chapman, ae 20y, free person
of color, d/o Robert Chapman & Betsy Dixon;
July 24 1862.

Richard Rilee, ae 44y, widower, s/o Wm. &
Sarah Walker Rilee; Martha Massey, ae 40y,
widow, of King and Queen Co VA, d/o Peyton &
Almenia Drummond Massey; Aug 12 1862 by Rev.
Stephen D. Howard at E. Massey's.

George W. Rowe, ae 24y, waterman, s/o
George & Catharine Rowe; Lucy J. Brown, ae
21y, d/o Wm. & Susan Brown; Sept 26 1862 at
John Hall's residence.

William Todd Robins, ae 26y 1m 7d, Capt.
in the Confederate Army, s/o A. W. & Maria
H. Todd Robins; Martha Tabb Smith, ae 22y,
of Fredericksburg VA, d/o Wm. P. & Marion
Seddon Smith; Oct 30 1862 by Rev. Chas. Mann
Rector of Ware Church at Ware Church.

John Samuel Cooke, ae 26y, 11m, 5d,
deputy clerk of Circuit Court of Gloucester
Co VA, s/o Thos. B. & Catherine C. Cary
Cooke; Robertnett V. Yates, ae 24y, d/o Ro.
& Mary A. B. Wood; Nov 6 1862 by Rev. A. F.
Scott at Newington Church.

William L. Bland, ae 43y, widower,
carpenter, s/o Wm. & Elizabeth Carlton
Bland; Mary Jane Smither, ae 46y, widow, of
King and Queen Co VA, d/o Whitaker & Sarah
Baytop Campbell; Nov 12 1862.

Augustine Harmons, ae 21y, farmer, s/o
Frank Lemon & Seignora Harmans; Martha Ann
Wilson, ae 22y, d/o Rich'd Easter & Mary
Wilson; Dec 20 1862 by Rev. Stephen D.
Howard at Mrs. John Lemmons'.

Alexander Atkins, ae 38y, widower, of
King and Queen Co VA, farmer, s/o John &
Nancy Taylor Atkins; Sarah Jane Roane, ae
20y, d/o Henry & Virginia Anderson Roane;
Dec 31 1862 by Rev. A. F. Scott at Henry
Roane's.

Claiborne T. Roane, ae 32y, widower,
carpenter, s/o Chas. & Mary Roane; Ann E.
Medlicott, ae 23y, d/o Sam'l R. & Elizabeth
C. Medlicott; Feb 5 1863 .

Richard Shackelford, ae 51y, widower,
shoe maker, of King and Queen Co VA, s/o Lee
& Rachel Shackelford; Juliet Ann Massey, ae
17y, d/o Robert & Mary Massey; Feb 10 1863
by Rev. James C. Crittenden at Mr. Boss'.

William L. Ware, ae 24y, farmer, of
Middlesex Co VA, s/o Reuben & Sarah Ware;
Maria Ann West, ae 23y, d/o Isaac & Harriet
E. West; Feb 19 1863 by Rev. John Pollard .

Gideon S. Fary, ae 32y, blacksmith, s/o
Thos. & Sarah Fary; Ann E. Pearce, ae 42y,
widow, of King and Queen Co VA, d/o Elijah &
---Brushwood; June 17 1863 at John W.
Stubbs'.

C. M. Swann, ae 31y, soldier Confederate
Army, of Nottingham ENGLAND, s/o Christopher
& Elizabeth L. Swann; Matilda C. Owen, ae
26y, d/o Rob't C. & Matilda Owen; Nov 12
1863 at Ebenezer Church.

Elias Easter, ae 22y, farmer, s/o Wm. &
Sarah Easter; Julia E. Dunston, ae 22y, d/o
James Soles & Elsey Dunston; Feb 21 1863 by
Rev. J. C. Crittenden at A. G. Huckstep's.

John W. Cringan, ae 29y, Capt. Confederate
States Army, of Richmond City VA, s/o R. P. &
Jane Cringan; Hally S. Curtis, ae 22y, d/o
Chas. C. & Harriet T. Curtis; Mar 5 1863 by
Rev. Chas. Mann, Rector of Abingdon and Ware
Parrishes at Wilson's Creek, residence of C.
C. Curtis.

Isaac Miles, ae 35y, widower, sailor, of
Indian Town, King William Co VA, s/o Pleasant
& Deborah Miles; Pinkey Eliza Lemon, ae 20y,
d/o Mordacai & Fanny Lemon; Mar 26 1863 by
Rev. A. F. Scott at Mr. Miles'.

Jacob Garlitts, ae 37y, widower, sailor,
of Preston Co VA, s/o Jacob & Rosannah
Garlitts; Sarah E. Medlicott, ae 18y, d/o
Benj. & Mary H. Medlicott; Feb 25 1863 by
Rev. A. F. Scott at John Rilee's.

Thomas B. Montague, ae 20y, teacher, s/o
Thos. B. & Sarah L. Montague; Josephine T.
Hill, ae 24y, of New Kent Co VA, d/o John &
Tabitha Hill; July 28 1864 by Rev. A. F.
Scott at Oswald S. Kemp's.

George P. Beazley, ae 23y, farmer, of
Middlesex Co VA, s/o John L. & Laura L.
Beazley; Indianna M. Broocke, ae 22y, d/o
Temple & Catharine Broocke; Oct 2 1864 by
Rev. John Pollard, Jr.

William C. Dutton, ae 22y, soldier,
Confederate Army, s/o John W. & Sarah Ann
Dutton; Maria F. Hibble, ae 18y, d/o Mat &
Letty Hibble; Nov 8 1861 by Rev. John W.
Tucker at Letty R. Hibble's.

Joseph Haynes, ae 45y, widower, farmer,
s/o Geo. & Nancy Haynes; Henrietta Dobson,
ae 24y, of Mathews Co VA, d/o John & Nancy
Dobson; Dec 28 1864 by Rev. Chas. Mann,
Rector of Abingdon & Ware Parrishes.

Frederick H. Wolfe, ae 22y, Lt. C. S.
Army, s/o John B. & Eliza A. Wolfe; Sarah E.
Thrift, ae 21y, d/o Thos. J. & Eliza Thrift;
Dec 29 1864 by Rev. John T. Tucker at Thos.
Thrift's.

James M. Bonnywell, ae 25y waterman, of
Accomac Co VA, s/o John & Sally Bonnywell;
Emily Bonnywell, ae 23y, widow, of Accomac
Co VA, d/o Leyburn & Nancy Sparrow; Feb 18
1866 by Rev. John W. Shield at my house in
York Co VA.

Addison Lemon, ae 32y, s/o John & Sally
Lemon; Martha A. Robinson, ae 24y, of King
and Queen Co VA, d/o --- Robinson; Mar 9
1865 by Rev. A. F. Scott at Cappahosic.

William D. Kelly, ae 28y, soldier,
Confederate Army, of Accomac Co VA, s/o Wm.
& Rebecca Kelly; Harriet E. West, ae 21y,
d/o Isaac & Harriet West; Mar 13 1865 by
Rev. W. G. Hammond at Mrs. West'.

Beverly Dunston, ae 40y, widower, farmer,
s/o John & Martha Dunston; Doretta C.
Drisgall, ae 30y, widow, d/o Thos. & ---
Marchant; Apr 11 1865 by Rev. A. F. Scott at
Benerly Dunston's.

Thomas J. Proctor, ae 20y, farmer, s/o
James H. Elizabeth Proctor; Lucretia
Fletcher, ae 19y, d/o James B. & Lilly S.
Fletcher; May 4 1865 by Rev. A. F. Scott.

Hiram L. Thrift, ae 26y, farmer, s/o John
& Frances Thrift;. Mary Frances Mason, ae
22y, d/o Leonard & Elizabeth Mason; May 11
1865 by Rev. A. F. Scott at Mr. Mason's.

Thomas F. Wilkins, ae 46y, carpenter, s/o
Nathan & Ann Wilkins; Ann Maria Robins, ae
23y, d/o Francis & Sarah Robins; May 16 1865
by Rev. A. F. Scott at Robert Walden's.

Hugh G. Wyatt, ae 22y, farmer, s/o James
B. & Helen E. Wyatt; Elizabeth Susan Singleton. ae 20y, d/o John F. & Eliza S. Singleton; May 16 1865 by Rev. W. G. Hammond at
Singleton's Chapel.

Benjamin P. Philips, ae 37y, widower,
merchant, of Elizabeth City Co VA, s/o Geo.
& Susan Philips; Julia Pointer, ae 22y, d/o
Cyrus C. & Martha Pointer; Aug 31 1865 by
Rev. John D. Tucker at Christian C.
Pointer's.

John W. Williams, ae 34y, farmer, of
Norfolk VA, s/o Wm. & Eliza Williams; Betty
H. Thornton, ae 24y, d/o Francis & Betsy
Thornton; Sept 20 1865 by Rev. A. F. Scott.

Joseph Green, ae 22y, oysterman, of York
Co VA, s/o Wm. & Dianna Green; Rebecca
Shackelford, ae 17y, d/o John W. & Sarah
Shackelford; Oct 4 1865 by Rev. W. S.
Hawkins at John Philip's.

John H. Smith, ae 27y, sailor, s/o Wm. C.
& Dolly C. Smith; Esther J. Edwards, ae 19y,
d/o Daniel & Susan Ann Edwards; Oct 5 1865
by Rev. W. S. Hawkins at Timberneck.

Charles E. C. Brooks, ae 29y, widower,
farmer, s/o James & Elizabeth Brooks;
Elizabeth F. Dutton, ae 21y, d/o Wm. H. &
Elizabeth Dutton; Oct 10 1865 by Rev. John
W. Tucker at Elizabeth Booker's.

William B. Catlett, ae 26y, farmer, s/o
John T. & Martha Catlett; Mary Booth, ae
22y, d/o Thos. B. & Margaret Booth; Oct 12
1865 by Rev. Chas. Mann, Rector of Ware
Parrish at Ware Church.

James H. Brown, ae 26y, widower, oyster,
s/o Chas. & Dorothy Brown; Susan E. Blake,
ae 19y. d/o John & Nancy Blake; Oct 19 1865
by Rev. W. G. Hammond at John Blake's.

John H. Curfman, ae 22y, oysterman, of
St. Mary's Co MD, s/o John Henry & Martha
Curfman; Charlotte E. Brown, ae 21y, d/o
Chas. & Dorothy E. Brown; Oct 19 1865 by
Rev. W. G. Hammond at Mrs. Brown's.

Joseph H. Lawson, ae 23y, farmer, s/o
Chas. & Fanny Coats Lawson; Mary E. Wyatt,
ae 22y, d/o Geo. W. & Sarah Wyatt; Oct 26
1865 by Rev. John W. Tucker at Geo. Wyatt's.

Horace A. Purcell, ae 38y, farmer, s/o
Wm. R. & Charity Purcell; Ann Maria Griffin,
ae 21y, d/o Thos. D. & Maria Griffin; Oct
31 1865 by Rev. John W. Tucker at Wm. D.
Griffin's.

Issac H. Carrington, ae 38y, widower,
lawyer, of Richmond VA, s/o Paul & Emma
Carrington; Ann Seddon Smith, ae 23y, of
Glen Roy, d/o Wm. P. & Marian Smith; Nov 7
1865 by Rev. Chas. Mann at Glen Roy.

Joseph H. Coats, ae 22y, farmer, s/o
Belchy & Nancy Coats; Sarah F. Lawson, ae
17y, d/o James W. & Jane Lawson; Nov 2 1865
by Rev. W. G. Hammond at Jane Lawson's.

Thomas Mason, ae 36y, widower, of York Co
VA, s/o Anthony & Elizabeth Mason; Mary
Elizabeth Elliott, ae 27y, d/o John & Elizabeth Elliott; Nov 2 1865 by Rev. A. F. Scott
at George W. Cruser's.

John Coats, ae 47y, widower, farmer, s/o
John & Mary Coats; Margaret Ann West, ae 28y,
d/o Wm. & Courtney West; Nov 7 1865 by Rev.
W. S. Hawkins at John Coats'.

Henry Smith, ae 47y, widower, farmer, s/o
Michael & Frances Smith' Mary Eliza Hornsby,
ae 25y, widow, of York Co VA, d/o Benjamin &
Jane Kelly; Nov 11 1865 by Rev. John W.
Tucker.

Nathaniel Wilkins, ae 20y, s/o Nathan F.
& Lilly A. Shackelford Wilkins; Frances A.
Moore, ae 14y, d/o Zack & Elizabeth A.
Moore; Nov 16 1865 by Rev. John W. Tucker .

Wilbert F. Ralph, ae 25y, of Kent Co MD,
lived Talbot Co MD, farmer, s/o Wm. H. &
Mary A. Ralph; Mollie A. Bray, ae 21y, d/o
Thos. J. & Martha A. Bray; Nov 21 1865 by
Rev. John D. Tucker at Thos. Bray's.

Samuel D. Pointer, ae 23y, harness maker,
s/o Seth & Gracy Pointer; Eugenia E. Harwood,
ae 17y, d/o John A. & Emma Harwood; Dec 6
1865 by Rev. W. G. Hammond at S. Pointer's.

George A. Roane, ae 31y, farmer, s/o
Major & Matilda Roane; Margaret A. Booth, ae
20y, d/o Thos. B. & Margaret M. Booth; Dec 7
1865 by Rev. A. F. Scott at Bellamy's Church.

Washington Cook, ae 35y, farmer, a freed
man, s/o Wm. & Jenny Cook; Lucy Blufoot, ae
35y, a freed woman of color, d/o Frank &
Lucy Blufoot; Dec 7 1865 by Rev. A. F. Scott.

Henry Sinclair, ae 21y, farmer, of Elizabeth City Co VA, s/o Jefferson B. & Georgianna Sinclair; Martha L. Catlett, ae 21, d/o
John Tabb & Martha S. Catlett; Dec 12 1865
by Rev. Chas. Mann, at Ware Church.

James H. Acra, ae 40y, widower, farmer,
s/o Jacob & Ann J. Acra; Matilda Ann Dutton,
ae 35y, widow, of Mathews Co VA, d/o Benja. &
Nancy Booker; Dec 12 1865 by Rev. Chs. Mann.

James L. Philpotts, ae 31y, farmer, s/o
John & Ann Philpots; Hester A. Hall, ae 21y,
d/o Thos. & Maria Hall; Dec 14 1865 by Rev.
W. G. Hammond at Mrs. Ann S. Amory's.
Jhaman M. Leavitt, ae 24y, harness maker,
s/o John S. & Frances Leavitt; Mary F.
Stubbs, ae 22y, d/o Lawrence S. & Mary
Stubbs; Dec 21 1865 by Rev. W. G. Hammond.
Washington Robins, ae 34y, widower,
mechanic, s/o Thos. & Elizabeth Robins;
Sarah Ann Thomas, ae 32y, widow, d/o Jesse &
Mary Thomas; Dec 24 1865 by Rev. David
Coulling at Mrs. Thomas'.
Edward A. Pippin, ae 38y, widower,
tailor, s/o Edward H. & Ann C. Pippin; Mary
Graham Hall, ae 29y, d/o John & Fanny Hall;
Dec 21 1865 by Rev. A. F. Scott at Henry
Burges'.
William C. Trevillian, ae 22y, farmer,
s/o Augustine S. & Emily Trevillian; Maria
G. Adams, ae 23y, d/o Geo. W. & Martha
Adams; Dec 25 1865 by Rev. W. G. Hammond at
Geo. W. Adam's.
Lorenzo Driver, ae 28y, oysterman, free
person of color, s/o John & Polly Cook; Mary
Ann Lancaster, ae 21y, free person of color,
d/o Isaac & Polly Lancaster; Dec 31 1865 by
Rev. A. F. Scott at Bethlehem Church.
John H. Nye, ae 29y, widower, oysterman,
of ENGLAND, s/o Wm. & Sarah Nye; Sarah
Euphanny Rilee, ae 22y, d/o Thos. R. & Susan
Rilee; Dec 28 1865 by Rev. John Pollard, Jr.
William S. Miller, ae 30y, farmer, of
Mathews Co VA, s/o Seth F. & Letitia Miller;
Virginia A. Dutton, ae 15y, d/o Wm. J. &
Mary Dutton; July 7 1864 by Rev. J. G.
Councill at Powatan L. Palmer's.
John Dobson, ae 53y, widower, farmer, of
Hanover Co VA, s/o Pitman & Martha Dobson;
Lucy Ann Dutton, ae 27y, d/o --- & ---
Mallory; Feb 14 1865 at Lucy A. Dutton's.
Edward Nuttall, ae 21y, farmer, s/o James
& Mary E. Nuttall; Frances Ann Hudgins, ae
18y, d/o Claiborne & Lucy Ann Hudgins; May
18 1865 by Rev. J. G. Councill at Mrs.
Dennis'.

John J. Chandler, ae 20y, clerk, of York
Co VA, lived Saluda Middlesex Co VA, s/o
James C. & Eliza C. Chandler; Lucy E. White,
ae 19y, d/o James H. & Susan White; Jan 4
1866 by Rev. David Coulling at J. H. White's.

Benjamin Bluford, ae 27y, oysterman,,
free person of color, s/o Sally Bluford;
Mary C. Douglas, ae 17y, free person of
color, d/o James & Daphne Douglas; Jan 5
1866 by Rev. A. F. Scott at Shelly Glo. VA.

Richard Croswell, ae 23y, widower, water-
man, s/o John W. & Nancy Croswell; Lucy
Harris, ae 19y, of York Co VA, d/o Robert &
Harriet Harris; Jan 12 1866 by Rev. W. S.
Hawkins at Wm. Williams'.

Patrick H. Dutton, ae 23y, farmer, s/o
Lorenzo D. & Frances F. Dutton; Emily R. B.
C. Kemp, ae 22y, d/o Gregory & Susan Kemp;
Jan 18 1866 by Rev. A. F. Scott at G. Kemp's.

John Z. Gale, ae 24y, sailor, of Middle-
sex Co VA, s/o Matthew & Ann E. Gayle; Jenny
F. Brown, ae 17y, d/o Austin & Louisa Brown;
Jan 18 1866 by Rev. W. G. Hammond at Ware
Neck.

Joel M. Rowe, ae 37y, sailor, s/o
Sterling & Frances Rowe; Martha Ellen Free-
man, ae 22y, d/o Wm. & Catharine Freeman;
Jan 18 1866 by Rev. W. G. Hammond in Guinea.

George Washington Driver, ae 23y, farmer,
colored person, s/o Sam & Fanny Driver;
Margaret Ann Morris, ae 20y, colored, d/o
Sye Carter & Jane Morris; Jan 25 1866 by
Rev. A. F. Scott at Jane Morris'.

William A. Hall, ae 33y, waterman, s/o
Wm. & Mary Hall; Susannah Howard, ae 25y,
d/o Thos. & Elizabeth Howard; Jan 25 1866 by
Rev. W. S. Hawkins at John Robins'.

J. Edward Bland, ae 27y, farmer, s/o
Thos. J. & Mildred Bland; Maggie A. Roane,
ae 20y, d/o Sam'l F. & Elizabeth Roane; Jan
28 1866 by Rev. W. G. Hammond at S. Roane's.

John R. Brown, ae 23y, farmer, of Middlesex Co VA, s/o Smith W. & Susan H. Brown;
Mary E. Carney, ae 23y, d/o Wm. S. & Elizabeth J. Carney; Jan 31 1866 by Rev. A. F.
Scott at Wm. Carney's.

William Chapman, ae 20y, colored, oyster-
man, s/o Robert & Gracy Chapman; Mary
Frances Gayle, ae 18y, colored, d/o Rachel
Gayle; Feb 6 1866 by Rev. A. F. Scott at
Cedar Bush Creek.

John F. Rowe, ae 33y, widower, merchant,
s/o Sterling & Frances A. Rowe; Martha Smith,
ae 28y, d/o Armistead & patsy Smith; Feb 6
1866 by Rev. W. S. Hawkins at A. Smith's.

Alexander Davenport, ae 23y, colored,
farmer, s/o Elizabeth Davenport; Rosetta
Whiting, ae 17y, colored, d/o John & Mary
Whiting; Feb 7 1866 by Rev. A. F. Scott at
my school house.

William H. Brown, ae 22y, oysterman, s/o
James & Susan Brown; Laura Lewis, ae 17y,
d/o Wm. I. & Lucy A. Lewis; Feb 15 1866 by
Rev. W. G. Hammond at Lucy Lewis'.

E. S. Shurtiff, ae 29y, seaman, of Oswego
N. Y, s/o J. B. & Elizabeth Shurtiff; P. V.
Summerson, ae 21y, d/o John & Mary Summer-
son; Feb 8 1866 by Rev. A. F. Scott at
Dragon Ordinary.

Thomas S. Stubblefield, ae 34y, farmer,
s/o Thos. M. & Elizabeth Stubblefield;
Amelia Emiline Robins, ae 31y, d/o Thos. C.
& Amelia Robins; Feb 14 1866 by Rev. A. F.
Scott at Newington Church.

Henry D. Rilee, ae 43y, widower, mechanic,
lived New Orleans LA, s/o Lewis & Annie
Rilee; Mary Jane Walker, ae 18y, d/o Richard
H. & Sarah C. Walker; Feb 14 1866 by Rev. W.
G. Hammond at Salem Church

Alexander H. Martin, ae 38y, widower,
farmer, s/o John & Maria Martin; Louisa
Jefferson Medlicott, ae 21y, d/o Sam'l R. &
Elizabeth Medlicott; Feb 25 1866 by Rev. W.
G. Hammond at Woods Cross Roads.

David Belvin, ae 22y, oysterman, s/o John
& Maria Belvin; Sally West, ae 25y, d/o
Ambrose & Hannah West; Apr 5 1866 by Rev.
Wm. E. Wiatt in Guinea.

Charles C. Chapman, ae 34y, farmer, s/o
John & Harriet J. Chapman; Susan Virginia
Kemp, ae 25y, d/o Gregory & Susan Kemp; Mar
1 1866 by Rev. A. F. Scott at Ebenezer Chrh.

A. L. Haynes, ae 28y, merchant, of
Lincoln Co N. C, s/o R. G. & Elizabeth
Haynes, Emily L. Davis, ae 24y, d/o Alfred
B. & Maria Davis; Mar 25 1866 by Rev. A. F.
Scott at Newington Church.

William R. Jones, ae 36y, carpenter, of
Middlesex Co VA, lived Glo. Co VA, s/o Lewis
& Sally Jones; Clara A. Sterling, ae 35y,
widow, of Albemarle Co VA, d/o Supry & Clara
Bunch; Mar 28 1866 by Rev. A. F. Scott at
Wm. R. Jones.

Robert Hall, ae 19y, colored, farmer, s/o
John & Tulip Ann Hall; Mary Walker, ae 20y,
colored, d/o Henry & Mary Walker; Mar 29
1866 by Rev. A. F. Scott at Walter T. Davis'.

George Winston, ae 24y, colored, oyster-
man, s/o Meredith & Dinah Winston; Mary
Eliza Wiatt, ae 25, colored, d/o Tom & Sally
Wiatt; Apr 2 1866 by Rev. A. F.Scott at
Poplar's Church.

Samuel Griffin, ae 30y, colored, farmer,
s/o Sam'l & Mary Griffin; Judy Rilee, ae 21y,
colored, d/o Geo. & Caroline Rilee; Apr 15
1866 by Rev. A. F. Scott at C. C. Curtis'.

James M. Hogg, ae 25y, oysterman, s/o Wm.
& Patsy Hogg; Susan M. Pointer, ae 23y, d/o
Daniel & --- Pointer; Apr 26 1866 by Rev. A.
F. Scott at James Brown's.

Palestine Hall, ae 21y, farmer, s/o Lewis
& Caty Hall; Annie E. Lowry, ae 22y, of
Portsmouth VA, d/o John & Sally Lowry; May
10 1866 by Rev. A. F. Scott at L. Hall's.

Charles Waller, ae 26y, colored, oyster-
man, s/o Robert & Clydia Waller; Harriet
Wiatt, ae 20y, colored, d/o Tom & Sally
Wiatt; May 22 1866 by Rev. A. F. Scott at
James K. Dabney's plantation.

Adam Harris, ae 24y, colored, farmer, s/o
Sam & Betsy Harris; Elizabeth Roy Baytop, ae
20y, colored, d/o Roy & Franky Baytop; June
14 1866 by Rev. A. F. Scott at Ebenezer Chrh.

William Jones, ae 20y, colored, dining
room servant, s/o Charles & Sally Jones;
Catharine Ann Grevais, ae 21y, colored, d/o
Philip & Fanny Grevais; June 24 1866 by Rev.
A. F. Scott at Col. Munford's residence.

Wm. Henry Keys, ae 43y, widower, farmer, s/o Cary Brown & Elizabeth Keys; Joannah Frances Massey, ae 27y, d/o Robert & Eliza Massey; June 16 1866 by Rev. A. F. Scott at Rev. Scott's.

John Wesley Morriss, ae 23y, colored, oysterman, s/o Billy Bluford & Mary Morriss; Mary Bluford, ae 22y, colored, d/o Tom & Harriet Bluford; June 28 1866 by Rev. A. F. Scott at Rev. Scott's.

James Burwell, ae 21y, colored, farmer, s/o John & Betsy Burwell; Mary Baker, ae 21y, colored, d/o Isaac & Lucy Baker; July 14 1866 by Rev. W. S. Hawkins.

John R. Bristow, ae 25y, farmer, s/o Richard H. & Mary S. Bristow; Mary E. Boswell, ae 22y, d/o Joseph & Eliza Boswell; Dec 7 1865 by Rev. J. G. Councill.

William Tilledge, ae 24y, oysterman, s/o Jefferson & Rebecca Tilledge; Georgianna Tilledge, ae 25y, widow, of York Co VA, d/o John & Nancy Belvin; July 19 1866 by Rev. W. S. Hawkins at Wm. Tilledge's.

John Burwell, ae 27y, colored, farmer, s/o George & Susan Burwell; Maria Carter, ae 21y, colored, d/o Sam & Louisa Carter; July 28 1866 by Rev. A. F. Scott.

Robert Colgate Selden Jr, ae 25y 11m, farmer, of Norfolk City VA, s/o Robert C. Selden & Courtney W. Seldon; Georgianna Wray Sinclair, ae 24y 6m, of Hampton Elizabeth City Co VA, d/o Jefferson B. & Georgianna W. Sinclair; Aug 9 1866 by Rev. Chas. Mann, Rector of Ware and Abingdon Parrishes at Jefferson Sinclair's.

Willoughby Wingfield Mason, ae 31y, farmer, s/o Milton W. & Elizabeth Mason; Emma Williams Thrift, ae 23y, of Norfolk City Va, lived Glo. Co VA, d/o Stephen & Rosa Thrift; Aug 29 1866 by Rev. W. G. Hammond at Thos. J. Thrift's.

Washington Hogg, ae 29y, oysterman, s/o Thos. & Rebecca Hogg; Emma Heywood, ae 16y, d/o Levi & Margaret Heywood; Aug 30 1866 by Rev. W. S. Hawkins at Rob't Thomas'.

Edmund Berry, ae 23y, colored, oysterman, s/o Edmund & Mary Berry; Usly Banks, ae 18y, colored, d/o Robert & Sally Banks; Aug 30 1866 by Rev. A. F. Scott at Newington M. E. Church.

Andrew Bohannon, ae 23y, farmer, s/o John & Susan Bohannon; Margaret Virginia Cooke, ae 16y, of Portsmouth VA, d/o Thos. & M. A. Cooke; Sept 6 1866 by Rev. Geo. E. Booker at Buena Vista King and Queen Co VA.

Richard Hall, ae 48y, widower, farmer, s/o John & Ann Hall; Elizabeth Robins, ae 35y, widow, of Nancock Co MD, lived Glo. Co VA, d/o Robert & Badger Robins; Sept 4 1866 by Rev. W. S. Hawkins.

J. H. Shackelford, ae 44y, widower, of King and Queen Co VA, merchant, s/o Warner & Joannah Shackelford; Martha A. Hunley, ae 33y, widow, d/o James & Gracy Belvin; Sept 16 1866 by Rev. W. S. Hawkins at M. Hunley's.

John Cary Wilson, ae 25y, colored, oysterman, s/o Polly Wilson, father unk, Sarah Cooke, ae 25y, colored, d/o Frank & Sarah Cooke; Sept 19 1866.

James R. Hogg, ae 21y, oysterman, s/o Washington & Elizabeth Hogg; Mary Catherine Townsend, ae 18y, d/o Kendall & Elizabeth Townsend; Feb 22 1866 by Rev. W. S. Hawkins at Carmine's Island.

Charles Grymes, ae 20y, colored, oyster, s/o Chas. Grymes & Daphney Whiting; Mary Bright, ae 21y, colored, d/o Wm. & Mary Bright; Feb 27 1866 by Rev. W. S. Hawkins at Mary Cooper's.

William Jenkins, ae 44y, widower, farmer, s/o Randall & Nancy Jenkins; Catherine West, ae 24y, d/o John & Catherine West; Mar 1 1866 by Rev. W. S. Hawkins at Rev. Hawkins school house.

George West, ae 25y, oysterman, s/o James & Mary West; Hannah Jenkins, ae 23y, d/o James & Charity Jenkins; Mar 6 1866 by Rev. W. S. Hawkins.

Joseph H. Smith, ae 40y, farmer, s/o Armistead & Patsy Smith; Lucy Ann Thomas, ae 27y, d/o Washington & Ann Thomas; Apr 10 1866 by Rev. W. S. Hawkins at Mrs. Thomas'.

Peyton G. Williams, ae 27y, merchant, s/o
Peyton G. & Nancy Williams; Mary E. Stubble-
field, ae 16y, d/o Augustine & Julia A.
Stubblefield; May 10 1866 by Rev. W. S.
Hawkins at Edward J. Carney's.

Zachariah Rufus Coates, ae 27y, farmer,
s/o Betsy & Lucy Coates; Martha Ann Corr, ae
27y, widow, d/o Thos. & Louisa Pearce; Oct
11 1866 by Rev. J. C. Crittenden at Mrs.
Corr's.

James Henry Vaughn, ae 24y, colored,
farmer, of Caroline Co VA, s/o Major & Mary
Vaughn; Elvia Spencer, ae 22y, colored, of
New Kent Co VA, d/o James & Eliza Spencer;
Oct 28 1866 by Rev. W. S. Hawkins at Union
Church.

Major Pendleton Dutton, ae 25y, farmer,
s/o Lorenzo D. & Fanny F. Dutton; Sarah Ann
Stubblefield, ae 19y, d/o Robert A. &
Virginia Stubblefield; Nov 8 1866 by Rev. W.
G. Hammond at R. A. Stubblefield's.

Jefferson Franklin Burke, ae 32y,
carpenter, s/o Jeremiah & Sarah Burke;
Elizabeth Frances Drisgall, ae 19y, d/o Wm.
H. & Frances Carpenter Drisgall; Dec 20 1866
by Rev. W. S. Hawkins at Crockett's.

Alpheus W. M. Johnson, ae 23y, colored,
farmer, of Cumberland Co VA, s/o Jacob &
Viney Johnson; Eliza Jane Fleming, ae 21y,
colored, d/o Harry & Nancy Fleming; Nov 7
1866 by Rev. J. L. Shipley.

Manny Whiting, ae 23y, colored, oyster,
s/o Lewis & Betsy Whiting; Henrietta Smith,
ae 21y, colored, d/o Peter & Elizabeth
Smith; Nov 7 1866 by Rev. W. S. Hawkins.

Richard Cary Sears, ae 22y, farmer, s/o
Beverly & Louisa Sears; Mary Virginia Ann
Nuttall, ae 17y, 9m 20d, d/o Wm. & Emily Ann
Nuttall; Nov 17 1866 by Rev. W. G. Hammond.

Thomas E. Lamberth, ae 28y, farmer, s/o
John & Mildred Lamberth; Maria Louisa
Bridges, ae 17y, d/o Francis G. & Mary C.
Bridges; Nov 22 1866 by Rev. David Coulling.

Armistead Hall, ae 48y, widower, oyster
and farm, s/o John & Ann Hall; Lizzie
Frances Henderson, ae 39y, widow, d/o Geo. &
Lizzie Frances Lewis; Dec 1 1866 by Rev. W.
S. Hawkins at Mrs. Henderson's.

Richard Allen Croswell, ae 22y, oyster, s/o Wm. & Matilda Croswell; Georgiana Robins, d/o Jesse & --- Robins; Dec 25 1866 by Rev. W. S. Hawkins at Poplar Church.

John Farinholt, ae 25y, farmer, of New Kent Co VA, s/o Rob't & Harriet Farinholt; Georgianna Roane, ae 18y, d/o Henry & Virginia Roane; Dec 13 1866 by Rev. G. W. Simcoe at the home of the bride.

George R. Murfee, ae 26y, farmer, of Greensville Co VA, s/o S. R. & E. R. Murfee; Sarah Margaret DeBerry, ae 23y, widow, d/o Edward H. & Susan Rowe; Dec 19 1866 by Rev. W. S. Hawkins at Edward Rowe's.

Elmer M. Roane, ae 22y, farmer, of King and Queen Co VA, s/o Allen & Nancy Roane; Lucy F. Bland, ae 20y, d/o Wm. L. &. Caroline S. Bland; Dec 20 1866 by Rev. Wm. E. Wiatt at Wm. Bland's.

William K. Perrin, ae 32y, farmer, s/o Wm. K. & Sarah T. Perrin; Lucy W. Jones, ae 25y, of Petersburg VA, lived Glo Co VA, d/o Walter F. & Fanny E. Jones; Dec 20 1866 by Rev. Chas. Mann, Rector of Ware Church at Waverly home of Dr. Walter F. Jones.

John Daniel, ae 26y, waterman, s/o John & Betsy Daniel; Mary E. Marchant, ae 21y, of Mathews Co VA, d/o Thos. & Mary Marchant; Dec 20 1866 by Rev. W. S. Hawkins at Crocket's home of Wm. T. Burke.

John Wesley Auld, ae 20y, waterman, of Baltimore City MD, s/o John W. & Anna Eliza Auld; Victoria Frances Griffin, ae 17y, d/o Thos. D. & --- Griffin; Dec 23 1866 by Rev. W. S. Hawkins .

John H. Rowe, ae 26y, farmer, s/o Benja. & Elizabeth Rowe; Mary S. Mouring, ae 25y, d/o Wm. T. & Susan Mouring; Dec 27 1866 by Rev. Wm. E. Wiatt at John Wm. Minor's.

Benjamin T. Rowe, ae 28y, merchant, s/o Benja. & Elizabeth Rowe; Dolly A. Minor, ae 19y, d/o John w. & Sarah V. Minor; Dec 27 1866 by Rev. Wm. E. Wiatt at Wm. Minor's.

John Sears, ae 21y, farmer, s/o Beverly & Louisa Sears; Eliza Ellen Haynes, ae 18y, d/o Wm. & Fanny Haynes; Dec 27 1866 by Rev. J. L. Shipley at Wm. Haynes'.

John Thomas Lemon, ae 23y, colored,
oysterman, s/o James & Patsy Lemon; Elleanor
Lee, ae 21y, colored, d/o John & Sarah Lee;
Dec 27 1866 by Rev. Wm. E. Wiatt .

James Carter, ae 26y, colored, oysterman,
s/o James & Judy Carter; Harriet Gregory,
ae 25y, widow, colored, d/o Overton Seldon;
Dec 26 1866 by Rev. W. S. Hawkins at Shelly.

Randall Carter, ae 21y, colored, oyster,
s/o James & Judy Carter; Mary Hughes, ae
24y, colored, d/o Ned & Kitty Hughes; Dec 27
1866 by Rev. W. S. Hawkins at Shelly.

Holeman Lewis, ae 26y, colored, miller,
Evelina Tazewell, ae 24y, colored;   Dec 26
1866 at Eagle Point.

Theodore W. Thrift, ae 22y, farmer, s/o
Thos J. & Eliza Thrift; Ann T. Rilee, ae
16y, d/o Thos. & Mary Rilee; Jan 3 1867 by
Rev. J. L. Shipley at Thos. Rilee's.

Braxton Washington, ae 21y, colored,
farmer, s/o Geo. & Maria Washington; Molly
Washington, ae 20y, colored, d/o Lucy
Washington; Dec 29 1866 by Rev. Wm. E. Wiatt
at John A. Bridges'.

George Lee, ae 23y, oysterman, colored,
s/o John & Sarah Lee; Fanny Sturges, ae 23y,
colored, d/o Tom & Fanny Sturges; Jan 3 1867
by Rev. J. L. Shipley.

George Noggin, ae 25y, colored, farmer,
of Dinwiddie Co VA, s/o Davy & Lucy Noggin;
Louisa Leamon, ae 24y, colored, d/o Daniel &
Lucy Leamon; Jan 3 1867 by Rev. Wm. E. Wiatt
at Jack Boothe's. (Colored)

George H. Haynes, ae 22y, farmer, s/o
Geo. H. & Mary Haynes; Lucy F. Pearce, ae
17y, d/o John & Mary Pearce;. Jan 10 1867 by
Rev. J. L. Shipley .

William Taliaferro, ae 23y, colored,
oysterman, s/o Sye & Jenny Taliaferro; Mary
Cooke, ae 19y, colored, d/o Godfrey Cooke;
Jan 10 1867 by Rev. W. S. Hawkins at
Providence Church.

William Auld, ae 22y, oysterman, s/o John
W. & Ann E. Auld; Martha A. Haynes, ae 18y,
d/o John W. & Frances Haynes; Jan 20 1867 by
Rev. W. S. Hawkins at Providence Church.

Thomas J. Rowe, ae 24y, waterman, s/o
Ralph & Mary Rowe; Joanna Thomas, ae 21y,
d/o James & Martha Thomas; Jan 10 1867 by
Rev. W. S. Hawkins at James Thomas'.

Edmund Gregory, ae 22y, oysterman, s/o
Daniel & Katy Gregory; Mary Harrison, ae
23y, d/o Harry & Martha Harrison; Jan 19
1867 by Rev. David Coulling at Thos. S.
Taliaferro's.

Guest Stokes, ae 22y, waterman, s/o Wm. &
Judy Stokes; Cordelia Ward, ae 22y, d/o
Billy & Maria Ward; Dec 27 1866 at Ben
Newcomb's.

Benjamin H. Williamson, ae 21y, farmer,
s/o James H. & Martha T. Williamson; Amelia
A. Pierce, ae 20y, d/o John M. & Ann T.
Pierce; Jan 15 1867 by Rev. J. L. Shipley.

John R. Coates, ae 25y, oysterman, s/o
John R. & S. E. Coates; Matilda J. Sparrow,
ae 20y, d/o Jacob & Delilah Sparrow; Jan 24
1867 by Rev. W. S. Hawkins at Capt. Wm.
Marshall's.

Robert T. Lambeth, ae 25y, farmer, s/o
James & Nancy Lambeth; Susan Rilee, ae 26y,
d/o Thos. R. & Susam Rilee; Jan 24 1867 by
Rev. J. L. Shipley at Capt. Jack Nye's.

John Read, ae 29y, colored, carpenter, of
Mathews Co VA, s/o Lucy Read, father unk,
Catharine Whiting, ae 20y, colored, d/o
Thos. & Esther Whiting; Jan 24 1867 by Rev.
J. L. Shipley at Capt. Jack Coleman's house
on Wm. S. Fields' farm.

Edward T. Darnell, ae 30y, widower,
farmer, s/o Isaac & Fanny Darnell; Sarah C.
Walker, ae 36y, widow, d/o Wm. & Sally
Rilee; Jan 31 1867 by Rev. J. L. Shipley.

Moses Mathews, ae 29y, colored, of
Cumberland Co VA, s/o Harry & Patsy Mathews;
Georgianna Cooke, ae 20y, d/o Peter & Agnes
Cooke; Jan 31 1867 by Rev. J. L. Shipley.

William Henry Belvin, ae 33y, farmer, s/o
James & Gracy Belvin; Georgianna Smith, ae
21y, d/o Anthony & Charlotte Smith; May 5
1866 by Rev. W. S. Hawkins at Mr. Belvin's.

Richard Grevis, ae 55y, widower, shoe
maker, of Mathews Co VA, s/o Pete & Arena
Grevis; Susan Leigh, ae 24y, of King William
Co Va, d/o Nat & Jenny Pride; Oct 28 1866.

Thomas A. Williams, ae 26y, oysterman,
s/o Thos. & Johannah Williams; Henrietta
Kiningham, ae 21y, d/o Clayborn & Susan
Kiningham; May 10 1866 by Rev. W. S. Hawkins
at Mr. Wilburn's.

Allen Robertson, ae 36y, widower, black-
Smith, colored, s/o Robin & Polly Robertson;
Fanny Collins, ae 25y, widow, of King and
Queen Co VA, d/o Thornton & Gabriella
Pollard; May 24 1866 by Rev. W. S. Hawkins
at Abingdon.

Joshua Richardson, ae 29y, farmer
colored, s/o Richard & Peggy Richardson;
Betsy King, ae 30y, colored, d/o Eliza; Oct
1 1866 by Rev. A. F. Scott.

Isaac Davis, ae 50y, colored, farmer, of
Farmville Va, s/o Thos. & Mary Davis;
Frances Ann Taliaferro, ae 25y, colored, of
King and Queen Co VA, d/o Warner Taliaferro;
Oct 4 1866 by Rev. A. F. Scott at Woods
Cross Roads.

William Jesse Thrift, ae 34y, widower,
coach maker, s/o Jeremiah & Ann Matilda
Groom Thrift; Ann Matilda Johnston, ae 23y,
d/o John R. & Catherine Johnston; Oct 4 1866
by Rev. A. F. Scott at E. Johnston's.

Albert Harleigh Robins, ae 24y, druggist,
lived Richmond VA, s/o Benja. J. C. &
Elizabeth Robins; Jane Frances Heywood, ae
23y, d/o Robert S. & Nancy Heywood; Oct 10
1866 by Rev. Wm. E. Wiatt at Rob't Heywood's.

Baylor Thornton, ae 21y, colored, oyster,
c/o Parrot & Sarah Thornton; Isabella Smith,
ae 20y, colored, d/o Wm. & Elizabeth Smith;
Feb 24 1867 by Rev. David Coulling at
Elmington.

Samuel Smith, ae 23y, oyster and fish,
s/o Henry & Sarah Smith; Elizabeth Hall, ae
23y, d/o Armistead & Sarah Hall; Feb 9 1867
by Rev. W. S. Hawkins at A. Hall's.

William Desmon, ae 28y, colored, farmer,
of Goochland Co VA, s/o Jack & Katy Desmon;
Amanda Gardner, ae 27y, d/o Daniel & Caty
Gardner; Feb 24 1867 by Rev. Chas. Mann at
Ware Parrish.

Joseph Lawton, ae 22y, colored, farmer, s/o James & Lucy Lawton; Sarah Gardner, ae 19y, colored, d/o Daniel & Caty Gardner; Feb 24 1867 by Rev. David Coulling at Elmington.

Peter Grevious, ae 26y, colored, oyster, of Mathews Co VA, s/o Richard & Sucky Grevious; Jane Carter, ae 23y, colored, d/o Billy & Sophy Carter; Feb 19 1867 by Rev. Chas. Mann at Ware Church Rectory.

John Robinson, ae 56y, widower, colored, blacksmith, s/o Jacob & Mary Robinson; Lucy Roy, ae 50y, widow, parents unk, Feb 16 1867 by Rev. W. S. Hawkins at J. Robinson's.

Albert Cooke, ae 22y, colored, farmer, s/o Cato & Caroline Cooke; Elleanor Kemp, ae 20y, colored, d/o Oswald & Minny Kemp; Feb 14 1867 by Rev. J. L. Shipley.

Edward F. Dutton, ae 29y, carpenter, s/o James & Nancy Dutton; Isabella Kemp, ae 18y, d/o Peter D. & Mary Kemp; Feb 7 1867 by Rev. J. L. Shipley at Salem Church.

James W. Lewis, ae 25y, oysterman, s/o Henry & Charlotte Lewis; Gracy A. Brown, ae 22y, d/o Chas. & Dorothy E. Brown; Feb 14 1867 by Rev. J. L. Shipley at Singleton's Chappel.

James Henry Corbin, ae 30y, widower, oysterman, s/o Sam & Betty Corbin; Viney Smith, ae ae 21y, widow, d/o Robert & Sally Banks; Feb 13 1867 by Rev. J. L. Shipley at Gloucester Parsonage at Belle Roy.

Samuel F. Roane, ae 45y, widower, of King and Queen Co VA, farmer, s/o Chas. & Frances Roane; Harriet E. Roane, ae 29y, of King and Queen Co VA, d/o Major & Matilda Roane; Feb 20 1867 by Rev. J. L. Shipley.

John Belvin, ae 34y, widower, oysterman, s/o John & Maria Belvin; Lizzie West, ae 21y, d/o Robert & Lucy West; Feb 22 1867 by Rev. W. S. Hawkins at J. Belvin's.

Churchill B. Roy, ae 22y, farmer, of Richmond City VA, s/o Thos. M. B. & Elizabeth Roy; Anna E. Muse, ae 33y, widow, d/o Robert & Matilda Owen; Feb 21 1867 by Rev. John Pollard Jr, at Dragon Ordinary.

Peter Thornton, ae 27y, colored, oyster,
s/o Parrot & Sarah Thornton; Evie Thornton,
ae 18y, colored, d/o Oliver & Milly Thornton;
Feb 21 1867 by Rev. Chas. Mann at Ware
Church Rectory.

Henry Blake, ae 20y, colord, farmer, s/o
Lewis Blake & Letty Burwell; Polly Dennis,
ae 21y, colored, d/o Phill Jones & Sally
Dennis; Feb 24 1867 by Rev. David Coulling.

George F. Goode, ae 27y, farmer, of
Middlesex Co VA, s/o John S. & Mary Goode;
Eudora A. Lewis, ae 24y, widow, d/o Frances
A. Gibbs, father unk, Feb 24 1867 by Rev.
John Pollard Jr. at Vernon Palmer's.

Beverly Smith, ae 25y, oysterman, of
Mathews Co VA, s/o Robin & Franky Smith;
Harriet Grevious, ae 24y, colored, of
Mathews Co VA, d/o Richard & Sucky Grevious
Feb 27 1867 by Rev. Chas. Mann at Ware
Church Rectory.

John Diggs, ae 23y, colored, farmer, s/o
Eliza Washington, father unk, Louisa Burwell,
ae 20y, colored, d/o Lucy Corbin, father unk,
Feb 28 1867 by Rev. Wm. E. Wiatt at Goshen,
home of Wm. K. Perrin.

Robert C. Hall, ae 25y, farmer, s/o Wm. M.
& Patsy Hall; Mary Ann Groom, ae 22y, of
King and Queen Co VA, d/o Beverly & Sarah
Matilda Groom; Feb 28 1867 by Rev. J. C.
Crittenden at B. Groom's.

Simon Tabb, ae 50y, colored, farmer, s/o
Fanny Tabb, father unk, Kitty Taliaferro, ae
47y, colored, d/o Phill & Caroline
Taliaferro; Mar 7 1867 by Rev. David
Coulling .

Jim Washington, ae 23y, farmer, s/o Isaac
& Fanny Washington; Maria Latimer, ae 23y,
of Mathews Co VA, d/o John & Mary Latimer;
Mar 7 1867 by Rev. W. S. Hawkins.

John Page, ae 60y, widower, colored,
chair maker and spinner, s/o Oliver & Judy
Page; Lucy Gallis, ae 70y, widow, colored,
parents unknown; Mar 17 1867 by Rev. W. S.
Hawkins .

William T. Hall, ae 26y, farmer, s/o Wm.
& Patsy Hall; Valinda C. Pearce, ae 20y, d/o
John & Mary Pearce; Mar 21 1867 by Rev.
James H. Crown.

James Sparrow, ae 23y, fish and oyster,
of Mathews Co VA, s/o Raymond & Sally
Sparrow; Martha Rowe, ae 22y, d/o Geo. &
Katy Rowe; Mar 17 1867 by Rev. W. S. Hawkins.

Lewis Taylor, ae 22y, farmer, of
Richmond City VA, s/o Harriet Taylor,
father unk, Amanda Wiatt, ae 22y, d/o Tom &
Sally Wiatt; Mar 17 1867 by Rev. David
Coulling at Rose Hill, Glo. Co VA.

Washington Byrd, ae 24y, colored, farmer,
of Halifax Co VA, s/o Washington & Nicy Byrd;
Susan Griffin, ae 23y, colored, d/o Sam &
Mary Griffin; Mar 27 1867 by Rev. W. S.
Hawkins .

Mann Johnson, ae 21y, colored, oysterman,
s/o Achilles & Sally Johnson; Sarah Ellen
Dabney, ae 21y, colored, d/o Jacob & Polly
Dabney; Apr 4 1867 by Rev. David Coulling at
Woodlawn, Gloucester Co VA.

Allen D. Reade, ae 47y, widower, farmer,
of Westmoreland Co VA, d/o Stephen & Nancy
Reade; Lucy Lambeth, ae 24y, d/o Wm. &
Elizabeth Lambeth; Apr 16 1867 by Rev. James
H. Crown.

Thomas Smith, ae 60y, widower, colored,
farmer, s/o Isaac & Matilda Smith; Frances
Smith, ae 24y, colored, d/o Thos. & Patsy
Smith; May 16 1867 by Rev. J. L. Shipley.

Harrison Ross, ae 22y, fireman at steam
mill, colored, s/o Adam & Ann Ross; Sarah
Cooke, ae 19y, colored, d/o James & Betsy
Cooke; May 12 1867 by Rev. Wm. E. Wiatt at
the home of the bride in Guinea.

Philip T. Yeatman, ae 39y, farmer, of
Mathews Co VA, s/o Thos. R. & Elizabeth
Yeatman; Jean C. W. Lloyd, ae 31, of
Alexandria Va, d/o John & Ann E. LLoyd; May
16 1867 by Rev. Chas. Mann , Rector of Ware
and Abingdon Parrishes at White Marsh, the
residence of D. J. P. Tabb.

George Edward Bristow, ae 21y, farmer,
s/o Wm. L. & Harriet Bristow; Ann Eliza
Bridges, ae 20y, d/o Robinson & Rosa Bridges;
May 16 1867 by Rev. David Coulling at James
H. Acra's.

Thomas Jefferson Oliver, ae 30y, widower, oysterman, s/o Wm. & Catharine Oliver; Sarah Wright, ae 28y, of York co VA, parents unk, May 16 1867 by Rev.W. S. Hawkins .

Thomas Binford, ae 32y, widower, colored, of Charles City Co VA, s/o Jasper & Mary Binford; Milly Peyton, ae 18y, colored, d/o Jack & Grace Peyton; June 2 1867 by Rev. W. S. Hawkins .

John Freet, ae 28y, cooper, of Washington Co MD, s/o Geo. & Margaret Freet; Adeline Bristow, ae 14y 9m 15d, d/o James B. & Lucy Ann Bristow; June 1 1867 by Rev. David Coulling at Lucy Bristow's.

William F. Thomas, ae 32, merchant, s/o Jesse & Nancy Thomas; Eliza Jane Thomas, ae 22y, d/o james & Martha Thomas; June 6 1867 by Rev. W. S. Hawkins.

John William Lawson, ae 40y, widower, farmer, s/o Richard B. K. & Elizabeth S. Lawson; Virginia Indianna Martin, ae 26y, widow, d.o Sam'l R. & Elizabeth C. Medlicott; June 9 1867 by Rev. J. L. Shipley at Woods Cross Roads.

Warner D. Chapman, ae 28y, physician, s/o Henry & Harriet W. Chapman; Lucy Agnes Medlicott, ae 19y, d/o Sam'l R. & Elizabeth C. Medlicott; June 9 1867 ny Rev. J. L. Shipley at Woods Cross Roads.

Edmund Carter, ae 28y, colored, oysterman, s/o Randall & Eliza Carter; Milly Taylor, ae 22y, colored, d/o Paul & Betsy Taylor; June 12 1867 by Rev. W. S. Hawkins at Mr. Pain's.

Charles H. Talbot, ae 27y, farmer, of Richmond City VA, lived Gloucester Co VA, s/o Chas. & Caroline W. Talbot; Sallie R. Munford, ae 25y, of Richmond City Va, lived Gloucester Co VA, d/o Col. Geo. & Elizabeth T. Munford; June 13 1867 by Rev. Chas. Mann. Rector of Ware Parrish assisted by Rev. D. Minnegerode of Richmond.

Cyrus Miller, ae 23y, colored, laborer, s/o Cyrus & Courtney Miller; Rebecca Wallace, ae 24y, colored, of James City co VA, d/o Davy & Nancy Wallace; June 18 1867 by Rev. J. L. Shipley at Belle Roi.

Sterling Morris, ae 64y, widower, farmer, colored, s/o Geo. & Sally Morris; Fanny Lemon, ae 40y, colored, d/o Jack & Milly Lemon; June 20 1867 by Rev. David Coulling at George Ashley's.

William T. Waddle, ae 33y, merchant, s/o Richard & Eliza Waddle; Ellen A. Williams, ae 18y, d/o Marcellas J. & Anne Williams; June 25 1867 by Rev. J. L. Shipley .

Henry Washington, ae 23y, colored, farmer, s/o Isaac & Fanny Washington; Catharine Burwell, ae 16y, colored, d/o Edmund & Sally Burwell; June 25 1867 by Rev. W. S. Hawkins at Hayes Mill, Glo. Co VA.

Lewis Monroe Kemp, ae 28y, coach maker, s/o Peter D. & Mary Kemp; Harriet E. B. Dutton, ae 19y, d/o Edw'd C. & Rebecca W. Dutton; June 27 1867 by Rev. J. L. Shipley.

James New Stubbs, ae 27y, atty at law, s/o Jefferson W. & Ann W. C. Stubbs; Eliza Medlicott, ae 23y, d/o Joseph & Hester Medlicott; Nov 20 1866 by Rev. W. G. Hammond at Bellomy's Church.

George G. Carneal, ae 35y, widower, farmer, of Caroline Co VA, s/o James & Mary Carneal; Clarissa F. Mason, ae 27y, d/o Milton & Elizabeth Mason; Feb 8 1864 by Rev. J. C. Crittenden at Elizabeth Mason's.

David Coulling, ae 50y, widower, dental surgeon, of Richmond City VA, s/o James M. & Mary W. Coulling; Harry Ann P. Cooke, ae 24y, d/o Thos. B. & Catharine C. Cooke; Nov 24 1864 by Rev. A. F. Scott at Ebenezer Ch.

George F. Massen, ae 25y, farmer, of Baltimore MD, s/o Wm. & Ellen Massen; Susan J. Roane, ae 28y, widow, of King and Queen Co VA, d/o Wm. F. & Lucy Adams; Jan 11 1866 by Rev. J. C. Crittenden at Wm. F. Adam's.

Lewis T. Wood, ae 23y, farmer, of Middlesex Co VA. s/o Lewis L. & Mary Ann Wood; Priscilla A. Bland, ae 22y, of King and Queen Co VA, d/o Zachariah & Delilah Bland; Jan 11 1866 by Rev. J. C. Crittenden.

James Foster, ae 23y, farmer, of King and Queen Co VA, s/o James & Betsy Foster; Sarah Bristow, ae 16y, d/o James B. & Elizabeth Bristow; Jan 13 1866 by Rev. J. C. Crittenden .

John W. Pitts, ae 20y, farmer, of King
and Queen Co VA, s/o John B. & Sarah C.
Pitts; Lavinia E. Fary, ae 16y, d/o Wm. C.
& Frances Fary; Dec 21 1865 by Rev. J. C.
Crittenden at Edwin Broaddus'.

James H. Pearce, ae 28y, farmer, s/o John
& Polly Pearce; Mary T. Pearce, ae 18y, d/o
Thos. & Louisa Groom Pearce; Jan 31 1866 by
Rev. J. C. Crittenden at J. A. P. Corr's.

William C. Broocke, ae 25y, blacksmith,
s/o Geo. & Julia Ann Broocke; Betty L. Rowe,
ae 19y, d/o Benjamin & Elizabeth Rowe; Apr
12 1866 by Rev. Wm. G. Hammond at B. Rowe's.

George W. Walker, ae 23y, farmer, s/o Wm.
M. & Margaret Walker; Catharine S. Taylor,
ae 15y 9m, d/o Geo. H. & Susan J. Taylor;
Aug 14 1867 by Rev. J. L. Shipley

John Cary Lawson, ae 22y, farmer, s/o
Chas. & Fanny Lawson; Fanny T. Wiatt, ae
22, d/o Geo. W. & Sarah Wiatt; Sept 5 1867
by Rev. J. L. Shipley.

George Catlett, ae 23y, colored, oyster,
s/o Wesley & Molley Catlett; Frances Tabb,
ae 17y, colored, d/o John & Fanny Tabb; Sept
5 1867 by Rev. W. S. Hawkins.

John W. Shackelford Jr, ae 26y, oyster,
s/o John W. & Sarah E. Shackelford; Mary Ann
Hardy, ae 25y, d/o Robert & Frances Hardy;
Sept 12 1867 by Rev. W. S. Hawkins

William Ison, ae 29y, farmer, of King and
Queen Co VA, s/o Reuben & Nancy Ison;
Harriet Potter, ae 32y, widow, of King and
Queen Co VA, d/o John & Mildred Banks; Sept
27 1867 by Rev. Wm. Eastwood at Bellamy's
Church.

Peter Perrin, ae 23y, colored, oysterman,
s/o Beverly & Diana Perrin; Lizzie Wiatt, ae
19y, colored, d/o Tom & Sally Wiatt; Oct 6
1867 by Rev. Chas. Mann at the Ware Church
Rectory.

William Thornton, ae 23y, colored, oyster,
s/o Anthony & Ann E. Thornton; Frances
Clarke, ae 17y, colored, d/o Humphrey & Aggy
Clarke; Oct 7 1867 by Rev. Chas. Mann at the
Ware Church Rectory.

Charles Stubbs, ae 22y, colored, farmer, s/o Lorenzo & Polly Stubbs; Margaret Sinclair, ae 21y, colored, d/o Wallace & Fanny Sinclair; July 23 1867 by Rev. W. S. Hawkins.

Alexander Elliott, ae 23y, oysterman, s/o Robert & Mary Elliott; Adaline Blasingame, ae 22y, d/o Henry L. & --- Blasingame; July 25 1867 by Rev. Wm. Eastwood at Ballamy's Church.

Frank Page, ae 22y, colored, laborer, s/o Isaac & Susan Page; Agnes Holmes, ae 17y, colored, d/o Geo. Walker & Judith Holmes; July 27 1867 by Rev. David Coulling.

William L. Bland, ae 49y, widower, carpenter, of King and Queen Co VA, s/o Wm. & Elizabeth Bland; Ann Eliza Spencer, ae 39y, of King and Queen Co VA, d/o Wm. & Sarah Spencer; July 31 1867 by Rev. James H. Crown at T. S. Cook's.

Richard Thomas Puller, ae 26y, waterman, s/o Thos. & Mary Ann Puller; Cordelia Read Wilkins, ae 17y, d/o John M. & Mary Wilkins; Sept 25 1867 by Rev. Wm. Eastwood at Bellamy's Church.

William S. Wroten, ae 28y, seaman, s/o Uriah & Polly F. Wroten; Elizabeth Purcell, ae 19y, d/o John & Susan Purcell; Aug 6 1867 by Rev. Wm. E. Wiatt at Bellamy's Church.

Roland Lawson, ae 25y, farmer, s/o John & Betsy Lawson; Lucy Ellen Bristow, ae 17y, d/o Peter & Lucy Ann Bristow; Aug 7 1867 by Rev. James H. Crown.

,   John B. Wolfe, ae 64y, farmer, of Prussia EUROPE, s/o John B. & Frances Wolfe; Mary E. Dutton, ae 42y, d/o James H. & Ann Dutton; Oct 10 1867 by Rev. Wm. Eastwood.

Benjamin Dabney, ae 30y, widower, laborer, colored, s/oGeo. & Edy Dabney; Martha Cole, ae 28y, colored, d/o Dick & Rosa Cole; Oct 17 1867 by Rev. J. L. Shipley.

Benjamin F. Howlett, ae 38y, widower, farm & oyster, s/o Isaac & Ann Howlett; Sarah E. Kemp, ae 27y, d/o Beverly & mary Kemp; Oct 24 1867 by Rev. J. L. Shipley.

Isaac Croswell, ae 42y, widower, waterman, s/o Wm. & Matilda Croswell; Charlotte Ann Smith, ae 18y, d/o Anthony & Charlotte Ann West Smith; Oct 31 1867 by Rev. W. S. Hawkins.

Cornelius Lawton, ae 25y, colored, carpenter, s/o Jas. & Lucy Lawton; Mary Baytop, ae 24y, colored, d/o Lewis & Maria Baytop; Nov 10 1867 by Rev. Chas. Mann, Rector of Ware Parrish at the Rectory.

Joshua Moore, ae 28y, farmer, of Goochland Co VA, s/o Bob & Jane Moore; Eliza Scott, ae 30y, widow, d/o Monroe & Sucky Page; Nov 17 1867 by Rev. W. S. Hawkins.

Joshua Brown, ae 24y, colored, farmer, s/o Edmund & Becky Brown; Mary Jane Cosby, ae 23y, d/o Gabriel & Fanny Cosby; Nov 17 1867 by Rev. Chas. Mann Rector of Ware Parrish.

Joseph H. Padgett, ae 40y, farmer, of King and Queen Co VA, s/o Wm. & Polly Padgett; Elleanora F. Webley, ae 26y, d/o Philip & Matilda Webley; Nov 21 1867 by Rev. David Coulling at Geo. W. Adams'.

James Morriss, ae 21y, widower, oyster and sailor, s/o James & Molly Morriss; Louisa Hall, ae 20y, d/o John & Matilda Hall; Nov 28 1867 by Rev. Wm. Eastwood.

James Smith, ae 21y, widower, oysterman, s/o Davy & Mary Smith; Mary Banks, ae 32y, widow, d/o John & Martha Hall; Nov 28 1867 by Rev. Wm. Eastwood at John Hall's.

John Frazier, ae 38y, colored, farmer, s/o Bob & Nancy Frazier; Lucy Gregory, ae 25y, d/o Peter & Emily Gregory; Dec 5 1867 by Rev. Chas. Mann at the Rectory of Ware Parrish.

Richard Thias, ae 32y, widower, carpenter, s/o Davy & Rebecca Thias; Jenny Foster, ae 23y, d/o Eliza Foster, father unk, Dec 17 1867 by Rev. Chas. Mann at the Rectory of Ware Parrish.

James A. Leavitt, ae 35y, carpenter, s/o Wm. & Mary Leavitt; Lucy V. Pointer, ae 20y, d/o Seth & Gracy Pointer; Dec 12 1867 by Rev. Wm. Eastwood at Seth Pointer's Eagle Point.

Mordacai Willis Robinson, ae 30y, colored, carpenter, s/o Addison & Indy Robinson; Mira Ann Burwell, ae 30y, colored, d/o Amy Burwell; Dec 25 1867.

Elijah Cook, ae 24y, colored, oysterman, s/o Elijah & Arena Cook; Frances Whiting, ae 24y, colored, d/o John & Polly Whiting; Dec 26 1867 by Rev. Chas. Mann at Ware Church Rectory.

Robert Noggins, ae 23y, colored, laborer, of Dinwiddiw Co Va, lived Glo. Co VA, s/o David & Lucy Noggins; Maria King, ae 27y, widow, d/o Elijah & Diana Hayes; Nov 24 1867 by Rev. Chas. Mann at Ware Church Rectory.

James Gardner, ae 22y, colored, oyster, s/o Baylor & Eliza Gardner; Susan Carter, ae 22y, colored, d/o Billy & Sophy Carter.

William H. Harris, ae 29y, farmer, s/o John T. & Susan A. Harris; Emeline F. Jenkins, ae 15y, d/o David & Susan Jenkins; Dec 26 1867 by Rev. W. S. Hawkins at Mrs. Jenkins'.

Benjamin Franklin Heywood, ae 30y, farmer, s/o Robert S. & Ann B. Heywood; Sarah C. Thruston, ae 24y, d/o Emanuel & Catherine Thruston; Dec 25 1867 by Rev. Wm. E. Wiatt at Millwood.

James Pratt, ae 22y, farmer, of PENN, s/o Benjamin Pratt; Mary Isabella Thawley, ae 17y, of Caroline Co Va, d/o John & Isabella Thawley; Dec 19 1867 by Rev. J. L. Shipley.

Frank Cooke, ae 50y, widower, colored, s/o Chas. & Sarah Cooke; Rebecca Lemon, ae 20y, colored, d/o Wm. & Mary A. Lemon; Dec 19 1867 by Rev. Wm. Eastwood at John Cary Wilson's.

Thomas Jefferson Whiting, ae 22y, oyster, colored, s/o Frank & Agnes Whiting; Sarah Williams, ae 21y, widow, colored, d/o James & Betsy Spurlock; Jan 9 1868 by Rev. W. S. Hawkins at Hickory Fork.

William Leigh, ae 21y, colored, oyster, of Mathews Co VA, s/o Jasper & Martha Leigh; Nelly Thornton, ae 22y, colored, d/o Oliver & Milly Thornton; Dec 21 1867 by Rev. Chas. Mann at Warner Taliaferro's.

Joseph C. Fleming, ae 25y, waterman, of
Princess Ann City VA, s/o James W. & Mildred
F. Fleming; Catharine A. Teagle, ae 21y, d/o
Thos. & Elizabeth Teagle; Dec 25 1867 by Rev.
J. L. Shipley.

William E. Fary, ae 26y, farmer, s/o Wm.
C. & Elizabeth Fary; Josena Lavinia Day
Fletcher, ae 21y, d/o Rowland & Frances A.
Fletcher; Dec 25 1867 by Rev. Wm. Eastwood.

William F. Eastwood, ae 41y, mechanic,
s/o Wm. & Jane Eastwood; Delia C. Harwood,
ae 27y, widow, d/o Richard D. & Dorothy
Leigh; Dec 19 1867 by Rev. David Coulling at
John Henry Leigh's.

Thomas E. Milby, ae 23y, farmer, of King
and Queen Co VA, s/o Thos. E. & Hannah E.
Milby; Sarah F. Corr, ae 30y, widow, d/o Wm.
& Elizabeth Lamberth; Dec 24 1867 by Rev.
David Coulling at Wm. Lamberth's.

Richard Upshur Roane, ae 21y, farmer, s/o
Samuel F. & Betty Roane; Mary F. Roane, ae
17y, d/o Henry & Virginia Roane; Dec 24 1867
by Rev. J. L. Shipley at Henry Roane's.

James Joyner Lewis, ae 24y, farmer,
colored, s/o --- & Franky Lewis; Betty Gwynn,
ae 18y, colored, d/o Philip & Sarah Gwynn;
Jan 4 1868 by Rev. W. E. Wiatt at Wareham.

William Robins, ae 26y, oysterman, s/o
Jesse & Chitty Robins; Mary Jane Smith, ae
19y, d/o James & Mary Ann Smith; Jan 9 1867
by Rev. Chas. Mann at Ware Church Rectory.

Stephen Jones, ae 21y, colored, laborer,
s/o Lewis & Nancy Jones; Lucy Carter, ae 21y,
colored, d/o John & Sarah Carter; Dec 25
1867 by Rev. W. S. Hawkins at Hickory Fork.

William J. Lawson. ae 28y, farmer, s/o
John & Elizabeth Lawson; Mary F. Coates, ae
22y, d/o Robert & Polly Coats; Dec 28 1867
by Rev. David Coulling at Robert Coat's.

Robert Ransome, ae 85y, widower, farmer,
s/o Peyton & Sarah Ransome; Fanny Gudmal, ae
75y, widow, d/o Anthony & Grace; Apr 6 1867
by Rev. W. S. Hawkins at Rosewell.

John William Robinson, ae 33y, colored,
carpenter, of Richmond City VA, s/o Moses &
Agnes Robinson; Charlotte Jones, ae 24y,
colored, d/o Abraham & Scilla Jones; Apr 7
1867 by Rev. David Coulling at Newington Ch.

James Gardner, ae 22y, oysterman, s/o
Baylor & Eliza Gardner; Susan Carter, ae 22y,
d/o Billy & Sophy Carter; Dec 17 1867 by Rev.
Chas. Mann.

Washington Chevis, ae 27y, colored,
farmer, s/o James & Peggy Chevis; Susan
Whiting, ae 21y, colored, d/o Tom & Esther
Whiting; Dec 26 1867, Certificate not signed.

John William Walker, ae 20y, colored,
farmer, s/o Harry & Mary Walker; Lucy Gwynn,
ae 18y, colored, d/o Philip & Susan Gwynn;
Dec 25 1867 by Rev. Wm. E. Wiatt.

John Smith, ae 23y, colored, farmer, of
Mathews Co VA, s/o Nathan & Milly Smith;
Maria Richardson, ae 24y, colored, d/o Milly
Richarsdson, father unk, Dec 29 1967 by Rev.
Certificate unsigned.

Randolph Carter, ae 23y, colored, s/o
Randolph & Eliza Carter; Nancy Cary, ae 19y,
d/o Miles & Polly Cary; Dec 28 1867 by Rev.
W. S. Hawkins.

Philip Morris, ae 22y, colored, oyster,
s/o Wade & Lucy Ann Morris; Mary Taylor, ae
22y, colored, d/o Henry & Betty Taylor; Jan
2 1868 by Rev. W. S. Hawkins.

William C. Taylor, ae 23y, farmer, of
Dorchester Co MD, s/o Littleton & Huldy
Taylor; Julia F. Holsten, ae 25y, widow, d/o
Robert C. & Polly Coates; Jan 4 1868 by Rev.
J. L. Shipley.

William Coats, ae 22y, oysterman, s/o
John R. & Ellen Ann Coats; Nancy West, ae
22y, d/o Wm. & Courtney West; Jan 7 1868 by
Rev. W. S. Hawkins.

Miles Henry Booker, ae 30y, farmer, s/o
Wm. C. & Elizabeth Frances Booker; Rosa Ann
Mason, ae 21y, d/o Philip & Rosa Mason; Jan
14 1868 by Rev. J. L. Shipley.

Thomas E. Johnston, ae 26y, farmer, s/o
John & Catherine Johnson; Indianna Taylor,
ae 18y, d/o Henry & Susan Taylor; Feb 2 1868
by Rev. David Coulling.

William J. Palmer, ae 24y, farmer, s/o
Vernon & Elizabeth Palmer; Mary E. Grooms,
ae 23y, d/o John L. & Martha E. Grooms; Feb
2 1868 by Rev. R. B. Beadles.

Addison Burwell, ae 32y, farmer, s/o
Philip & Sally Burwell; Martha Fox, ae 18y,
d/o Jim & Sarah Fox; Feb 5 1868 by Rev. W.
E. Wiatt.

Luke T. Shipley, ae 21y, waterman, of St.
Mary's MD, parents unk; Pinkey E. Brown, ae
17y, d/o Chas. & Dolly Brown; Feb 6 1868 by
Rev. Charles Mann.

Jerry Gregory, ae 56y, widower, farmer,
s/o Kemp & Catharine Dillard; Amy Bayal, ae
55y, widow, d/o Henry & Maria Jones; Apr 30
1868 by Rev. Wm. E. Wiatt.

Jacob A. Dillard, ae 22y, farmer, s/o
Kemp & Catharine Dillard; Sarah Jane Burton,
ae 21y, d/o Thos. B. & Jane Burton; Feb 4
1868 by Rev. Wm. E. Wiatt.

Joseph Brown, ae 31y, mechanic, s/o Thos.
& Mildred Brown; Betty E. Howard, ae 21y,
d/o James & Betsy Howard; Feb 13 1868 by
Rev. Wm. E. Wiatt.

James Cook, ae 24y, colored, farmer, s/o
Anthony & Maria Cook; Emeline Ross, ae 19y,
colored, d/o Peter & Frances Ross; Feb 8
1868 by Rev. David Coulling.

James Rice, ae 21y, farmer, of Halifax Co
Va, s/o Billy & Biddy Rice; Amanda Montague,
ae 17y, d/o Tilleun & Kitty Montague; Feb 13
1868 by Rev. J. L. Shipley.

Miles Seawell, ae 35y, oysterman, s/o
Abraham & Lucinda Seawell; Martha Curtis, ae
18y, d/o Robin & Maud Curtis; Feb 20 1868.

Thomas C. Cooke, ae 34y, farmer, s/o Thos.
B. & Catharine Cooke; Mary J. Vaughan, ae
19y, d/o Wm. & A. F. Vaughan; Feb 27 1868 by
Rev. David Coulling.

Thomas C. Enos, ae 31y, merchant, s/o
Francis & Catherine Enos; Martha C. Lowry,
ae 24y, d/o Wm. & Martha Lowry; Feb 25 1868
by Rev. Wm. E. Wiatt.

Hugh A. South, ae 42y, widower, farmer,
s/o Andrew & Mary H. South; Ada L. Hall, ae
22y, of King and Queen Co VA, d/o Thos B. &
Sarah R. Hall; Mar 4 1868 by Rev. David
Coulling.

Benjamin Marbles, ae 40y, widower, farmer,
colored, of Southampton Co VA, s/o Harry &
Violet Marbles; Fanny Randolph, ae 38y,
widow, colored, parents unk; Mar 1 1868.

James P. Wallace, ae 21y, oysterman, s/o
Joseph & Lilia Ann Wallace; Maria Susan
Hardy, ae 18y, d/o Robert Hardy, mother unk;
Mar 5 1868 by Rev. W. S. Hawkins.

William W. Gressitt, ae 47y, farmer, s/o
John M. & Ann W. Gressitt; Emeline L.
Blasingame, ae 36y, widow, d/o Richard D. &
Catharine Dunston; Mar 5 1868 by Rev. J. L.
Shipley.

Powatan Elliott, ae 25y, shoe maker, of
King and Queen Co Va, s/o Robert & Mary
Elliott; Susan R. Blasingame, ae 21y, d/o
Thos. & Martha Blasingame; Mar 5 1868 by
Rev. J. L. Shipley.

James Brown, ae 23y, oysterman, s/o James
& Susanna Brown; Rebecca A. Lewis, ae 16y,
d/o Wm. J. & Lucy Lewis; Mar 24 1868 by Rev.
J. L. Shipley.

Benjamin A. Rowe, ae 27y, merchant, s/o
Sterling & Frances A. Rowe; Cornelia E. Rowe,
ae 19y, d/o Benjamin & Elizabeth Rowe; Apr
2 1868 by Rev. Wm. E. Wiatt.

Thomas B. Burton, ae 47y, widower, farmer,
s/o Chas. R. & Nancy Burton; Rosa Ann Hibble,
ae 27y, widoe, d/o Cary & Nancy Booker; Apr
2 1868 by Rev. Wm. E. Wiatt.

Benjamin P. Dobson, ae 40y, widower,
waterman, of Middlesex Co VA, s/o Wm. &
Eliza Dobson; Martha Sampson, ae 29y,
widow, d/o Simon & Elizabeth Green; Apr
6 1868 by Rev. Charles Mann.

James H. Harris, ae 20y, colored, farmer,
s/o Wm. & Dinah Harris; Mary Ellen Jackson,
ae 17y, colored, d/o Philip & Mary Jenkins;
Apr 21 1868 by Rev. W. S. Hawkins.

George Brown, ae 40y, widower, farmer,
s/o Geo. & Susan Brown; Martha Ann Jenkins,
ae 36y, d/o John & Melvinia Jenkins; Apr 21
1868 by Rev. W. S. Hawkins.

Isaac Thornton, ae 23y, colored, farmer,
s/o Paul & Kesiah Thornton; Julia Lewis, ae
18y, colored, d/o Warner & Fanny Lewis; Apr
25 1868 by Rev. Wm. E. Wiatt.

Charles L. Gwynn, ae 29y, physician, of
Norfolk VA, s/o Chas. R. & Mary Gwynn;
Margaret B. Taliaferro, ae 19y, d/o Thos.
B. & Mary M. Taliaferro; Apr 28 1868 by Rev.
Charles Mann.

James Thompson, ae 42y, colored, widower, oysterman, s/o Lewis & Minerva Thompson; Rachel Fleming, ae 21y, colored, widow, d/o Essen & Betsy Guthrie; June 19 1868 by Rev. Wm. E. Wiatt.

James Baytop, ae 65y, widower, colored, farmer, s/o James & Amy Tuck; Mary Wormley, ae 40y, widow, colored, parents unk, July 2 1868 by Rev. J. L. Shipley.

William H. Holt, ae 30y, farmer, s/o Wm. & Sarah Holt; Ann Eliza Baytop, ae 24y, d/o Jim Baytop; July 2 1868 by Rev. J. L. Baytop.

Nathaniel Gregory, ae 23y, oysterman, s/o Daniel & Caty Gregory; Lucy Dixon, ae 21y, d/o John & Nancy Dixon; June 25 1868 by Rev. Chas. Mann.

William Shackelford, ae 30y, widower, coach maker, s/o Wm. & Eliza Shackelford; Margaret Cooke, ae 30y, d/o John Mordacai & Julia Ellen Cooke; July 7 1868 by Rev. J. L. Shipley.

James A. Goalder, ae 24y, coach maker, of King and Queen Co VA, s/o Augustine & Rosa Goalder; Julia Ann Acra, ae 21y, d/o Wm. J. & Julia C. Acra; July 9 1868 by Rev. Wm. E. Wiatt.

Gary Stokes, ae 23y, colored, farmer, s/o Wm. & Judy Stokes; Mary Todd, ae 20y, colored, d/o Philip A. Todd; July 18 1868 by Rev. W. S. Hawkins.

James H. Brooks, ae 23y, colored, oyster, s/o Cesar & Dianna Brooks; Louisa Tazewell, ae 20y, colored, d/o Winston & Patty Tazewell; July 25 1868 by Rev. Wm. E. Wiatt.

Alexander Stoakes, ae 24y, colored, boat man, s/o Christopher & Ann Stoakes; Martha Wiatt, ae 30y, widow, d/o Randall & Eliza Carter; Aug 13 1868 by Rev. W. S. Hawkins.

Robert Borum, ae 22y, oysterman, s/o Daniel & Polly Borum; Cathrine Davis, ae 22y, widow, of Middlesex Co VA, d/o Jack & Laura Davis; Aug 20 1868 by Rev. W. S. Hawkins.

Taylor Whiting, ae 21y, colored, farmer, s/o Daniel & Hannah Whiting; Louisa Singleton, ae 21y, colored, d/o Wallace & Fanny Singleton; Aug 29 1868 by Rev. Wm. E. Wiatt.

John Dutton Clayton, ae 20y, farmer, s/o
Joseph & Sarah Ann Clayton; Mary E. Baker, ae
19y, d/o Wm. P. & Elizabeth F. Baker; Sept
6 1868 by Rev. R. B. Beadly.

George W. Horseley, ae 26y, farmer, s/o
Kilingham & Elizabeth Horseley; Lucy Jane
Sheppard, ae 18y, d/o John D. & Ann Sheppard;
Sept 10 1868 by Rev. David Coulling.

John W. Booth, ae 20y, farmer, s/o Jack &
Betsy Booth; Bettie Muse, ae 20y, d/o Esson
& Nancy Muse; Sept 12 1868 by Rev. Wm. E.
Wiatt.

William Monroe, ae 23y, colored, farmer,
s/o Iverson & Grace Monroe; Fanny Dudley,
ae 24y, colored, d/o Thias & Isabella Dudley;
Sept 19 1868 by Rev. W. S. Hawkins.

George Owens, ae 49y, widower, oysterman,
s/o Reed & Jane Owens; Mildred West, ae
29y, d/o Christopher & Fanny West; Nov 19
1868 by Rev. W. S. Hawkins.

Carrel Tompkins, ae 23y, colored, farmer,
s/o Isaac & ROse Tompkins; Margaret Jones,
ae 26y, colored, d/o Billy & Martha Sparks;
Sept 26 1868 by Rev. David Coulling.

Armstead Hall Jr, ae 19y, farmer, s/o
Armstead & Sarah Jane Hall; Kitty Hogg, ae
22y, d/o Tho. & Betsy Hogg; Sept 24 1868 by
Rev. W. S. Hawkins.

Joseph Thomas Mathews, ae 25y, farmer,
s/o Jack & Betsy Mathews; Rosa Rilee, ae
23y, d/o Wm. & Mary Rilee; Oct 8 1868 by
Rev. David Coulling.

Archibald Hayes, ae 27y, waterman, s/o
Geo. & Martha Hayes; Hester E. Croswell, ae
14y, d/o John T. & Ann Croswell; Oct 21 1868
by Rev. W. S. Hawkins.

George W. Shackelford. ae 38y, widower,
waterman, s/o Benja. & Tabitha Shackelford;
Sarah Amanda Dews, ae 18, d/o Zachariah &
Elizabeth Dews; Oct 21 1868 by Rev. W. S.
Hawkins.

John W. Watkins, ae 25y, oysterman, s/o
David & Elizabeth A. Watkins; Julia A.
McLane, ae 22y, d/o Wm. & Elizabeth McLane;
Oct 21 1868 by Rev. Wm. E. Wiatt.

Edward T. Massey, ae 25y, farmer, s/o
Edward G. & Mary Massey; Mary A. C. Haynes,
ae 19y, d/o Geo. & Mary Haynes; Nov 1 1868
by Rev. R. B. Beadles.

John Portlock, ae 27y, colored, farmer,
of Norfolk Co VA, s/o Sam & Rachel Coy; Rose
Smith, ae 22y, colored, d/o Thos. & Sally
Smith; Nov 5 1868 by Rev. Chas. Mann.

Richard Cooke, ae 29y, colored, oyster,
s/o James & Chloe Cooke; Louisianna Rowe, ae
21y, colored, d/o Wm. & Maud Monroe; Nov 5
1868 by Rev. J. T. Wallace.

Harry A. Atkinson Jr, ae 23y, attorney at
law, of Richmond VA, s/o Henry A. & Gracy E.
Atkinson; Belle V. Dobson, ae 20y, d/o Wm. &
Mary M. Dobson; Nov 4 1868 by Rev. Wm. E.
Wiatt.

George Cosby, ae 25y, colored, farmer, s/o
Gabriel & Fanny Cosby; Jane Jones, ae 21y,
colored, d/o Lucy Ann Jones; Nov 7 1868 by
Rev. J. T. Wallace.

John Burns, ae 26y, farmer, of upper
CANADA, lived G1ô. Co VA, s/o Michael &
Catharine Burns; Catharine Norton, ae 35y,
widow, d/o Wm. Bristow; Nov 12 1868 by Rev.
Charles Mann.

Thomas S. Beckwith, ae 26y, merchant, of
Petersburg VA, s/o Thos. L. & Agnes Beck-
with; Emma Cary, ae 25y, d/o Sam'l B. & B.
W. Cary; Nov 17 1868 by Rev. Chas. Mann.

W. Henry Curry, ae 34y, widower, farmer,
s/o Sowersby & Mary A. Curry; Octavia Jane
Stubbs, ae 16y, d/o Edward S. & Jane A. S.
Stubbs; Dec 3 1868 by Rev. David Coulling.

Shepard G. Miller, ae 21y, farmer, of
Mathews Co VA, s/o Shepard G. & Mary Miller;
Ada G. Catlett, ae 21y, d/o Temple G. &
Martha S. Catlett; Dec 3 1868 by Rev. J. L.
Shipley.

William R. Stubbs, ae 69y, widower,
farmer, s/o Francis & Susannah Stubbs; Mary
J. Stubbs, ae 57y, widow, d/o John & Mary
Stubbs; Dec 4 1868 by Rev. J. L. Shipley.

Philip A. Taliaferro, ae 41y, physician,
s/o Warner T. & Leah S. Taliaferro; Sarah L.
McCandish, d/o Geo. I. McCandish; Dec 10
1868 by Rev. Charles Mann.

Joel Heywood, ae 25y, oysterman, s/o
Charles & Peggy Heywood; Sarah Greene, ae
18y, d/o Geo. & Millie Greene; Dec 10 1868
by Rev. W. S. Hawkins.

Robert Carter, ae 28y, colored, oyster,
s/o Henry & Polly Carter; Pinkey Lockley, ae
21y, colored, d/o Betsy Davenport, father
unk, Dec 10 1868 by Rev. David Coulling.

James T. Gray, ae 24y, farmer, of Somerset Co MD, s/o Major Johnson & Margaret
Gray; Mary R. Trevilian, ae 19y, d/o
Augustine S. & Julia Ann Trevilian; Dec 15
1868 by Rev. J. T. Wallace.

Lewis West, ae 25y, oysterman, s/o Wm. &
Courtney West; Hester Smith, ae 21y, d/o
Tayler & Fanny Smith; Dec 17 1868 by Rev. W.
S. Hawkins.

William H. Seawell, ae 24y, farmer, of
KENTUCKY, s/o Wm. H. & Mary Seawell; Laura
O. Johnston, ae 21y, d/o Thos. E. & Eliza-
beth Johnston; Dec 17 1868 by Rev. J. T.
Wallace.

Cicero L. Blake, ae 24y, farmer, of
Middlesex Co VA, s/o James & Ann K. Blake;
Mary K. Johnston, ae 20y, d/o Thos. E. &
Elizabeth Johnston; Dec 17 1868 by Rev. J.
T. Wallace.

Beverly Jackson, ae 22y, colored, farmer,
s/o Edward & Becky Jackson; Sarah F. Bristow;
ae 20y, d/o Billy & Catharine Bristow; Dec
20 1868 by Rev. J. T. Wallace.

Isaac Cook, ae 22y, colored, oysterman,
s/o Anthony & Milly Cooke; Mary Sturges, ae
23y, d/o Godfrey & Fanny Chapman; Dec 22
1868 by Rev. David Coulling.

John Tabb, ae 18y, oysterman, s/o John &
Fanny Tabb; Ellen Hearns, ae 18y, d/o Henry
& Fanny Hearns; Dec 24 1868 by Rev. E. S.
Hawkins.

Charles H. Thomson, ae 26y, farmer, of
Shenandoah VA, s/o James & Mary A. Thomson;
Grace Foster, ae 21y, of Mathews Co VA, ./.
parents unk; Dec 25 1868 by Rev. R. B.
Beaddly.

James Monroe, ae 21y, farmer, s/o Elijah
& Nancy Monroe; Susan Page, ae 23y, widow,
d/o Mon & Sucky Page; Dec 25 1868 by Rev.
S. H. Phillips.

Richard B. Roberts, ae 48y, house carpenter, of Mathews Co VA, s/o John B. & Patsy Roberts; Elizabeth Brown, ae 33y, widow, d/o Thos. Howard; Dec 31 1868 by Rev. Wm. E. Wiatt.

John A. Blake, ae 22y, farmer, of Middlesex Co Va, s/o Barkley R. & Susan Blake; Mary E. Massey, ae 32y, widow, d/o John Buchannon & Susan Wilson; Dec 24 1868 by Rev. R. B. Beadde.

George Gregory, ae 21y, oysterman, s/o Peter & Emery Gregory; Lizzie Morris, ae 20y, d/o Geo. & Mary Dixon Morris; Dec 31 1868 by Rev. W. S. Hawkins.

Frank Brown, ae 35y, widower, colored, farmer, s/o Edmund & Rebecca Brown; Lucy F. Lemon, ae 19y, colored, d/o John & Sally B. Lemon; Dec 31 1868 by Rev. J. T. Wallace.

John F. Chapman, ae 35y, widower, clerk, of St. Mary's MD, s/o John H. & Martha Chapman; Laura Jane Ransone, ae 16y, d/o James R. & Susan H. Ransone; Dec 31 1868 by Rev. Charles Mann.

James Henry Robinson, ae 24y, farmer, of King and Queen Co VA, s/o Wm. & Ony Robinson; Nancy Meads, ae 30y, parents unk, Dec 31 1868 by Rev. David Coulling.

Lorenzo D. Cooke, ae 21y, oysterman, s/o Wm. L. Cooke; Mary Ellen Lockley, ae 21y, d/o Wm. & Emiline Lockley; jan 16 1869 by Rev. David Coulling.

Ned Carter, ae 28y, oysterman, s/o Wm. & Sophy Carter; Maria Gardner, ae 21y, d/o Baylor & Eliza Gardner; Jan 2 1869 by Rev. Charles Mann.

Isaac Brigerson, ae 38y, widower, slave getter, of Northampton VA, s/o Benjamin & Eliza Brigerson; Lucy Washington, ae 38y, d/o George Washington & Franky; Jan 9 1869 by Rev. J. T. Wallace.

William Henry Booth, ae 38y, widower, farmer, s/o Wm. & Rose Booth; Betsy Allen, ae 25y, widow, d/o Robert & Maria Curtis; Jan 6 1869 by Rev. David Coulling.

William Coats, ae 22y, oysterman, s/o John R. & Ellen Ann Coats; Nancy West, ae 21y, d/o Wm. & Courtney West; Jan 7 1869 by No Rev. listed.

Currell Holmes, ae 52y, widower, farmer, of King William Co VA, s/o Addison & Lucy King; Mariah Stubbs, ae 50y, widow, parents unk, Jan 7 1869 by Rev. Samuel H. Phillips.

Benjamin Lindsey, ae 22y, waterman, of James City Co VA, s/o Wm. J. & Mary C. Lindsey; Julia Blasingham, ae 18y, d/o John & Emiline Blasingame; Jan 13 1869 by Rev. E. M. Peterson.

James Thomas Banks, ae 28y, farmer, s/o John D. & Mildred Banks; Harriet Elizabeth Jones, ae 22y, d/o Thos. L. & Elizabeth Jones; Jan 14 1869 by Rev. E. M. Peterson.

Warner Henry Hogg, ae 26y, farmer, s/o Warner H. & Susan Hogg; Susan Brown, ae 22y, d/o Geo. & Nancy Brown; Jan 14 1869 by Rev. W. S. Hawkins.

Christopher West, ae 26y, farmer, s/o Christopher & Nancy West; Lillia Ann Hogg, ae 22y, d/o Warner H. & Susan Hogg; Jan 14 1869 by Rev. W. S. Hawkins.

Marcellus J. Williams, ae 45y, widower, seaman, d/o Wm. & Frances Williams; Georgia P. White, ae 18y, d/o James & Susan F. White; Jan 20 1869 by Rev. George E. Thomas.

Edward Henry Rowe, ae 39y, farmer, s/o Hansford & Gracie Rowe; Mary Susan Williams, ae 20y, d/o Wm. & Martha E. Williams; Jan 21 1869 by Rev. W. S. Hawkins.

John T. Rilee, ae 29y, farmer, s/o Wm. K. & Mary C. Rilee; Sarah C. Haynes, ae 24y, d/o Wm. & Fanny Haynes; Jan 21 1869 by Rev. R. B. Beaddles.

Christopher Washington, ae 21y, farmer, s/o Washington & Nancy Washington; Laura Jane Grimes, ae 18y, d/o Jefferson Grimes; Jan 21 1869 by Rev. Wm. E. Wiatt.

William Smith, ae 26y, oyster, of Mathews Co VA, s/o Adam & Nancy Smith; Judy Wormley, ae 21y, d/o Armstead & --- Wormley; Jan 26 1869 by Rev. E. M. Peterson.

Andrew W, Wright, ae 27y, hotel keeper, s/o Henry P. & Mary A. Wright; Lucy Ellen Leavitt, ae 25y, d/o W. A. & L. E. Leavitt; Feb 4 1869 by Rev. E. M. Peterson.

Samuel Banks, ae 54y, widower, farmer, s/o Adam & Jenny Banks; Lucy Lockley, ae 54y, widow, d/o Bailey & Nanny Lockley; Jan 29 1869 by Rev. Chas. Mann.

Frank Thornton, ae 48y, widower, farmer, s/o Sam & Betsy Thornton; Catharine Burwell, ae 19y, d/o John & Harriet Burwell; Jan 30 1869 by Rev. E. M. Peterson.

Charles Smith, ae 32y, farm hand, of Norfolk VA, s/o Dorius & Mariah Saunders; Mary Jane Lemon, ae 30y, widow, parents unk; Feb 4 1869 by Rev. E. M. Peterson.

Alexander W. Pearce, ae 28y, millwright, s/o Wm. B. & Ann E. Pearce; Georgia C. & Pointer, ae 20y, d/o Wm. D. & Mary E. Pointer; Feb 4 1869 by Rev. E. M. Peterson.

Ransom Evens Dudley, ae 20y, farmer, s/o Ransom & Mariah Dudley; Mary Frances Baytop, ae 17y, d/o Peter & Rebecca Baytop; Feb 11 1869 by Rev. E. M. Peterson.

Alexander Washington Anderson, ae 20y, farmer, s/o Ned Holles; Ann Thomas Morris, ae 18y, d/o -- & Mariah Griffin; Feb 11 1869 by Rev. E. M. Peterson.

John Anderson Hogg, ae 38y, oysterman, s/o Thos. & Mollie Hogg; Susanna Shackelford, ae 25y, d/o Geo. & Betsy Shackelford; Feb 18 1869 by Rev. W. S. Hawkins.

John Henry Kelly, ae 25y, widower, miller, s/o Susan Kelly; Martha Pollard, ae 24y, d/o Philip & Sally Pollard; Feb 28 1869 by Rev. J. T. Wallace.

John H. Figg, ae 28y, wheelwright, s/o James & Polly Figg; Tiney Blake, ae 17y, of Middlesex Co VA, d/oW. L. & -- Blake; Mar 3 1869 by Rev. J. T. Wallace.

William King, ae 30y, oysterman, s/o Henry Taylor & Rebecca King; Lucy Jane Driver, ae 19y, d/o Lorenzo &-Sally Driver; Mar 4 1869 by Rev. David Coulling.

Benjamin West, ae 25y, oysterman, s/o Ambrose & Hannah West; Nancy West, ae 22y, d/o Christopher & Nancy West; Mar 11 1869 by Rev. Wm. E. Wiatt.

Ralph Belvin, ae 27y, oyster & farm, s/o Lewis & Nancy Belvin; Nancy West, ae 22y, d/o Howard & Nancy West; Mar 18 1869 by Rev. Samuel H. Phillips.

George Washington Smith, ae 39y, fireman at steam mill, of Mathews Co VA, s/o James & Rosa Smith; Louisa Wiatt, ae 31y, widow, parents unk; Jan 31 1869 by Rev. Chas. H. Page.

George Augustine Bruce, ae 26y, ship caulker, of Norfolk Co VA, s/o Lodurick & Elizabeth Bruce; Mary Catharine Watkins, ae 24y, d/o David & Elizabeth Watkins; Mar 8 1869 by Rev. Wm. E. Wiatt.

Joe Stevens, ae 35y, widower, oyster and farm, of Northampton Co VA, s/o John Gayle & Leah Stevens; Jane Carter, ae 24y, d/o Daniel & Sarah Willis; Mar 18 1869 by Rev. Chas. Mann.

Richard Harris, ae 21y, laborer, s/o Wm. & Dinah Harris; Martha Washington, ae 21y, d/o Sally Washington; Mar 20 1868 by Rev. E. M. Peterson.

John Archer Brown, ae 29y, oysterman, s/o James & Susan Brown; Mary Jane West, ae 21y, d/o Frank & Frances West; Mar 20 1869 by Rev. W. S. Hawkins.

John Dobson Rowe, ae 22y, oysterman, d/o Wm. A. & Caroline Rowe; Emma Robins, ae 17y, d/o Wm. Robins & Elizabeth W. (now E. W. Hall); Mar 25 1869 by Rev. W. S. Hawkins.

Charles Henry Morris Whitington, ae 22y, colored, sailor, s/o Geo. & Hetty Whitington; Henrietta Ross, ae 21y, colored, d/o Betsy Ross; Mar 28 1869 by Rev. Chas. Mann.

Richard Thomas Shepard, ae 24y, sailor, s/o Geo. & Polly Shepard; Alice Maria Banks, ae 21y, d/o Thos. & Catharine Banks; Mar 31 1869 by Rev. E. M. Peterson.

John A. Robinson, ae 24y, oysterman, s/o Lewis & Susanna Robinson; Clara Jackson, ae 21y, d/o Henry & Emiline Jackson; Apr 10 1869 by Rev. E. M. Peterson.

Benjamin B. Belvin, ae 30y, farmer, s/o Geo. & Fanny Belvin; Mary Green, ae 28y, d/o Geo. & Nancy Green; Mar 29 1869 by Rev. Wm. E. Wiatt.

William Brooks, ae 21y, oysterman, s/o Hester Brooks; Sarah Gregory, ae 20y, d/o Peter & Emily Gregory; Apr 6 1869 by Rev. E. M. Peterson.

James Thomas Jordan, ae 22y, oysterman,
s/o Wm. & Mariah J. Jordan; Margaret Ann
Purcell, ae 26y, widow, d/o John B. & Isabella James; Apr 19 1869 by Rev. W. S.
Hawkins.

Robert J. Hudgins, ae 21y, farmer, of
Mathews Co VA, s/o Wm. & Frances Hudgins;
Vandelia Hudgins, ae 23y, d/o Wm. H. & Mary
E. Hudgins; Apr 19 1869 by Rev. J. T.
Wallace.

L. M. Ironmonger, ae 25y, waterman, of
York Co VA, s/o L. D. & Elizabeth Ironmonger;
Sue Templeman, ae 20y, d/o Wm. H. & Mildred
Templeman; Apr 22 1869 by Rev. E. M/
Peterson.

Joseph Smith, ae 22y, farmer, s/o Henry
& Priscilla Smith; Adeline Semore, ae 21y,
d/o Daniel & Lucy Semore; Apr 24 1869 by
Rev. J. T. Wallace.

John D. Buckins, ae 30y, wheelwright, of
Lancaster PENN, lived King and Queen,s/o
Geo. & Ann Buckins; Martha A. Booker, ae
25y, d/o Geo. Pillsbury, mother unk, May 3
1869 by Rev. E. M. Peterson.

James Green, ae 25, oysterman, s/o Geo. &
Nancy Green; Elizabeth Belvin, ae 24y, d/o
Geo. & Frances Belvin; May 11 1869 by Rev.
Wm. E. Wiatt.

Joseph Carter, ae 23y, oysterman, s/o
Samuel & Betsy Carter; Sally Carter, ae 37y,
widow, d/o James & Nancy Fox; May 20 1869 by
Rev. W. S. Hawkins.

Si Jones, ae 21y, oysterman, s/o Si &
Fannie Jones; Grace Lee, ae 14y, d/o John &
Martha Lee; May 23 1869 by Rev. Chas. Mann.

David Grimes, ae 22y, oysterman, s/o
Chas. & Daffany Grimes; Mary Ellen Dixon, ae
19y, d/o Wm. & Betsy Dixon; June 3 1869 by
Rev. W. S. Hawkins.

William C. Edwards, ae 40y, farmer, s/o
Thos. C. & Nancy Edwards; Mary Ann Haynes,
ae 26y, d/o Wm. & Frances Haynes; June 17
1869 by Rev. E. M. Peterson.

Albert M. Stubbs, ae 26y, wright clerk,
s/o John W. & Ellen Stubbs; Sarah J. Hughes,
ae 25y, d/o Wm. C. & Jane Hughes; June 27
1869 by Rev. David Coulling.

Robert Lockley, ae 27y, oysterman, s/o
Daniel & Milly Lockley; Melvina Robinson, ae
20y, d/o John & Mary Robinson; June 29 1869
by Rev. David Coulling.

Munford Howard, ae 60y, farmer, of York
Co Va, parents unk; Margaret Page, ae 35y,
d/o Daniel & Franky Page; July 8 1869 by
Rev. Wm. E. Wiatt.

Robert Roades Berry, ae 45y, merchant,
s/o James & Ann Berry; Martha Glass, ae 24y,
of Mathews Co VA, d/o Andrew & Sarah Glass;
July 13 1869 by Rev. E. M. Peterson.

John Mince Wilkins, ae 45y, widower,
farmer, s/o Nathan & Nancy Wilkins; Elizabeth Frances Howlett, ae 24y, d/o Isaac &
Ann Howlett; July 16 1869 by Rev. E. M.
Peterson.

Thomas Jefferson, ae 23y, parents unk;
Frances Slaughter, ae 21y, d/o Jefferson &
Betsy Slaughter; July 29 1869 by Rev. E. M.
Peterson.

Washington Evans, ae 19y, oysterman, s/o
Wm. & Clara Evans; Harriet Dixon, ae 19y,
d/o Robert & Sally Dixon; Aug 2 1869 by Rev.
Charles Mann.

James Henry Dutton, ae 31y, carpenter,
s/o James & Jane Dutton; Mollie Virginia
Massenburg, ae 22y, d/o Wm. H. & Harriet
Massenburg; Aug 6 1869 by Rev. Chas. Mann.

Edward Carter, ae 53y, widower, farmer,
s/o Sam & Phillis Carter; Betsy Burnette, ae
40y, widow, d/o Philip Moody; Aug 8 1869 by
Rev. Samuel H. Phillips.

Richard Bird, ae 23y, farmer, s/o Sam &
Amy Bird; Catharine Braxton, ae 17y, d/o
Geo. & Catharine Braxton; Aug 8 1869 by Rev.
J. C. Crittenden.

Albert Williams, ae 49y, widower, house
carpenter, of Mathews Co VA, s/o Wm. & Susan
Williams; Parnelia A. Chapman, ae 29y, d/o
John W. & Harriet Chapman; Aug 26 1869 by
Rev. F. W. Edwards.

Alexander Carter, ae 22y, oysterman, s/o
Henry & Polly Carter; Silva Robinson, ae
19y, d/o John W. & Chance Robinson; Sept 7
1869 by Rev. Charles Mann.

Oliver Dudley, ae 48y, widower, farmer, s/o Ransone & Nancy Dudley; Mary J. Johnson, ae 20y, d/o Lewis & Mary Johnson; Sept 7 1869 by Rev. E. M. Peterson.

Edward Huell, ae 21y, farmer, s/o John & Susan Huell; Sarah Jane Smith, ae 15y, parents unk; Sept 16 1869 by Rev. F. W. Edwards.

Ferry Bird, ae 45y, farmer, of Warren Co TENN, s/o Cornelius & Timpy Bird; Elizabeth Lockley, ae 21y, d/o Richard & Lidia Ann Whitin; Sept 23 1869 by Rev. David Coulling.

Edward Henry Rowe, ae 47y, widower, merchant, s/o Wm. & Margaret Rowe; Lizzie Glass, ae 35y, d/o Andrew & Sarah Glass; Sept 28 1869 by Rev. Wm. E. Wiatt.

William Thomas Tyler, ae 21y, oysterman, of New Kent Co VA, s/o Marshall & Mary Tyler; Gracie Lockley, ae 21y, d/o Daniel & Nellie Lockley; Sept 30 1869 by Rev. David Coulling.

Alfred Jackson, ae 23y, laborer, of Richmond VA, s/o Mathew & Mariah Jackson; Martha Laws, ae 16y, parents unk; Oct 2 1869 by Rev. David Coulling.

Baylor Fleet, ae 60y, widower, farmer, of King and Queen Co VA, s/o Ben & Rose Fleet; Nancy Hughes, ae 50y, widow, parents unk; Oct 7 1869 by Rev. W. S. Hawkins.

Thomas Henry Dunston, ae 22y, farmer, s/o John & Mary Dunston; Mary Louisa Cavan, ae 18y, d/o John W. & Mary F. Cavan; Oct 7 1869 by Rev. W. S. Hawkins.

Thomas Mason, ae 38y, farmer, widower, of York Co VA, s/o Anthony Mason & Elizabeth, his wife who was E. H; Lucinda Connelly, ae 33y, d/o Richard & Elizabeth Banks; Oct 12 1869 by Rev. David Coulling.

John M. Pierce, ae 46y, widower, farmer, of Isle of Wight Co VA; s/o Nathan & Patunia Pierce; Adaline Amanda Amory, ae 30y, d/o Dennis & Anna S. Amory, who was Anna S. Wood; Oct 14 1869 by Rev. David Coulling.

William Whiting, ae 21y, farmer, s/o
Lewis & Laurance Whiting; Lucy Ellen
Whiting, ae 18y, d/o Frank & Dafney Whiting;
Oct 14 1869 by Rev. W. S. Hawkins.

Beverly Wilson, ae 32y, widower, farmer,
s/o Robert & Betsy Wilson; Caroline Berry,
ae 27y, parents unk; Oct 17 1869 by Rev.
David Coulling.

John T. Perrin, ae 32y, farmer, s/o Wm.
K. & Sarah T. Perrin; Matilda Prosser Tabb,
ae 20y, d/o John P. & Rebecca Tabb; Oct 20
1869 by Rev. Chas. Mann.

Americus V. Rowe, ae 22y, merchant, s/o
Jasper C. & Julia B. Stubblefield; Tabitha
V. Rowe, ae 18y, d/o Edmund & Susan H.
Hayes; Oct 26 1869 by Rev. Wm. E. Wiatt.

John H. Dudley, ae 23y, farmer, s/o Cyrus
& Isabella Dudley; Ann Davis Whiting, ae
21y, d/o Lewis & Betsy Whiting; Oct 27 1869
by Rev. W. S. Hawkins.

Carter Jones, ae 39y, widower, oysterman,
s/o Daniel & Milly Jones; Nannie Thias, ae
17y, d/o Brittian & Nellie Thias; Nov 2 1869
by Rev. Chas. Mann.

David Cornelius Jenkins, ae 20y, oyster,
s/o David & Susan Jenkins; Ann Thomas Riley,
ae 21y, d/o John M. Sarah V. Riley; Nov 7
1869 by Rev. W. S. Hawkins.

John H. Leigh, ae 33y, farmer, s/o John &
Frances Leigh; Margaret A. Roane, ae 24y,
widow, d/o Thomas Booth & Margaret Sinclair;
Nov 8 1869 by Rev. E. M. Peterson.

William F. Maddox, ae 27y, widower,
oysterman, s/o James & Matilda Garrett;
Julia E. Puller, ae 17y, d/o Thos. & Mary A.
Puller; Nov 11 1869 by Rev. David Coulling.

Richard A. Bramble, ae 23y, oysterman,
s/ Adam & Catharine Bramble; Elnora Hayes,
ae 23y, d/o Geo. & Lucy Hayes; Nov 11 1869
by Rev. W. S. Hawkins.

William Burwell, ae 70y, widower, carpenter, s/o Wm. & Milly Burwell; Ann Curtis,
ae 60y, widow, of Mathews Co VA, parents
unk; Nov 18 1869 by Rev. Wm. E. Wiatt.

Alexander Brooks, ae 45y, widower,
laborer, of Mathews Co VA, s/o Wyatt & Lucy
Brooks; Jenny Peterson, ae 40y, widow,
parents unk; Nov 18 1869.

Dr. Albert Johnson Terrell, ae 42y,
widower, physician, of Caroline Co VA, s/o
Geo. B. & Louisa Terrell; Mary Elizabeth
Guest, ae 32y, of Richmond VA, d/o James &
Mary Z. Guest; Nov 17 1869 by Rev. J. T.
Wallace.

Gordon Miller, ae 26y, waterman, of
Portsmouth, VA, s/o Linsey & Martha J.
Miller; Louisianna Teagle, ae 21y, d/o Thos.
& Elizabeth Teagle; Nov 24 1869 by Rev. Wm.
E. Wiatt.

Abner F. Dutton, ae 32y, merchant, s/o
Lorenzo L. & Fanny F. Chapman Dutton; Eliza-
beth L. Callis, ae 28y, d/o Lewis B. &
Elizabeth L. Leavitt Callis; Nov 25 1869 by
Rev. E. M. Peterson.

Robert Wilbur Taylor, ae 30y, waterman,
s/o Henry & Betsy Taylor; Lucy Jane Morris,
ae 21y, d/o -- & Jane Carter; Nov 25 1869 by
Rev. David Coulling.

Robert Burwell, ae 23y, farmer, s/o
Philip Burwell; Mary Susan Howard, ae 19y,
d/o Martha Lewis; Dec 2 1869 by Rev. W. S.
Hawkins.

Samuel Gayle, ae 25y, sailor, of Eastern
Shore MD, parents unk; Lucy Washington, ae
23y, d/o Henry & Maria Washington; Dec 3
1869.

James Belcher, ae 25y, farmer, s/o James
& Nancy Belcher; Lucretia Burwell, ae 21y,
of Mathews Co VA, d/o John & Harriet
Burwell; Dec 4 1869 by Rev. David Coulling.

James L. Williams, ae 47y, teacher, of
Middlesex Co VA, s/o Carter & Nancy
Williams; Mary West, ae 36y, widow, of
Mathews Co VA, d/o Richard & Sarah Careles;
Dec 7 1869 by Rev. Wm. E. Wiatt.

John William Blake, ae 47y, widower,
farmer, s/o Thos. & Mary Blake; Mary Smith,
ae 19y, of Baltimore MD, d/o Wm. & Sarah
Smith; Dec 9 1869 by Rev. E. M. Peterson.

Peter Kemp, ae 22y, oysterman, s/o John &
Judy Kemp; Margaret Corbin, ae 19y, d/o Jack
& Judy Corbin; Dec 6 1869 by Rev. E. M.
Peterson.

Thomas Smith, ae 24y, oysterman, s/o Michael & Eliza Smith; Lucretia Ann West, ae 17y, d/o Robert & Lucy West; Dec 12 1869 by Rev. E. M.Peterson.

Henry Lemon, ae 21y, colored,oysterman, s/o James & Patsy Lemon; Lucy Baytop, ae 18y, colored, d/o Harry & Milly Baytop; Dec 15 1869 by Rev. David Coulling.

William West, ae 21y, oysterman, s/o Wm. & Courtney Brown West; Sarah A. Brown, ae 23y, d/o Robert & Mary Brown; Dec 18 1869 by Rev. Wm. S. Hawkins.

George Washington Leigh, ae 26y, widower, oysterman, of King and Queen Co VA, s/o John & Sarah Leigh; Elizabeth Morris, ae 17y, of York Co VA, d/o Thos. & Mary Morris; Dec 13 1869 by Rev. E. M. Peterson.

William T. Jenkins, ae 23y, boatsman, s/o Wm. & Mary Williams Jenkins; Viana West, ae 24y, d/o Christopher & Hannah Green West; Dec 25 1869 by Rev. Wm. E. Wiatt.

George Thomas Smither, ae 24y, farmer, of Essex Co VA, s/o Geo. K. & Cordelia Smither; Lucy Emily Moore, ae 17y, d/o Geo.& Williamouth G. Moore; Dec 22 1869 by Rev. E. M. Peterson.

Godfrey Cooke, ae 24y, oysterman, s/o Wm. & Virginia Cooke; Sarah Lockley, ae 23y, of Middlesex Co VA, d/o Daniel & Milly Lockley; Dec 23 1869 by Rev. David Coulling.

Benjamin Franklin Stubblefield, ae 22y, ousterman, s/o Simeon & Martha Stubblefield; Susan Ellen Smither, ae 22y, d/o Geo. & Cordelia Smither; Dec 23 1869 by Rev. E. M. Peterson.

William G. Graves, ae 21y, farmer, s/o Wm. G. & Eliza Elliott Graves; Sarah Frances Dunston, ae 22y, d/o John H. & Mary F. Bridges Dunston; Dec 23 1869 by Rev. W. S. Hawkins.

Benjamin W. Thornton, ae 23y, farmer, s/o Francis & Harriet E. Cluverious Thornton; Catharine C. Cooke, ae 19y, d/o Thos. D. & Catharine C. Cary Cooke; Dec 23 1869 by Rev. David Coulling.

Jinks Sparks, ae 25y, farmer, s/o Wm.&
Martha Sparks; Jennie Alice Williams, ae
21y, d/o Henry & Judy Williams; Dec 26 1869
by Rev. E. M. Peterson.

Robert Jones Clements, ae 27y, mechanic,
s/o Robert Y. & J. A. P. Clements; Mary
Louisa Williams, ae 25y, d/o Andrew &
Pauline Williams; Dec 25 1869 by Rev. David
Coulling.

Charles Homes, ae 35y, widower,
oysterman, s/o John & Easter Homes; Lena
Lemon, ae 30y, widow, d/o Nancy Freeman; Dec
22 1869 by Rev. E. M. Peterson.

Sam Richerson, ae 25y, farmer, s/o Sam &
Louisa Richerson; Betty Bird, ae 22y, d/o
Fanny Bird; Dec 26 1869 by Rev. E. M.
Peterson.

John William Smither, ae 26y, farmer,
s/o Wm. T. & Elizabeth H. Smither; Lucy D.
Hannah A. Leigh Stubblefield; Dec 26 1869 by
Rev. David Coulling.

Mordecai T. Cooke, ae 32y, farner, s/o
Francis W. & Fanny Cavan Cooke; Sarah E.
Powers, ae 21y, d/o Wm. H. & Nancy Shield
Powers; Dec 28 1869 by Rev. David Coulling.

Thomas J. Ash Jr, ae 28y, farmer, s/o
Thos. & Lucy A. Ransone Ash; Mary E. Minor,
ae 18y, d/o John W. & Frances A. Mouring
Minor; Dec 26 1869 by Rev. Wm. E. Wiatt.

William Hayes Atkinson, ae 22y, clerk, of
Richmond Va, s/o Henry A. & G. E. Belvin
Atkinson; Alice Boyd Rowe, ae 20y, d/o
Jasper C. Rowe; Dec 29 1869 by Rev. E. M.
Peterson.

James Monroe Selden, ae 27y, oysterman,
Jasper & Lucy Selden; Mary Elizabeth
Thornton, ae 22y, d/o Anthony & Ann Eliza
Thornton; Dec 30 1869 by Rev. W. S. Hawkins.

Achilles Rowe, ae 33y, widower, waterman,
s/o Ralph & Mary Williams Rowe; Elizabeth
Hogg, ae 29y, d/o Geo. A. & Rachel King
Hogg; Dec 30 1869 by Rev. W. E. Wiatt.

James Borden, ae 24y, laborer, of N. C,
d/o Willis & Eliza Borden; Anna Pennington
Cooke, ae 20y, d/o Reubin & Betty Pennington;
Dec 30 1869 by Rev. David Coulling.

George W. Sterling, ae 21y, oysterman, of
Mathews Co Va, s/o Noah & Elizabeth Respess
Sterling; Ellen Deal, ae 17y, d/o John A. &
Elizabeth Brown Deal; Dec 30 1869 by Rev.
Samuel H. Phillips.

Philip Moody, ae 26y, farmer, s/o Philip
& Nancy Moody; Sally Corbin, ae 26y, widow,
d/o Chas. & Delphy Reed; Dec 30 1869 by Rev.
W. S. Hawkins.

David Burwell, ae 25y, farmer, s/o Peyton
& Mary Burwell; Sidney Hayes, ae 25y, widow,
-- & Mary Hayes; Jan 1 1870 by Rev. Samuel
H. Phillips.

James T. Banks, ae 28y, widower, farmer,
s/o John D. & Mildred Banks; Harriet E.
Jones, ae 22y, widow, d/o Thos. L. & Elizabeth Jones; Jan 13 1869 by Rev. E. M.
Peterson.

William Smith, ae 26y, of Mathews Co VA,
s/o Adam & Mary Smith; Judy Wormley, ae 21y,
of Middlesex Co VA, d/o Armistead ° Wormley;
Jan 26 1869 by Rev. E. M. Peterson.

Andrew J. Wright, ae 27y, keeper of
restaurant, s/o H. P. & Mary A. Wright; Lucy
Ellen Leavitt, ae 25y, d/o W. A. & L. E.
Leavitt; Feb 4 1869.

Charles Smith, ae 32y, of Norfolk VA;
Mary Jane Lemon, ae 30y, widow; Feb 1 1869.

John Henry Rowe, ae 35y, merchant, s/o
John L. & Lucy L. Rowe; Fanny C. Hall, ae
26y, d/o Lorenzo & Catharine C. Hall; Dec 8
1868 by Rev. J. L. Shipley

Frank Reed, ae 22y, farmer, of Mathews Co
VA, s/o Frank & Fanny Reed; Lucy Wiatt, ae
21y, d/o Lewis & Rachel West; Nov 27 1869 by
Rev. E. M. Peterson.

Robert Jones, ae 21y, farmer, s/o Tan &
Judy Jones; Mary Eliza Hayes, ae 21y, d/o
Peyton & Mary Hayes; Jan 1 1870 by Rev.
Samuel H. Phillips.

James Richard Corsey, ae 26y, sailor, of
Baltimore MD, s/o Jas. & Ann Kemp Corsey;
Mary Frances Haynes, ae 17y, d/o John W. &
Frances Ann Nuttall Haynes; Jan 1 1870 by
Rev. W. S. Hawkins.

Beverly W. Kemp, ae 21y, waterman, s/o Beverly W. & Mary B. Kemp; Rosa Belle Dunston, ae 18y, d/o Rich'd & Susan Dunston; Jan 6 1870 by Rev. E. M. Peterson.

Poindexter Booker, ae 26y, house carpenter, s/o James & Elizabeth Newcomb Booker; Sally V. Sears, ae 21y, of Middlesex Co VA, d/o Henry & Hester A. Booker Sears; Jan 6 1870 by Rev. Wm. E. Wiatt.

George Barney Redcrop, ae 29y, oysterman, of York Co VA, s/o George & Lucritia Redcrop; Mary Ellen Sampson, ae 17y, d/o Susan Sampson; Jan 6 1870 by Rev. W. S. Hawkins.

John Maury, ae 22y, oysterman, s/o John & Elizabeth Hogg Maury; Willie Ann Harvey, ae 18y, d/o John & Frances Harvey; Jan 6 1870 by Rev. W. S. Hawkins.

George T. Newbille, ae 28y, plasterer, of King and Queen Co VA, s/o John & Elizabeth Newbille; Mary Margaret Hughes, ae 19y, d/o Thos. H. & Julia E. Hughes; Jan 9 1870.

Henry Thomas, ae 21y, farmer, s/o Abraham & Eliza Thomas; Molly Jones, ae 22y, d/o George & Sally Jones; Jan 9 1870 by Rev. David Coulling.

Luther Major Roane, ae 30y, merchant, of King and Queen Co VA, s/o Charles & Sarah R. Roane; Demarius Ann Fary, ae 18y, d/o Wm. C. & Frances Corr Fary; Jan 13 1870 by Rev. J. C. Crittenden.

William Henry Bridges, ae 22y, farmer, s/o Elijah & Mary F. Kemp Bridges; Agnes Ann Brown, ae 19y, of Middlesex Co VA, d/o Smith W. & Susan H. Garrett Brown; Jan 18 1870 by Rev. J. T. Wallace.

William A. Haynes, ae 24y, farmer, s/o Wm. & Frances Padgett Haynes; Harriet S. Milby, ae 21y, of King and Queen Co VA, d/o Thos. E. & Mary E. Bland Milby; Jan 18 1870 by Rev. E. M. Peterson.

Daniel Parker, ae 26y, laborer, of Chesterfield Co VA, s/o George & Betsy Parker; Cuetta Batcher, ae 50y, widow, d/o James & Nelly Davenport; Jan 20 1890 by Rev. W. S. Hawkins.

David Smith, ae 66y, widower, laborer, of
Norfolk, VA, s/o David & Channy Smith;
Hannah Harrison, ae 50y, parents unk; Feb 6
1870 by Rev. W. S. Hawkins.

John Wm. Cooke, ae 35y, oysterman, s/o
James & Elizabeth Cooke; Margaret Ann Smith,
ae 20y, of Mathews Co VA, d/o Nutty & Isaac
Smith; Feb 9 1890 by Rev. Wm. E. Wiatt.

Joseph Gardener, ae 23y, oysterman, of
Richmond VA, s/o James & Betsy Gardener;
Fanny Willis, ae 18y, of Mathews Co VA, d/o
Farmer & Cordelia Willis; Feb 12 1870 by
Rev. Charles Mann.

John Hairston Seawell, ae 29y, attorney
at law, s/o John T. & Elizabeth Hairston
Seawell; Henrietta M. Smith, ae 20y, of
Worcester Co MD, d/o George R. & Amelia
Jackson Smith; Feb 16 1870 by Rev. Charles
Mann.

George Kidd, ae 22y, farmer, of King and
Queen Co VA, s/o John And Eliza Booker Kidd;
Eliza Tyler, ae 18y, of James City Co VA,
d/o Mary Carter; Feb 16 1870 by Rev. E. M.
Peterson.

Peter Hogg, ae 24y, oysterman, s/o John &
Judy Dunston Hogg; Rosa A. Oliver, ae 16y,
d/o Ryland & Fanny Seawell Oliver; Feb 16
1870 by Rev. W. S. Hawkins.

William Heywood, ae 24y oysterman, s/o
Wm. & Eliza Heywood; Catherine Brown, ae
25y, d/o Wm. & Milly Brown; Feb 17 1870 by
Rev. W. S. Hawkins.

Benjamin A. Hogg, ae 21y, oysterman, s/o
Washington & Elizabeth Bosby Hogg; Henrietta
C. Hogg, ae 20y, d/o John & Judy Dunston
Hogg; Feb 16 1870 by Rev. W. S. Hawkins.

John Richard Cavan, ae 27y, merchant, s/o
John W. & Fanny Moore Cavan; Mary Catharine
Smither, ae 22y, d/o Wm. T. & Elizabeth
Crittenden Smither; Feb 16 1870 by Rev. E.
M. Peterson.

Robert W. Bristow, ae 22y, farmer, s/o
Rich'd & Mary Carney Bristow; Betty Ann
Mason, ae 17y, d/o Thos. & Harriet Didlake
Mason; Feb 20 1870 by Rev. David Coulling.

Charles Collier, ae 25y, farmer, of King
and Queen Co VA, s/o Charles & Mary Didlake
Collier; Catharine Coates, ae 21y, d/o John
& Fanny Lawson Coates; Feb 23 1870 by Rev.
David Coulling.

William Gordon, ae 24y, farmer, s/o
Beverly & Betsy Gordon; Rebecca Fields, ae
21y, d/o Albert & Lucy Fields; Mar 26 1870
by Rev. W. S. Hawkins.

George Cottee, ae 31y, oysterman, s/o
Catharine Cottee; Virginia A. Oliver, ae
21y, d/o Robert & Catharine Oliver; Mar 31
1870 by Rev. Samuel Henry Phillips, Rector
of Abingdon.

Willaim Gabriel Starr, ae 29y, minister
of the gospel, of Rappahannock Co VA, s/o
Wm. H. & Frances Starr; Lizzie A. Leigh, ae
21y, d/o John & Jane B. Leigh; Apr 5 1870 by
Rev. E. M. Peterson.

William Collins Washington, ae 22y,
oysterman, s/o David & Colnette Washington;
Mary Ransom, ae 22y, d/o George W. & Jenny
Ransom; Apr 7 1870 by Rev. W. S. Hawkins.

Thomas Henry Lewis, ae 22y, oysterman,
s/o George & Sarah Lewis; Indiana Robins,
ae 27y, widow, d/o Thos. & Mary Ransone; Apr
13 1870 by Rev. Wm. E. Wiatt.

Randal Robinson, ae 23y, oysterman, s/o
John & Lucy Robinson; Lizzie Cole, ae 21y,
d/o Moses & Nancy Cole; Apr 10 1870 by Rev.
David Coulling.

George Collins, ae 37y, widower, shoe-
maker, of E. S. MD, s/o Johnathan & Mary
Collins; Margaret Fields, ae 29y, widow, d/o
John R. & Judy Hogg; Apr7 1870 by Rev. W. S.
Hawkins.

Alexander Washington Gordon, ae 36y,
oysterman, s/o Beverly & Betsy Gordon;
Frances Hall, ae 17y, d/o John & Elizabeth
Ann Hall; Apr 14 1870 by Rev. W. S. Hawkins.

Alfred J. Ward, ae 33y, sailor, of
Accomack Co VA, s/o Wm. Ward & Mary Summers;
Martha A. Bayley, ae 25y, d/o John H. &
Maria Williams Bayley; Apr 14 1870 by Rev.
Wm.E. Wiatt.

Nicholas Robinson, ae 24y, oysterman, s/o Seth & Matilda Robinson; Margaret Morris, ae 21y, d/o John & Lucie Morris; Apr 20 1870 by Rev. E. M. Peterson.

Harry Carter, ae 25y, oysterman, s/o John & Mary Carter; Mary Page, ae 26y, widow, parents unk; Apr 28 1870 by Rev. W. S. Hawkins.

Henry Page, ae 30y, widower, farmer, of King and Queen Co VA, s/o Moses & Nancy Page; Mary Susan Kemp, ae 25y, of King and Queen Co VA, d/o Cary & Lucie Ann Kemp; July 12 1870 by Rev. Thos. Nopper.

William Franklin Hogg, ae 29y, farmer, s/o Richard & Catharine Hogg; Julia Frances Bray, ae 21y, d/o Thos. J. & Martha A. Bray; May 5 1870 by Rev. E. M. Peterson.

Frank Carter, ae 21y, laborer, s/o John & Sarah Carter; Frances Gibbs, ae 21y, parents unk; Sept 9 1870 by Rev. W. S. Hawkins.

James Jester, ae 29y, farmer, of Cecil Co MD, s/o John & Hannah Cystergres Jester; Mary Thomas Carr, ae 26y, d/o Fanny Coates; May 7 1870 by Rev. David Coulling.

John Henry Field, ae 22y, farmer, s/o Albert & Lucy Field; Rebecca Stubbs, ae 21y, d/o Lorenzo & Polly Stubbs; May 14 1870 by Rev. W. S. Hawkins.

William Henry Davies, ae 27y, clerk, s/o Alfred B. & Maria E. Pryor Davies; Indiana Hughes, ae 18y, d/o John H. & Julia Leavit Hughes; May 17 1870 by Rev. E. M. Peterson.

John Lawson, ae 27y, sailor, of Somerset Co Md, lived in Mathews Co Va, s/o Josiah & Leah Johnston Lawson; Sarah Page, 21y, d/o Oliver & Becky Page; May 21 1870 by Rev. W. S. Hawkins.

Joseph Stokes, ae 23y, oysterman, s/o Christopher & Ann Stokes; Ellen Gage, ae 21y, d/o Philip & Ellen Gage; June 2 1870 by Rev. W. S. Hawkins.

Isaac Tabb, ae 30y, laborer, of King and Queen Co VA, parents unk; Martha Cary, ae 21y, of King and Queen Co VA, parents unk; June 18 1870 by Rev. J. C. Crittenden.

Henry Seawell, ae 22y, oysterman &
sailor, s/o Miles & Dinah Seawell; Alicy
Ward, ae 16y, d/o Billy & Maria Ward; June 9
1870 by Rev. E. M. Peterson.

Daniel Graham, ae 30y, farmer, s/o John &
Alicy Graham; Martha Carter, ae 22y, d/o
Delia Ann Jackson; June 30 1870 by Rev. S. H.
Phillips.

John Pollard, ae 21y, farmer, s/o Martha
Shackelford; Elizabeth Guthrie, ae 21y, d/o
Peter & Milly Guthrie; June 18 1870 by Rev.
David Coulling.

Lewis Curdly, ae 21y, farmer, s/o
Winchester & Nancy Curdly; Lucy Graham, ae
21y, d/o John & Nancy Graham; July 22 1870
by Rev. S. H. Phillips.

Samuel Ransone, ae 27y, oysterman, s/o
Daniel & Delphey Ransone; Sally Carter, ae
19y, d/o Edward & Harriet Carter; July 30
1870 by Rev. W. S. Hawkins.

Miles Carter, ae 30y, oysterman, s/o
George & Jenny Carter; Indiana Hall, ae 21y,
d/o John & Eliza Hall; Aug 4 1870 by Rev. W.
S. Hawkins.

James Montague, ae 24y, oysterman, s/o
Soloman & Sarah Montague; Emily Page, ae
22y, d/o Isaac & Frankie Page; Aug 11 1870
by Rev. W. S. Hawkins.

Lad S. Stubbs, ae 24y, merchant, lived in
King and Queen Co VA, s/o Lawrence S. & Mary
Dame Stubbs; Agnes J. Hall, ae 22y, d/o John
F. & Elizabeth Hall; Aug 11 1870 by Rev.
David Coulling.

John Dennis, ae 25y, fireman for steam
mill, of MD, parents unk; Letty Nickerson,
ae 22y, widow, of King and Queen Co VA,
parents unk; Aug 21 1870 by Rev. Wm. E.
Wiatt.

James Claiborne, ae 21y, farmer, s/o
Daniel & Polly Claiborne; Milly Robinson, ae
23y, parents unk; Aug 21 1870 by Rev. Wm. E.
Wiatt.

Arthur Walker, ae 30y, farmer, s/o Harry
& Mary Walker; Ellen Burwell, ae 20y, d/o
Kender & Easter Burwell; Aug 25 1870 by Rev.
A. F. Scott.

Aaron Stubbs, ae 22y, farmer, s/o Lorenzo & Polly Stubbs; Mary Fields, ae 21y, d/o Albert & Lucy Fields; Sept 16 1870 by Rev. Samuel Henry Phillips, Rector of Abingdon.

James Whiting, ae 22y, oysterman, lived in York Co, VA, s/o Beverly & Nancy Whiting; Fanny Booker, ae 23y, widow, d/o Cain & Polly Evans; Sept 22 1870 by Rev. Wm. E. Wiatt.

Wilson Lewis, ae 62y, widower, farmer, of King and Queen Co VA, s/o Lewny & Rosa Madison Lewis; Nany Griffin, ae 30y, widow, parents unk; Sept 29 1870 by Rev. David Coulling.

Richard Taliaferro, ae 22y, oysterman, s/o James & Louisa Taliaferro; Georgetta Bright, ae 18y, d/o Wm. & Lucy Bright; Sept 28 1870 by Rev. S. H. Phillips.

Thornton Walker, ae 24y, farmer, of Fluvannah VA, s/o Phill & Judy Walker; Daphney Jackson, ae 26y, d/o York & Suckey Jackson; Oct 1 1870 by Rev. E. W. Page.

Lewis W. Fletcher, ae 35y, farmer, s/o Lewis & Eliza Fletcher; Lucie C. Bristow, d/o John A. & Elizabeth Soles Bristow; Oct 2 1870 by Rev. Thos. H. Boggs.

Adam Whiting, ae 21y, farmer, s/o Adam & Betsy Whiting; Maria Booth, ae 2oy, d/o Wm. H. & Mary Whiting; Oct 14 1870 by Rev. David Coulling.

George C. Coates, ae 21y, oysterman, s/o John R. & Ella Coates; Mary S. West, ae 21y, d/o Wm. & Courtney West; Oct 28 1870 by Rev. W. S. Hawkins.

Isaac H. Auld, ae 21y, waterman, of Baltimore City MD, s/o John W. & Ann E. Crosswell Auld; Sally Lega, ae 21y, of Caroline Co MD, d/o Joseph & Mary Vincent Legar; Oct 27 1870 by Rev. W. S. Hawkins.

James Hogg, ae 63y, widower, oysterman, s/o Thos. & Milcy Hogg; Mary Smith, ae 63y, widow, d/o James & Sarah Smith; Oct 2 1870 by Rev. Wm. E. Wiatt.

Robert Spurlark, ae 22y, farmer, s/o
Charles & Martha Spurlark; Emiline Lightfoot,
ae 21y, parents unk; Nov 3 1870 by Rev. E.
M. Peterson.

Sylvester Pilsberry, ae 26y, widower,
farmer, of King and Queen Co VA, s/o Wm. &
Sarah Milby Pilsberry; Catharine F. Fary, ae
23y, d/o James & Rebecca Newble Fary; Nov 12
1870 by Rev. Jas. C. Crittenden.

Cyrus Griffin, ae 30y, waterman, of
Accomack Co VA, s/o Isaiah & Betsy Griffin;
Maria Tabb, ae 28y, parents unk; Nov 16 1870
by Rev, W. S. Hawkins.

John W. Kay, ae 23y, sailor, of Somerset
MD, s/o George & Jennett Kay; Sally E.
Campbell, ae 17y, d/o Thos. W. & Louisa
Dunston Campbell; Oct 18 1870 by Rev. E. M.
Peterson.

William M. Peyton, ae 31y, farmer, of
Roanoke Co VA, lived in Albemarle Co VA, s/o
Wm. M. & Sallie A. E. Taylor Peyton; Nannie
H. Mann, ae 25y, d/o Rev. Charles & Mary
Jackson Mann; Oct 27 1870 by Rev. Wm. G.
Jackson.

Warner Washington, ae 50y, widower,
farmer, s/o Lot & Fanny Washington; Hannah
Gregory, ae 24y, widow, d/o Henry & Sarah
Gregory; Dec 7 1870, no Rev. listed.

Thomas Massenburg, ae 21y, farmer, s/o
Wm. H. & Harriet Smith Massenburg; Elizabeth
Carmines, ae 19y, d/o Daniel & Susan T.
Drenn Carmines; Dec 8 1870 by Rev. W. S.
Hawkins.

Augustine Hammond, ae 28y, widower,
farmer, s/o Frank Lemon & Lena Hammond;
Sylva Harwood, ae 18y, d/o Wm. & Arena
Harwood; Dec 11 1870 by Rev. Thos. Nopper.

James Nuttall, ae 28y, capt of vessel,
s/o Wm. & Emily Haywood Nuttall; Fanny
Elizabeth Acra, ae 19y, d/o John & Emily
Nuttal Acra; Dec 15 1870 by Rev. W. S.
Hawkins.

Coleman Bell, ae 28y, farmer, s/o John &
Lucy Bell; Agnes Ransone, ae 21y, d/o Sam &
Delsa Ransone; Dec 18 1870 by Rev. Elder Wm.
Thomas.

Thomas A. Leigh, ae 25y, farmer, s/o Rich'd D. & Dorothy L. Pointer Leigh; Emma Jane Howard, ae 20y, d/o Henry A. & Martha A. Curry Howard; Dec 22 1870 by Rev. J. C. Martin.

William Thomas Bluford, ae 26y, oysterman, s/o Billy & Mary Bluford; Alice Stubbs, ae 23y, d/o Adam & Catharine Stubbs; Dec 22 1870 by Rev. J. C. Martin.

George Ward, ae 22y, oysterman, of Middlesex Co VA, s/o Billy & Delia Ward; Martha Allmand, ae 17y, d/o Sam & Manerva Allmand; Dec 22 1870 by Rev. W. S. Hawkins.

Washington Smith, ae 22y, oysterman, s/o Henry & Sarah Robins Smith; Frances Jenkins, ae 21y, d/o Wm. & Betsy Ross Jenkins; Dec 22 1870 by Rev. W. S. Hawkins.

Zachariah Dews Jr, ae 29y, farmer, s/o Zachariah & Elizabeth Insley Dews; Mary E. Shackelford, ae 21y, d/o Zachariah & Frances T. Bew Shackelford; Dec 22 1870 by Rev. J. C. Martin.

Thomas Booth, ae 19y, farmer, s/o Jack & Betsy Booth; Laura Hall, ae 18y, d/o John & Martha Hall; Dec 24 1870 by Rev. J. C. Martin.

Pleasance Singleton, ae 21y, farmer, s/o Wallace & Fanny Singleton; Eliza Curdly, ae 21y, d/o Winchester & Nancy Curdly; Dec 19 1870 by Rev. S. H. Phillips.

Miles Winfrey Corr, ae 24y, farmer, of King and Queen Co VA, s/o James & Mary Fary Corr; Emma C. Roane, ae 19y, d/o Warner & Frances A. Bland Roane; Dec 25 1870 by Rev. J. C. Martin.

James Scott, ae 21y, farmer, of King and Queen Co VA, s/o Ben & Manerva Scott; Lucy Jackson, ae 16y, d/o John & Delia Jackson; Dec 25 1870 by Rev. David Coulling.

Ransone Dudley, ae 72y, widow, farmer, s/o John Harris & Polly Dudley; Rosanna Holmes, ae 21y, parents unk; Dec 26 1870 by J. C. Martin.

Aaron Lewis, ae 27y, laborer, s/o Wm. & Martha Lewis; Mollie Baytop, ae 19y, d/o Thos. & Lucy A. Baytop; Dec 24 1870 by Rev. David Coulling.

James D. Pointer, ae 36y, coach maker,
s/o Wm. D. & Mary Elwood Pointer; Mary
Marion Minor, ae 20y, d/o John W. & Jennie
Mouring Minor; Dec 27 1870 by Rev. Wm. E.
Wiatt.

Robert Adams, ae 56y, widower, farmer,
s/o James & Lucy Adams; Catharine Williams,
ae 39y, widow, d/o James & Mary Carter; Dec
28 1870 by Rev. Wm. E. Wiatt.

John C. Walker; ae 24y, oysterman, s/o
Meade & Maria Hutson Walker; Margaret Sarah
McLane, ae 22y, d/o Wm. & Betsy Cobbs
McLane; Dec 29 1870 by Rev. Wm. E. Wiatt.

Frank Reed , ae 22y, laborer, s/o Frank &
Mary Reed; Mary Walker, ae 21y, parents unk;
Dec 29 1870 by Rev. David Coulling.

Thomas C. Johnston, ae 29y, widower,
farmer, s/o John R. & Catharine Graves Johnston; Julia W. Massey, ae 16y, d/o Wm. Y. &
Julia Wright Massey; Jan 3 1871 by Rev.
James C. Martin.

Thomas Crew, ae 24y, sailor, s/o John &
Ava Dunston Crew; Adda Woodley, ae 19y, d/o
John & Lucy Woodley; Jan 5 1871 by Rev. Wm.
E. Wiatt.

Benjamin Ransom, ae 21y, oyster and farm;
s/o Geo. & Frances Ransom; Hester E.
Ransone, ae 16y, d/o Sam'l & Dephia Ransone;
Jan 12 1871 by Rev. W. S. Hawkins.

James Seawell, ae 22y, oyster and fish,
s/o Benjamin & Mary Oliver Seawell; Frances
Moore, ae 21y, of Richmond VA, d/o John &
Mary Irvin Moore; Jan 12 1871 by Rev. W. S.
Hawkins.

William Irvin Sedgewick, ae 35y, farmer,
of Richmond City VA, s/o Wm. & Jane Irvin
Sedgewick; Emily Foxwell, ae 16y, d/o Geo. &
Frances Seawell Foxwell; Jan 12 1871 by Rev.
W. S. Hawkins.

Thomas Chapman, ae 21y, farmer, s/o
Richard & Caroline Jackman Chapman; Sarah E.
Shackelford, ae 18y, d/o Wm. & Leah Proctor
Shackelford; Jan 17 1871 by Rev. David
Coulling.

George Fields, ae 21y, farmer, s/o Humphrey & Matilda Fields; Elizabeth Fields, ae
19y, d/o Ned & Elizabeth Fields; Jan 24 1871
by Rev. J. C. Crittenden.

George T. Hutchinson, ae 22y, oysterman,
of Accomac Co VA, s/o Geo. & Lovey S.
Stevens Hutchinson; Frances Gibson, ae 17y,
d/o Alex & Mary Seawell Gibson; Jan 18 1871
by Rev. W. S. Hawkins.

Stephen Decatur Rowe, ae 26y, merchant,
s/o Jasper C. & Julia B. Stubblefield Rowe;
Nannie McKain Thornton, ae 23y, d/o John A.
B. & Sarah E. Hayes Thornton; Jan 19 1871 by
Rev. Wm. E. Wiatt.

Edward E. Nuttall, ae 26y, widower,
sailor, s/o James & Mary E. Figg Nuttall;
Maria E. Robin , ae 16y, d/o Uriah & Mary A.
Robin; Jan 22 1871 by James C. Martin.

John T. Soles, ae 22y, farmer, s/o Thos.
& Mary Lawson Soles; Cordelia Walker, ae
24y, d/o Geo. & Ann Southern Walker; Jan 22
1871 by Rev. James C. Martin.

Stephen H. Boston, ae 22y, sailor, of
Eastern Shore MD, parents unk; Susan Clay-
ton, ae 22y, parents unk; Jan 24 1871 by Rev.
J. C. Crittenden.

Washington Hogg, ae 27y, farmer, s/o
Richard & Mildred West Hogg; Elizabeth Hall,
ae 21y, d/o Wm. F. & Mary A. Rowe Hall; Jan
26 1871 by Rev. Wm. E. Wiatt.

John Thawley, ae 46y, widower, farmer, of
Caroline Co MD, s/o John & Martha Thawley;
Mary Lillie Temple Lewis, ae 17y, of Middle-
sex Co VA, d/o Thos. J. & Sarah F. Edwards
Lewis; Jan 26 1871 by Rev. J. C. Martin.

Albert T. Gaya, ae 21y, oysterman, s/o
Robin & Keziah Gaya; Ellen Seawell, ae 19y,
d/o Miles & Dinah Smith Seawell; Jan 26 1871
by Rev. Thos. Nopper.

Peter Johnson, ae 22y, farmer, s/o Amos &
Anna Johnson; Rosa Jane Smith, ae 19y, d/o
Emanuel & Caroline Smith; Jan 29 1871 by
Rev. W, S. Hawkins.

George Hogg, ae 28y, oysterman, s/o Wm. &
Patsy Hogg; Elvina Blake, ae 19y, d/o John &
Mary Louisa Blake; Feb 13 1871 by Rev. w.
S. Hawkins.

William Andrew Washington, ae 21y, farms,
s/o Bass & Eliza Washington; Matilda Carter,
ae 21y, d/o Edward & Harriet Carter; Feb 9
1871 by Rev. W. S. Hawkins.

Adam Page, ae 28y, oysterman, of Rich-
mond VA, s/o Joshua & Martha Page; Harriet
Dennis, ae 17y, of GEORGIA, d/o Susan
Daniel; Feb 16 1871 by Rev. David Coulling.

Edward Roberson, ae 21y, sailor, s/o
Isaac & Priscilla Roberson; Adaline Jones,
ae 23y, d/o Henry & Sally Jones; Mar 2 1871
by Rev. J. C. Martin.

Frank Page, ae 23y, laborer, s/o Frank &
Harriet Page; Fanny Davenport, ae 21y, d/o
Emanuel & Maria Davenport; Mar 4 1871 by
Rev. David Coulling.

Carter B. Williams, ae 26y, farmer, s/o
Edmund & Margaret Seaborn Williams; Rebecca
Alice Williams, ae 22y, d/o Andrew & Paulina
Jones Williams; Mar 5 1871 by Rev. W. S.
Hawkins.

John Thomas Massey, ae 23y, farmer, s/o
Chas. A. & Mary Haynes Massey; Bridget
Pearce, ae 15y, d/o Geo. & Polly Pearce; Mar
9 1871 by Rev. Thos. H. Boggs.

Andrew Davis, ae 31y, widower, laborer,
of Isle of Wight Co VA, parents unk; Martha
Shackelford, ae 31y, parents unk; Mar 8 1871
by Rev. David Coulling.

Robert Green, ae 27y, farmer, of Richmond
City VA, s/o Geo. & Sarah Greene; Jane
Duval, ae 24y, widow, d/o James & Betsy
Stoakes; Mar 16 1871 by Rev. David Coulling.

Lawson Brooks, ae 50y, widower, farmer,
of Middlesex Co VA, s/o Elijah & Molly
Brooks; Mary Ann Fox, ae 30y, widow, d/o
James & Nancy Fox; Mar 24 1871 by Rev. W. S.
Hawkins.

Stephen Fields, ae 23y, waterman, s/o
Sally Fields; Sarah Jane Tilman, ae 18y, d/o
Jefferson & Maria J. Tilmon; Mar 23 1871 by
Rev. W. S. Hawkins.

Charles Cosby, ae 21y, farmer, of Mathews
Co VA, s/o Harriet Parker; Harriet Gardener,
ae 24y, d/o Daniel & Charlotte Gardener; Mar
26 1871 by Rev. Thos. Nopper.

Rufus A. Duer, ae 31y, waterman, of
Somerset Co MD, s/o Edward & Nancy Sturges
Duer; Martha Steptoe Fitzhugh, ae 19y, d/o
Patrick H. & Mary S. Christian Fitzhugh; Mar
28 1871 by Rev. David Coulling.

George W. Owens, ae 24y, oysterman, s/o
Geo. & Nancy Doggett Owens; Elizabeth
Jenkins, ae 27y, d/o Armistead & Dolly
Jenkins; Apr 1 1871 by Rev. Wm. E. Wiatt.

William Pollard, ae 21y, farmer, s/o
Henry & Betsy Pollard; Sarah Robinson, ae
21y, d/o Soloman & Kitty Robinson; Mar 30
1871 by Rev. James C. Martin.

Alfred Evans, ae 25y, farmer, s/o Wm. &
Clara Evans; Amanda Brown, ae 20y, d/o Henry
& Ella Brown; Mar 30 1871 by Rev. Sam'l S.
Harden.

John W. Brooking, ae 37y, farmer, s/o
Benja. R. & Courtney Blake Brooking; Mary F.
Powers, ae 20y, d/o Wm. W. J. & Nancy A.
Powers; Apr 6 1871 by Rev. James G. Councill.

William Johnson, ae 23y, farmer, s/o
Corbin & Maria Johnson; Lucy Baker, ae 21y,
d/o Tour & Chloe Baker; Apr 8 1871 by Rev.
Wm. E. Wiatt.

Alexander Cooke, ae 21y, farmer, s/o
Anthony & Maria Cooke; Fanny Pryor, ae 21y,
d/o Philip & Fannie Jane Pryor; Apr 8 1871
by Rev. David Coulling.

Beverly Wilson, ae 30y, farmer, s/o
Robert & Betsy Wilson; Jane Lowden, ae 18y,
d/o Beverly & Susan Lowden; Apr 10 1871.

Lewis Richerson, ae 21y, farmer, s/o Joe
& Mary Richerson; Ann West, ae 21y, d/o
Thos. & Hannah West; Apr 9 1871 by Rev.
David Coulling.

Brittain Grevius, ae 21y, farmer, of
Mathews Co VA, s/o Philip & Fanny Grevius;
Mary Jane Ruff, ae 21y, d/o Jack & Betsy
Ruff; Apr 23 1871 by Rev. Thos. Nopper.

Peter Norton, ae 22y, farmer, s/o Jim &
Lucy Norton; Eleanora Harwood, ae 17y, d/o
Wm. & Arena Harwood; Apr 23 1871 by Rev.
Thos. Nopper.

Joseph Gwynn, ae 21y, laborer, s/o Robert
& Betsy Gwynn; Fanny Ann Holmes, ae 18y, d/o
Wm. & Dorothy Holmes; Sept 29 1871 by Rev.
Wm. E. Wiatt.

George Smith, ae 22y, oysterman, s/o
Anthony & Charlotte Smith; Mary West, ae
23y, d/o Ambrose & Hannah West; May 7 1871.

Winston Tazewell, ae 40y, widower, farmer,
s/o John & Sarah Tazewell; Manerva Burwell,
ae 26y, d/o Wm. & Amy Burwell; May 26 1871
by Rev. Samuel S. Harden.

Robert Staley, ae 22y, laborer, of NORTH
CAROLINA, s/o Wesley & Mary Staley; Sally
Thrift, ae 17y, d/o Benj. & Catharine
Thrift; Jun 8 1871 by Rev. James C. Martin.

Phill Montague, ae 43y, widower, farmer,
s/o Harry & Katy Montague; Sarah Fleming, ae
22y, d/o Harry & Nancy Fleming; Jun 8 1871
by Rev. W. S. Hawkins.

Beverly Thornton, ae 21y, oysterman, s/o
Rich'd & Octavia Thornton; Martha Cary, ae
18y, d/o Miles & Louisa; Jun 11 1871 by
Rev. Samuel S. Harden.

Alexander Madison, ae 24y, widower,
farmer, of Louisa Co VA, s/o Harman & Lucy
Madison; Margarit Clarke, ae 18y, d/o Wm. &
Violet Clarke; Jun 15 1871 by Rev. W. S.
Hawkins.

Richard Munford, ae 36y, widower,
farmer, of New Kent Co VA, s/o Dick & Eliza
Munford; Clara Ann Hughes, ae 24y, widow,
parents unk; Jun 24 1871 by Rev. James C.
Martin.

James Reade, ae 22y, farmer, of King and
Queen Co VA, s/o Wm. & Phillis Reade; Mary
Byrd, ae 24y, parents unk; Jun 28 1871 by
Rev. James C. Martin.

George W. Deal, ae 23y, farmer, s/o John
A. & Elizabeth Brown Deal; Laura Frances
Williams, ae 19y, d/o Samuel & Mary Robins
Williams; Jun 24 1871 by Rev. Samuel Henry
Phillips.

Thomas J. Owens, ae 24y, waterman, s/o
Cary & Mary Owens; Margaret Ann Heywood, ae
21y, d/o John & Eliza Ann Heywood; Aug 12
1871 by Rev. Wm. E. Wiatt.

Samuel M. Montague, ae 35y, widower,
farmer, s/o Ned & Mary Montague; Lucie Lee
Burwell, ae 31y, widow, d/o Louy & Betsy
Jones Burwell; Aug 10 1871 by Rev. J. C.
Martin.

William Patterson, ae 24y, farmer, s/o
Henry & Frances Patterson; Martha Lee, ae
23y, parents unk; Sept 14 1871 by Rev. J. G.
Councill.

Gary P. Seawell, ae 21y, sailor, s/o Joseph & Sarah Carmines Seawell; Virginia Carmines, ae 16y, d/o James M. & Margaret Fosque Carmines; Aug 17 1871 by Rev. W. S. Hawkins.

George Griffin, ae 23y, oysterman, of King and Queen Co VA, s/o George & Diana Griffin; Mary Wormly, ae 22y, d/o Ralph & Sally Wormly; Sept 14 1871 by Rev. S. H. Phillips.

William E. Wiatt, ae 44y, widower, minister of the gospel, s/o Wm. G. & Louisa C. Stubbs Wiatt; Nancy B. Heywood, ae 31y, d/o Robert S. & Nancy Robins Heywood; Jul 18 1871 by Rev. W. S. Hawkins.

Harrison Selden, ae 22y, widower, laborer, s/o Jasper & Peggy Selden; Esther Holmes, ae 19y, of King and Queen Co VA, d/o Walker & Judy Holmes; Sept 17 1871 by Rev. David Coulling.

William Henry Harris, ae 20y, oysterman, s/o Ro. & Mary Spaun Harris; Lucy Ann Wise, ae 18y, d/o John & Mary Jane Dews Wise; Oct 2 1871 by Rev. James C. Martin.

Philip Jackson, ae 22y, colored, of Middlesex Co VA, s/o Phill & Mary Carter Jackson; Mary Eliza Patterson, ae 21y, colored, d/o Henry & Frances Patterson; Oct 15 1871 by Rev. Samuel S. Harden.

Robert Allen Hudgin, ae 24y, farmer, s/o Claiborne & Lucy Ann Hayes Hudgin; Sarah Lewis Nuttall, ae 22y, d/o Iverson & Lucy Bristow Nuttall; Oct 15 1871 by Rev. J. B. Councill.

William D. Mouring, ae 26y, constable & collector, s/o Wm. T. & Susan A. Leavitt Mouring; Susan B. Thornton, ae 21y, d/o John A. B. & Sarah Elizabeth Hayes Thornton; Oct 25 1871 by Rev. Wm. E. Wiatt.

John Lewis, ae 21y, colored, laborer, s/o Billy & Dolly Lewis; Mary Bundy, ae 23y, colored, d/o Billy & Jane Bundy; Oct 24 1871 by Rev. Samuel S. Harden.

John William Allmand, ae 22y, colored, oysterman, s/o Sam & Malvena Allmand; Sarah Stoakes, ae 18y, colored, d/o Ket & Ann Stoakes; Oct 26 1871 by Rev. W. S. Hawkins.

William Lockley, ae 23y, widower, farmer,
of Middlesex Co VA, s/o Daniel & Milly
Lockley; Ann Eliza Whiting, ae 22y, d/o Thos.
& Easter Whiting; Oct 26 1871 by Rev. J. C.
Martin.

James Henry Carter, ae 20y 9m, farmer,
s/o Frances Ann Carter; Lucy Frances
Davenport, ae 21y 3m, d/o Thos. & Mary
Davenport; Oct 26 1871 by Rev. David
Coulling.

Beverly Wilson, ae 30y, widower, colored,
farmer, s/o Robert & Betsy Wilson; Lula Ann
Meggs, ae 21y, colored, of King and Queen Co
VA, parents unk; Oct 29 1871 by Rev. David
Coulling.

James Roane, ae 25y, colored, oysterman,
of King and Queen Co VA, s/o Sam & Milly
Roane; Nancy Lemon, ae 19y, colored, d/o
Robert & Hester Lemon, now Hester Berry; Oct
26 1871 by Rev. David Coulling.

Beverly Dunston, ae 43y, widower, farmer,
s/o John & Martha Dunston; Ann Maria
Wilkins, ae 30y, widow, d/o Frank & Sarah
Robins; Nov 2 1871 by Rev. James C. Martin.

Dr. Thomas Latane, ae 47y, widower,
physician, of Essex Co VA, lived King and
Queen Co VA, s/o Henry W. & Susannah Allen
Latane; Mary E. Robins, ae 30y, d/o
Augustine W. & Elizabeth P. Todd Robins; Nov
1 1871 by Rev. A. F. Scott.

Iverson Bland, ae 22y, colored, farmer,
of Fluvannah Co VA, s/o John & Rose Bland;
Lizzie Anderson, ae 20y, colored, d/o Geo. &
Diana Anderson; Nov 4 1871 by Rev. Edward
Page.

Henry Kelly, ae 30y, colored, laborer, s/o
Allen T. & Courtney Kelly; Matilda Bundy, ae
25y, colored, of Middlesex Co VA, d/o Sam &
Jane Bundy; Nov 7 1871 by Rev. J. G.
Councill.

Robert Goodchild, ae 61y, widower, farmer,
of Mathews Co VA, s/o Peter & Milly
Goodchild; Selena Wilson, ae 60y, widow,
parents unk; Nov 7 1871 by Rev. J. G.
Councill.

Lewis Mayer, ae 38y, lawyer, of Baltimore City MD, s/o Chas. F. & Eliza C. Blackwell Mayer; Virginia Deans, ae 26y, d/o Josiah & Mary Yeatman Deans; Nov 9 1871 by Rev. S. H. Phillips.

Jack Peyton, ae 65y, colored, widower, carpenter, s/o Nelson & Lavinia Peyton; Mary Roy, ae 65y, widow, colored, d/o Jerry & Betsy Ellis; Nov 15 1871 by Rev. Samuel H. Harden.

William Rowe, ae 27y, waterman, s/o Wm. & Caroline Rowe; Elizabeth Hogg, ae 22y, d/o Thos. & Betsy Hogg; Nov 14 1871 by Rev. W. S. Hawkins.

Doctor Garland, ae 24y, farmer, of Milton N. C, s/o Richard & Rhoda Garland; Sarah Carter, ae 19y, d/o Gabriel & Ann Carter; Nov 23 1871 by Rev. Edward Page.

George Frank Struther, ae 36y, supt. of penitentiary of Va, of Rappahannock Co VA, lived Richmond City VA, s/o James F. & Elizabeth R. Roberts Struther; Lessie Elizabeth Cary, ae 22y, d/o E. B. S. & Eliza A. Smith Cary; Nov 19 1871 by Rev. Chas. Mann, Rector of Ware Parrish.

James Driver, ae 23y, colored, oysterman, s/o Sam & Fanny Driver; Matilda Washington, ae 22y, colored, d/o Voss & Elizabeth Washington; Nov 30 1871 by Rev. W. S. Hawkins.

Robert R. Rowe, ae 28y, widower, farmer, s/o Robert S. & Catharine D. Rowe; Larla Ruth Coles Massey, ae 15y, d/o Wm. C. & Mary Massey; Dec 15 1871 by Rev. J. G. Councill.

Samuel Rowe, ae 23y, oysterman, s/o Zack & Fanny Rowe; Alice Brown, ae 18y, d/o Rob't & Mary Brown; Dec 7 1871 by Rev. W. S. Hawkins.

R. H. Hogg, ae 30y, merchant, s/o Richard & Catharine Hogg; Mary F. Hall, ae 23y, d/o Lozenzo & Catharine Hall; Dec 10 1871 by Rev. James C. Martin.

Emanuel J. Stubblefield, ae 55y, widower, farmer, of Middlesex Co VA, s/o Wm. & Elizabeth Jones Stubblefield; Julia A. Leigh, ae 33y, widow, d/o Archer & Mary Bland; Dec 13 1871 by Rev. J. G. Councill.

Henry Turpin, ae 30y, farmer, of MD,
parents unk; Polly Jones, ae 30y, d/o Sam &
Louisa Richerson Jones; Dec 11 1871 by Elder
Thos. Washington.

J. C. Heywood, ae 27y, merchant, s/o Wm.
B. & Julia A. Heywood; Bettie P. Hawkins, ae
19y, d/o Wm. S. & Louisa Hawkins by Rev. W.
S. Hawkins.

Albert F. Coleman, ae 23y, farmer, s/o
John F. & Mildred B. Coleman; Mary Louisa
Gaskins, ae 19y, of Norfolk VA, d/o J. W. &
Louisa Gaskins; Dec 14 1871 by Rev. James C.
Martin.

William Graves, ae 21y, colored, oyster,
s/o John & Betsy Graves; Betsy Robinson, ae
21y, colored, d/o John & Lucy Robinson; Dec
20 1871 by Rev. Edward Page.

Francis Jefferson Kemp, ae 25y, coach
maker, s/o Peter D. & Mary Booker Kemp; Lucy
Berry Richesen, ae 19y, d/o Fleming W. &
Ellen Marchant Richesen; Dec 21 1871 by Rev.
J. G. Councill.

Gabriel Carter, ae 23y, colored, oyster,
s/o Gabriel & Ann Carter; Georgiana Hills,
ae 20y, colored, d/o Geo. & Georgiana Hills;
Dec 24 1871 by Rev. Wm. E. Wiatt.

James Webb, ae 29y, colored, oysterman,
s/o James & Mary Webb; Milly French, ae 21y,
colored, d/o Peter & Eliza French; Dec 21
1871 by Rev. Wm. E. Wiatt.

Zachariah Shackelford, ae 50y, widower,
sail maker, s/o Berry & Tabitha Steed Shackelford; Julia A. Stubblefield, ae 40y,
widow, d/o Edward J. & Mary A. Davis Carney
Stubblefield; Dec 24 1871 by Rev. W. S.
Hawkins.

Edmund Gales, ae 21y, colored, farmer,
s/o Randall & Jenny Gales; Eliza Williams,
ae 23y, colored, d/o Sam & Catharine
Williams; Dec 16 1871 by Rev. Edward Page.

Larkey Page, ae 21y, colored, oysterman,
s/o James & Louisa Page; Polly Tazewell, ae
20y, colored, d/o Winston & Patsy Tazewell;
Dec 23 1871 by Rev. Edward Page.

Thomas Frank Cary, ae 21y, colored,
farmer, s/o Chas. & Isabella Cary; Lucy
Thornton, ae 21y, colored, d/o Richard &
Octavia Thornton; Dec 23 1871 by Rev. E. Page.

Joseph F. Hall, ae 34y, merchant, s/o Lorenzo & Catharine White Hall; Sarah Josephine Walker, ae 19y, d/o Wineder G. & Alvina Glass Walker; Dec 26 1871 by Rev. James C. Martin.

Brittian Gardner, ae 21y, oysterman, s/o Daniel & Charlotte Gardner; Maria Willis, ae 20y, of Mathews Co VA, d/o Fanner & Cordelia Willis; Dec 30 1871 by Rev. Chas. Mann.

Harry Tabb, ae 24y, colored, oysterman, parents unk; Amanda Taliaferro, ae 19y, colored, d/o George & Fanny Taliaferro; Dec 25 1871 by Rev. Edward Page.

George Jackson, ae 34y, colored, widower, farmer, of New Kent Co VA, s/o Billy & Jenny Jackson; Susannah Shackleford, ae 19y, colored, d/o George & Courtney Shackleford; Dec 28 1871 by Rev. James C. Martin.

Alexander King, ae 21y 9m, colored, farmer, s/o Buck & Violet King; Catharine Whiting, ae 21y, colored, d/o John & Mary Jane Whiting; Dec 28 1871 by Rev. J. C. Martin.

George Marble, ae 21y, colored, farmer, s/o Ben Marble; Pinky Johnson, ae 17y, colored, d/o Henry & Mary Johnson; Dec 30 1871 by Rev. William Thomas.

Andrew German, ae 21y, farmer, s/o Wm. & Alithia Bridges German; Annie E. Hewell, ae 19y, d/o John & Susan Framan Hewell; Dec 31 1871 by Rev. J. G. Councill.

William Yates, ae 22y, colored, farmer, of King and Queen Co VA, s/o Bob & Mary Yates; Julia Feilds, ae 20y, colored, d/o Humphrey & Matilda Feilds; Dec 30 1871 by Rev. W. S. Hawkins.

James P. Wallace, ae 24y, oysterman, s/o Joseph & Lillie Ann Wallace; Mary S. Green, ae 21y, of York Co VA, d/o Joseph & Mary Susan Green; Dec 31 1871 by Rev. J. C. Crittenden.

Thomas Cosby, ae 22y, colored, farmer, s/o Gabreil & Fanny Cosby; Leddy King, ae 23y, widow, colored, d/o George & Farna King; Jan 2 1871 by Rev. Charles Mann.

Augustine W. Ware, ae 40y, widower,
farmer, s/o Robert & Jane Leavitt Ware;
Maria F. Dutton, ae 30y, d/o James & Nancy
Chapman Dutton; Jan 3 1872 by Rev. David
Coulling.

Tom Gwynn, ae 21y, colored, farmer, s/o
Phil & Rosana Gwynn; Mary Whiting, ae 18y,
colored, d/o John & Sarah Smith Whiting; Jan
4 1872 by Rev. David Coulling.

George W. Croswell, ae 22y, oysterman,
s/o John & Ann Croswell; Catharine Finis, ae
16y, d/o Wm. & Sarah Finis; Jan 4 1872 by
Rev. W. S. Hawkins.

Simon Wright, ae 60y, widower, colored,
farmer, of Craney Island,VA, s/o Chas. & Caty
Wright; Judy Walker, ae 60y, widow, colored,
of Fluvannah Co VA, d/o John & Caty Butler;
Jan 6 1872 by Rev. Edward Page.

Washington Cary, ae 21y, colored, farmer,
s/o Tom & Mary Cary; Polly Blake, ae 22y,
colored, d/o Sally Dennis; Jan 6 1872 by
Rev. David Coulling.

George W. Shelton, ae 27y, sailor, of King
and Queen Co VA, s/o John P. & Sarah M.
George Shelton; Hester Hall, ae 21y, d/o
Rich'd & Martha Jenkins Hall; Dec 3 1871 by
Rev. W. S. Hawkins.

Lafayette Burton, ae 22y, colored, farmer,
s/o Sye & Jane Burton; Lucy West, ae 22y,
colored, d/o Tom & Lucy West; Jan 7 1872 by
Rev. David Coulling.

William Thomas Hall, ae 32y, farmer, of
King and Queen Co VA, s/o Thos. B. & Sarah R.
Clarke Hall; Martha Ellen Smith, ae 20y, of
Middlesex Co VA, d/o Hugh A. & Julia A. E.
Bland South Smith; Jan 9 1872 by Rev. Wm. E.
Wiatt.

Zachary Lewis, ae 24y, colored, oysterman,
of Middlesex Co VA, s/o Iverson & Mary Lewis;
Frances Lewis, ae 18y, colored, d/o Zachary
& Aggy Lewis; Jan 11 1872 by Rev. W. S.
Hawkins.

Richard Harrison Horner, ae 32y, farmer,
of Flauquier Co VA, s/o Rich'd B. & Mary
Little Horner; Virginia Ann Cary, ae 15y, d/o
E. B. S. & Elizabeth Smith Cary; Jan 11 1872
by Rev. Charles Mann, Rector of Ware Parish.

Curtis Milby, ae 31y, farmer, of King and Queen Co VA, parents unk; Mary A. E. Bland, ae 17y, d/o Zachariah & Delilah A. E. Bland; Jan 11 1872 by Rev. J. C. Crittenden.

Cary Davis, ae 23y, colored, farmer, of Newbern Co N. C, s/o Geo. & Betty Davis; Catharine Reed, ae 21y, colored, d/o Spencer & Mary Reed; Jan 13 1872 by Rev. David Coulling.

Harry Bland, ae 25y, merchant, s/o Thos. J. & Mildred Bland; Sarah Hester Rowe, ae 18y, d/o Robert J. & Catharine D. Rowe; Jan 18 1872 by Rev. James C. Martin.

Thomas Jefferson Davis, ae 25y, farmer, of Mathews Co VA, s/o Wm. K. & Sarah Deal Davis; Sarah Jane Thornton, ae 27y, d/o Francis & Elizabeth Cluverius Thornton; Jan 25 1872 by Rev. David Coulling.

William Henry Davenport, ae 22y, oysters, s/o Thos. & Mary Davenport; Moses Ann Rowe, ae 21y, d/o Moses & Nancy Rowe; Jan 29 1872 by Rev. James C. Martin.

Thomas H. Dunston, ae 24y, widower, farms, s/o John & Mary Dunston; Coris Ann Walker, ae 21y, d/o John & Elizabeth F. Walker; Feb 1 1872 by Rev. J. G. Councill.

James Robinson Bridges, ae 29y, farmer, s/o Rich'd M. & Caroline Clarke Bridges; Florence Ann Hughes, ae 21y, d/o John H. & Julia A. F. Leavitt Hughes; Feb 1872 by Rev. W. S. Hawkins.

Randall Green, ae 45y, laborer, of Isle of Wight Co VA, s/o Jim & Maria Green; Betsy Foster, ae 30y, widow, d/o Samson & Polly Dennis; Feb 6 1872 by Rev. J. G. Councill.

John Harvery Pfister, ae 28y, farmer, of SWITZERLAND, s/o Sam'l & Maria Pfister; Anna M. Chapman, ae 21y, d/o Henry & Harriet Chapman; Feb 7 1872 by Rev. David Coulling.

William Booth, ae 21y, colored, farmer, s/o Geo. & Martha Booth; Polly Ann Thornton, ae 21y, colored, d/o Clay & Peggy Thornton; Feb 14 1872 by Rev. James C. Martin.

Davy Jones, ae 22y, colored, oysterman, s/o David & Mary Jones; Jane Jackson, ae 18y, colored, d/o Glouster & Betsy Bassett; Feb 17 1872 by Rev. Edward Page.

Benjamin F. Leigh, ae 25y, farmer, s/o
Thos. R. & Martha J. Hall Leigh; Laura A.
Leavitt, ae 20y, d/o John W. & Elizabeth
Stubblefield Leavitt; Feb 20 1872 by Rev.
W. S. Hawkins.

Isaac Thornton, ae 22y, colored, oysters,
s/o Paul & Mary Thornton; Charity Braxton, ae
21y, colored, d/o Temple & Rebecca Braxton;
Feb 18 1872 by Rev. Samuel S. Harden.

George Washington Hughes, ae 74y, widower,
colored, House of Senate, s/o Jasper & Agnes
Hughes; Maria Tabb, ae 41y, parents unk; Feb
20 1872.

Westcum Hudgins, ae 22y, oysterman, of
Mathews Co VA, s/o Thos. L. & Mary Frances
Blake Hudgins; Lucy A. Rilee, ae 21y, d/o
Thos. R. & Mary T. Rilee; Feb 22 1872 by Rev.
David Coulling.

Robert H. Marble, ae 47y, widower, farms,
of Caroline Co MD, s/o George W. & Elizabeth
Sisk Marble; Elizabeth Jane Pratt, ae 19y, of
Caroline Co MD, d/o Benja. Pratt; Feb 21 1872
by Rev. James C. Martin.

Harry Lowry, ae 70y, widower, farmer, of
York Co VA, s/o Jack & Nancy Lowry; Mary
Davenport, ae 40y, parents unk; May 1 1873 by
Rev. David Coulling.

Ralph Jackson, ae 24y, colored, farmer,
s/o Edward & Milly Jackson; Betty Washington,
ae 23y, colored, d/o Geo. & Rebecca Washington; June 15 1873 by Rev. Charles Mann.

Sye Jones, ae 22y, colored, oysterman,
s/o Isaac & Charlotte Jones; Charlotte Gardner, colored, d/o Dan'l & Charlotte Gardner;
June 24 1873 by Rev. Samuel S. Harden.

Joe Young, ae 28y, colored, laborer, s.o
Wm. & Mollie Young; Mary Braxton, ae 26y,
colored, parents unk; July 8 1873 by Rev.
James C. Martin.

Robert Smith, ae 24y, oysterman, s/o John
& Ann Smith; Sarah Sparrow, ae 21y, d/o Ray-
mond & Sally Sparrow; July 10 1873 by Rev. W.
S. Hawkins.

William Booth, ae 41y, widower, sailor,
s/o Milan & Milly Booth; Mary Field, ae 40y,
widow, d/o Thompson & Mary Baytop; Aug 2 1873
by Rev. Wm. E. Wiatt.

John Kidd, ae 27y, farmer, of King and
Queen Co VA, s/o Eliza Booker, father unk;
Mary Catharine West, ae 19y, of King and
Queen Co VA, d/o David & Grace West; Aug 2
1873 by Rev. James C. Martin.

John R. Singleton, ae 22y, merchant, s/o
John & Eliza Singleton; Mary F. Hibble, ae
21y, d/o Henry H. & Ellen Hibble; Aug 6 1873
by Rev. James C. Martin.

Edmund Burwell, ae 24y, oysterman, s/o
Edmund & Sally Burwell; Susan Allen, ae 21y,
d/o Emory Green; July 31 1873 by Rev. W. S.
Hawkins.

James Kemp, ae 21y, oysterman, s/o James
& Betsy Kemp; Pinkey Dixon, ae 21y, d/o
James & Mary Dixon; Aug 14 1873 by Rev. W.
S. Hawkins.

John Stoaks, ae 27y, oysterman, s/o Wm. &
Judy Stoaks; Mattie J. Smith, ae 23y, d/o
Warner & Eliza Smith; Aug 19 1873 by Rev. W.
S. Hawkins.

Buy Bright, ae 19y, farmer, s/o Tom &
Agnes Bright; Molly WAshington, ae 17y, d/o
Warner & Jane Washington; Aug 21 1873 by Rev.
Sam'l S. Harden.

Richard Green, ae 20y, colored, oyster,
s/o Wm. & Margaret Green; Jenny Crittenden,
ae 21y, of York Co VA, d/o Joseph & Nettie
Crittenden; Dec 12 1872 by Rev. W. S.
Hawkins.

Wyndham Smith Haynes, ae 21y, farmer, s/o
Wm. & Fanny Padgett Haynes; Louisa Thomas
South, ae 20y, d/o Thos. D. & Harriet Rilee
South; Nov 28 1872 by Rev. David Coulling.

William Cook, ae 23y, colored, shoemaker,
s/o Peter & Agnes Cook; Catharine Talia-
farro. ae 18y, of New Kent Co VA, d/o Cell &
Jane Taliaferro; Nov 28 1872 by Rev. Sam'l
S. Harden.

Edward Smith, ae 23y, colored, teamster,
s/o Agnes Wiatt; Zula Oryor, ae 17y, d/o
Betsy Cook; Dec 5 1872 by Rev. Sam'l S.
Harden.

Davy Corbin, ae 25y, colored, laborer at
steam mill, of King and Queen Co VA, s/o
Cary & Susan Corbin; Easter Lee, ae 21y, d/o
Lucy; Dec 21 1872 by Rev. David Coulling.

James Wilson, ae 21y, colored, farmer,
parents unk; Harriet Brown, ae 17y, colored,
d/o Sam & Eliza Brown; Dec 19 1872 by Rev.
David Coulling.

Forrester Thompson, ae 24y, colored, car-
penter, of Boston MASS, parents unk; Amanda
Ellis, ae 26y, colored, d/o Lewis & Maria
Carpender Baytop Ellis; Dec 24 1872 by Rev.
Chas. Mann, Rector of Ware.

Andrew T. Stubbs, ae 24y, clerk, s/o
Edward S. & Jane S. Coleman Stubbs; Delia J.
Stubbs, ae 21y, d/o Lawrence S. & Mary A.
Darne Stubbs; Dec 25 1872 by Rev. James C.
Martin.

John W. Gregg, ae 25y, farmer, of Essex
Co VA, s/o Peter J. & Mary South Gregg;
Alice A. Howard, ae 24y, d/o Henry A. &
Martha Curry Howard; Dec 26 1872 by Rev.
James C. Martin.

Charley C. Poole, ae 23y, farmer, of
Mathews Co VA, s/o Thos. & Paulina Sibley
Poole; Emma A. Trevilian, ae 18y, d/o
Augustine & Julia A. Dutton Trevilian; Dec
25 1872 by Rev. David Coulling.

Will Selden, ae 81y, widower, colored,
Blacksmith, s/o Will & Jenny Selden; Sally
Cooke, ae 56y, widow, colored, parents unk;
Jan 5 1873 by Rev. Edward Page.

Joseph Smith, ae 41y, widower, colored,
laborer, s/o Henry & Scilla Smith; Agnes
Thornton, ae 17y, colored, d/o Paul & Mary
Thornton; Dec 26 1872 by Rev. Samuel S.
Harden.

Lewis Jones, ae 25y, colored, farmer, s/o
Leroy & Betsy Jones; Judy Washington, ae
24y, colored, d/o Geo. & Becky Washington;
Dec 29 1872.

James Smith, ae 28y, farmer, s/o Hannah
Carter; Martha Ellen Braxton, ae 25y, of
King and Queen Co VA, d/o Virginia Braxton;
Jan 4 1873.

Randall Brown, ae 50y, widower, colored,
farmer, s/o Edmund & Becky Brown; Winney
Scott, ae 35y, widow, colored, d/o Essex &
Patty Smith; Jan 2 1873 by Rev. David
Coulling.

George B. Bohannon, ae 23y, sailor, of
Mathews Co Va, s/o W. & Lucy Bohannon;
Lavinia Alice Crismond, ae 23y, d/o John &
Louisa Crismond; Jan 7 1873 by Rev. James C.
Martin.

Christopher West, ae 24y, oysterman, s/o
Christopher & Fanny Jenkins West; Mary West,
ae 22y, d/o James & Nancy West; Jan 9 1873
by Rev. W, S, Hawkins.

Reuben Berkley, ae 24y, colored, school
teacher, Spotsylvania Co VA, s/o Reuben &
Brayner Berkley; Easter Green, ae 15y,
colored, d/o Henry & Elizabeth Green; Oct 24
1872.

Moses Grimes, ae 22y, colored, farmer, of
Mathews Co VA, s/o Joshua & Dianna Grimes;
Maria Willis, ae 23y, colored, d/o Daniel &
Sarah Wilson Willis; Jan 11 1873 by Rev.
Samuel S. Harden.

Thomas Crew, ae 31y, widower, oysterman,
s/o John & Amy Dunston Crew; Ellen Blake, ae
18y, d/o John & Mary E. Blake; Jan 12 1873
by Rev. W. S. Hawkins.

H. Palestin Hall, ae 27y, farmer, s/o
Lewis & Catharine Newbill Hall; Nannie Minor,
ae 17y, d/o Wm. T. & Fanny Enos Minor; Jan 15
1873 by Rev. James C. Martin.

James A. Fletcher, ae 24y, lumber getter,
s/o Wm. R. & Frances A. Fary Fletcher; Lizzie
C. Purcell, ae 19y, d/o Wm. A. & Martha A.
Blake Purcell; Jan 15 1873 by Rev. James C.
Martin.

William Thomas Burwell, ae 36y, widower,
colored, farmer, s/o Lucy Burwell; Mary
Scott, ae 22y, widow, d/o Peter & Agnes Cooke
Scott; Jan 18 1873 by Rev. Jas, C. Martin.

Benjamin Dixon, ae 21y, colored, water-
man, s/o Aaron & Roberta Dixon; Lucinda
Robinson, ae 22y, colored, d/o John R.
Robinson; Jan 19 1873 by Rev. W. S. Hawkins.

Washington Thomas, ae 24y, oysterman, s/o
James & Martha Smith Thomas; Harriet A.
Thomas, ae 18y, d/o Washington & Elizabeth
Thomas; Jan 23 1873 by Rev. W. S. Hawkins.

Jeff Wilson, ae 22y, colored, waterman,
s/o Rob't & Matilda Wilson; Lucy Jamison, ae
21y, colored, d/o Wm. & Mary Jamison; Jan 23
1873 by Rev. James C. Martin.

Anthony Hamilton, ae 24y, colored, farm, of Charlotte Co VA, s/o James & Susan Hamilton; Jennett Thornton, ae 23y, colored, d/o Oliver & Milly Thornton; Jan 26 1873 by Rev. Chas. Mann, Rector of Ware.

Edward Fields, ae 50y, colored, widower, farmer, of King and Queen Co VA, s/o Geo. & Maria Fields; Mary Yates, ae 35y, colored, widow, parents unk; Jan 23 1873 by Rev. Sam'l Harden.

George Shackelford, ae 45y, colored, widower, farmer, s/o Neptune & Lucy Shackelford; Judy Garrett, ae 40y, colored, widow, d/o Frank & Mary Ellis Garrett; Jan 23 1873 by Rev. Sam'l S. Harden.

John Patterson, ae 22y, colored, oyster, s/o Raney Patterson; Dolly Jones, ae 25y, colored, widow, d/o Armistead Jones; Feb 20 1873 by Rev. W. S. Hawkins.

William H. Bristow, farmer, s/o Wm. L. & Elizabeth Bristow; Martha A. Brown, of Middlesex Co VA, d/o Thos. S. & Mary Daniel Brown; Feb 6 1873 by Rev. J. G. Councill.

Samuel D. Puller, ae 33y, merchant, s/o Sam'l & Mary W. Hall Puller; Ella P. Duncan, ae 19y, of St. Louis MISSOURI, lived in Gloucester Co VA, d/o James & Mary Franklin Duncan; Feb 5 1873 by Rev. Chas. Mann.

John N. Martin, ae 38y, widower, farmer, of Nelson Co VA, s/o N. S. & E. A. Dickenson Martin; Catharine C. Tayler, ae 21y, d/o Fielding S. & E. T. Fauntleroy Tayler; Feb 11 1873 by Rev. Chas Mann, Rector of Ware.

William Lemon, ae 24y, colored, oyster., s/o James & Elizabeth Lemon; Margaret Bolling, ae 22y, colored, d/o Bob & Easter Bolling; Feb 12 1873 by Rev. Jas. C. Martin.

George Yates, ae 42y, colored, farmer, s/o Rob't & Rachel Yates; Maria L. Muse, ae 18y, colored, d/o Essex & Nancy Muse; Feb 13 1873 by Rev. Samuel S, Harden.

Milton S. Mason, ae 24y, carpenter, s/o Philip S. & Amanda Bland Mason; Emma A. Graves, ae 18y, d/o Lewis T. & Rosa A. Taylor Graves; Feb 13 1873 by Rev. Jas. C. Martin.

Charles Jones, ae 22y, colored, oyster, s/o James Smith; Susan Smith, ae 20y, color, d/o Isaac & Jennie Smith; Feb 20 1873 by Rev. Samuel S. Harden.

Isaac Henry King, ae 23y, farmer, s/o Thos. & Susan Drummond King; Sarah Jane Belvin, ae 22y, d/o John & Harriet Heywood Belvin; Feb 20 1873 by Rev. W. S. Hawkins.

Jacob Warden, ae 21y, colored, waterman, of Williamsburg VA, s/o Jack & Maria Warden; Mary Bright, ae 22y, colored, d/o Wm. & Mary Bright; Feb 27 1873 by Rev. Edward Page.

Samuel Carter, ae 23y, colored, oysters, s/o Randall & Eliza Carter; Nancy Talia-ferro, ae 21y, colored, parents unk; Feb 27 1873 by Rev. Edward Page.

John E. Smith, ae 29y, pilot, of Ports-mouth VA, s/o John W. & Elizabeth S. Dennis Smith; Grace Elizabeth Smith, ae 19y, widow, d/o Peter & Frances Jane Rowe Smith; Feb 27 1873 by Rev. W. S. Hawkins.

Albert J. Wilkins, ae 21y, farmer, s/o Nathan & Lilly Coleman Wilkins; Susannah Robins, ae 26y, widow, of Mathews Co VA, parents unk; Mar 13 1873 by Rev. Wm. E. Wiatt.

William Smith, ae 22y, colored, oysters, s/o Isaac & Jane Smith; Rosa Hayes, ae 21y, colored, d/o Robert & Betsy Hayes; Mar 15 1873 by Rev. David Coulling.

Randall Kellis, ae 24y, colored, oysters, of York Co VA, s/o Robert & Ellen Kellis; Susannah Thruston, ae 21y, colored, d/o Mat & Ann Burwell Thruston; Mar 20 1873 by Rev, W. S. Hawkins.

George Williams, ae 21y, colored, oysterman, s/o John & Mary Williams; Mahlaey Bright, ae 21y, colored, d/o Thomas & Agnes Bright; Mar 27 1873 by Rev. Samuel S. Harden.

Joseph W. Peters, ae 34y, widower, farmer, of Queen Anne Co MD, s/o Wm. S. & Catharine Peters; Mary E. Booker, ae 22y, of Caroline Co MD, d/o Wm. H. Booker; Mar 27 1873 by Rev. Charles Mann, Rector of Ware.

Thomas H. Dunston, ae 25y, widower, steam
mill hand, s/o John & Mary Dunston; Sarah A.
Fletcher, ae 22y, d/o James B. & Lilly A.
Fletcher; Apr 3 1873 by Rev. J. C. Martin.

Robert J. Rowe, ae 33y, carpenter, s/o
Benj. & Elizabeth Purcell Rowe; Mary S. Rowe,
ae 30y, d/o Wm. T. & Susan Leavitt Mouring
Rowe; Apr 6 1873 by Rev. W. S. Hawkins.

Wallace Harwood, ae 26y, colored, laborer,
s/o Wm. & Anna Harwood; Alice Lee, ae 21y,
colored, of King and Queen Co VA, d/o Henry
& Louisa Lee; Mar 6 1873 by Rev. David
Coulling.

Robert Meggs, ae 42y, colored, ship timber
getter, s/o Peter & Jane Meggs; Adaline
Banks, ae 24y, widow, colored,d/o Wm. &
Harriet Banks; Apr 7 1873 by Rev. David
Coulling.

Peter Carter Bolden, ae 28y, colored,
farmer, s/o Robert & Easter Carter; Lucy
Frances Lemon, ae 28y, d/o James & Patsy
Lemon; Apr 9 1873 by Rev. James C. Martin.

Frank Bright, ae 22y, colored, oysterman,
s/o Nat & Mary Bright; Margaret Dixon, ae
25y, colored, d/o Thos. & Sally Dixon; Apr 10
1873 by Rev. James C. Martin.

Columbus Anderson, ae 31y, oysterman, s/o
Benj. & Elizabeth Davis Anderton; Lucy A.
Gayle, ae 24y, d/o Zelotes & Eliza White
Gayle; Apr 24 1873 by Rev. James C. Martin.

Richard C. Rilee, ae 23y, farmer, s/o
Rich'd & Mary Hibble Rilee; Laura C. Massey,
ae 21y, d/o Wm. Y. & Julia Wright Massey; Apr
13 1873 by Rev. David Coulling.

John J. Graves, ae 37y, widower, farmer,
s/o W. J. & Eliza Graves; Hester J. Smith, ae
27y, widow, d/o David & Susan Edwards Smith;
Apr 28 1873 by Rev. David Coulling.

A. W. Smith, ae 21y, sailor, s/o Peter W.
& Frances J. Rowe Smith; Laura L. Hughes, ae
20y, d/o Henry & Mary Hughes; Apr 29 1873 by
Rev. James C. Martin.

Martin Lockley, ae 25y, colored, farmer,
of Williamsburg, VA, s/o Martin & Lucinda
Lockley; Betty Duval, ae 23y, colored,
parents unk; May 15 1873 by Rev. Wm. E.
Wiatt.

Michael Scanlon, ae 47y, widower, farmer, of Wilmington DEL, s/o Ed & Betsy Scalon; Harriet Roane, ae 42y, widow, d/o James & Ann Dutton Roane; May 27 1873 by Rev. James C. Martin.

George T. Hibble, ae 27y, farmer, s/o Mathew & Lilly R. Thrift Hibble; Emily J. Lamberth, ae 19y, d/o A. C. & Sarah Lamberth; May 27 1873 by Rev. James C. Martin.

Cassius M. Enos, ae 24y, s/o Geo. & Sarah A. E. Moore Enos; Hetty H. Kerns, ae 21y, of Lancaster PA, d/o Maris C. & Emma J. Liffaur Kerns; June 3 1873 by Rev. J. C. Martin.

Joseph Brown, ae 36y, widower, mechanic, s/o Thos. & Milly Brown; Catharine Rowe, ae 33y, d/o Ralph & Mary Rowe; June 18 1873 by Rev. W. S. Hawkins.

James Bright, ae 22y, oysterman, s/o Nat & Mary Bright; Lucy Robinson, ae 21y, d/o Lewis & Susan Robinson; Mar 20 1873 by Rev. James C. Martin.

Virginius H. Fletcher, ae 21y, farmer, s/o Wm. R. & Frances A. Fary Fletcher; Harriet G. Fary, ae 21y, d/o Wm. C. & Mary F. Corr Fary; Aug 28 1873 by Rev. James C. Martin.

Ambrose West Jr, ae 22y, farmer, s/o Ambrose & Hannah West; Elizabeth Green, ae 21y, d/o Geo. W. & Molly Green; Sept 7 1873 by Rev. W. S. Hawkins.

George Washington Williams, ae 35y, oysterman, s/o Elisha Williams; Sarah Isabella Jones, ae 19y, of Baltimore MD, d/o Ferdinand & Sally Jones; Sept 14 1873 by Rev. W. S. Hawkins.
John H. Dye, ae 31y, widower, minister of the gospel, of Independence Co ARK, s/o Henry C. & D. J. Mathews Dye; Kate L. Sinclair, ae 23y, d/o John & Lucy Baytop Sinclair; Sept 23 1873 by Rev. Wm. E. Wiatt.

John Bristow, ae 22y, laborer, s/o Wm. & Katie Bristow; Georgiana West, ae 21y, d/o London & Catharine West; Sept 25 1873 by Rev. W. S. Hawkins.

John J. Floyd, ae 23y, studying for ministry, of Alexandria VA, s/o John J. & Eliza A. Seldon Floyd; Ella G. Hubbard, ae 23y, of Richmond VA, d/o Wm. J. & Maria McTabb Hubbard; Sept 25 1873 by Rev. Robert A. Gibson.

James E. Ransone, ae 23y, farmer, s/o
John W. & Mary Ransone; Joicy F. Limbrough,
ae 26y, d/o Wm. & Susan J. Ransone Limbrough;
Oct 1 1873 by Rev. David Coulling.

Robert Robinson, ae 48y, widower, farmer,
s/o Peter & Fanny Robinson; Rachel Ann
Allmond, ae 57y, d/o Fanny Allmond, father
unk; Oct 4 1873 by Rev. W. S. Hawkins.

Christopher C. Wilkins, ae 24y, oyster,
s/o John & Mollie Howlett Wilkins; Rosa Lee
Jenkins, ae 21y, d/o Wm. A. & Elizabeth
Belvin Jenkins; Jan 1 1894 by Rev. Paul
Bradley.

William Robert Reed, ae 22y, laborer, s/o
H. Bush & Mary Reed; Marilla Stokes, ae 22y,
d/o Guest & Delia Stokes; Jan 4 1894 by Rev.
J. W. Booth.

Elias Kemp, ae 24y, widower, farmer, s/o
Henry & Elizabeth Kemp; Fanny Montague, ae
22y, d/o Phill & Mary E. Montague; Jan 3
1887 by Rev. Z. T. Whiting.

Jefferson Sinclair Jr, ae 42y, widower,
farmer, of Elizabeth City VA, s/o Jefferson
& Frances Lowry Sinclair; Mary Graham Jones,
ae 33y, d/o Walker F. & Mary Agnes Baytop
Jones; Jan 9 1894 by Rev. J. D. Hanks.

James Shipley Brown, ae 23y, oysterman,
s/o L. T. & Maria F. Savage Brown; Catharine
E. Walker, ae 19y, d/o Enock W. & Elizabeth
A. Brown Walker; Jan 10 1894 by Rev. Paul
Bradley.

Willie W. Bright, ae 27y, street car
driver, of Currituck Co N. C, s/o Wesley &
Sarah Powers Bright; Anna Florence Fleming,
ae 21y, d/o Joseph C. & Catharine A. Teagle
Fleming; Jan 14 1894 by Rev. Paul Bradley.

William Henry Bryan, ae 24y, farmer, of
Kent Co MD, s/o Rich'd H. & Mary C. Birch
Bryan; Barbara C. Erdman, ae 25y, of Balto
Co MD, d/o Chas. & Emma E. Reed Erdman; Jan
15 1894 by Rev. J. D. Hank.

J. V. Bray, ae 40y, widow, mechanic, of
King and Queen Co VA, s/o John & Mira New-
comb Bray; Emma J. Leigh, ae 30y, widow, d/o
James R. & Rebecca E. Adams Claytor Leigh;
Jan 16 1894 by Rev. J. D. Hank.

James W. George, ae 27y, merchant, of Lancaster Co VA, s/o James M. & Margaret Lanas George; Mary E. Haynes, ae 18y, of King and Queen Co VA, d/o Chas. E. & Virginia D. Milby Haynes; Jan 17 1894 by Rev. R. H. Younger.

Thomas R. Brothers, ae 38y, widower, merchant, of Pasquotank N. C, s/o T. P. & Dicey Brothers; Elizabeth P. Chandler, ae 23y, d/o J. J. & Lucy Chandler; Jan 18 1894 by Rev. W. E. Wiatt.

George R. Jarvis, ae 38y, farmer, s/o Geo. & M. R. Singleton Jarvis; Maggie V. C. Chandler, ae 21y, d/o J. J. & Lucy Chandler; Jan 18 1894 by Rev. W. E. Wiatt.

John F. Thomas, ae 25y, fisherman, s/o Rob't & Mira Hogg Thomas; Nannie E. Thomas, ae 23y, d/o Wm. F. & Eliza Jane Thomas; Jan 21 1894 by Rev. R. A. Folkes.

Daniel Ellis, ae 22y, oysterman, s/o Frank & Johannah Ellis; Fanny Reed, ae 22y, of King and Queen Co VA, d/o Harry & Martha Taliaferro Reed; Jan 25 1894 by Rev. Z. Taylor Whiting.

Albert Kelly, ae 20y, farmer, s/o John & Martha Kelly; Margarit Carter, ae 20y, d/o Davy & Georgianna Adams Carter; Feb 4 1894 by Rev. J. W. Booth.

Harrison Stubbs, ae 46y, widower, farmer, s/o Harrison & Clara Stubbs; Laura L. Booth, ae 39y, widow, d/o John Hall; Feb 6 1894 by Rev. J. W. Booth.

Charles F. S. Hall, ae 24y, oysterman, s/o Rich'd & Elizabeth Bridges Hall; Sarah Robins, ae 23y, d/o John & Caroline Howard Robins; Feb 11 1894 by Rev. R. A. Folkes.

Charles E. Harper, ae 30y, farmer, s/o Edward & Elizabeth Sheppard Harper; Ada R. Kemp, ae 21y, d/o S. M. & Harriet E. B. Dutton Kemp; Feb 18 1894 by Rev. J. D. Hank.

Tyler Brown, ae 21y, oysterman, s/o Rob't & Mary Smith Brown; Margaret Sarah West, ae 17y, d/o Davy & Susan Sparrow West; Feb 27 1872 by Rev. W, S, Hawkins.

Roy Smith, ae 22y, colored, farmer, parents unk; Elizabeth Yates, ae 20y, colored, d/o Mary Yates; Mar 7 1872 by Rev. Wm. E. Wiatt.

Emanuel J. Thruston, ae 34y, farmer, s/o
Emanuel J. & Catharine P. Cooke Thruston;
Sarah Ann Rootes, ae 30y, d/o Jacquline &
Emily Robins Rootes; Feb 28 1872 by Rev. J.
G. Councill.

Jeff Cooke, ae 22y, waterman, s/o Billy &
Fisher Cooke; Ann Braxton, ae 23y, d/o
Marlow & Sarah Cooke; Mar 2 1872 by Rev.
Edward Page.

Richard L. Nuttall, ae 22y, farmer, s/o
Iverson & Lucy Bristow Nuttall; Betty Brown,
ae 22y, widow, of Middlesex Co CA, parents
unk; Mar 14 1872 by Rev. J. G. Councill.

Braxton Taylor, ae 21y, colored, oyster,
s/o John & Lucy Taylor; Martha Banks, ae
21y, colored, d/o Wm. & Lucy Banks; Mar 20
1872 by Rev. Samuel S. Harden.

George Washington Hughes, ae 74y, colored,
widower, house servant, s/o Jasper & Agnes
Hughes; Maria Tabb, ae 41y, colored, widow,
parents unk; Feb 22 1872 by Rev. W. S.
Hawkins.

Armistead Jones, ae 55y, colored, oyster,
s/o Armistead & Dolly Jones; Polly Bolling,
ae 30y, colored, d/o John & Courtney Collins
Bolling; Mar 23 1872 by Rev. W. S. Hawkins.

John Deal, ae 23y, oysterman, s/o John &
Elizabeth Brown Deal; Louisiana Bonnywell,
ae 21y, d/o Geo. & Nancy Robins Bonnywell;
Mar 23 1872 by Rev. Samuel Henry Phillips.

Robert Stubbs, ae 21y, colored, oyster,
s/o Rob't & Katy Stubbs; Violet Johnson, ae
21y, colored, parents unk; Apr 6 1872 by
Rev. James C. Martin.

Richard Allen Fitzhugh, ae 27y, farmer,
of Middlesex Co VA, s/o Patrick H. & Mary S.
Christian Fitzhugh; Matilda E. Johnston, ae
21y, d/o Thos. E. & Elizabeth Ransone Johnston; Apr 7 1872 by Rev. J. G. Councill.

Benjamin F. Oliver, ae 27y, oysterman,
s/o Regault & Mildred Oliver; Eliza Larke,
ae 27y, d/o Geo. & Maria Larke; Apr 11 1872
by Rev. W. S. Hawkins.

James W. Oliver, ae 22y, oysterman, s/o
Regault & Mildred Oliver; Lucy Woodley, ae
18y, d/o, John & Lucy Woodley; Apr 1 1872 by
Rev. W. S. Hawkins.

Frank Reed Jr, ae 25y, widower, farmer, s/o Frank & Mary Reed; Elsy Harrison, ae 17y, d/o Joe & Nancy Harrison; Apr 18 1872 by Rev. Samuel S. Harden.

Abraham Hughes, ae 31y, colored, farmer, of Elizabeth City Co VA, s/o James & Matilda Hughes, Emily Hughes, ae 20y, colored, d/o Mary Frances Hughes; Apr 28 1872 by Rev. W. S. Hawkins.

John A. Williams, ae 25y, farmer, s/o Andrew & Paulina Williams; Annie M. Peatross, ae 21y, of Caroline Co VA, d/o Geo. & Maria Peatross; Apr 14 1872 by Rev. W. S. Hawkins.

Beverly Jones, ae 23y, oysterman, s/o Jack & Delia Jones; Lucy Carter, ae 21y, d/o Gabriel & Ann Carter; May 2 1872 by Rev. David Coulling.

Alexander Emmerson, ae 50y, widower, farm, of King and Queen Co VA, s/o Wm. & Susan Emmerson; Julia A. Stafford, ae 18y, of Talbot Co MD, d/o Theodore & Eliza Stafford; May 14 1872 by Rev. W,. E. Wiatt.

William Dean, ae 25y, colored, farmer, of Lancaster Co VA, s/o Besick & Aggy Dean; Mary Wormley, ae 23y, colored, d/o Rose Wormley, father unk; May 6 1872 by Rev. James C. Martin.

Serian Evans, ae 27y, colored, oysterman, s/o Wm. & Clara Evans; Betty Leigh, ae 17y, colored, of Mathews Co VA, d/o Jasper & Martha Leigh; May 12 1872 by Rev. Chas. Mann, Rector of Ware Church.

Thomas Jefferson Woodland, ae 23y, sailor, s/o John & Catharine Lewellan Woodland; Mary Ellen Robins, ae 18y, d/o James W. & Virginia Ann Rowe Robins; May 13 1872 by Rev. James C. Martin.

John Curtis, ae 21y, colored, laborer, s/o Jim & Ann Curtis; Frances Leigh, ae 25y, colored, parents unk; June 1 1872 by Rev. Samuel S. Harden.

Jasper Leigh, ae 21y, colored, oysterman, of Mathews Co VA, s/o Jasper & Martha Leigh; Maria Scott, ae 20y, colored, of King and Queen Co VA, d/o Jane Scott; June 2 1872 by Samuel S. Harden.

Richard L. Padgett, ae 47y, widower,
farmer, s/o Fleming & Susan Padget; Mary
Louisa Drisgall, ae 18y, d/o Wm. & Dolly
Drisgall; June 30 1872 by Rev. David
Coulling.

Joe Smith, ae 20y, colored, oysterman,
of Mathews Co VA, s/o Henry & Delia Smith;
Catharine Tabb, ae 21y, colored, of King and
Queen Co VA, d/o Andrew & Maria Tabb; June 6
1872 by Rev. David Coulling.

Wilson D. Williams, ae 31y, merchant, of
Richmond VA, s/o Wilson & Elizabeth H.
Collins Williams; Martha C. Woller, ae 41y,
widow, d/o John & Ann W. C. Catlett Field;
June 11 1872 by Rev. Chas. Mann, Rector of
Ware Church.

Warrington Mathias, ae 38y, widower,
oysterman, s/o Davy & Becky Warrington;
Georgianna Smith, ae 24y, colored, d/o
Werter & Delphy Smith; June 13 1872 by Rev.
Sam'l S. Harden.

Adam Dorsey, ae 23y, colored, farmer, of
Alexandria VA, s/o Moses & Matilda Dorsey;
Letty Clark, ae 19y, colored, d/o Wm. &
Violet Clark Clarke; June 13 1872 by Rev.
Edward Page.

Aska Irgerson, ae 28y, colored, farmer,
of Northampton Co N. C, lived York Co VA,
s/o Bristow & Lenna Blue; Rebecca Bolden, ae
25y, colored, d/o Samuel & Harriet Bolden;
June 17 1872 by Rev. Edward Page.

Franklin J. Huel, ae 25y, farmer, s/o
John & Susan Huel; Sarah E. Huel, ae 25y, of
King and Queen Co VA, parents unk; July 7
1872 by Rev. J. G. Councill.

John W. Ennis, ae 26y, stock dealer, of
New Castle DELAWARE, lived Middlesex Co VA,
s/o B. B. & Elizabeth Ennis; Mary E. Rilee,
ae 22y, d/o Rob't L. & Susan Rilee; July 9
1872 by Rev. David Coulling.

George Washington Heywood, ae 24y,
oysterman, s/o Levi & Martha J. Diggs Heywood; Harriet Alice Brown, ae 19y, d/o Lewis
& Catharine Ann Brown; July 18 1872 by Rev.
Chas. Mann, Rector.

James Polk Ash, ae 26y, ferryman, s/o
Thos. & Lucy Ransone Ash; Adelaide Singleton
Minor, ae 18y, d/o John W. & Frances A.
Mouring Minor; Oct 22 1872 by Rev. W. S.
Hawkins.

Albert Berry, ae 22y, colored, oysterman,
s/o John & Patsy Berry; Ann Gregory, ae 21y,
colored, d/o Geo. & Sally Gregory; Oct 19
1872 by Rev. Samuel S. Harden.

Peyton N. Page, ae 32y, attorney, s/o
Mann & Lucy Ann Jones Page; Emily D. Kemp,
ae 25y, d/o Wyndham & Ann L. Perrin Kemp;
Nov 7 1872 by Rev. Chas. Mann.

William E. Brooks, ae 24y, farmer, of
Mathews Co VA, s/o James B. & Elizabeth
Johnson Brooks; Fannie White, ae 24y, d/o
James H. & Susan F. Thomas White; Nov 25
1872 by Rev. Geo. E. Thomas.

Miles H. Rilee, ae 27y, farmer, s/o
Richard & Nancy Hibble Rilee; Julia F.
Philips, ae 29y, widow, d/o C. C. & Martha
D. Wright Pointer; Nov 10 1872 by Rev. David
Coulling.

Beverly Jackson, ae 24y, widower, farmer,
s/o Edw'd & Becky Jackson; Harriet Gage, ae
22y, widow, parents unk; Nov 23 1872 by Rev.
Wm. E. Wiatt.

Richard Green, ae 20y, colored, oystered,
s/o Wm. & Margaret Green; Jenny Crittenden,
ae 21y, colored, of York Co. VA, d/o Joseph &
Nettie Crittenden; Dec 12 1872 by REv. W. S.
Hawkins.

Wyndham Smith Haynes, ae 21y, farmer, s/o
Wm. & Fanny Padgett Haynes; Louisa Thosmas,
South, ae 20y, d/o Thos. B. & Harriet Rilee
South; Nov 28 1872 by Rev. David Coulling.

William Cook, Ae 23y, colored, shoemaker,
s/o Peter & Agnes Cook; Catharine Taliaferro,
ae 18y, colored, d/o Cell & Jane Taliaferro;
Nov 28 1872 by Rev. Samuel S. Harden.

Edward Smith, ae 23y, colored, teamster,
s/o Agnes Wiatt; Bula Pryor, ae 17y, colored,
d/o Betsy Cook; Dec 5 1872 by Rev. Samuel S.
Harden.

James Wilson, ae 21y, colored, farmer,
parents unk; Harriet Brown, ae 17y, colored,
d/o Sam & Eliza Brown; Dec 19 1872 by Rev.
David Coulling.

Forrester Thompson, ae 24y, colored, carpenter, of Boston MASS, parents unk; Amanda Ellis, ae 26y, colored, widow, d/o Lewis & Maria Baytop; Dec 24 1872 by Rev. Chas. Mann, Rector of Ware Church.

Andrew Stubbs, ae 23y, clerk, s/o E. E. & Jane A. Coleman Stubbs; Delia J. Stubbs, ae 24y, d/o Lawrence S. & Mary A. Dame Stubbs; Dec 25 1872 by Rev. James C. Martin.

John W. Gregg, ae 25y, farmer, of Essex Co VA, s/o Peter J. & Mary South Gregg; Alice A. Howard, ae 24y, d/o Henry A. & Martha Curry Howard; Dec 26 1872 by Rev. James C. Martin.

Charley C. Poole, ae 23y, farmer, of Mathews Co VA, s/o Thos. & Paulina Sibley Poole; Emma A. Trevillian, ae 18y, d/o Augustine S. & Julia A. Dutton Trevillian; Dec 25 1872 by Rev. David Coulling.

Will Selden, ae 81y, widower, colored, blacksmith, s/o Will & Jenny Selden; Sally Cook, ae 56y, widow, colored, parents unk; Jan 5 1873 by Rev. Edward Page.

Joseph Smith, ae 40y, colored, widower, laborer, s/o Harry & Scilla Smith; Agnes Thornton, ae 17y, colored, d/o Paul & Mary Thornton; Jan 5 1873 by Rev. Sam'l S. Harden.

Lewis Jones, ae 25y, colored, farmer, s/o Leroy & Betsy Jones; Judy Washington, ae 22y, colored, d/o Geo. & Becky Washington; Dec 29 1872.

James Smith, ae 28y, farmer, s/o Hannah Carter, father unk; Martha Ellen Braxton, ae 25y, of King and Queen Co VA, d/o Virginia Braxton; Jan 4 1873.

Randall Brown, ae 50y, colored, widower, farmer, s/o Edmund & Becky Brown; Nancy Scott, ae 35y, colored, d/o Essex & Polly Smith; Jan 2 1873 by Rev. David Coulling.

George B. Bohannon, ae 23y, sailor, of Mathews Co VA, s/o Geo. W. & Lucy Bohannon; Lavinia Crismond, ae 23y, d/o John & Louisa Crismond; Jan 7 1873 by Rev. Jas. C. Martin.

Christopher West, ae 24y, oysterman, s/o Christopher & Fanny West; Mary West, ae 22y, d/o Jas. & Nancy West; Jan 9 1873 by Rev. W. S. Hawkins.

Reuben Berkeley, ae 24y, colored, school
teacher, of Spotsylvania Co VA, s/o Reuben &
Brayner Berkeley; Easter Green, ae 15y,
colored, d/o Henry & Elizabeth Green; Oct
24 1873 by Rev. Jas. C. Martin.

Moses Grimes, ae 22y, colored, farmer, of
Mathews Co VA, s/o Joshua & Diana Grimes;
Maria Willis, ae 23y, colored, d/o Daniel &
Sarah Wilson; Jan 11 1873 by Rev. Samuel S.
Harden.

Thomas Crew, ae 31y, oysterman, s/o John
& Ary Dunston Crew; Ellen Blake, ae 18y, d/o
John & Mary Blake; Jan 12 1873 by Rev. W. S.
Hawkins.

Palestine Hall, ae 27y, farmer, s/o Lewis
& Catharine Newbill Hall; Nannie Minor, ae
17y, d/o Wm. T. & Fanny Enos Minor; Jan 15
1873 by Rev. James C. Martin.

James A. Fletcher, ae 24y, lumber getter,
s/o Wm. R. & Frances A. Fary Fletcher;
Lizzie C. Purcell, ae 19y, d/o Wm. A. &
Martha A. Blake; Jan 16 1873 by Rev. Jas. C.
Martin.

William Thomas Burwell, ae 36y, colored,
widower, farmer, s/o Lucy Burwell, father
unk; Mary Scott, ae 22y, colored, widow, d/o
Peter & Agnes Cooke; Jan 18 1873 by Rev.
James C. Martin.

Benjamin Dixon, ae 21y, colored, water-
man, s/o Aaron & Roberta Dixon; Lucinda
Robinson, ae 22y, colored, d/o John R.
Robinson, mother unk; Jan 19 1873 by Rev.
W. S. Hawkins.

Washington Thomas, ae 24y, oysterman, s/o
James & Martha Smith Thomas; Harriet Ann
Thomas, ae 18y, d/o Washington & Elizabeth
Thomas; Jan 23 1873 by Rev. W. S. Hawkins.

Jeff Wilson, ae 22y, colored, waterman,
s/o Rob't & Matilda Wilson; Lucy Jamison, ae
21y, colored, d/o Wm. & Mary Jamison; Jan 23
1873 by Rev. James C. Martin.

Anthony Hamilton, ae 24y, colored, farm,
of Charlotte Co VA, s/o Jas. & Susan Hamilton; Jennett Thornton, ae 23y, colored, d/o
Oliver & Milly Thornton; Jan 26 1873 by Rev.
Chas. Mann.

Edward Fields, ae 50y, colored, widower, farmer, of King and Queen Co VA, s/o Geo. & Maria Fields; Mary Yates, ae 35y, colored, widow, parents unk; Jan 23 1873 by Rev. Samuel S. Harden.

George Shackelford, ae 45y, colored, widower, farmer, s/o Neptune & Lucy Shackelford; Judy Garrett, ae 40y, colored, widow, d/o Frank & Mary Ellis; Jan 23 1873 by Rev. James C. Martin.

John Patterson, ae 22y, colored, oyster, s/o Raney Patterson; Dolly Jones, ae 25y, widow, d/o Armistead Jones; Feb 20 1873 by Rev. W. S. Hawkins.

William H. Bristow, ae 22y, farmer, s/o Wm. L. & Elizabeth Bristow; Martha A. Brown, ae 22y, of Misddlesex Co VA, d/o Thos. S. & Mary Daniel Brown; Feb 6 1873 by Rev. J. G. Councill.

Samuel D. Puller, ae 33y, merchant, s/o Sam'l D. & Mary W. Hall Puller; Ella P. Duncan, ae 19y, of St. Louis MO, d/o James & Mary Franklin Duncan; Feb 5 1873 by Rev. Chas. Mann, Rector of Ware.

John N. Martin, ae 38y, widower, farmer, of Nelson Co VA, s/o N. S. & E. A. Dickenson Martin; Catharine C. Taylor, ae 21y, d/o Fielding L. & E. F. Fauntleroy Taylor; Feb 11 1873 by Rev. Chas. Mann, Rector of Ware.

William Lemon ae.24y, colored, oyster, s/o James & Elizabeth Lemon; Margaret Bolling, ae 22y, colored, d/o Bob & Easter Bolling; Feb 12 1873 by Rev. Jas. C. Martin.

George Yates, ae 42y, widower, farmer, s/o Robert & Rachel Yates; Maria L. Muse, ae 18y, d/o Essex & Nancy Muse; Feb 13 1873 by Rev. Sam'l S. Harden.

Milton S. Mason, ae 24y, carpenter, s/o Philip S. & Amanda Bland Mason; Emma A. Graves, ae 18y, d/o Lewis T. & Rosa A. Taylor Graves; Feb 13 1873 by Rev. James C. Martin.

Charles Jones, ae 22y, colored, oyster, s/o Jane Smith, father unk; Susan Smith, ae 20y, colored, d/o Isaac & Jennie Smith; Feb 20 1873 by Rev. Sam'l S. Harden.

Isaac Henry King, ae 23y, farm, s/o Thos.
& Susan Drummond King; Jane Belvin, ae 22y,
d/o John & Harriet Heywood Belvin; Feb 20
1873 by Rev. W. S. Hawkins.

Jacob Warden, ae 21y, col'rd, waterman,
of Williamsburg VA, s/o Jack & Maria Warden;
Mary Bright, ae 22y, col'rd, d/o Wm. & Mary
Bright; Feb 27 1873 by Rev. Edward Page.

Samuel Carter, ae 23y, col'rd, oyster,
s/o Randall & Eliza Carter; Nancy Talia-
farro, ae 21y, col'rd, parents unk; Dec 27
1873 by Rev. Edward Page.

John E. Smith, ae 19y, widower, pilot, of
Portsmouth VA, lived Norfolk VA, s/o John W.
& Elizabeth S. Dennis Smith; Grace Elizabeth
Smith, ae 19y, d/o Peter W. & Frances Jane
Rowe Smith; Feb 23 1873 by Rev, W. S.
Hawkins.

Albert J. Wilkins, ae 21y, farm, of
Mathews Co VA, s/o Nathan & Lilly Coleman
Wilkins; Susannah Robins, ae 26y, col'rd,
parents unk; May 13 1873 by Rev. Wm. E.
Wiatt.

William Smith, ae 22y, col'rd, oyster,
s/o Isaac & Jane Smith; Rosa Hayes, ae 21y,
col'rd, d/o Rob't & Betsy Hayes; Mar 15 1873
by Rev. David Coulling.

Randall Kellis, ae 24y, col'rd, oyster,
of York Co VA, s/o Rob't & Ellen Kellis;
Susannah Thruston, ae 21y, col'rd, d/o Mat &
Ann Burwell Thruston; May 20 1873 by Rev.
Wm. S. Hawkins.

George Williams, 21y, col'rd, oyster, s/o
John & Mary Williams; Mahaley Bright, ae
20y, col'rd, d/o Thos. & Agnes Bright; May
27 1873 by Rev. Samuel S. Harden.

Joseph H. Peters, ae 34y, widower, farm,
of Queen Ann Co MD, s/o Wm. L. & Catharine
Peters; Mary E. Booker, ae 22y, d/o Wm. H.
Booker, mother unk; May 27 1873 by Rev.
Chas. Mann, Rector of Ware.

Thomas H. Dunston, ae 25y, widower, steam
mill hand, s/o John & Mary Dunston; Sarah A.
Fletcher, ae 22y, d/o Jas. B. & Lilly A.
Fletcher; Apr 3 1873 by Rev. Jas. C. Martin.

Wallace Harwood, ae 26y, colored, worker, s/o Wm. & Anna Harwood; Alice Lee, ae 21y, colored, of King and Queen Co VA, d/o Henry & Louisa Lee; Mar 6 1873 by Rev. David Coulling.

Robert Meggs, ae 42y, colored, timber getter for ships, s/o Peter & Jane Meggs; Adaline Banks, ae 24y, colored, d/o Wm. & Harriet Banks; Apr 7 1873 by Rev. David Coulling.

Peter Carter Bolden, ae 28y, colored, s/o Rob't & Easter Bolden; Lucy Frances Lemon, ae 28y, colored, d/o Jas. & Patsy Lemon; Apr 9 1873 by Rev. Jas. C. Martin.

Frank Bright, ae 22y, colored, oysterman, s/o Wat & Mary Bright; Margaret Dixon, ae 25y, colored, d/o Thos. & Sally Dixon; Apr 10 1873 by Rev. Jas. C. Martin.

Columbus Anderton, ae 31y, oysterman, s/o Benja. & Elizabeth Davis Anderton; Lucy A. Gayle; ae 24y, d/o Zelotes & Eliza White Gayle; Apr 24 1873 by Rev. Jas. C. Martin.

Richard C. Rilee, ae 23y, farmer, s/o Rich'd & Nancy Hibble Rilee; Laura C. Massey, ae 21y, d/o Wm. Y. & Julia Wright Massey; Apr 13 1873 by Rev. David Coulling.

John J. Graves, ae 37y, widower, farmer, s/o W. J. & Eliza Graves; Hester J. Smith, ae 27y, widow, d/o Daniel & Susan Edwards; Apr 28 1873 by Rev. David Coulling.

A. W. Smith, ae 21y, sailor, s/o Peter W. & Frances Rowe Smith; Laura L. Hughes, ae 20y, d/o Henry E. & Mary E. Hughes; Apr 29 1873 by Rev. Jas. C. Martin.

Martin Lockley, ae 25y, colored, farmer, of Williamsburg VA, s/o Martin & Lucinda Lockley, Betsy Duval, ae 23y, colored, parents unk; May 15 1873 by Rev. Wm. E. Wiatt.

Michael Scanlon, ae 47y, widower, farmer, of Wilmington DELAWARE, s/o Edward & Betsy Scanlon; Harriet Roane, ae 42y, widow, d/o Jane & Ann Dutton; May 27 1873 by Rev. James C. Martin.

George T. Hibble, ae 27y, farmer, s/o Mathew & Letty R. Thrift Hibble; Emily J. Lamberth, ae 19y, d/o A. C. & Sarah Lial Lamberth; May 27 1873 by Rev. Jas. C. Martin.

Cassius W. Enos, ae 24y, brick layer, s/o
Geo. & Sarah A. E. Moore Enos; Hetty H.
Kerns, ae 21y, of Lancaster Co PA, d/o Maris
& Emma J. Liffaur Kerns; June 3 1873 by Rev.
James C. Martin.

Joseph Brown, ae 36y, widower, mechanic,
s/o Thos. & Milly Brown; Catharine Rowe, ae
33y, d/o Ralph & Mary Rowe; June 18 1873 by
Rev. W. S. Hawkins.

James Bright, ae 22y, oysterman, s/o Nat
& Mary Bright; Lucy Robinson, ae 21y, d/o
Lewis & Susan Robinson; Mar 20 1873 by Rev.
James C. Martin.

Harry Lowry, ae 70y, colored, widower, of
York Co VA, farmer, s/o Jack & Nancy Lowry;
Mary Davenport, ae 40y, parents unk; May 1
1873 by Rev. David Coulling.

Ralph Jackson, ae 24y, colored, farmer,
s/o Edw'd & Milly Jackson; Betty Washington,
ae 23y, s/o Geo. & Rebecca Washington; June
15 1873 by Rev. Chas. Mann.

Sye Jones, ae 22y, colored, oysterman,
s/o Isaac & Charlotte Jones; Charlotte Gardner, ae 20y, colored, d/o Dan'l & Charlotte
Gardner; June 24 1873 by Rev. Sam'l S.
Harden.

Joe Young, ae 28y, colored, laborer, s/o
Wm. & Mollie Young; Mary Braxton, ae 26y,
colored, parents unk; July 8 1873 by Rev.
James C. Martin.

Robert Smith, ae 20y, oysterman, s/o John
& Ann Smith; Sarah Sparrow, ae 21y, d/o Ray-
mond & Sally Sparrow; July 10 1873 by Rev.
W. S. Hawkins.

John Kidd, ae 27y, farmer, of King and
Queen Co VA, s/o Eliza Booker, father unk;
Mary Catharine West, ae 19y, of King and
Queen Co VA, d/o David & Grace West; Aug 2
1873 by Rev. James C. Martin.

William Booth, ae 41y, widower, sailor,
s/o Milan & Milly Booth; Mary Field, ae 40y,
widow, d/o Thompson & Mary Baytop; Aug 5
1873 by Rev. Wm. E. Wiatt.

John R. Singleton, ae 22y, merchant, s/o
John & Eliza Singleton; Mary F. Hibble, ae
21y, d/o Henry H. & Ellen Hibble; Aug 6 1873
by Rev. James C. Martin.

Edmund Burwell, ae 24y, oysterman, s/o Edmund & Sally Burwell; ae 24y, oysterman, s/o Edmund & Sally Ann Burwell; Susan Allen, ae 21y, d/o Emory Green, father unk; July 31 1873 by Rev. W.S. Hawkins.

James Kemp, ae 21y, oysterman, s/o James & Betsy Kemp; Pinkey Dixon, ae 21y, d/o Jas. & Mary Dixon; Aug 14 1873 by Rev. W. S. Hawkins.

John Stoakes, ae 27y, oysterman, s/o Wm. & Judy Stoakes; Mattie J. Smith, ae 23y, d/o Warner & Elizabeth Smith; Aug 19 1873 by Rev. W. S. Hawkins.

Buy Bright, ae 19y, farmer, s/o Tom & Agnes Bright; Molly Washington, ae 17y, d/o Warner & Jane Washington; Aug 21 1873 by Rev. Samuel S. Harden.

Virginius H. Fletcher, ae 21y, farmer, s/o Wm. R. & Frances A. Fary Fletcher; Harriet G. Fary, ae 21y, d/o Wm. C. & Mary F. Corr Fary; Aug 28 1873 by Rev. Jas. C. Martin.

Ambrose West Jr, ae 22y, s/o Ambrose & Hannah West; Elizabeth Green, ae 21y, d/o Geo. W. & Molly Green; Sept 7 1873 by Rev. W. S. Hawkins.

George Washington Williams, ae 35y, oysterman, s/o Elisha Williams, father unk; Sarah Gabella Jones, ae 19y, of Baltimore MD, d/o Ferdinand & Sally Jones; Sept 7 1873 by Rev. W. S. Hawkins.

John H. Dye, ae 31y, widower, minister of the gospel, of Independence Co AKS, s/o Henry C. & D. J. Matthews Dye; Kate L. Sinclair, ae 23y, d/o John & Lucy Baytop Sinclair; Sept 23 1873 by Rev. Wm. E. Wiatt.

John Bristow, ae 22y, laborer, s/o Wm. & Katie Bristow; Georgianna West, ae 21y, d/o London & Catharine West; Sept 25 1873 by Rev. W. S. Hawkins.

John J. Lloyd, ae 23y, studying for ministry, of Alexandria VA, s/o John J. & Eliza A. Selden Lloyd; Ella G. Hubard, ae 23y, of Richmond VA, d/o Wm. J. & Maria McTabb Hubard; Sept 25 1873 by Rev. Rob't A. Gibson.

James E. Ransone, ae 23y, farmer, s/o
John W. & Mary A. Ransone; Joicy F. Lem-
brough, ae 26y, d/o Wm. & Susan J. Ransone
Lembrough; Oct 1 1873 by Rev. David
Coulling.

Robert Robertson, ae 57y, widower, farm,
s/o Peter & Fanny Robertson; Rachel Ann
Allmand, ae 57y, d/o Fanny Allmond, father
unk; Oct 4 1873 by Rev. W. S. Hawkins.

Lewis Jones, ae 26y, farmer, s/o Lewis &
Betsy Jones; Judith Washington, ae 26y, d/o
Geo. & Rebecca Washington; Oct 12 1873 by
Rev. Chas. Mann, Rector of Ware.

William Brown, ae 25y, farmer, s/o Geo. &
Nancy Brown; Lucretia Brown, ae 25y, d/o Wm.
& Amelia Brown; Oct 19 1873 by Rev. W. S.
Hawkins.

Americus V. Rowe, ae 25y, widower,
merchant, s/o Jasper C. & Julia Stubblefield
Rowe; Henrietta Pointer, ae 23y, d/o Henry
L. & Fanny Leigh Pointer; Oct 27 1873 by
Rev. James C. Martin.

William Fox, ae 21y, colored, oysterman,
s/o Sarn & Martha Fox; Maria Kemp, ae 16y,
colored, d/o John & Mary Stokes Kemp; Nov 1
1873 by Rev. Edward Page.

Thomas Ward, ae 30y, colored, farmer, s/o
Wm. & Maria Ward; Susan Smith, ae 40y, widow,
colored, parents unk; Nov 3 1873 by Rev.
David Coulling.

William C. Monroe, ae 21y, colored,
laborer, s/o James & Betsy Monroe; Elizabeth
Hall, ae 23y, colored, d/o M. Fanny Dixon;
Nov 15 1873 by Rev. Edward Page.

Moses Reed, ae 22y, colored, oysterman,
s/o Austin & Matilda Reed; Sarah Lawton, ae
25y, widow, of Middlesex Co VA, d/o Daniel &
Charlotte Gardner Lawton; Nov 15 1873 by
Rev. Samuel S. Harden.

William L. Pointer, ae 23y, collector of
Ware Township, s/o C. C. & Martha Pointer;
Mary J. Landes, ae 23y, of Lancaster Co PA,
d/o John G. & Martha Landes; Nov 18 1873 by
Rev. James C. Martin.

Reid Jenkins, ae 20y, oysterman, s/o
Mitchell & Anna Jenkins; Anna Jenkins, ae
18y, d/o Vincent & Dicey Jenkins; Nov 23
1873 by Rev. W. S. Hawkins.

Augustine Hughes, ae 33y, merchant, s/o
Henry & Mary E. D. Hall Hughes; Linda Godwin, ae 21y, of Hampton/Elizabeth City Co
VA, d/o John W. Godwin, mother unk; Nov 18
1873 by Rev. Jas. C. Martin.

Alexander Berry, ae 22y, colored, oyster,
s/o John & Hester Berry; Charlotte Morriss,
ae 17y, colored, Thos. & Mary Morriss; Dec 4
1873 by Rev. Samuel S. Harden.

Alexander Green, ae 30y, colored, farmer,
s/o Henry & Elizabeth Green; Emily Kemp, ae
24y, colored, d/o Oswald & Mina Kemp; Dec 4
1873 by Rev. Edward Page.

John Baylor Jones, ae 23y, colored,
laborer, s/o Lewis & Betsy Jones; Amanda
Shackelford, ae 18y, colored, d/o Wm. &
Martha Shackelford; Dec 14 1873 by Rev. Wm.
E. Wiatt.

Edward Smith, ae 53y, widower, colored,
farmer, s/o Phill & Peggy Smith; Mary Hane-
son, ae 40y, widow, d/o Henry & Hannah Hane-
son; Dec 11 1873 by Rev. W. S. Hawkins.

Maryus Jones, ae 29y, attorney at law,
s/o Catesby & M. A. B. Pollard Jones; Mary
Armistead Burwell Catlett, ae 23y, d/o John
W. C. & Fanny K. Burwell Catlett; Dec 10
1873 by Rev. Chas. Mann, Rector of Ware.

John W. Walker, ae 21y, farmer, s/o
Rich'd & Sarah Rilee Walker; Lilly A.
Walker, ae 21y, d/o Geo. & Emily S. Mason
Walker; Dec 11 1873 by Rev. Wm. E. Wiatt.

Wahington Lancaster, ae 24y, colored,
sailor, s/o Isaac & Polly Lancaster; Ann
Sturges, ae 21y, d/o Tom & Fanny Sturges;
Dec 18 1873 by Rev. Wm. E. Wiatt.

Wm. Augustus Robins, ae 30y, merchant,
s/o Thos. C. & Amelia E. Armistead Robins;
Flora Harwood, ae 20y, d/o Thos. S. & Lucy
E. Stubblefield Harwood; Dec 18 1873 by Rev.
Chas. Mann, Rector of Ware.

William Thomas Harwood, ae 25y, farmer,
of Warwick Co VA, s/o Ed & Rebecca Harwood;
Caroline V. Peatross, ae 21y, of Caroline Co
Va, d/o G. W. & Maria Peatross; Dec 18 1873
by Rev. W. S. Hawkins.

William C. Lawson, ae 21y, farmer, s/o
James W. & Mary J. Lawson; Mary S. Bristow,
ae 14y, d/o Rich'd & Sarah M. Bristow; Dec 18
1873 by Rev. John McClelland.

Thomas Bluford, ae 28y, colored, farmer,
s/o Thos. & Harriet Bluford; Adaline Green,
ae 21y, d/o Henry & Betsy Green; Dec 23 1873
by Rev. James C. Martin.

Armistead Smith, ae 30y, colored, farmer,
s/o Essex & Polly Smith; Frances Smith, ae
30y, colored, d/o Robert & Senny Noggin; Dec
23 1873 by Rev. Charles Mann, Rector.

Thomas Hogg, ae 24y, farmer, s/o John &
Julia Dunston Hogg; Virginia Edwards, ae 23y,
d/o Dan'l & Susan West Edwards; Dec 23 1873
by Rev. W. S. Hawkins.

Jasper C. Rowe, ae 22y, oysterman, s/o
Zachariah & Johannah Rowe; Elizabeth Belvin,
ae 21y, d/o Lewis & Mary Belvin; Dec 24 1873
by Rev. W. S. Hawkins.

Thomas Smith, ae 24y, colored, farmer, s/o
Johnson & Patsy Smith; Julia Jackman, ae 21y,
colored, parents unk; Dec 24 1873 by Rev.
Edward Page.

Jack Peyton, ae 65y, widower, colored,
carpenter, s/o Nelson & Lavenia Peyton; Sucky
Smith, ae 45y, widow, colored, d/o Wm. &
Betty Allen; Dec 24 1873 by Rev. David
Coulling.

Edmund Cook, ae 21y, colored, farmer, s/o
Peyton & Frances A. Cook; Loula Frances
Goaldman, ae 18y, colored, d/o Pinky Daven-
port; Dec 25 1873 by Rev. Edward Page.

Meaux Thornton, ae 23y, farmer, s/o John
A. B. & Sarah E. Hayes Thornton; Sarah M.
Minor, ae 22y, d/o John W. & Sarah J. Mour-
ing Minor; Dec 25 1873 by Rev. Wm. E. Wiatt.

Aaron Harwood, ae 25y, colored, farmer,
s/o Tawney & Gracy Harwood; Susan Billups, ae
30y, parents unk; Dec 27 1873 by Rev. W. S.
Hawkins.

William C. Bland, ae 24y, clerking, of
King and Queen Co VA, lived York Co VA, s/o
Cary T. & Maria H. Mouring Bland; Sarah A.
Thomas, ae 22y, d/o James & Martha E. Smith
Thomas; Dec 25 1873 by Rev. W. S. Hawkins.

Frank Whiting, ae 36y, widower, colored,
farmer, s/o John & Mary J. Whiting; Frances
Davenport, ae 29y, Of King and Queen Co VA,
d/o Geo. & Hannah Davenport; Dec 25 1873 by
Rev. Edward Page.

Richard A. Allard, ae 48y, coachmaker, s/o
Richard & Sarah Fleming Allard; Julia E.
Leigh, ae 37y, widow, d/o Jasper C. & Sarah
A. Wilson Hughes; Dec 25 1873 by Rev. James
C. Martin.

Robert C. Stubbs, ae 22y, colored, farmer,
s/o Wm. & Clara Stubbs; Clara Thornton, ae
17y, colored, d/o Rich'd & Sarah Thornton;
Dec 27 1873 by Rev. James C. Martin.

Parker Robinson, ae 22y, colored, farmer,
s/o John & Lucy Robinson; Kate Cary, ae 20y,
d/o Charles & Isabella Cary; Dec 27 1873 by
Rev. W. S. Hawkins.

Monroe Booth, ae 22y, colored, oysterman,
s/o Wm. H. & Mary Booth; Mary Robinson, ae
16y, colored, d/o Soloman & Mary Robinson;
Dec 27 1873 by Rev. Edward Page.

James Edward Ford, ae 21y, mariner, of
Portsmouth Va, s/o Wm. H. & Lavenia Gaskins
Ford; Eudora Fosque, ae 16y, d/o John L. &
Mary H. Hogg Fosque; Jan 7 1874 by Rev. W. S.
Hawkins.

Washington Pane, ae 22y, colored, oyster-
man, of Fluvannah Co VA, s/o Dick & Rebecca
Pane; Mary Wiatt, ae 18y, colored, d/o John &
Louisa White; Jan 3 1874 by Rev. Edward Page.

Jasper Seawell, ae 22y, oysterman, s/o
James & Sally Carmines Seawell; Dora Wilburn,
ae 16y, d/o Jesse & Mary Davis Wilburn; Jan 6
1874 by Rev. W. S. Hawkins.

William Brown, ae 24y, colored, farmer,
s/o Sam & Eliza Brown; Mary Eliza Thomas, ae
19y, colored, d/o Abraham & Eliza Thomas; Jan
7 1874 by Rev. John W. Booth.

John W. Cooke, ae 21y, colored, oysterman,
s/o Jesse & Sarah Cooke; Margaret Jane Hall,
ae 18y, colored, d/o John & Eliza Ann Hall;
Jan 8 1874 by Rev. W. S. Hawkins.

Abram Jones, ae 20y, colored, oysterman,
s/o Lewey & Betsy Jones; Lee Carter, ae 16y,
colored, d/o Scipio & Betsy Carter; Jan 17
1874 by Rev. John W. Booth.

Henry Tabb, ae 21y, colored, farmer, s/o Wilis & Betty Tabb; Charlotte Patterson, ae 18y, colored, d/o Henry & Frances Patterson; Jan 17 1874 by John W. Booth.

Richard Ware, ae 21y, colored, farmer, s/o James Henry & Nancy Ware; Rose King, ae 22y, colored, parents unk; Jan 29 1874 by Rev. Samuel S. Harden.

Christman Borum, ae 22y, colored, oyster, s/o Daniel & Polly Borum; Lizzie Reed, ae 23y, colored, d/o Matilda, father unk; Jan 22 1874 by Rev. Edward Page.

Hansford Foster Stubblefield, ae 25y, merchant, s/o Ro. H. & Dorinda A. Leigh Stubblefield; Edler Susan Rowe, ae 20y, d/o Ed H. & Susan A. Hayes Rowe; Jan 20 1874 by Rev. James C. Martin.

Albert Segar, ae 21y, colored, of King and Queen Co VA, s/o David & Dinah; Hester Thornton, ae 25y, colored, parents unk; Jan 18 1874 by Rev. John W. Booth. He was a waterman.

Jerry Williams, ae 22y, colored, oyster, s/o Lewis & Nancy; Louisa Suiter, ae 24y, colored, d/o Dan'l & Sarah; Jan 24 1874 by Rev. Samuel S. Harden.

Frank West, ae 21y, oysterman, s/o Frank & Fanny Smith West; Emily Parkerson, ae 23y, of Richmond VA, d/o Geo. & Nancy Parkerson; Jan 24 1874 by Rev. W. S. Hawkins.

Charles Bright, ae 21y, colored, oyster, s/o Arthur & Annie Bright; Margaret J. Clarke, ae 21y, colored, d/o Thos. Clarke, mother unk; Jan 29 1874 by Rev. Edward Page.

Thomas Brown, ae 21y, mail carrier, s/o Geo. & Nancy West Brown; Ellen Belvin, ae 18y, d/o John & Harriet Heywood Belvin; Jan 29 1874 by Rev. Wm. E. Wiatt.

Joseph Whiting, ae 21y, colored, oyster, s/o Lewis & Betsy Whiting; Martha Billups, ae 23y, colored, d/o John & Susan Billups; Jan 31 1874 by Rev. Edward Page.

William Taliaferro. ae 21y, colored, farmer, s/o Wm. & Jane Taliaferro; Frances Tazewell, ae 21y, colored, d/o Frank & Judy; Jan 31 1874 by Rev. Edward Page.

Luther W. Davis, ae 23y, seaman, s/o Wm. K. & Sarah E. Deal Davis; Fanny O. Thornton, ae 22y, d/o Francis & Elizabeth Cluverius Thornton; Feb 3 1874 by Rev. Jas. C. Martin.

John Richard Foster, ae 25y, mail carrier, of Mathews Co VA, s/o R. W. & Frances A. Foster; Virginia E. Pointer, ae 24y, d/o Cyrus C. & Martha D. Pointer; Feb 5 1874 by Rev. Jas. C. Martin.

Wilson Brown, ae 23y, colored, farmer, of Charles City Co VA, s/o Ned Brown; Roberta Corbin, ae 21y, colored, d/o Wm. & Hannah Corbin; Feb 5 1874 by Rev. Jas. C. Martin.

Henry Brooks, ae 21y, colored, teamster, s/o Betsy Cook; Eleanora Page, ae 17y, colored, d/o Jane Page; Feb 12 1874 by Rev. Samuel S. Harden.

John Thomas Donnell, ae 21y, waterman, s/o Wm. W. & Mary Ann Dunston Darnell; Margaret T. Larkin, ae 20y, d/o Geo. & Maria Seawell; Feb 12 1874 by Rev. W. S. Hawkins.

Pleasant Singleton, ae 22y, widower, colored, s/o Wallace & Fanny Singleton; Sytone Brown, ae 21y, colored, d/o Dan'l & Lizzie Brown; Feb 18 1874 by Rev. Edward Page. He was an oysterman.

William Stuart, ae 23y, farmer, of Essex Co VA, s/o Ben & Sally Stuart; Clara Thornton, ae 18y, colored, d/o Oliver & Molly Thornton; Feb 13 1874 by Rev. Samuel S. Harden.

William Jones, ae 21y, colored, oysters, s/o Chloe Jones; Elsey Montague, ae 20y, colored, d/o Phill & Margaret Montague; Feb 22 1874 by Rev. Edward Page.

John C. Cooke, ae 22y, oysterman, s/o Sarah T. Cooke; Mary Frances Williams, ae 18y, colored, d/o Lewis & Caroline Williams; Feb 22 1874 by Rev. John W. Booth.

William Seawell, ae 27y, oysterman, s/o John & Eliza Stevens Seawell; Mary Williams, ae 21y, d/o Thos. & Elizabeth Dunn Williams; Feb 22 1874 by Rev. W. S. Hawkins.

Warner Smith, ae 21y, colored, sailor, s/o Tom & Harriet Smith; Patty Williams, ae 21y, colored, d/o John & Mary Williams; Mar 3 1874 by Rev. John W. Booth.

Robert Johnson, ae 21y, colored, steam mill hand, of King and Queen Co VA, s/o Joe & Julia Johnson; Agnes Lee, ae 19y, colored, d/o Henry & Louisa Lee; Feb 26 1874 by Rev. John W. Booth.

Christopher Columbus Smith, ae 19y, oysterman, s/o Anthony & Charlotte A. Smith; Elizabeth Ann Lewis, ae 15y, d/o Benjamin & Martha Jenkins Lewis; Feb 26 1874 by Rev. W. S. Hawkins.

Major Scott, ae 26y, colored, farmer, s/o Henry & Lucy Ann Scott; Charry Lockley, ae 24y, colored, d/o Wm. & Emiline Lockley; Feb 28 1874 by Rev. John W. Booth.

Alexander Brown, ae 23y, colored, farmer, of Charles City Co VA, s/o Jarvis & Dinah Brown; Fanny Paine, ae 18y, colored, of Fluvannah Co VA, d/o Rich'd & Becky Paine; Feb 28 1874 by Rev. Edward Page.

John T. Rilee, ae 38y, widower, farmer, s/o Wm. & Mary C. Rilee; Emily T. Haynes, ae 18y, d/o Geo. P. & Mildred P. Haynes; Mar 3 1874 by Rev. Wm. E. Wiatt.

James K. P. Smith, ae 27y, oysterman, s/o Peyton & Sally Hogg Smith; Sarah Morey, ae 19y, d/o John W. & Elizabeth Hogg Morey; Mar 11 1874 by Rev. W. S. Hawkins.

Robert Rowe, ae 26y, sailor, s/o Rich'd & Mildred Rowe; Mildred Hogg, ae 17y, d/o Thos. & Betsy Hogg; Mar 17 1874 by Rev. W. S. Hawkins.

Henry Fields, ae 23y, mill hand, of Eastern Shore, parents unk; Mary Clayton, ae 21y, colored, d/o Rob't & Nancy Clayton; Mar 19 1874 by Rev. John W. Booth.

Joseph Cooke, ae 26y, colored, farmer, s/o Billy & Tisher Cooke; Catharine Jones, ae 26y, colored, d/o Gabriel & Lucy Jones; Mar 26 1874 by Rev. John W. Booth.

James Page, ae 28y, colored, farmer, s/o Armistead & Rachel Page; Jane Page, ae 24y, colored, d/o Deleware & Viney Page; Apr 2 1874 by Rev. W. S. Hawkins.

William C. Lewis, ae 24y, oysterman, s/o Wm. & Lucy A. Tillage Lewis; Eudora A. Templeman, ae 18y, d/o Jackson & Frances A. Minor Templeman; Apr 7 1874 by Rev. James C. Martin.

Lewis Stubbs, ae 24y, colored, oysterman, s/o Adam & Catharine Stubbs; Georgianna Booth, ae 21y, colored, d/o Geo. & Hannah Booth; Apr 9 1874 by Rev. James C. Martin.

John Henderson, ae 20y, oysterman, s/o Thos. J. & Elizabeth Lewis Henderson; Elizabeth F. Jenkins, ae 22y, d/o Thos. & Mary West Jenkins; Apr 9 1874 by Rev. W. S. Hawkins.

Philip Walker, ae 21y, colored, farmer, s/o Philip & Judy Walker; Eliza Perrin, ae 16y, d/o Wm. & Polly Perrin; Apr 9 1874 by Rev. Edward Page.

John W. Rowe, ae 21y, farmer, s/o Lee & Julia Ann West Rowe; Julia Jenkins, ae 23y, d/o Gracy Jenkins, father unk; Apr 30 1874 by Rev. W. S. Hawkins.

Robert B. Howlett, ae 35y, widower, of Mathews Co VA, merchant, s/o Wm. & Ann J. Hodges Howlett; Lucy D. Kemp, ae 23y, d/o Oswald S. & P. A. Christian Kemp; Apr 28 1874 by Rev. J. G. Councill.

Robert Oliver, ae 30y, farmer, s/o Thomas & Catharine Belvin Oliver; Susan West, ae 23y, d/o Howard & Nancy Green West; Apr 22 1874 by Rev. A. Y. Hundley.

Thomas C. Atkins, ae 25y, carpenter, of Fredericksburg CA, lived Middlesex Co VA, s/o Wm. & Elizabeth M. Layton Atkins; Georgia Pierce Williams, ae 21y, widow, d/o James & Susan Thomas White; Apr 30 1874 by Rev. James C. Martin.

George W. Miller, ae 27y, sailor, of Gloucester Co VA, lived Portsmouth VA, s/o Lindsay & Martha J. Camp Miller; Mary E. Teagle, ae 21y, d/o Thos E. & Elizabeth Evans Teagle; May 5 1874 by Rev. James C. Martin.

William Miller, ae 30y, colored, seaman, s/o Wm. & Rebecca Miller; Martha Ann Bluford, ae 27y, d/o Billy & Mary Bluford; May 7 1874 by Rev. James C. Martin.

Henry King, ae 25y, colored, farmer, s/o Wm. & Betty King; Betty Scipio, ae 21y, colored, d/o Tom Scipio, mother unk; May 7 1874 by Rev. J. G. Councill in Mathews Co.

William Kellinberger, ae 40y, s/o Peter &
Mary Kellenberger; Elizabeth Dutton, ae 22y,
d/o Philip T. & -- Dutton; May 19 1874.
    Charles F. Nuttall, ae 28y, widower,
farmer, s/o Chas. & Fanny Nuttall; Charlotte
Elizabeth Birch, ae 26y, of Kent Co MD, d/o
Wm. & Caroline Birch; May 28 1874 by Rev.'W.
S. Hawkins.
    William Jones, ae 23y, colored, sailor,
s/o Sye & Fanny Jones; Rosetta Harwood, ae
21y, d/o Wm. & Arena Harwood; May 28 1874 by
Rev. John W. Booth.
    Thomas T. Nelson, ae 18y, oysterman, of
Somerset Co MD, s/o Zariah & Mary C.
McCready Nelson; Lucretia Hogg, ae 18y, d/o
Lewis & Martha E. Hall Hogg; May 10 1874 by
Rev. A. Y. Hundley.
    Benjamin F. Rowe, ae 23y, oysterman, s/o
Geo. W. & Louisa Rowe; Susan Shackelford, ae
18y, d/o Archer Shackelford; June 4 1874 by
Rev. Charles Mann.
    Edward W. Scanlon, ae 22y, colored,
farmer, of Middlesex Co VA, s/o Michael &
Emily Bland Scanlon; Eufelia E. Trevillian,
ae 22y, d/o Roscow C. & Eliza Clements Tre-
villian; June 4 1874 by Rev. Jas. C. Martin.
    George Steurer, ae 27y, sailor, of New
York City N. Y, s/o Geo. & Catharine
Steurer; Martha E. Collier, ae 21y, d/o
Chas. & Mary F. Didlake Collier; June 6 1874
by Rev. Wm. E. Wiatt.
    Frank Collins, ae 23y, farmer, of King
William Co VA, s/o Richmond & Mary Collins;
Frances Smith, ae 21y, d/o Harry & Scilla
Smith; June 14 1874 by Rev. Sam'l S.
Harwood.
    Joseph A. Williams, ae 23y, colored, ┊· ·⁖·⸱⁓
teacher, s/o Robin & Jane Williams; Mary
Jane Walker, ae 22y, of Fluvannah Co VA, d/o
Phill & Judy Walker; June 18 1874 by Rev. E.
W. Page.
    John W. Tonkins, ae 25y, colored, oyster,
s/o Frank & Jenny Tonkins; Lucy Roy, ae 27y,
widow, d/o Pleasant & Venus Perrin; June 20
1874 by Rev. Samuel S. Harden.
    John Thomas, ae 22y, colored, oysterman,
s/o Nancy Thomas; Virginia Bright, ae 21y,
parents unk; July 5 1874 by Rev. E. W. Page.

William Rayfield, ae 60y, widower, farm,
of Accomack Co VA, s/o Wm. & Susannah Kelly
Rayfield; Robert E. Mason, ae 23y, d/o
Philip F. & Amanda Bland Mason; June 27 1874
by Rev. James C. Martin.

Andrew Nickons, ae 23y, colored, wood
cutter, of Columbus OHIO, s/o Wm. & Sarah
Nickôns; Harriet Sheppard, ae 16y, colored,
d/o Peter & Abby Sheppard; June 29 1874 by
Rev. Wm. E. Wiatt.

John L. Fox, ae 40y, farmer, s/o John W.
& Mary Frances Ball Fox; Annie Lee Marnex,
ae 19y, d/o Wm. W. & Mary F. Pippin Marnex;
June 30 1874 by Rev. James C. Martin.

Alfred Major, ae 33y, colored, farmer, of
Halifax Co VA, s/o Jack & Dicey Major; Maria
Brown, ae 23y, colored, of Mathews Co VA,
s/o Reede & Dinah Armistead; July 11 1874 by
Rev. Charles Mann.

William Bidwell, ae 31y, carpenter,ℯ of
Marion Co VA, s/o Moses & Lucy A. Craft Bidwell; Virginia H. White, ae 17y, parents
unk; Oct 15 1874 by Rev. James C. Martin.

James Belvin, ae 23y, farmer, s/o James &
Rebecca Heywood Belvin; Emiline Hall, ae 20y,
d/o John D. & Mary S. Brown Hall; July 28
1874 by Rev. James C. Martin.

Lemuel Blake, ae 21y, colored, farmer,
s/o Lewis & Letty Blake; Matilda Thomas, ae
21y, colored, d/o Abraham & Eliza Thomas;
Aug 2 1874 by Rev. John W. Booth.

Benjamin Dobson, ae 21y, oysterman, s/o
John & Eliza Rider Dobson; Georgianna Lark-
in, ae 17y, d/o Geo. & Maria Seawell Larkin;
Aug 2 1874 by Rev. W. S. Hawkins.

Banks Spencer, ae 40y, colored, widower,
oysterman, parents unk; Jane Allmand, ae 35y,
colored, d/o Miles & Courtney Allmand; Aug 6
1874 by Rev. W. S. Hawkins.

Francis Deal, ae 32y, miscellanius, s/o
John & Betsy Deal; Catharine West, ae 27y,
d/o Wm. & Betsy West; Aug 26 1874 by Rev.
A. Y. Hundley.

Cary Bluford, ae 33y, colored, farmer,
s/o Frank & Lucy Bluford; Nancy Dean, ae
30y, colored, d/o Joe & Polly Dean; Sept 4
1874 by Rev. Samuel S. Harden.

Newmiah Fleming, ae 40y, widower, farmer, of King and Queen Co VA, s/o Alex & Ellender Hall Fleming; Robert Alexander Gains, ae 25y, farmer, s/o Tom & Sarah Fleming; Sept 6 1874 by Rev. C. D. Cranley.

Edward W. Dunston, ae 25y, farmer, s/o Rich'd & Sarah Hughes Dunston; Asenath Elizabeth Teagle, ae 21y, d/o John A. & Martha J. Hall Teagle; Sept 8 1874 by Rev. James C. Martin.

Henry Ambrose, ae 38y, widower, farmer, s/o Michael & Elizabeth Haywood Ambrose; Virginia Seawell, ae 19y, widow, d/o James M. & Margaret A. Fosque Carmines; Sept 17 1874 by Rev. W. S. Hawkins.

George Washington Field, ae 50y, colored, shoe maker, s/o Betty Lane, father unk; Fanny Field, ae 45y, colored, d/o Betsy Field, father unk; Oct 18 1874 by Rev. John W. Booth.

Robert Hayes, ae 21y, colored, laborer, s/o Currell & Harriet Hayes; Hannah Coleman, ae 21y, colored, of Richmond VA, parents unk; Oct 25 1874.

Joseph Towns, ae 35y, widower, farmer, of York Co VA, s/o Wilson & Rhoda Towns; Jane Curtis, ae 40y, d/o James & Nancy Tylrt; Oct 25 1874.

Isaac Carter, ae 22y, colored, farmer, s/o John & Sarah Carter; Margaret Page, ae 21y, colored, d/o Jane Page, father unk; Oct 29 1874 by Rev. E. W. Page.

William F. Eastwood, ae 45y, widower, merchant, s/o Wm. & Jane Eastwood; Frances A. Payne, ae 27y, d/o Dan'l & Elizabeth Payne; Nov 1 1874 by Rev. Jas. C. Martin.

Len Driver, ae 20y, colored, oysterman, s/o Miles & Hannah Driver; Caroline Seawell, ae 20y, colored, d/o Aug. & Frances Driver; Nov 1 1874 by Rev. John W. Booth.

Spencer Reed, ae 22y, colored, laborer, s/o Spencer & Mary Reed; Harriet Leigh, ae 19y, d/o Lucy Briggerson, father unk; Nov 7 1874 by Rev. John W. Booth.

John Brown, ae 20y, oysterman, s/o Geo. & Nancy West Brown; Lilly Ann Smith, ae 19y, d/o Michael & Eliza Smith; Nov 8 1874 by Rev. W. S. Hawkins.

Peyton Brooks, ae 26y, sailor, of James
City Co, s/o Wm. & Catharine Brooks; Hester
Graves, ae 27y, widow, parents unk; Nov 8
1874 by Rev. Wm. E. Wiatt.

James Taylor, ae 35y, colored, laborer,
of Prince George Co VA, s/o Moses & Nancy
Taylor; Jane Scott, ae 35y, colored, widow,
d/o Jerry & Bathia Gregory; Nov 30 1874 by
Rev. Charles Mann.

Arthur Smith, ae 22y, colored, laborer,
s/o Dan'l & Pinky Smith; Harriet Winn, ae
21y, colored, d/o Margaret Winn, father unk;
Nov 29 1874 by Rev. John W. Booth.

William Courtney Dimmock, ae 28y, engineer, of Richmond VA, s/o Chas. & Henrietta
F. Johnson Dimmock; Mary Byrd Seldon, ae
26y, d/o Robert C. & Courtney W. Brooke
Seldon; Dec 3 1874 by Rev. A. Y. Hundley.

Edward Wiatt, ae 24y, colored, oyster, of
Petersburg VA, s/o Alfred & Chloe Wiatt;
Julia Burwell, ae 21y, colored, d/o Kinder &
Easter Burwell; Dec 3 1874 by Rev. John W.
Booth.

John Henry Blake, ae 23y, farmer, of
Middlesex Co VA, s/o John L. & Margaret A.
Howard Blake; Susie E. Howard, ae 22y, d/o
Henry A. & Martha A. Curry Howard; Dec 18
1874 by Rev. James C. Martin.

Davy Thornton, ae 23y, colored, oyster-
s/o Thos. & Margaret Thornton; Grace Willis,
ae 21y, colored, d/o John & Margaret Willis;
Dec 10 1874 by Rev. John W. Booth.

James Henry Buford, ae 25y, colored,
oysterman, s/o Billy & Mary Buford; Martha
Langster, ae 21y, colored, d/o Keziah Langster, father unk; Dec 17 1874 by Rev. O.
Littleton.

Thomas J. Ash, ae 41y, merchant, s/o Wm.
& Sarah Kemp Ash; Susie Carter Williams, ae
19y, d/o Andrew & Paulina Jones Williams;
Dec 17 1874 by Rev. W. S. Hawkins.

Joseph H. Heywood, ae 20y, farmer, s/o
John & Eliza Hogg Heywood; Susannah Hall, ae
22y, d/o Rich'd & Martha Jenkins Hall; Dec
17 1874 by Rev. W. S. Hawkins.

Richard H. Hogg, ae 33y, widower, merchant, s/o Rich'd & Catharine Hogg; Elizabeth Thornton, ae 21y, d/o John A. B. & Elizabeth Thornton; Dec 22 1874 by Rev. W. S. Hawkins.

Wyatt W. Farinholt, ae 25y, of York Co VA, lumber dealer, s/o Lynes & Anna Christian; Victoria E. Roane, ae 16y, d/o Henry & Virginia Roane; Dec 23 1874 by Rev, O. Littleton.

Silas Williams, ae 22y, colored, oyster, s/o Lewis & Caroline Williams; Lucy C. Stubbs, ae 20y, colored, d/o Clara Stubbs, father unk; Dec 24 1874 by Rev. John W. Booth.

Edward Bannister Rowe, ae 26y, sailor and oysterman, s/o Ralph & Mary Williams Rowe; Missouri M. Rowe, ae 23y, d/o Sterling & Frances A. Belvin Rowe; Dec 24 1874 by Rev. W. S. Hawkins.

Alex Emerson, ae 45y, farmer, of Queen Anne's Co MD, s/o Wm. & Susan Emerson; Mary Catharine Leager, ae 35y, of Caroline Co MD, parents unk; Dec 24 1874 by Rev. J. G. Councill.

Wilmer J. Rowe, ae 26y, farmer, s/o John L. & Lucy L. Rowe; Frances C. Ward, ae 18y, d/o John A. & Elizabeth J. Ward; Dec 24 1874 by Rev. O. Littleton.

George W. Moore, ae 29y, miller, s/o Geo. & Willemouth Carlton Miller; Virginia F. Fleming, ae 24y, d/o Jas. W. & Mildred F. Hobday Fleming; Dec 24 1874 by Rev. O. Littleton.

Warner Reed, ae 21y, colored, laborer, of King and Queen Co VA, s/o Wm. & Phillis Reed; Sally Ann Guthrie, ae 21y, colored, d/o Peter & Milly Ann Guthrie; Dec 25 1874 by Rev. John Wm. Booth.

Philip Tabb, ae 21y, colored, laborer, parents unk; Sally Dabney, ae 18y, colored, d/o Davy & Hannah Whiting; Dec 26 1874 by Rev. John Wm. Booth.

Alex Cook, ae 21y, colored, laborer, s/o Peter & Mary Cook; Jane Buckner, ae 21y, colored, d/o Tom Buckner, mother unk; Dec 28 1874 by Rev. J. G. Councill.

John W. Kellis, ae 22y, colored, oyster,
of York Co VA, s/o Rob't & Ellen Kellis;
Nancy Ransome, ae 17y, colored, d/o Sam &
Delphy Ransome; Dec 26 1874 by Rev. W. S.
Hawkins.

Joseph Massey, ae 22y, farmer, s/o Robert
& Rebecca Cox Massey; Peggy S. Gunter, ae
26y, of Accomac Co VA, d/o Laven J. &
Isabella Gunter; Dec 27 1874 by Rev. W. S.
Hawkins.

John W. Thomas, ae 22y, oysterman, s/o
Jesse & Nancy Williams Thomas; Sarah Jose-
phine Hogg, ae 21y, d/o Stephen & Nancy
Robins Hogg; Dec 29 1874 by Rev. W. S.
Hawkins.

Robert McLane, ae 26y, sailor, s/o Wm. &
Elizabeth Cobb McLane; Nancy Robbins, ae
19y, d/o John & Caroline Howard Williams;
Dec 31 1874 by Rev. W. S. Hawkins.

William H. Bristow, ae 24y, widower,
farmer, s/o Wm. L. & Eliza Boswell Bristow;
Louisa V. Brown, ae 25y, of Middlesex Co VA,
d/o Thos. S. & Mary Elizabeth Daniel Brown;
Dec 31 1874 by Rev. J. G. Councill.

George Morriss, ae 28y, colored, widower,
farmer, s/o Sterling & Mary Morriss; Elizabeth Bluford, ae 22y, colored, d/o Thos. &
Maria Bluford; Dec 31 1874 by Rev. John W.
Booth.

George Ward, ae 27y, colored, oysterman,
s/o Jimmy & Scilla Ward; Patsy Harrison, ae
22y, colored, d/o Martha Travers, father
unk; Dec 31 1874 by Rev. Chas. Mann.

Henry Jones, ae 62y, colored, widower,
farmer, s/o Harry & Maria Jones; Agnes
Cooke, ae 45y, colored, widow, parents unk;
Dec 31 1874 by Rev. John W. Booth.

Beverly Randolph, ae 23y, colored,
laborer, of York Co VA, s/o Beverly & Susan
Randolph; Fanny Claiborne, ae 17y, colorded,
d/o Daniel & Polly Claiborne; Jan 2 1875 by
Rev. John W. Booth.

James Robinson, ae 20y, colored, farmer,
s/o Soloman & Kitty Robinson; Caroline
Curtis, ae 22y, colored, d/o Robins & Maria
Curtis; Jan 7 1875 by Rev. John W. Booth.

Patrick H. Gwynn, ae 24y, farmer, s/o Robert H. & Eliza Booker Gwynn; Roxey E. Acra, ae 23y, d/o Wm. J. & Julia A. Booker Acra; Jan 7 1875 by Rev. Wm. E. Wiatt.

Eli Conway, ae 35y, widower, sailor, of Baltimore MD, s/o John & Celestine Conway; Matilda Coats, ae 24y, widow, d/o Jacob & Delilah Sparrow; Jan 7 1875 by Rev. W. S. Hawkins.

James C. Graves, ae 44y, widower, farmer, of King and Queen Co VA, s/o John & Frances Bew Graves; Henrietta Williams, ae 30y, widow, of Middlesex Co VA, parents unk; Jan 10 1875 by Rev. Wm. E. Wiatt.

Edward C. Sears, ae 24y, carpenter, of Middlesex Co VA, s/o Henry L. & Mira A. Edwards Sears; Josie E. Kemp, ae 20y, d/o Overton J. & Emeline Fary Kemp; Jan 26 1875 by Rev. David Coulling.

John T. Fosque, ae 30y, widower, merchant, of Accomack Co VA, s/o Nathaniel R. & Margaret A. Stevens Fosque; Anna M. Seawell, ae 20y, d/o John H. P. & Mary Seawell; Jan 27 1875 by Rev. W. S. Hawkins.

Thomas B. German, ae 25y, farmer, s/o Wm. & Sarah L. Bridges German; Eleanora Bridges, ae 24y, d/o Elijah & Mary F. Kemp Bridges; Jan 28 1875 by Rev. J. G. Councill.

William H. Harwood, ae 24y, farmer, s/o John A. Emiline Enos Harwood; Addie V. Sterling, ae 18y, of Middlesex Co VA, d/o Rob't & Clara Jones Sterling; Feb 7 1874 by Rev. O. Littleton.

John Burwell, ae 38y, colored, farmer, widower, s/o Philip & Sallie Burwell; Maria Fleet, ae 18y, colored, d/o Geo. & Mary Fleet; Feb 9 1875 by Rev. John W. Booth.

James Henry Jones, ae 26y, colored, house servant, s/o Harriet Philips, father unk; Agnes Jones, ae 18y, colored, d/o John & Julia Jones; Feb 10 1875 by Rev. John W. Booth.

Wyndham H. Leavitt, ae 33y, widower, farmer, s/o Wm. A. & Lucy Hodges Leavitt; Bettie A. Pointer, ae 28y, d/o Henry & Fanny D. Leigh Pointer; Feb 10 1875 by Rev. O. Littleton.

Elias Holmes, ae 21y, colored, sailor, s/o Chas. & Seny Holmes; Mary Ellen Harrison, ae 18y, colored, d/o Rebecca Harrison, father unk; Feb 10 1875 by Rev. E. W. Page.

Alex Carter, ae 25y, colored, oysterman, s/o Henry & Polly Carter; Maria Foster, ae 21y, colored, widow, d/o Jeff & Katy Foster; Feb 14 1875 by Rev. Chas. Mann.

Jack Tazewell, ae 22y, colored, of Fluvannah Co VA, s/o David & Judy Tazewell; Sarah F. Curtis, ae 24y, colored, d/o Scipio & Betsy Curtis; Feb 20 1875 by Rev. E. W. Page. He was a farmer.

John Thomas Robinson. ae 21y, colored, farmer, s/o Henry & Louisa Robinson; Lucy Hall, ae 21y, colored, d/o John & Tulip Hall; Feb 25 1875 by Rev. John W. Booth.

George T. King, ae 23y, colored, oyster, s/o Thos. & Mary King; Martha Jane Tomkins, ae 20y, colored, d/o James Tomkins & Lucy Cook; Feb 25 1875 by Rev. Wm. Thomas.

Cato Smith, ae 21y, colored, oysterman, s/o Edw'd & Sally Seldon Smith; Agnes Pendleton, ae 21y, colored, d/o John & Judy Pendleton; Feb 27 1875 by Rev. E. W. Page.

Hiram Oscar Kerns, ae 22y, miller, of Lancaster Co VA, s/o Maris V. & Emma J. Leffevre Kerns; Julia Florence Trevilian, ae 17y, d/o A. S. & Julia A. Dutton Trevilian; Feb 28 1875 by Rev. O. Littleton.

Beverly W. Kemp, ae 25y, widower, waterman, s/o Beverly W. & Mary Dunston Kemp; Rebecca T. Fletcher, ae 25y, d/o James B. & Lilly Minor Fletcher; Mar 9 1875 by Rev. O. Littleton.

Iverson Hogg, ae 25y, oysterman, s/o Geo. A. & Rachel Hogg; Delia Brown, ae 19y, d/o John & Elizabeth Brown; Mar 9 1875 by Rev. W. S. Hawkins.

William T. Sparrow, ae 24y, oysterman, of Mathews Co VA, s/o Raymond & Sally Sparrow; Margaret S. East, ae 17y, of Northampton Co VA, d/o John & Ann East; Mar 4 1875 by Rev. W. S. Hawkins.

J. M. Goalder, ae 29y, carpenter, of King and Queen Co VA, s/o Augustine & Rosa Kemp Goalder; Fanny E. Acra, ae 19y, d/o Jas. H. & Lilly A. R. Acra; Mar 11 1875 Rev. Wiatt.

James C. Soles, ae 32y, farmer, s/o Wm.
H. & Lucy A. Fary Soles; Dorinda A. Blake,
ae 22y, d/o Austin & Mary A. Blake; Mar 18
1875 by Rev. O. Littleton.

Gabriel Garrett, ae 29y, colored, oyster,
s/o Davy & Sally Garrett; Georgianna
Mathews, ae 30y, colored, d/o Agnes Cook,
father un; Mar 24 1875 by Rev. E. W. Page.

James Randall, ae 26y, widower, cooper,
of Dinwiddie Co VA, s/o Gilbert & Betsy Randall; Eliza Washington, ae 21y, d/o Bob &
Kitty Washington; Mar 25 1875.

Francis Booth, ae 40y, colored, farmer,
s/o Augustine & Rose Booth; Ann Thomas
Anderson, ae 23y, d/o Geo. & Dianna Anderson, Apr 7 1875 by Rev. John W. Booth.

Henry Allen, ae 29y, colored, oysterman,
of Middlesex Co VA, lived Mathews Co VA, s/o
Henry & Betsy Bundy Allen; Mary Susan
Mathias, ae 19y, colored, parents unk; Apr
7 1875 by Rev. E. W. Page.

George Morriss, ae 21y, colored, oyster,
s/o John & Mary Morriss; Polly Ann Borum, ae
18y, colored, d/o Amos & Betsy; Apr 13 1875
by Rev. E. W. Page.

James Hopkins, ae 52y, widower, merchant,
of York Co VA, s/o Davis & Marg't Anderton
Hopkins; Emily Shackelford, ae 23y, d/o
Archer Shackelford; Apr 16 1875 by Rev. Wm.
E. Wiatt.

Daniel Wynn, ae 26y, colored, laborer,
s/o Chas. & Margaret Wynn; Cordelia Patterson, ae 21y, d/o Henry & Frances Patterson;
Apr 20 1875 by Rev. John W. Booth.

James S. Benson, ae 22y, farmer, of Ann
Arundell Co MD, s/o Besir S. & Mary A. Smith
Benson; Mollie E. Thomas, ae 19y, of Ann
Arundell Co MD, d/o Helen & Eleanor Linthi-
cum Thomas; Apr 20 1875 by Rev. A. Y.
Hundley.

Ira S. Hall, ae 23y, farmer, s/o Stephen
& Elizabeth Leamon Hall; Milly A. Kinning-
ham, ae 23y, parnets unk; Apr 29 1875 by
Rev. Wm. E. Wiatt.

John Carter, ae 24y, colored, oysterman,
s/o Wm. & Sophy Carter; Mary Eliza Gardner,
ae 21y, colored, d/o Amanda Carter, father
unk; Apr 29 1875 by Rev. R. A. Fox.

Edmund Jefferson, ae 23y, colored, oyster, of Morthumberland Co VA, s/o Thos. & Sarah Jefferson; Clara Cooke, ae 17y, colored, d/o Jesse & Sarah Cooke; May 2 1875 by Rev. Wm. Thomas.

John Purcell, ae 23y, oysterman, s/o John & Susan Brown Purcell; Indianna Figg, ae 15y, d/o Mathew & Starr Ann Jones Figg; May 13 1875 by Rev. O. Littleton.

John F. Mattox, ae 24y, sailor, s/o Wm. & Matilda Garrett Mattox; Adaline Virginia Robins, ae 19y, d/o James W. & Virginia Rowe Robins; May 18 1875 by Rev. O. Littleton.

George Washington Rowe, ae 28y, sailor, s/o Washington & Susan Rowe; Matilda J. Ransone, ae 20y, d/o John W. & Mary A. Hall Ransone; May 27 1875 by Rev. A. Y. Hundley.

John Evans, ae 21y, colored, oysterman, s/o John & Betsy Evans; Lucinda Williams, ae 21y, colored, d/o John & Mary Williams; June 9 1875 by Rev. R. A. Fox.

John Pollard, ae 31y, colored, farmer, s/o Henry & Betsy Pollard; Louisa Carter, ae 21y, colored, d/o Sam & Louisa Carter; June 13 1875 by Rev. E. W. Page.

William D. Bristow, ae 22y, miller, s/o Wm. D. & Fanny A. Bristow; Jessie A. Rilee, ae 16y, d/o Thos. R. & Mary F. Rilee; July 5 1875 by Rev. J. D. Hanks.

John Bolden, ae 44y, colored, widower, oysterman, s/o Sam & Harriet Bolden; Nancy Bright, ae 46y, widow, colored, parents unk; of Richmond Va, June 23 1875 by Rev. E. W. Page.

William B. Seawell, ae 24y, sailor, s/o John & Eliza Seawell; Eudora Hogg, ae 18y, d/o John R. & Sarah Hogg; July 1 1875 by Rev. Wm. E. Wiatt.

John W. Yates, ae 32y, colored, oyster, s/o Wm. & Sally Yates; Jane Frances Young, ae 28y, colored, of James City Co VA, d/o Venus Young, father unk; July 18 1875 by Rev. W. S. Hawkins.

Virgil Gardner Weaver, ae 35y, farmer, of Selma ALABAMA, s/o Philip John & Ann P. Gardner Weaver; Rosa Burnet Deans, ae 25y, d/o Josiah L. & Mary Yeatman Deans; July 14 1875 by Rev. A. Y. Hundley.

Andrew B. Foxwell, ae 23y, blacksmith,
s/o John & Louisa Foxwell; Emma J. Oliver,
ae 23y, d/o Washington & Sally Oliver; July
15 1875 by Rev. W. S. Hawkins.

Warner Rowe, ae 28y, colored, widower,
farmer, s/o Warner & Matilda Rowe; Diza Taylor, ae 21y, colored, d/o Henry & Polly Taylor; July 18 1875 by Rev. John W. Booth.

William H. Williams, ae 24y, sailor, s/o
Ed & Martha Ann Williams; Mary S. Hall, ae
20y, d/o John & Mary S. Hall; July 21 1875
by Rev. W. S. Hawkins.

William Jesse Thrift, ae 44y, widower,
carpenter, s/o Jeremiah & Ann Groom Thrift;
Elizabeth S. Hibble, ae 22y, d/o Chas. W. &
Mary E. Hibble; July 22 1875 by Rev. Wm. E.
Wiatt.

John William Washington, ae 24y, colored,
oysterman, s/o Nancy Washington, father unk;
Keziah Grimes, ae 20y, of Northumberland Co
VA, d/o Thos. F. & Sarah Grimes; July 29
1875 by Rev. Wm. Thomas.

Emanuel Pollard, ae 29y, colored, widower,
farmer, of King and Queen Co VA, s/o Thornton & Harriet Pollard; Susan Payne, ae 23y,
colored, d/o Rich'd & Rebecca Payne; Aug 14
1875 by Rev. A. Y. Hundley.

Robert Belvin, ae 25y, farmer, s/o Lewis
& Nancy Belvin; Matilda Jane (Julia Matilda)
Hudgins, ae 23y, of Mathews Co VA, d/o Wm.
O. & Mary Hudgins; Aug 16 1875 by Rev. A. Y.
Hundley.

John Francis, ae 71y, colored, farmer,
s/o Jas. & Mary Frances; Mary Scott, ae 60y,
colored, d/o Henry & Betty Spurlock; Sept 2
1875 by Rev. W. S. Hawkins.

George Booth, ae 48y, colored, widower,
farmer, s/o Miler & Milly Booth; Lover Wilson, ae 35y, of Princess Ann Co VA, d/o
Aggy Wilson, father unk; Sept 8 1875 by Rev.
John W. Booth.

John W. Bonewell, ae 26y, farmer, s/o
Geo. W. & Ann F. Robins Bonewell; Ellen S.
Williams, ae 22y, widow, d/o James & Eliza-
beth Hogg Howard; Sept 12 1875 by Rev. W. S.
Hawkins.

George Jacobs, ae 22y, colored, sailor,
of Accomack Co VA, lived Mathews Co VA, s/o
Daniel & Polly Jacobs; Jane Gardner, ae 21y,
colored, d/o Bailey & Eliza Gardner; Sept 16
1875 by Rev. John W. Booth.

William Hundley, ae 26y, oysterman, of
King and Queen Co VA, s/o Fields & Peggy
Hundley; Mary Washington, ae 23y, d/o David
& Colnett Washington; Sept 30 1875 by Rev.
W. S. Hawkins.

Harvey Temple, ae 22y, colored, farmer,
of King and Queen Co VA, s/o Davy & Louisa
Temple; Chloe Todd, ae 22y, colored, d/o
Aaron & Jennett Todd; Oct 9 1875 by Rev.
John W. Booth.

George E. Bristow, ae 31y, widower, farm,
s/o Wm. L. & Harriet Bristow; Mary Jane
Bridges, ae 25y, d/o Robinson & Rosa Bridges; Oct 14 1875 by Rev. David Coulling.

Warner H. Jenkins, ae 19y, oysterman,
s/o Winston & Georgianna Jenkins; Frances A.
West, ae 18y, d/o James & Ann C. West; Oct
17 1875 by Rev. W. S. Hawkins.

Winter Washington, ae 22y, colored, farm,
s/o Geo. & Becky; Molly Mathias, ae 23y,
colored, d/o Brittain Mathias, mother unk;
Oct 20 1875 by Rev. John W. Booth.

Peter I. Gregg, ae 52y, widower, farmer,
of Essex Co VA, s/o Philip & Catharine Brooks
Gregg; Parke F. Shackelford, ae 42y, widow,
d/o Ro. Y. & Jaza A. P. Jones Clements; Oct
26 1875 by Rev. David Coulling.

John William Chapman, ae 24y, colored,
oysterman, s/o Godfrey & Nancy Chapman;
Cerris Ann Lemon, ae 22y, colored, d/o Bell
& Mary A. Lemon; Oct 28 1875 by Rev. Wm. E.
Wiatt.

Spencer Laws, ae 22y, colored, farmer,
s/o James & Harriet Laws; Jenny Bates, ae
18y, colored, parents unk; Nov 7 1875 by
Rev. Chas. Mann.

Peter Jackson, ae 23y, colored, farmer,
of Middlesex Co VA, s/o Phill & Mary Jackson; Lucy Pryor, ae 23y, colored, d/o Philip
& Jane Pryor; Nov 10 1875 by Rev. John W.
Booth.

Warner Burwell, ae 62y, colored, widower, cook, s/o Harry & Milly; Mary Spurlock, ae 30y, colored, d/o Chas. & Martha; Nov 11 1875 by Rev. Sam'l S. Harden.

James Hanley, ae 29y, broom maker, of Baltimore MD, s/o Michael & Ellen Hanley; Margaret Henderson, ae 18y, d/o Thos. J. & Elizabeth Henderson; Nov 24 1875 by Rev. W. S. Hawkins.

Phill Burton, ae 24y, colored, farmer, s/o Jne, father unk; Hannah Ranson, ae 18y, colored, d/o Sanko & Hannah; Nov 24 1875 by Rev. John W. Booth.

Samuel M. Rowe, ae 41y, farmer, s/o Hansford & Gracy Dobson Rowe; Ann & Elizabeth Williams Diggs; Nov 23 1875 by Rev. W. S. Hawkins.

Soloman Braxton, ae 36y, colored, farmer, of King William Co VA, s/o Jacob & Louisa; Martha Taliaferro, ae 23y, colored, d/o Caroline Taliaferrro, father unk; Nov 25 1875 by Rev. Chas. Mann.

Allen Hogg, ae 23y, farmer, s/o Warner & Susan Hogg; Georgia West, ae 19y, d/o James & Nancy West; Nov 28 1875 by Rev. W. S. Hawkins.

Thomas Crew, ae 34y, widower, farmer, s/o John & Evy Dunston Crew; Julia Ann Mory, ae 22y, d/o John & Elizabeth Hogg Mory; Dec 2 1875 by Rev. Wm. E. Wiatt;

William Ruffin, ae 45y, colored, laborer, of King and Queen Co VA, s/o Jesse & Ailcy Ruffin; Betsy Cook, ae 39y, widow, parents unk; Dec 2 1875 by Rev. Sam'l S. Harden.

William Smith, ae 26y, colored, oyster, s/o Isaac & Jenny; Fanny Gwynn, ae 23y, parents unk; Dec 2 1875 by Rev. Samuel S. Harden.

John W. Hill, ae 24y, colored, oyster, s/o Robert Hill & Lucy Cooke; Ann Reed, ae 17y, colored, d/o Frank & Fanny Reed; Dec 12 1875 by Rev. John W. Booth.

Thomas E. Lamberth, ae 38y, widower, farmer, s/o John & Mildred Walker Lamberth; Betty V. Shackelford, ae 30y, d/o William & Eliza Shackelford; Dec 15 1875 by Rev. O. Littleton.

Robert Gregory, ae 45y, colored, farmer,
widower, s/o Mary Gregor, father unk; Catharine Brown, ae 35y, widow, d/o Robert &
Sally Banks; Feb 3 1876 by Rev. O. Littleton.

Peter H. Spandow, ae 25y, farmer, s/o
Peter H. & Mary Spandow; Julia A. Collins,
ae 25y, parents unk; Jan 4 1876 by Rev. J.
G. Councill.

Henry Willis, ae 33y, colored, cooper, of
Petersbutg VA, s/o Robert & Patience Willis;
Eliza Ann Selden, ae 23y, colored, d/o James
& Katie Selden; Jan 6 1876 by Rev. O. Lit-
tleton.

Henry Elright, ae 48y, widower, fence
maker, of Franklin Co PA, s/o Jacob & Eliza
Schafner Elright; Ellen Shackelford, ae 28y,
parents unk; Jan 16 1876 by Rev. David
Coulling.

George W. Sterling, ae 27y, merchant, of
Mathews Co VA, s/o Noah & Eliza Respess
Sterling; Alice Deal, ae 18y, d/o John A. &
Elizabeth Brown Deal; Jan 19 1876 by Rev.A.
Y. Hundley.

Richard Thomas, ae 22y, colored, sailor,
s/o Henry & Hester Thomas; Lucy Ann Walker,
ae 21y, colored, d/o Phill & Judy Walker;
Jan 23 1876 by Rev. E. W. Page.

George Yates, ae 21y, colored, farmer,
s/o Rob't & Mary Yates; Milly Meredith, ae
16y, colored, d/o James & Ailcy Meredith;
Feb 20 1876 by Rev. John Wm. Booth.

Alexander Dixon, ae 22y, colored, oyster,
s/o Chas. & Fanny Dixon; Martha Scott, ae
20y, colored, d/o Reuben & Easter Scott; Feb
24 1876 by Rev. E. W. Page.

Richard Upshur, ae 25y, colored, farmer,
of King and Queen Co VA, s/o Henry & Keziah
Upshur; Johannah Washington, ae 22y, col'rd,
d/o Voss & Eliza wahington; Mar 2 1876 by
Rev. W. S. Hawkins.

Wm. Washington, ae 21y, col'rd, oyster   ,
s/o Parker & Fanny Langston; Lucy Carter, ae
19y, col'rd, d/o Parker & maria Carter; Mar
9 1876 by Rev. John W. Booth.

Samuel M. Blake, ae 26y, farmer, d/o Austin & Mary Minor Blake; Mary F.Hogg, ae 21y, d/o Washington & Elizabeth Hall Hogg; Dec 15 1875 by Rev. W. S. Hawkins.

Richard Dabney, ae 22y, colored, farmer, of KIng William Co VA, s/o Major & Caroline Dabney; Laura Banks, ae 19y, colored, d/o Wm. & Grace Sparks Banks; Dec 18 1875 by Rev. Sam'l S. Harden.

John Travis, ae 25y, colored, farmer, s/o Jack & Mary Travis; Sarah Thornton, ae 24y, widow, d/o Parrott & Sarah Thornton; Dec 19 1875.

William G. Bayliss, ae 23y, merchant, of Essex Co VA, s/o Chas. F. & M. J. Coghill Bayliss; Bettie P. Robinson, ae 20y, of Essex Co VA. d/o Philemon & Virginia M. Robinson; Dec 21 1875 by Rev. J. D. Hank.

Randall Cooke, ae 20y, colored, farmer, s/o Peyton & Frances A. Cooke; Lee Cooke, ae 15y, colored, d/o Chas. & Caroline M. Cooke; Dec 25 1875 by Rev. John W. Booth.

Wilbur L. Dutton, ae 23y, farmer, s/o Edward C. & Rebecca Chapman Dutton; Rebecca Jane Ware, ae 17y, d/o A. S. & Sarah E. Walden Ware; Dec 26 1875 by Rev. David Coulling.

Willis Scott, ae 35y, colored, shoemaker, of Hanover Co VA, s/o John & Maria Scott; Susan Wormley, ae 30y, colored, d/o James & Peggy WOrmley; Dec 28 1875 by Rev. Sam'l S. Harden.

James Selden, ae 28y, colored, widower, waterman, s/o Jasper & Lucy; Betsy Jackson, ae 21y, colored, d/o Ceasar & Mary; Dec 30 1875 by Rev. John W. Booth.

Richard Hopkins, ae 21y, sailor, of Dorchester Co MD, s/o Wm. & Eliza Brooks Hopkins; Georgia White, ae 20y, d/o John & ---- Gressitt White; Dec 30 1875 by Rev. O. Littleton.

William H. Birch, ae 26y, farmer, of Queen Ann Co MD, s/o Wm. H. & Caroline Seward Birch; Margaret A. Willett, ae 21y, d/o Jesse & Sarah A. Cobb Willett; Dec 30 1875 by Rev. W. S. Hawkins.

John Henry Jones, ae 43y, col'd, widower,
farmer, s/o Jim & Maria Jones; Lilly Pendleton, ae 21y, col'rd, d/o Geo. & Peggy; Mar 9
1876 by Rev. John W. Booth.

Walter Brookins, ae 22y, col'rd, sailor,
s/o Lewis & Emory Brookins; Anna Berry, ae
18y, col'rd, d/o James & Polly Jones; Jan
26 1876 by Rev. W. S. Hawkins.

James Grimes, ae 22y, col'rd, farmer, of
Mathews Co VA, parents unk; Courtney Todd,
ae 18y, col'rd, d/o Aaron & Jenny Todd; Mar
16 1876 by Rev. Sam'l S. Harden.

Samuel Whiting, ae 24y, col'rd, farmer,
s/o Jane Washington, father unk; Nancy Hall,
ae 19y, col'rd, d/o John & Tulip Ann Hall;
Mar 30 1876 by Rev. Sam'l S. Harden.

Samuel Johnston, ae 23y, col'rd, farmer,
of Middlesex Co VA, s/o Henry & Betsy Johnson; Lucy Jane Braxton, ae 21y, col'rd, d/o
Geo. & Judy Braxton; Apr 2 1876 by Rev. O.
Littleton.

William R. Purcell, ae 27y, col'rd, farm,
s/o Wm. N. & Martha Purcell; Margaret Walden, ae 21y, col'rd, d/o Rob't & Sarah A.
Walden; Mar 30 1876 by Rev. O. Littleton,
Methodist Minister.

John Edwin, ae 25y, col'rd, wood cutter,
of Norfolk VA, s/o Gerard & Rose; Sarah
Palmer, ae 21y, col'rd, parents unk; Apr 3
1876 by Rev. J. G. Councill.

Robert Jones, ae 25y, col'rd, oysterman,
of James City Co VA, s/o Wm. & Letty Jones;
Alice Griffin, ae 25y, col'rd, d/o Jim & Lucy
Ann Griffin; May 18 1876 by Rev. John Wm.
Booth.

Robert Cook, ae 27y, col'rd, farmer, s/o
Tony & Milly Cook; Mary Elizabeth Dabney, ae
19y, col'rd, d/o Washington & Martha; May 21
1876 by Rev. John Wm. Booth.

Charles E. Coleman, ae 21y, laborer, s/o
David & Ann Minor Coleman; Margaret A. Musey,
ae 23y, d/o Andrew & Sarah Nusey; May 25
1876 by Rev. David Coulling.

George Carter, ae 24y, col'rd, sailor,
s/o Gabriel & Ann Carter; Easter Hunley, ae
22y, col'rd, d/o Frederick & Crissey Hunley;
now Crissey Marshall; May 25 1876 by Rev.
John Wm. Booth.

Frank Brown, ae 21y, col'rd, waterman, s/o Frank & Nancy Brown; Mary Bentley, ae 21y, col'rd, d/o Daniel & Isabella Bentley; May 24 1876 by Rev. Sam'l S. Harden.

Corbin Stubbs, ae 22y, col'rd, oysterman, s/o Adam & Catharine Stubbs; Fannie Burwell, ae 21y, col'rd, d/o Beverly & Catharine Stubbs; June 4 1876 by Rev. John W. Booth.

John E. Clarke, ae 21y, merchant, of Jacksonville FLA, s/o John & Amanda E. Ellender Clarke; Eva H. Taliaferro, ae 22y, d/o Henry P. & Emily H. Harsinding Talia-ferro; June 12 1876 by Rev. Chas. Mann, Rector of Ware Church.

Beverly Jones, ae 25y, col'rd, widower, oysterman, s/o Jack & Cordelia Jones; Polly Hunley, ae 22y, col'rd, d/o Frederick & Polly Hunley; June 21 1876 by Rev. Sam'l S. Harden.

William Tazewell, ae 22y, col'rd, oyster, s/o Winston & Patty Tazewell; Sarah Carter, ae 18y, col'rd, d/o Rob't Henry & Charlotte; June 22 1876 by Rev. Samuel S. Harden.

Charles H. Bristow, ae 26y, farmer, s/o Dick & Mary Bristow; Mary J. Palmer, ae 18y, d/o P. S. & Mary A. Palmer; May 25 1876 by Rev. J. G. Councill.

Thomas J. Bonnywell, ae 25y, sailor, s/o Burwell B. & Emeline Bonnywell; Ellen Brown, ae 18y, d/o Geo. & Nancy Brown; June 18 1876 by Rev. W. S. Hawkins.

Robert Whiting, ae 22y, col'rd, sailor, s/o John & Lucy Whiting; Betty Jones, ae 17y, col'rd, d/o Chas. H. & Agnes Jones; Apr 16 1876 by Rev. Sam'l S. Harden.

John H. Bluford, ae 24y, col'rd, seaman, s/o Tom & Harriet Bluford; Margaret Lemon, ae 18y, col'rd, d/o James & Eliza Lemon; Apr 20 1876 by Rev. John Wm. Booth.

Frank Billups, ae 22y, col'rd, farmer, s/o Tom & Milly Billups; Cinty Lewis, ae 24y, col'rd, d/o Geo. & Rose Lewis; July 1 1876 by Rev. Sam'l S. Harden.

Thomas Henry Shackelford, ae 21y, oyster, s/o John W. & Julia A. Brown Shackelford; Elizabeth A. Hunley, ae 21y, d/o Geo. L. & Martha A. Belvin Hunley; June 29 1876 by Rev. W. S. Hawkins.

Albert Corbin, ae 23y, col'rd, sailor,
s/o Geo. & Judy Corbin; Lizzie Smith, ae
24y, col'rd, d/o Warner & Elizabeth Smith;
July 6 1876 by Rev. W. S. Hawkins.

Reuben Wyatt, ae 25y, col'rd, farmer,
parents unk; Susan Gardner, ae 21y, col'rd,
d/o Alfred & Aggy Gardner; July 7 1876 by
Rev. Sam'l S. Harden.

John Thomas Enos, ae 29y, merchant, s/o
Sam'l P. & Ann E. Atkins Enos; Vandalia
Amelia Kemp, ae 19y, d/o John & Catharine D.
Coleman Kemp; Aug 2 1876 by Rev. O. Little-
ton, Methodist minister.

Benjamin C. Newcomb, ae 25y, merchant,
s/o John C. & Joann S. Enos Newcomb; Martha
J. Coleman, ae 24y, d/o John F. & Mildred B.
Philpotts Coleman; Aug 2 1876 by Rev. O.
Littleton, Methodist minister.

Robert King, ae 23y, col'rd, farmer, s/o
Wm. & Eliza King; Lucy Smith, ae 40y,
col'rd, d/o Dan'l & Pinky Smith; Aug 9 1876
by Rev. John Wm. Booth.

John Franklin Braxton, ae 23y, col'rd,
laborer, s/o Ellen Roy, father unk; Ginty
Holmes, ae 18y, col'rd, d/o Walker & Judy
Holmes; Aug 9 1876 by Rev. John Wm. Booth.

John Thomas Haynes, ae 29y, farmer, s/o
Geo. P. & Emily T. Edwards Haynes; Joanna
Groom, ae 19y, d/o Albert & Mary Frances
Bristow Groom; Aug 15 1876 by Rev. W. W.
Wood.

Samuel B. Walker, ae 20y, oysterman, s/o
Peter & Louisa Jenkins Walker; Rebecca Jen-
kins, ae 21y, d/o Edmund & Martha Jenkins;
Aug 17 1876 by Rev. W. S. Hawkins.

Lewis Harrison, ae 23y, col'rd, oyster,
s/o Chas. & Lucy Harrison; Ann Reed, ae 21y,
col'rd, d/o Wm. & Maria Reed; Aug 27 1876 by
Rev. W. S. Hawkins.

Ned Carter, ae 22y, col'rd, oysterman,
s/o Edward & Harriet Carter; Hannah Williams, ae 22y, col'rd, d/o Dan'l & Susan
Williams; Sept 7 1876 by Rev. W. S. Hawkins.

George Johnson, ae 25y, col'rd, widower,
miller, of Middlesex Co VA, s/o Phill & Judy
Johnson; Milly Grimes, ae 25, col'rd, d/o
parents unk, of Caroline Co VA; Mar 25 1877
by Rev. J. G. Councill.

Samuel V. Corbell, ae 33y, farmer, Nansemond Co VA, s/o Henry & Arabella Corbin; Fannie C. Hughes, ae 24y, d/o Thos. & Julia E. Hughes; Sept 12 1877 by Rev. O. Littleton, Methodist minister.

Thomas Bentley, ae 21y, col'rd, farmer, s/o Dan'l & Isabella Bentley; Emily Smith, ae 21y, col'rd, d/o Wm. & Martha A. Turner; Sept 14 1876 by Rev. Sam'l S. Harden.

James Dabney, ae 50y, col'rd, widower, farmer, s/o Abram & Lucinda Dabney; Rebecca Cheeseman, ae 45y, widow, parents unk; Sept 16 1876 by Rev. E. W. Page.

Isaac Lancaster, ae 40y, col'rd, widower, farmer, s/o Isaac & Maria Lancaster; Eudora Palmer, ae 21y, col'rd, d/o Phill & Rebecca Palmer; Sept 16 1876 by Rev. John Wm. Booth.

William Kemp, ae 35y, col'rd, widower, farmer, s/o Lynes & Diana; Lucy Ann Smith, ae 37y, col'rd, parents unk; Sept 19 1876 by Rev. John Wm. Booth.

William Patterson, ae 26y, col'rd, oysterman, of Richmond VA, s/o John & Keziah Patterson; Edith Roberson, ae 20y, col'rd, d/o John & Lucy Roberson; Sept 27 1876 by Rev. W. S. Hawkins.

Wade Driver, ae 21y, col'rd, farmer, s/o Sam & Sally Driver; Rosa Baytop, ae 21y, col'rd, d/o Thompson & Mary Baytop; Sept 24 1876 by Rev. John Wm. Booth.

John Jefferson, ae 30y, col'rd, widower, farmer, of Mathews Co VA, s/o John & Jane; Margaret Billups, ae 25y, col'rd, widow, d/o John & Leah; Sept 28 1876 by Rev. J. G. Councill.

Cary Bluford, ae 37y, col'rd, widower, oysterman, s/o Frank & Lucy; Nancy Lewis, ae 30y, col'rd, widow, d/o Henry & Nancy Corbin; Sept 28 1876 by Rev. John Wm. Booth.

Zachariah Jones, ae 23y, col'rd, farmer, s/o Isaac & Charlotte; Nannie Williams, ae 21y, col'rd, d/o John & Mary; Sept 30 1876 by Rev. R. A. Fox.

Stephen Burwell, ae 27y, col'rd, farmer, s/o Kinder & Easter Burwell; Earsley Berry, ae 26y, col'rd, widow, d/o Sye & Sally Moody; Oct 5 1876 by Rev. O. Littleton.

Rufus A. Duer, ae 28y, widower, mariner, of Somerset Co MD, lived Baltimore MD, s/o Edward & Mary Sturges Duer; Elmire Shelton Fitzhugh, ae 28y, of Middlesex Co VA, d/o Patrick & Mary Christian Fitzhugh; Oct 4 1876 by Rev. J. G. Councill.

Major H. Harris, ae 20y, col'rd, farmer, s/o Wm. H. & Dianah Harris; Adelaide Washington, ae 18y, col'rd, d/o Henry & Dianah Washington; Oct 15 1876 by Rev. John Wm. Booth.

Benjamin F. Wilson, ae 41y, widower, of Adams Co PA, lived Norfolk VA, s/o Benjamin F. & Susan Wierman Wilson; Maria M. Seawell, ae 28y, d/o Wat W. & Jane R. Seawell; Oct 18 1876 by Rev. Wm. E. Wiatt. He was a trucker and fruit grower.

Milton Redman, ae 30y, col'rd, farmer, of Burbon Co KY, s/o Stuban & Phebe Redman; Eliza Banks, ae 22y, col'rd, d/o Sam & Lucky Banks; Oct 19 1876 by Rev. Richard Andrew Fox.

Prophet Thornton, ae 23y, col'rd, oyster, s/o Oliver &Milly Thornton; Betsy Jones, ae 18y, col'rd, d/o Paroy & Eliza Jones; Oct 21 1876 by Rev. R. A. Fox.

Isaac Carter, ae 21y, col'rd, oysterman, s/o Sam & Judy; Lucy Ann Williams, ae 19y, col'rd, d/o Simon & Caty; Oct 26 1876 by Rev. E. W. Page.

Charles Blackburn, ae 22y, col'rd, timber getter for ships, of Essex Co VA, s/o Edw'rd & Jenny Blackburn; Henrietta Allmand, ae 18y, col'rd, d/o Rachel Allmand, father unk; Oct 28 1876 by Rev. E. W. Page.

George Washington, ae 22y, col'rd, farmer, s/o Catharine; father unk; Lucinda Brown, ae 21y, col'rd, of Charleston S. C, d/o James & Jane Brown; Oct 28 1876.

Seth F. Bray, ae 26y, wharf agent, s/o Rich'd & Emily Bray; Lucy Thornton, ae 22y, d/o John A. B. & Elizabeth Thornton; Nov 2 1876 by Rev. W. S. Hawkins.

Fielding W. Bayne, ae 24y, carpenter, s/o Dan'l & Betsy Curry Bayne; Mary E. Pearce, ae 24y, d/o John H. & Mary F. Gresitt Pearce; Nov 5 1876 by Rev. O. Littleton.

Robert Green, ae 21y, col'rd, oysterman, s/o John & Maria Green; Elizabeth Almand, ae 21y, col'rd, parents unk; Nov 7 1876 by Rev. E. W. Page.

John Smith, ae 23y, oysterman, s/o Michael & Eliza West Smith; Emiline West, ae 20y, d/o Turner & Frances A. Haven West; Oct 23 1876 by Rev. W. S. Hawkins.

Jefferson Sinclair, ae 24y, farmer, of Elizabeth City Co VA, s/o Jefferson & Frances Lowry Sinclair; Lucy Roena Sinclair, ae 24y, d/o John & Lucy Baytop Sinclair; Nov 8 1876 by Rev. Alex Y. Hundley.

Robert Hudgins, ae 30y, widower, farmer, s/o Claiborne & Lucy Ann Hudgins; Isa Dora Padgett, ae 14y, d/o Rich'd 1. & Matilda Padgett; Nov 9 1876 by Rev. J. G. Councill.

Thomas M. Cary, ae 38y, bookkeeper, of Zanesville OHIO, s/o Thos. & Hannah Moore Cary; Sarah E. Thurston, ae 35y, d/o Ed T. & Julia P. Cary Thurston; Nov 22 1876 by Rev. Alex Y. Hundley.

John Robinson, ae 21y, col'rd. farmer, s/o John & Chaney Robinson; Alice Hall, ae 18y, col'rd, d/o John & Tulip Hall; Nov 23 1876 by Rev. John Wm. Booth.

John Hundley, ae 43y, widower, col'rd, of King and Queen Co VA, farmer, s/o Ephraim & Milcy Hundley; Sarah Miller, ae 24y, col'rd, of King and Queen Co VA, d/o John & Betsy Miller; Nov 26 1876 by Rev. John Wm. Booth.

David Dixon, ae 22y, col'rd, oysterman, s/o Chas. & Fanny Dixon; Sarah Thornton, ae 21y, col'rd, d/o Rich'd & Octavia Thornton; Nov 27 1876 by Rev. Sam'l S. Harden.

M. W. Tinsley, ae 29y, col'rd, lumber dealer of Hanover Co VA, s/o S. H. & Sarah K. Davis Tinsley; Mary Lee Wiatt, ae 23y, of Montgomery ALA, d/o Wm. E. & Charlotte Laura Coleman Wiatt; Nov 29 1876 by Rev. Wm. E. Wiatt.

Charles P. Roane, ae 21y, farmer, of Middlesex Co VA, s/o Wm. P. & Mary S. Bland Roane; Susanna Aherron, ae 19y, d/o Wm. F.& Frances Ann Stubblefield Aherron; Dec 3 1876 by Rev. O. Littleton.

James H. Walton, ae 24y, farmer, of King
and Queen Co VA, lived Middlesex Co VA, s/o
Wm. & Sarah Ann Walton; Eliza C. Sears, ae
28y, widow, d/o Wm. & Fanny E. Haynes; Dec 5
1876 by Rev. Wm. E. Wiatt.

Charles Smith, ae 32y, col'rd, widower,
farmer, s/o Isaac & Scilla Smith; Sarah Lawson, ae 27y, col'rd, d/o Oliver & Elizabeth
Page; Dec 8 1876 by Rev. Alex Y. Hundley.

James C. Bristow, ae 22y, farmer, s/o
James B. & Lucy Bristow; Lucie C. Groom, ae
18y, d/o Albert & Mary F. Groom; Dec 14 1876
by Rev. Wm. E. Wiatt.

George H. Enos, ae 32y, farmer, s/o Geo.
& Sarah A. E. Moore Enos; Mary E. Fletcher,
ae 21y, d/o Caleb M. & Martha Purcell Fletcher; Dec 20 1876 by Rev. O. Littleton.

William Brooks, ae 21y, col'rd, oyster,
s/o Addison & Frances Brooks; Sarah Driver,
ae 18y, col'rd, d/o Sam & Sarah Driver; Dec
21 1876 by Rev. John Wm. Booth.

William Cook, ae 21y, col'rd, farmer,
s/o Dan'l & Rebecca ; Peggy Smith, ae 17y,
col'rd, d/o James & Mary; Dec 23 1876 by
Rev. Alex Y. Hundley.

John S. Wright, ae 23y, blacksmith, of
New Kent Co VA, s/o W. D. & Sarah Minor
Wright; Lizzie C. Fosque, ae 16y, d/o John
L. & Mary H. Hogg Fosque; Dec 24 1876 by
Rev. Wm. E. Wiatt.

Frank Robinson, ae 23y, col'rd, farmer,
s/o Addison & Sarah Lemon; Mary Gasby, ae
21y, col'rd, d/o Peter & Eliza Gasby; Dec 24
1876 by Rev. John Wm. Booth.

James L. Henderson, ae 19y, shoe maker,
s/o Laben & Martha E. West Henderson; Ozella
Blake, ae 18y, d/o Thos. B. & Eliza R. Coleman Blake; Dec 25 1876 by Rev. John Wm.
Booth.

Warner W. Cooke, ae 20y, col'rd, farmer,
s/o Peter & Agnes Cooke; Gracie Ann Lockley,
ae 21y, col'rd, of King and Queen Co VA, d/o
James & Mary Lockley; Dec 25 1876 by Rev.
John Wm. Booth.

James T. Davenport, ae 23y, col'rd, farm,
s/o Thos. & Mary Davenport; Eugenia Goldman,
ae 17y, d/o Pinky Davenport; Dec 25 1876 by
Rev. John Wm. Booth.

Joe Washington, ae 22y, col'rd, teamster, of King and Queen Co VA, s/o John & Martha; Louisa Cosby, ae 22y, col'rd, d/o Harriet Parker; Dec 26 1876 by Rev. R. A. Fox.

Guest Stoaks, ae 21y, col'rd, widower, oysterman, d/o Wm. & Judy Stoaks; Mary T. Lockley, ae 21y, col'rd, of Middlesex Co VA, d/o James & Mary Lockley; Dec 30 1876 by Rev. E. W. Page.

Charles Field, ae 20y, col'rd, farmer, s/o Humphrey & Tilla Field; Fanny Patterson, ae 18y, col'rd, d/o Mary F. Patterson; Dec 24 1876 by Rev. John WM. Booth.

Robert Ward, ae 28y, col'rd, laborer, of Richmond City VA, s/o Wm. & Nancy Ward; Julia Frances Hayes, ae 21y, col'rd, of Mathews CO VA, d/o Robert & Sally Hayes; Dec 28 1876 by Rev. Sam'l S. Harden.

James Whiting, ae 23y, col'rd, oysterman, s/o Jack & Betsy; Sarah Hubbard, ae 17y, of King and Queen Co VA, d/o Wm. & Nancy; Dec 28 1876 by Rev. John Wm. Booth.

William Burwell, ae 21y, col'rd, farmer, s/o Julia Ward; Susan Carter, ae 16y, col'rd; d/o Anthony & Lucy Ann Carter; Dec 30 1876 by Rev. John Wm. Booth.

William Payne , ae 70y, col'rd, widower, oysterman, s/o Humphrey & Mary Payne; Kitty Throckmorton, ae 65y, col'rd, d/o Harry & Mary Carter; Jan 4 1877 by Rev. E. W. Page.

Anthony Anderson, ae 21y, col'rd, s/o Lony & Peggy Anderson; Charlotte Scott, ae 21y, col'rd, d/o John & Rose Scott; Jan 7 1877 by Rev. Sam'l S. Harden.

Edward T. Ripley, ae 28y, fisherman, of Mathews Co VA, s/o Wm. & Nancy Diggs Ripley; Julia Pugh, ae 29y, of Mathews Co VA, d/o Wm. & Adda Hudgins Pugh; Jan 11 1877 by Rev. W. S. Hawkins.

A. F. Shackelford, ae 30y, col'rd, mechanic, s/o Zachariah & Frances T. Bew Shackelford; Mary C. Wallace, ae 20y, d/o Wm. & Elizabeth T. Williams Wallace; Jan 14 1877 by Rev. Wm. E. Wiatt.

Billy Curtis, ae 25y, col'rd, laborer, s/o James & Ann; Fanny Washington, ae 29y, col'rd, d/o Geo. & Becky; Jan 14 1877 by Rev. Charles Mann.

James R. Thomas, ae 36y, oysterman, s/o
Washington & Elizabeth Thomas; Nannie Hogg,
ae 21y, d/o Stephen & Nancy Robins Hogg; Jan
16 1877 by Rev. W. S. Hawkins.

Felix Smith, ae 26y, col'rd, oysterman,
s/o Wm. & Elizabeth Smith; Mary Eliza Anderson, ae 21y, of Norfolk VA, d/o Ellen Anderson; Jan 18 1877 by Rev. Sam'l S. Harden.

John W. Phillips, ae 18y, col'rd, sailor,
s/o Henry & Kitty Phillips; Mary M. Johnson,
ae 20y, col'rd, d/o Thos. & Elizabeth A.
Johnson; Jan 18 1877 by Rev. E. W. Page.

Robert Baytop, ae 21y, col'rd, farmer,
s/o Bob & Franky Baytop; Rich'd Anna Stubbs'
ae 21y, col'rd, d/o Wm. & Nelly Stubbs; Jan
25 1877 by Rev. John W. Booth.

Charles Henry Morris, ae 26y, col'rd,
widower, of Eastern Shore MD, s/o Geo. &
Hettie Whittington; Becky Banks, ae 17y,
col'rd, d/o Jas. & Lucy Banks; Jan 30 1877
by Rev. Samuel S. Harden.

Benjamin F. Blasingame, ae 29y, farmer,
s/o John & Emiline Blasingame; Missouri B.
Templeman, ae 19y, d/o Jackson & Frances A.
Templeman; Feb 1 1877 by Rev. O. Littleton.

Currell Pryor, ae 21y, col'rd, oyster and
sailor, s/o Jim & Betty Pryor; Pheby Gardner;
ae 22y, col'rd, d/o Harry & Amanda; Feb 3
1877 by Rev. Sam'l S. Harden.

George Ransone, ae 23y, col'rd, oyster,
s/o Geo & Frances Ransone; Nora Anderson, ae
22y, col'rd, parents unk; Feb 8 1877 by Rev.
John Wm. Booth.

George Thornton, ae 24y, col'rd, oyster,
s/o Frank & Peggy Thornton; Mary Fox, ae
17y, col'rd; Feb 10 1877 by Rev. Sam'l S.
Harden.

William F. Robins, ae 26y, farmer, s/o
John Wm. & Mary M. Robins; Mary Lavinia Dunston, ae 21y, d/o John & Mary Dunston; Feb
17 1877 by Rev. Wm. E. Wiatt.

William H. Hogg, ae 21y, oysterman, s/o
Washington & Elizabeth Hogg; Annie F. Car-
mines, ae 17y, d/o James M. & Margaret A.
Carmines; Feb 13 1877 by Rev. W. S. Hawkins.

William Cully, ae 21y, col'rd, oysterman,
s/o Jack & Joan Cully; Ella Whiting, ae 21y,
col'rd, d/o Dick & Lilly Ann Whiting; Feb 15
1877 by Rev. John Wm. Booth.

Amos T. Graves, ae 22y, farmer, s/o Wm.
J. & Eliza Graves; Alice J. Fletcher, ae
22y, d/o James B. & Lily A. Fletcher; Feb 18
1877 by Rev. Wm. E. Wiatt.

Tyler Booker, ae 21y, col'rd, farmer, s/o
Isaac & Mary Booker; Molly Davis, ae 21y,
col'rd, d/o Tom & Betsy Davis; Feb 18 1877
by Rev. John Wm. Booth.

E. F. Landis, ae 23y, farmer, of Lancas-
ter Co PA, s/o John G. & Martha Barr Landis;
Roxanna Trevilian, ae 22y, d/o Roscoe C. &
Elizabeth Clements Trevilian; Feb 18 1877 by
Rev. David Coulling.

Robert F. Fary, ae 22y, col'rd, lumber
dealer, s/o Wm. C. & Mary F. Corr Fary;
Maria F. Clayton, ae 17y, col'rd, d/o Joseph
& Sarah A. Dutton Clayton; Feb 22 1877 by
Rev. David Coulling.

Robert Latimor, ae 31y, col'rd, minister
of the gospel, of Elizabeth Co VA, s/o Thom-
asia Webb, Sarah Catharine Gregory, ae 25y,
parents unk; Feb 22 1877 by Rev. J. G.
Councill.

John H. Brown, ae 25y, farmer, of Middle-
sex Co VA, col'rd, s/o Sam & Ann Eliza Brown;
Elvira Louisa Jones, ae 16y, col'rd, d/o
Cary & Courtney; Feb 28 1877 by Rev. John
Wm. Booth.

Dennis Fleming, ae 45y, widower, farmer,
s/o Thos. & Sarah Dare Fleming; Eugenia E.
Goode, ae 18y, d/o Andrew W. & Frances
Croom Goode; Mar 1 1877 by Rev. A. Wiles.

George Stewart, ae 24y, col'rd, farmer,
of Richmond VA, s/o Jim & Annie Stewart;
Lizzie Perrin, ae 30y, col'rd, d/o Wm. &
Rebecca Perrin; Mar 4 1877 by Rev. Wm. E.
Wiatt.

John Lloyd Tabb, ae 25y, merchant, s/o
John Prosser & Rebecca Lloyd Tabb; Susan
Selden, ae 24y, d/o Robert C. & Courtney W.
Brooke Selden; Mar 6 1877 by Rev. Alex Y.
Hundley.

William L. Meredith, ae 25y, farmer, of
King and Queen Co VA, s/o Miles C. & Frances
A. Roane Meredith; Virginia A. Roane, ae
21y, d/o Henry & Virginia Anderson Roane;
Mar 11 1877 by Rev. Wm. E. Wiatt.

Cornelius Davenport, ae 21y, col'rd,
farmer, s/o Thos. & Mary Davenport; Annie
Lawson, ae 21y, col'rd, d/o Emma Cooke; Mar
11 1877 by Rev. John Wm. Booth.

Robert Brown, ae 23y, col'rd, farmer, of
Middlesex Co VA, s/o Sam'l & Ann Eliza
Brown; Luvy Duval, ae 22y, col'rd, d/o Chas.
& Mary Duval; Mar 4 1877 by Rev. John Wm.
Booth.

Isaac Smith, ae 21y, col'rd, oysterman,
s/o Wm. & Mary Smith; Rebecca S. Stubbs, ae
17y, col'rd, d/o Clara Stubbs; Mar 15 1877
by Rev. O. Littleton.

Robert Henry Carter, ae 22y, col'rd,
boatman, s/o Peter & Caroline Carter; Maria
Jones, ae 19y, col'rd, d/o Alex Jones & Rose
Chapman; Mar 29 1877 by Rev. John Wm. Booth.

Joseph Schevery, ae 29y, engineer, of
SWITZERLAND, s/o Joseph & Thace Schevery;
Mary J. Lawson, ae 22y, d/o James & Mary J.
Lawson; Apr 1 1877 by Rev. J. G. Councill.

Hezekiah Monroe, ae 25y, col'rd, farmer,
s/o James & Betsy Monroe; Judy Kedley, ae
21y, col'rd, d/o Washington & Nancy Kedley;
Apr 7 1877 by Rev. E. W. Page.

James M. Hobday, ae 23y, col'rd, farmer,
s/o John & Nancy Hobday; Mary A. Johnson, ae
18y, col'rd, d/o Henry & Mary Johnson; Apr
12 1877 by Rev. Wm. Thomas.

David Washington, ae 21y, col'rd, farmer,
s/o Isaac & Frances Washington; Frances
Johnson, ae 21y, col'rd, d/o Henry & Mary ;
Apr 12 1877 by Rev. Wm. Thomas.

William Jackson Mann, ae 33y, farmer, s/o
Chas. Mann & Mary Jackson; Sallie Bruce
Smith, ae 24y, d/o Wm. P. & Marian Seddon
Smith; Apr 18 1877 by Rev. Wm. Munford,
Priest in Fauquier Co VA.

Cary Olvis, ae 42y, col'rd, widowed, of
York Co VA, lived Gloucester Co VA, oyster,
s/o Dick & Sally Willis; Martha Brooks, ae
30y, widow, d/o Billy 7 Patsy; Apr 19 1877
by Rev. E. W. Page.

George E. Williams, ae 26y, waterman, s/o
Ed & Margaret Williams; Laura F. East, ae
17y, of Accomack Co VA, d/o John T. & Nancy
East; Aug 16 1877 by Rev. W. S. Hawkins.

Joseph Henry Seawell, ae 25y, farmer, s/o
Wat W. & Jane R. Seawell; Lucy J. Peatross,
ae 21y, of Caroline Co VA, d/o Geo. W. &
Maria L. Peatross; Aug 21 1877 by Rev. Wm.
E. Wiatt.

Frederick Jefferson, ae 25y, col'rd, farm,
of N. C, near Danville VA, s/o Rich'd &
Rhody Jefferson; Frances Ann Tabb, ae 30y,
col'rd, widow, d/o Gabriel & Ann Carter; Aug
21 1877 by Rev. Sam'l S. Harden.

Charles Taliaferro, ae 21y, col'rd, farm,
of King and Queen Co VA, s/o Warner & Dian-
nah Taliaferro; Harriet Lockley, ae 21y,
col'rd, d/o Sam'l & Matilda Lockley; Aug 23
1877 by Rev. John W. Booth.

Charles T. Moore, ae 28y, farmer, s/o
Geo. & Williamouth Carlton Moore; Harriet
Fleming, ae 18y, d/o Jas. W. & Mildred Hob-
day Fleming; Sept 4 1877 by Rev. W. S.
Hawkins.

Peter Perrin, ae 30y, col'rd, widower,
farmer, s/o Beverly & Dinah Perrin; Nettie
Harrison, ae 19y, col'rd, d/o Joe & Nancy
Harrison; Sept 22 1877 by Rev. W. S. Hawkins.

Beverly Sears, ae 60y, widower, farmer,
s/o John & Caroline Hobday Sears; Elizabeth
F. Lamberth, ae 37y, d/o John & Mildred
Walker Lamberth; Oct 11 1877 by Rev. O.
Littleton.

James R. Brushwood, ae 24y, clerk in
store, s/o James & Elvira Brushwood; Sue A.
Wolfe, ae 21y, d/o John B. & Eliza Wolfe;
Oct 10 1877 by Rev. O. Littleton.

John William Tillage, ae 21y, farmer,
oysterman, s/o Joseph & Georgianna Belvin
Tillage; Mary Jane Phillips, ae 22y,d/o John
E. & Catharine A. Shackelford Phillips; Oct
11 1877 by Rev. W. S. Hawkins.

John Field, ae 27y, farmer, s/o Chas. C.
& Harriet Taliaferro Field; Louisa Turner
Cary, ae 25y, d/o Dr. Sam'l B. & Catharine
Y. Kemp Fary; Oct 17 1877 by Rev. Wm. M.
Munford at Ware Parrish.

Henry Chapman, ae 38y, colored, oyster, s/o Robert & Betsy Chapman; Mary Jackson, ae 22y, colored, d/o Ceasar & Mary Jackson; Apr 19 1877 Rev. E. W. Page.

James Henry Haynes, ae 26y, farmer, s/o John W. & Francis A. Nuttall Haynes; Martha Catharine Stubblefield, ae 22y, daughter of Jas. B. & Susan Enos Stubblefield; May 15 1877 by Rev. Wm. E. Wiatt.

William Isaac Collins, ae 26y, col'rd, sailor, of Somerset Co MD, s/o John & Leah Collins; Daphney Thornton, ae 18y, d/o Paul & Mary Thornton; May 20 1877 by Rev. Sam'l S. Harden.

Philip Morris, ae 26y, col'rd, sailor, s/o Philip & Lucy Morris; Elizabeth Dixon, ae 21y, col'rd, d/o Wm. & Patsy Dixon; May 24 1877 by Rev. Sam'l S. Harden.

Isaac Garnett, ae 21y, col'rd, timber getter, of Fredericksburg VA, s/o Jim & Julia Garnett; Johnetta Adams, ae 21y, d/o Georgia & Harriet Adams; May 31 1877 by Rev. E. W. Page.

John H. Dunston, ae 58y, widower, farmer, s/o John & Matilda Waddle Dunston; Lilly A. Fletcher, ae 40y, widow, parents unk; May 31 1877 by Rev. O. Littleton.

John Wilson, ae 23y, farmer, of Surry Co VA, s/o Lewis & Louisa Anna Wilson; Mary Eliza Smith, ae 21y, d/oEmanuel & Caroline Smith; June 6 1877 by Rev. Wm. Thomas.

William H. Martin, ae 42y, widower, farm, s/o John & Maria Stubbs Martin; Addie C. Leigh, ae 38y, d/o John Leigh; June 12 1877 by Rev. O. Littleton.

Cuffy Tazewell, ae 21y, col'rd, farmer, s/o Winston & Patsy Tazewell; Elizabeth Daniels, ae 16y, col'rd, d/o Susan Daniels; June 13 1877 by Rev. Sam'l S. Harden.

Alfred G. Huckstep. ae 62y, widower, lived King and Queen Co VA, farmer, s/o Jas. S. & Elizabeth Jackson Huckstep; Sarah A. E. T. Howard, ae 21y, of King William Co VA, d/o Thos. & Sarah Kemp Howard; June 16 1877 by David Coulling.

Washington Ross, ae 22y, col'rd, farmer, s/o Peter & Frances Ross; Jenny Baytop, ae 21y, col'rd, parents unk; June 4 1877 by Rev. John Wm. Booth.

John Edward Saunders, ae 29y, col'rd, waiter, of Roanoke Co VA, parents unk; Jenny Linde Cooke, ae 26y, col'rd, d/o Chas. & Rachel Cooke; June 21 1877 by Rev. E. W. Page.

Ralph Washington, ae 65y, col'rd, widower, farmer, s/o Isaac & Dinah Washington; Betsy Braxton, ae 34y, col'rd, d/o Jack & Lucy; June 24 1877 by Rev. John Wm. Booth.

John H. Stevens, ae 34y, ship carpenter, of Dorchester Co MD, s/o Wm. & Hannah Stevens; Indianna Townsend, ae 21y, d/o Kendall & Elizabeth Carnes Townsend; June 28 1877 by Rev. W. S. Hawkins.

Frank Lemon, ae 24y, col'rd, farmer, s/o John & Sally Lemon; Frances Reed, ae 21y, col'rd, d/o Spencer & Mary Reed; June 29 1877 by Rev. Wm. E. Wiatt.

Christopher C. Moore, ae 26y, working saw mill, s/o Henry M. & Mary Bridges Moore; Sallie E. Clements, ae 20y, of Middlesex Co VA, d/o John Clements; July 1 1877 by Rev. Wm. E. Wiatt.

Temple Page, ae 21y, col'rd, farmer, of King and Queen Co VA, s/o Henry & Mary Page; Hannah Fox, ae 21y, col'rd, d/o Sam & Martha; July 7 1877 by Rev. Sam'l S. Harden.

Edward Croswell, ae 24y, oysterman, s/o John & Ann L. Carmines Croswell; Sophronia White, ae 21y, d/o John & Elizabeth Oliver White; July 19 1877 by Rev. W. S. Hawkins.

James L. Clements, ae 27y, farmer, s/o John W. & Sarah L. Smither Clements; Caroline Bridges, ae 26y, d/o Richard M. & Caroline Clarke Bridges; Aug 14 1877 by Rev. O. Littleton.

Charles Pannell, ae 40y, col'rd, farmer, of King William Co VA, s/o Edmund & Milly Pannell; Ellen Mantley, ae 21y, d/o Geo. & Caroline Mantley; Aug 14 1877 by Rev. Sam'l S. Harden.

William H. Cary, ae 24y, state officer,
s/o E. B. S. & Eliza A. Smith Cary; Kate
Field, ae 21y, of Baltimore MD, d/o Chas. C.
& Harriet A. Taliaferro Field; Oct 17 1877
by Rev. Wm. M. Munford, Abingdon Rector.

Charles Jones, ae 21y, col'rd, oysterman,
s/o Sye & Fanny Jones, Fanny Braxton, ae
19y, col'rd, of Mathews Co VA, d/o Lee &
Martha Braxton; Oct 27 1877 by Rev. R. A.
Fox.

William Henry Horseley, ae 37y, farmer,
s/o John W. & Mary A. Rilee Horseley; Virginia Walker, ae 21y, d/o Rich'd H. & Sarah
C. Rilee Walker; Nov 1 1877 by Rev. O.
Littleton.

Warner Whiting, ae 21y, col'rd, farmer,
s/o John & Mary Jane Whiting; Indianna Baytop, ae 15y, d/o Peter & Rebecca Baytop; Nov
4 1877 by Rev. John W. Booth.

Shurley Baylor, ae 24y, col'rd, farmer,
of Chesterfield Co VA, s/o Armistead & Johannah Baylor; Catharine Banks, ae 22y,
col'rd, parents unk; Nov 8 1877 by Rev. E.
W. Page.

William Lockley, ae 26y, col'rd, farmer,
s/o Wm. & Emiline Lockley; Mary Jones, ae
21y, col'rd, d/o Wm. & Monday Jones; Nov 8
1877 by Rev. E. W. Page.

George T. Brooking, ae 22y, farmer, s/o
Henry W. & Verlinda E. Brooking; Sarah E.
Rilee, ae 17y, of Middlesex Co VA, d/o
Joshua & Catharine Rilee; Nov 11 1877 by
Rev. Wm. E. Wiatt.

William Milby, ae 38y, widower, farmer,
of King and Queen Co VA, s/o Thos. & Elizabeth Bland Milby; Sarah Howard, ae 39y, d/o
Jas. & Susan Powers Howard; Nov 13 1877 by
Rev. David Coulling.

Carter B. Williams, ae 32y, widower,
farmer, s/o Edmund & Margaret Seaborne Williams; Emma F. Leavitt, ae 17y, d/o Wm. F. &
Emily F. Pointer Leavitt; Nov 15 1877 by
Rev. Wm. E. Wiatt.

Joseph A. West, ae 23y, farmer, s/o Jos.
& Nancy West; Mary S. West, ae 21y, d/o
Chas. & Peggy Haywood; Nov 8 1877 by Rev. W.
S. Hawkins.

Algernon S. Varden, ae 30y, farmer, of
New Kent Co VA, s/o Henry & Malvina Stubble-
field Varden; Tabitha C. Kemp, ae 20y, d/o
O. S. Kemp & P. A. Christian; Nov 21 1877 by
Rev. J. G. Councill.

Robert Bright, ae 21y, col'rd, oysterman,
s/o Thos. & Agnes Bright; Lucy Goldman, ae
17y, col'rd, d/o John & Roberta Coldman; Nov
22 1877 by Rev. Sam'l S. Harden.

Charles L. Leake, ae 27y, farmer, of
Goochland Co VA, s/o W. D. & I. M. Kean
Leake; Sue H. Shield, ae 24y, of York Co VA,
d/o Wm. H. & Sue A. Howard Shield; Nov 22
1877 by Rev. Alex Y. Hundley.

George Kemp, ae 40y, widower, col'rd,
farmer, s/o Henry & Milly Kemp; Mary Washington, ae 26y, col'rd, of King and Queen Co
VA, d/o John & Martha Washington; Nov 28
1877 by Rev. R. A. Fox.

William P. Roane, ae 54y, widower, farm,
of Gloucester Co VA, lived Middlesex Co VA,
s/o Chas. & Mary Roane; Mary Jane Harper, ae
40y, widow, d/o Henry & Harriet Chapman; Nov
28 1877 by Rev. A. Wiles.

Gibson Hogg, ae 25y, farmer, s/o Thos. &
Betsy Hogg; Matilda Jenkins, ae 26y, d/o
John & Winey Jenkins; Nov 29 1877 by Rev. W.
S. Hawkins.

Sye Carter, ae 60y, widower, col'rd,
farmer, s/o Jacob & Mary Carter; Eliza Kidd,
ae 33y, col'rd, d/o Sarah Leigh; Dec 13 1877
by Rev. John W. Booth.

William Henry Harrison Palmer, ae 25y,
col'rd, farm and Oyster, s/o Phill & Rebecca
Palmer; Polly Jones, ae 21y, col'rd, d/o
Gabriel & Lucy Jones; Dec 20 1877 by Rev.
John Wm. Booth.

Wiliam J. Minor, ae 21y, farmer, s/o John
W. & Sarah J. Mouring Minor; Bettie C. Ash,
ae 25y, d/o Thos. & Lucie Ransone Ash; Dec
20 1877 by Rev. W. S. Hawkins.

George D. Ash. ae 30y, farmer, s/o Thos.
& Lucy Ransone Ash; Harriet S. Minor, ae
22y, d/o John W. & Sarah J. Mouring Minor;
Dec 25 1877 by Rev. W. S. Hawkins.

George D. Stubbs, ae 25y, farmer, s/o
Lawrence S. & Mary Darne Stubbs; Hetty R.
Stubbs, ae 19y, d/o Edw'rd S. & Jane Coleman
Stubbs; Dec 25 1877 by Rev. Geo. E. Booker.

Joshua T. Bland, ae 20y, farmer, s/o
Zachariah & Delilah Ann Didlake Bland; Sarah
Frances Fletcher, ae 23y, d/o Wm. R. &
Frances Ann Fary Fletcher; Dec 25 1877 by
Rev. Wm. E. Wiatt.

Jasper Burwell, ae 23y, col'rd, laborer,
s/o Phill & Sarah Burwell; Julia Reed, ae
24y, col'rd, of Essex Co VA, d/o Washington
& Betty Reed; Dec 25 1877 by Rev. John Wm.
Booth.

Augustine S. Trevilian, ae 55y, widower,
farmer, s/o Christopher & Elizabeth Massey
Trevilian; Josephine T. Montague, ae 40y,
widow, d/o J. T. & Tabitha Christian Hill;
of New Kent Co VA, Dec 25 1877 by Rev. Geo.
E. Booker.

John Green, ae 25y, col'rd, laborer, of
Essex Co VA, s/o Tom & Emiline Green; Hester
Whiting, ae 21y, col'rd, d/o Aaron & Margar-
et Whiting; Dec 25 1877 by Rev. John Wm.
Booth.

Claiborne Lemon, ae 22y, col'rd, farmer,
s/o Wade & Emiline Lemon; Georgianna Lemon,
ae 18y, col'rd, d/o Theodore & Louisa Heath
Lemon; Dec 27 1877 by Rev. John Wm. Booth.

Eugene Streagle, ae 23y, farmer, s/o Lan-
don & Lily Ann Haynes Streagle; Mary Susan
Dunston, ae 19y, d/o Beverly & Eliza Jane
Hurst Dunston; Dec 27 1877 by Rev. Wm. E.
Wiatt.

Edward S. Stubbs, ae 27y, farmer, s/o
Edw'rd S. & Jane Coleman Stubbs; Mary Ella
Smith, ae 22y, d/o Geo. W. & Catharine S.
Hughes Smith; Dec 27 1877 by Rev. Geo. E.
Booker.

Joseph Anderson, ae 23y, col'rd, laborer,
of Norfolk Co VA, parents unk; Betsy Smith,
ae 19y, col'rd, d/o Rich'rd & Sarah Smith;
Dec 20 1877 by Rev. Sam'l S. Harden.

Albert Brown, ae 28y, sailor, of Wicomico
Co MD, s/o John W. & Sarah Jane Walter
Brown; Martha A. Leavitt, ae 19y, d/o Wm. F.
& Emily F. Pointer Leavitt; Jan 10 1878 by
Rev. W. S. Hawkins.

Essex T. Jones, ae 21y, col'rd, farmer, s/o Dan'l & Mary Jones; Virgin M. Bright, ae 18y, col'rd, parents unk; Jan 8 1878 by Rev. Sam'l S. Harden.

Richard H. Bryan, ae 37y, widower, farm, of Queen Anne's Co MD, s/o Henry & Louisa Sparks Bryan; Catharine A. Griffin; ae 35y, widow, d/o Dennis & Anna S. Wood Amory; Jan 13 1878 by Rev. Wm. E. Wiatt.

Lewellan M. Bristow, ae 37y, farmer, of Middlesex CO VA, s/o Thos. S. & Mary S. Garrett Bristow; Mary Louisa Streagle, ae 21y, d/o Landon & Lily Ann Haynes Streagle; Jan 15 1878 by Rev. J. G. Councill.

John Franklin Pointer, ae 37y, farmer, s/o Henry S. & Fanny D. Leigh Pointer; Virginia Smither, ae 22y, d/o Wm. T. & Elizabeth Crittenden Smither; Jan 16 1878 by Rev. Wm. E. Wiatt.

William Noggin, ae 25y, col'rd, laborer, s/o Rob't & Seny Noggin; Julia Hooks, ae 22y, col'rd, d/o Elizabeth Tibbs; Jan 16 1878 by Rev. John Wm. Booth.

Augustine Gregory, ae 24y, col'rd, farm, s/o Henry & Sarah Gregory; Sarah Monroe, ae 24y, col'rd, d/o Iverson & Grace Monroe; Jan 16 1878 by Rev. Sam'l S. Harden.

Elijah Morris, ae 42y, col'rd, widower, oysterman, s/o Seth & Polly Morris; Jane Mathias, ae 44y, col'rd, widow, d/o Jeff & Rainy Bowls; Jan 17 1878 by Rev. E. W. Page.

Braxton Richardson, ae 23y, col'rd, farm, s/o Sam & Louisa Richardson; Lizzie Thornton, ae 19y, col'rd, d/o John & Milly Thornton; Jan 17 1878 by Rev. Sam'l S. Harden.

John Henry Green, ae 22y, col'rd, oyster, s/o Lucy Jones; Hannah Holmes, ae 24y, col'rd, d/o Charlotte Holmes; Jan 17 1878 by Rev. John Wm. Booth.

William J. Oliver, ae 21y, farmer, s/o Washington J. H. & Sarah Dunston Oliver; Lucy A. Brown, ae 21y, d/o James & Ann Brown; Jan 17 1878 by Rev. Wm. E. Wiatt.

James William Heywood, ae 22y, sailor and oyster, s/o John & Eliza A. Hogg Heywood; Mary Ellen Owens, ae 22y, d/o Geo. & Nancy Doggin Owens; Jan 22 1878 by Rev. W. S. Hawkins.

Thaddeus M. Robins, ae 25y, works at saw mill, s/o John W. Mary M. Moore Robins; Martha E. Dunston, ae 20y, d/o Beverly & Eliza Hurst Dunston; Jan 24 1878 by Rev. Wm. E. Wiatt.

Rob't Henry Banks, ae 22y, col'rd, waterman, s/o Wm. & Lucy Banks; Frances Banks, ae 16y, col'rd, d/o Henry & Elizabeth Banks; Feb 2 1878 by Rev. John Wm. Booth.

George Montague, ae 23y, col'rd, oyster, s/o Chas. & Hester Montague; Nannie Bet Holmes, ae 18y, col'rd, d/o Currell & Betsie Holmes; Jan 31 1878 by Rev. Sam'l S. Harden.

George Noggin, ae 33y, col'rd, widower, farmer, of Dinwiddie Co Va, s/o Davy & Lucy Noggin; Frances Roberson, ae 19y, col'rd, d/o Dan'l & Eve Roberson; Jan 31 1878 by Rev. John Wm. Booth.

William King, ae 21y, widower, farmer, s/o Wm. & Betsy King; Dolly Burwell, ae 18y, d/o Philip & Sarah Burwell; Feb 2 1878 by Rev. John Wm. Booth.

Ralph Claiborne, ae 23y, col'rd, cutting lumber, s/o Dan'l & Polly Claiborne; Harriet Lee Burwell, ae 16y, col'rd, d/o John E. & Eliza Burwell; Feb 2 1878 by Rev. John Wm. Booth.

James W. Oliver, ae 27y, oysterman, s/o Regold & Mildred Brown Oliver; Martha E. Hogg, ae 19y, d/o Wm. & Mildred Reynolds Hogg; Feb 4 1878 by Rev. Wm. E. Wiatt.

Lee Rosser Peterson Lewis, ae 22y, oysterman, s/o Wm. & Lucy Ann Tillage Lewis; Emily Jane Jordan, ae 18y, d/o Wm. & Maria J. Oliver Jordan; Feb 5 1878 by Rev. Geo. E. Booker.

Lewis Lane, ae 22y, farmer, s/o Rob't & Lucy Hugen Lane; Willentina Parrottm ae 18y, of Mathews Co VA, d/o Wm. & Maria Bohannon Parrott; Feb 8 1878 by Rev. Geo. E. Booker.

William H. Willis, ae 24y, farmer, of King and Queen Co VA, s/o Algernon S. & Willentina Crittenden Willis; Edler Rebecca Leavitt, ae 24y, d/o Ed A. & Rebecca Leavitt; Feb 12 1878 by Rev. Geo. E. Booker.

John W. Padgett, ae 48y, widower, carpenter, of King and Queen Co VA, s/o Fleming & Susan Brown Padgett; Georgianna Horseley, ae 19y, d/o Kinningham & Martha A. Hibble Horseley; Feb 13 1878 by Rev. Wm. E. Wiatt.

William Thomas Williams, ae 29y, oyster, s/o Sam'l & Mary Williams; Elberta Cotter, ae 18y, d/o Andrew J. & Catharine Adams Cotter; Feb 14 1878 by Rev. R. A. Fox.

William Lockley, ae 19y, col'rd, oyster, s/o Albert & Hester Lockley; Eliza Gasby, ae 19y, col'rd, of Middlesex Co VA, d/o Peter Lockley & Eliza Gasby; Feb 17 1878 by Rev. John Wm. Booth.

Albert West, ae 22y, oysterman, s/o Wm. & Frances Jenkins West; Rachel West, ae 22y, d/o Cary & Ellen Virginia Cox West; Feb 8 1878 by Rev. W. S. Hawkins.

Emanuel Gorden, ae 28y, col'rd, oyster, s/o Gloucester & Nancy; Bettie Ann Lewis, ae 20y, col'rd, d/o Dennis & Luetta; Feb 21 1878 by Rev. W. S. Hawkins.

Charles Hogg, ae 24y, sailor, s/o Jack & Julia Dunston Hogg; Ann Matilda Seawell, ae 21y, d/o Benjamin & Mary A. Oliver Seawell; Feb 26 1878 by Rev. W. S. Hawkins.

Alexander Gregory, ae 21y, col'rd, farm, s/o Henry & Sarah Gregory; Catharine A. Jefferson, ae 14y, d/o Thos. W. & Emily Jefferson; Feb 28 1878 by Rev. E. W. Page.

George W. Deal, ae 23y, merchant, of Mathews Co VA, s/o Wm. & Nancy C. Eddings Deal; Maria Maud Miller, ae 17y, d/o Rob't D. & Maria G. Thornton Miller; Feb 28 1878 by Rev. R. A. Fox.

Peyton Jones, ae 28y, col'rd, widower, farmer, of York Co VA, s/o Eastman & Peggy Jones; Lucy Ann Taylor, ae 19y, col'rd, d/o John & Lucinda Taylor; Feb 28 1878 by Rev. R. A. Fox.

Benjamin Baylor, ae 30y, col'rd, carpenter, of Caroline Co VA, s/o Smith & Henrietta Baylor; Elizabeth West, ae 23y, col'rd, d/o John & Elizabeth West; Mar 2 1878 by Rev. Geo. E. Booker.

Jacob Acra, ae 70y, col'rd, farmer, s/o
Tom & Sarah; Julia Miller, ae 30y, d/o John
& Susan; Mar 9 1878 by Rev. David Coulling.

Malvin Fagans, ae 25y, col'rd, farmer, of
N. C, s/o Warner & Argey; Elizabeth Smith,
ae 29y, col'rd, parents unk; Mar 8 1878 by
Rev. Sam'l S. Harden.

Wesley Sturges, ae 24y, col'rd, oyster,
s/o Rachel Sturges; Mollie Berry, ae 21y,
col'rd, d/o Bob & Lucinda Berry; Mar 10 1878
by Rev. John Wm. Booth.

William P. Jordan, ae 23y, oysterman, s/o
Wm. & Maria J. Oliver Jordan; Eleanor Lee
Purcell, ae 15y, d/o John & Margaret Ann
Jones Purcell; Mar 14 1878 by Rev. W. S.
Hawkins.

William Thomas, ae 28y, fisherman, s/o
James & Martha E. Smith Thomas; Maggie Quil-
len, ae 16y, of Portsmouth VA, d/o Thos. &
Pinky Hogg; Mar 21 1878 by Rev. W. S.
Hawkins.

Andrew H. Soles, ae 28y, farmer, s/o Thom
& Mary Lawson Soles; Henrietta w. Rilee, ae
27y, d/o Pascal D. & Nancy Walker Rilee; Mar
24 1878 by Rev. Geo. E. Booker.

Edward Gayle, ae 21y, col'rd, oysterman,
s/o Peter & Judy Gayle; Catharine Gordon, ae
21y, d/o Wm. Henry & Elsey Gordon; Mar 24
1878 by Rev. Sam'l S. Harden.

Lewis F. Stubblefield, ae 27y, bl'ksmith,
s/o Jas. B. & Susan Enos Stubblefield; Sarah
F. Graves, ae 30y, widow, d/o John & Mary
Bridges Graves; Mar 26 1878 by Rev. Wm. E.
Wiatt.

John R. Lamberth, ae 34y, farmer, s/o
John & Mildred Walker Lamberth; Lizzie L.
Chapman, ae 16y, d/o Sam'l B. Chapman; Mar
27 1878 by Rev. Sam'l S. Harden.

John Haskins, ae 23y, col'rd, teamster,
of Middlesex Co VA, s/o Wash & Rebecca Haskins; Elmira Goldman, ae 19y, d/o Jack &
Roberta Goldman; Mar 28 1878 by Rev. Sam'l
S. Harden.

Robert Morris, ae 27y, col'rd, farm, s/o
Barbary Morriss; Julia Stokes, ae 18y,
col'rd, d/o Ben & Manerva Stokes; Apr 4 1878
by Rev. E. W. Page.

John H. King, ae 23y, sailor, s/o Wm. &
Martha West King; Susan Rowe, ae 19y, d/o
Livingston & Lucy Spencer; Apr 4 1878 by
Rev. W. S. Hawkins.

Richard Brown, ae 38y, widower, pressman,
of Richmond City VA, s/o Christopher &
Susan Brown; Polly Randolph, ae 28y, col'rd,
d/o Ralph & Netty; Apr 24 1878 by Rev. Sam'l
S. Harden.

Davy Thias, ae 23y, col'rd, farmer, s/o
Davy & Becky Thais; Patsy Smith, ae 27y,
col'rd, d/o Essex & Phillis Smith; May 2
1878 by Rev. Sam'l S. Harden.

Joseph H. Hall, ae 33y, farmer, s/o Wm. &
Polly Rowe Hall; Mary Elizabeth Shackelford,
ae 19y, d/o John & Julia A. Brown Shackelford; May 8 1878 by Rev. Wm. E. Wiatt.

Wilmore T. Heywood, ae 28y, farmer, s/o
Wm. B. Julia Ann Enos Heywood; Lucinda F.
Pointer, ae 30y, d/o Henry & Frances D.
Leigh Pointer; May 8 1878 by Rev. Wm. E.
Wiatt.

George Lockly, ae 22y, col'rd, farmer,
s/o Wm. & Emiline Lockly; Matilda Taliaferro, ae 21y, col'rd, d/o Wm. & Betsy Taliaferro; Aug 3 1878 by Rev. Geo. E. Booker.

W. J. Diggs, ae 47y, widower, waterman,
of Mathews Co VA, s/o Henry & Mary A. Diggs;
Margaret S. Croswell, ae 23y, d/o Isaac &
Elizabeth Croswell; Aug 6 1878 by Rev. W. S.
Hawkins.

George E. Emerson, ae 21y, farmer, of
Queen Anne Co MD, s/o Alexander & Elizabeth
Emerson; Ida C. Goode, ae 19y, d/o James
Thomas & Mary C. Goode; Aug 15 1878 by Rev.
M. S. Colonna.

Thomas W. Lawson, ae 26y, farmer, s/o
John W. & Euphamia Mann Lawson; Emma S. Tuttle, ae 18y 5m, of Fair Haven CONN, d/o
Horace S. & Cornelia S. Lewis Tuttle; Aug 24
1878 by Rev. Wm. E. Wiatt.

Benjamin Jackson, ae 25y, col'rd, farmer,
parents unk; Martha Ellen Cheeseman, ae 21y,
col'rd, d/o Chas. & Rebecca; Aug 26 1878 by
Rev. John Wm. Booth.

Benjamin Lewis, ae 48y, widower, farmer,
s/o Wm. J. & Rebecca James Lewis; Catharine
Alice Belvin, ae 22y, d/o John P. & Mary
Walker Belvin; Aug 27 1878 by Rev. W. S.
Hawkins.

Alexander Walker, ae 28y, col'rd, farmer,
of Richmond City VA, s/o Philip & Rachel
Walker; Belle Coleman, ae 24y, col'rd, of
Fredericksburg VA, d/o Mary Wallace; Aug 28
1878 by Rev. Sam'l S. Harden.

Humphrey Ware, ae 31y, col'rd, laborer,
of Elizabeth City Co VA, s/o Thos. & Polly
Ware; Charity Banks, ae 21y, col'rd, d/o
Thos. Hawkins & Susan Banks; Aug 30 1878 by
Rev. Sam'l S. Harden.

Samuel B. Taylor, ae 29y, school teacher,
of Northumberland Co VA, s/o Joseph H. &
Frances Taylor; Lucy A. Powers, ae 18y, d/o
Wm. F. & Mary C. Powers; Sept 17 1878 by
Rev. J. G. Councill.

Thomas Billups, ae 54y, col'rd, widower,
farm, of Mathews Co VA, s/o Bailey & Polly;
Mary Laws, ae 40y, widow, d/o Joshua & Diana
Brown; Oct 2 1878 by Rev. Sam'l S. Harden.

Michael W. Pointer, ae 30y, farmer, s/o
Henry S. & Frances D. Leigh Pointer; Frances
J. Leigh, ae 18y, of King and Queen Co VA,
d/o Dr. John H. S. & Mattie A. Harwood
Leigh; Oct 2 1878 by Rev. Geo. E. Booker.

Edgar E. Emerson, ae 30y, farmer, of Lancaster Co PA, lived Middlesex Co VA, s/o Alex
& Elizabeth Emerson; Ellie Leager, ae 17y,
of Caroline Co MD, d/o Kate Leager; Oct 6
1878 by Rev. M. S. Colonna.

Jerome Washington, ae 21y, col'rd, farm,
s/o Geo. Washington & Rebecca Smith; Susan
Harrison, ae 18y, col'rd, d/o Joseph & Nancy
Harrison; Oct 10 1878 by Rev. Sam'l S.
Harden.

Richard Mann Page, ae 40y, farmer, s/o
Mann & Lucy A. Jones Page; Kate Mallory
Wray, ae 27y, of Hampton VA, d/o Jacob K. &
Mary Frances Booker Wray; Oct 10 1878 by
Rev. Alex Y. Hundley.

James Perrin, ae 22y, col'rd, farmer, s/o
Bill & Becky Perrin; Ellen Jackson, ae 25y,
col'rd, d/o Henry & Emiline Jackson; Oct 19
1878 by Rev. E. W. Page.

Sam Jackson, ae 40y, widower, col'rd, farmer, s/o Isaac & Letty Jackson; Charlotte Jackson, ae 25y, col'rd, d/o Mary Baytop; Oct 21 1878 by Rev. Sam'l S. Harden.

James A. Davenport, ae 22y, col'rd, waterman, of King and Queen Co VA, s/o Wm. & Mary Davenport; Amy Cooke, ae 17y, col'rd, d/o Addison & Sally Cooke; May 12 1878 by Rev. E. W. Page.

William Todd Robins, ae 42y, attormey at law, of King and Queen Co VA, s/o Augustine W. & Maria H. Todd Robins; Sally Berkely Nelson, ae 23y, d/o Wilmer W. & Sally B. Catlett Nelson; Nov 23 1878 by Rev. Alex Y. Hundley.

George King, ae 28y, col'rd, farmer, of Henrico Co VA, s/o Billy & Jane King; Eliza Dunlavy, ae 30y, col'rd, d/o John & Margaret Dunlavy; June 2 1878 by Rev. John W. Booth.

David Washington, ae 27y, col'rd, oyster, s/o David & Collinette Washington; Peggy Orrill, ae 25y, d/o Matt & Nancy; June 4 1878 by Rev. W. S. Hawkins.

Simon Stokes, ae 23y, col'rd, oysterman, s/o Kit & Ann Stokes; Henrietta Lewis, ae 22y, col'rd, d/o John & Mary Lewis; June 6 1878 by Rev. W. S. Hawkins.

Daniel Gardner, ae 23y, col'rd, oyster, s/o Bailey & Eliza Gardner; Rosetta Jones, ae 21y, col'rd, d/o Chas. & Sally Jones; June 8 1878 by Rev. R. A. Fox.

Thomas Walker, ae 60y, col'rd, widower, farmer, s/o Billy & Chloe Walker; Becky Miller, ae 30y, widow, col'rd, of James City Co VA, d/o Wallace & Matilda Miller; June 13 1878 by Rev. Geo. E. Booker.

William Iverson, ae 55y, widower, farmer, of Mathews Co VA, s/o Geo. & Dorothy Smith Iverson; Rosetta Nuttall, ae 26y, d/o Wm. Nuttall; June 13 1878 by Rev. Geo. E. Booker.

William Burnett, ae 24y, col'rd, laborer, of Chesterfield Co VA, s/o Wm. & Jane; Helen Thornton, ae 22y, col'rd, d/o Parrot & Sarah Thornton; June 20 1878 by Rev. Sam'l S. Harden.

Stephen T. Hogg, ae 20y, farmer, s/o Stephen & Nancy Robins Hogg; Catharine M. Ash, ae 26y, of Portsmouth VA, d/o Wm. & Mary Ash; June 20 1878 by Rev. W. S. Hawkins.

Alfred Kelly, ae 24y, col'rd, farmer, s/o Courtney Kelly; Hillie Peed, ae 22y, col'rd, d/o Lizzie Peed; July 3 1878 by Rev. Rev. Latimore.

Robert Dixon, ae 22y, col'rd, oysterman, s/o Chas. & Fanny Dixon; Lucy Carter, ae 24y, col'rd, d/o John & Sarah Carter; July 18 1878 by Rev. Sam'l S. Harden.

Nelson Douglass, ae 25y, col'rd, farmer, of Henrico Co VA, s/o Hampton & Ennis Douglass; Amanda Wiatt, ae 25y, col'rd, d/o Tom & Sally Wiatt; July 18 1878 by Rev. Sam'l S. Harden.

Muscoe R. Booker, ae 21y, farmer, s/o Lewis T. & Lucy F. Fary Booker; Emma A. Walker, ae 19y, d/o John & Elizabeth Booker Walker; July 28 1878 by Rev. Wm. E. Wiatt.

John W. Shackelford, ae 21y, waterman, s/o John W. & Julia Brown Shackelford; Bettie McLane, ae 22y, d/o Wm. & Betsy Cobbs McLane; July 2 1878 by Rev. W. S. Hawkins.

George W. Green, ae 21y, waterman, s/o Geo. & Molly West Green; Georgianna West, ae 21y, d/o Howard & Nancy Green West; July 28 1878 by Rev. W. S. Hawkins.

Charles Thomas, ae 22y, col'rd, oyster, s/o Henry & Easter Thomas; Flora Cary, ae 21y, col'rd, d/o Chas. & Isabella Cary; Oct 26 1878 by Rev. E. W. Page.

Davy Banks, ae 22y, col'rd, farmer, s/o Wm. & Grace Sparks Banks; Indianna King, ae 18y, col'rd, d/o Wm. & Violet King; Oct 27 1878 by Rev. John Wm. Booth. Violet King is now Baytop.

Henry Clarke, ae 25y, col'rd, oysterman, s/o s/o Wm. & Violet Clarke; Caroline Anderson, ae 21y, col'rd, d/o Wm. & Sarah Anderson; Nov 3 1878 by Rev. E. W. Page.

Jas. Henry Ware, ae 49y, widower, col'rd, farmer, of Mathews Co VA, s/o Rich'd & Judy Ware; Nancy Cole, ae 49y, widow, col'rd, d/o Abram & Charity; Nov 5 1878 by Rev. Sam'l S. Harden.

George T. Walker, ae 28y, farmer, s/o
Geo. & Ann Walker; Lucy F. Horseley, ae 22y,
d/o John & Mary Horseley; Nov 6 1878 by Rev.
Geo. E. Booker.

William S. Wroten, ae 39y, widower, farm,
s/o Uriah & Polly Wroten; Alice Coloney, ae
21y, of York Co VA, d/o Edw'd & Lucinda; Nov
12 1878 by Rev. Wm. E. Wiatt.

George W. Harwood, ae 38y, farmer, s/o
Christopher C. & Judith D. Hall Harwood;
Anna S. Acra, ae 26y, d/o James H. & Lilly
Roane Acra; Nov 14 1878 by Rev. Wm. E. Wiatt.

William Carter, ae 23y, col'rd, farmer,
s/o John & Rebecca Carter; Milly Jones, ae
18y, col'rd, d/o Alexander & Martha Jones;
Nov 17 1878 by Rev. John W. Booth.

David West, ae 21y, sailor, s/o Margaret
West; Georgianna Robins, ae 18y, d/o Jefferson & Catharine Ransone Robins; Nov 21 1878
by Rev. W. S. Hawkins.

Jesse Cooke, ae 23y, col'rd, oysterman,
s/o Jesse & Sarah Cooke; Henrietta Lee, ae
21y, col'rd, of James City Co VA, d/o Rich'd
& Louisa Lee; Nov 24 1878 by Rev. Wm. Thomas.

Thomas Lewis, ae 21y, col'rd, farm, s/o
Wilson & Rebecca Lewis; Ann Reed, ae 21y,
col'rd, d/o Frank & Mary Reed; Nov 28 1878
by Rev. John W. Booth.

William Jerniston, ae 23y, col'rd, labor,
of Henry Co VA, s/o Geo. & Sally Jerniston;
Mary Eliza Gardner, ae 20y, col'rd, d/o
Bailey & Eliza Gardner; Nov 30 1878 by Rev.
Sam'l S. Harden.

Thomas Fox Wiatt, ae 21y, col'rd, oyster,
s/o Wm. & Martha Ann Wiatt; Fannie Cary, ae
19y, col'rd, d/o Miles & Polly Cary; Dec 1
1878 by Rev. E. W. Page.

C. B. Roy, ae 34y, widower, of Richmond
City VA, farmer, s/o T. M. B. & Jane E. Roy;
Willentina West, ae 28y, d/o Isaac & Harriet
West; Dec 30 1878 by Rev. M. S. Colonna.

Gideon S. Chapman, ae 34y, lumber busi-
ness, s/o Henry & Harriet W. Davis Chapman;
Emiline C. Sears, ae 24y, d/o Rich'd & Arena
Dutton Sears; Dec 4 1878 by Rev. Wm. E.
Wiatt.

John Andrew Smith, ae 22y, col'rd, oyster,
s/o Emanuel & Caroline Smith; Sarah Washington, ae 27y, col'rd, s/o Jacob & Eliza Washington; Dec 12 1878 by Rev. Wm. Thomas.

Beverly Roane, ae 25y, farmer, s/o Henry
& Virginia Anderson Roane; Sarah Bell Hudson,
ae 21y, of Sussex Co DELAWARE, d/o C. W. &
Mary A. Cannon Hudson; Dec 22 1878 by Rev.
Geo. E. Booker.

Richard W. Roane, ae 32y, widower, farm,
s/o Sam'l F. & Elizabeth Booker Roane; Mary
L. Kemp, ae 18y, d/o Oswald S. & Park A.
Christian Kemp; Dec 22 1878 by Rev. Wm. E.
Wiatt.

Robert Johnson, ae 22y, col'rd, laborer,
of King and Queen Co VA, s/o Lewis & Mary
Johnson; Alice Moody, ae 21y, col'rd, d/o
Peter & Ann Moody; Dec 24 1878 by Rev. Sam'l
S. Harden.

Zachariah T. Whiting, ae 28y, col'rd,
farmer, s/o Dan'l & Hannah Whiting; Clara
Jackson, ae 19y, col'rd, d/o John & Laura
Jackson; Dec 24 1878 by Rev. E. W. Page.

James Meredith, ae 46y, widower, farmer,
col'rd, s/o Jim & Jennie Meredith; Rose Chapman, ae 43y, col'rd, d/o Robin & Maria Curtis; Dec 25 1878 by Rev. John W. Booth.

Isaac Cooke, ae 19y, col'rd, farmer, s/o
Peyton & Frances Ann Cooke; Mary Jane Daven-
port, ae 20y, col'rd, d/o Thos. & Mary Ann
Davenport; Dec 25 1878 by Rev. John W. Booth.

John Howard, ae 22y, oysterman, s/o Henry
& Pinky Fletcher Howard; Virginia Ann Belvin,
ae 19y, d/o Edw'rd & Mary A. Aherron Belvin;
Dec 25 1878 by Rev. W. S. Hawkins.

Lorenzo King, ae 21y, oysterman, s/o Thos.
& Susan Smith King; Amanda Belvin, ae 21y,
d/o John & Harriet Heywood Belvin; Dec 25
1878 by Rev. W. S. Hawkins.

William H. Hogg, ae 29y, farmer, s/o Stephen & Nancy Robins Hogg; Leah Frances Hogg,
ae 21y, d/o Lewis & Martha E. Hall Hogg; Dec
25 1878 by Rev. W. S. Hawkins..

John B. Rank, ae 21y, carpenter, of Lancaster Co PA, s/o Philip & Margaret Buffen-
moyers Rank; Mary Pratt, ae 21y, of Caroline
Co MD, d/o Benj. & Elizabeth Leager Pratt;
Dec 26 1878 by Rev. J. G. Councill.

Clinton Peterson Howlett, ae 22y, farmer, s/o Benjamin F. & Virginia Kemp Howlett; Ophelia Jane Dunston, ae 17y, d/o Beverly & Eliza Hurst Dunston; Dec 26 1878 by Rev. Alex Y. Hundley.

Simon Lancaster, ae 23y, col'rd, sailor, s/o Wm. & Clara Lancaster; Sarah Phillips, ae 19y, col'rd, d/o Henry & Kitty Phillips; Dec 26 1878 by Rev. John W. Booth.

John Brown, ae 23y, oysterman, s/o John & Bethesda Brown; Susan Ann Robins, ae 18y, d/o Joel & Mary Rowe Robins; Dec 26 1878 by Rev. W. S. Hawkins.

John W. Thomas, ae 21y, fisherman, s/o Washington & Betsy Thomas; Lulie E. Robins, ae 19y, d/o John & Becky Ash Robins; Dec 29 1878 by Rev. W. S. Hawkins.

Julius C. Walker, ae 24y, farmer, s/o Elijah & Margaret Walker; Julia V. Walker, ae 24y, d/o John & Elizabeth Walker; Dec 31 1878 by Rev. Wm. E. Wiatt.

Jacob A. Dillard, ae 33y, widower, farm, s/o Kemp & Catharine Sears Dillard; Mary Catharine Blake, ae 30y, widow, d/o Thos E. & Elizabeth Ransone Johnston; Jan 1 1879.

Carter Anderson, ae 23y, col'rd, farmer, of King William Co VA, s/o Carter & Martha Anderson; Lavinia Jones, ae 21y, col'rd, d/o Geo. & Sally Jones; Jan 2 1879 by Rev. J. W. Booth.

James P. Palmer, ae 30y, col'rd, laborer, s/o Philip & Rebecca Palmer; Kate Johnson, ae 30y, col'rd, widow, of King William Co VA, d/o Sam & Betsy; Jan 15 1879 by Rev. J. W. Booth.

Americus V. Prince, ae 25y, farmer, s/o Rich'd J. & Catharine Bridges Prince; Willie Ann Norton, ae 20y, d/o Wm. & Catharine G. Bristow Norton; Jan 16 1879.

William Wallace Williams, ae 33y, farmer, s/o Andrew & Paulina A. Jones Williams; Mary Alice Peatross, ae 30y, of Caroline Co VA, d/o Geo. W. & Maria Peatross; Jan 17 1879 by Rev. Wm. E. Wiatt.

John Henry Williams, ae 30y, col'rd, farmer, of Terrell Co N. C, s/o Cely & Sam'l Williams; Willie Whiting, ae 35y, widow, of Caroline VA, d/o Wm. Lightfoot; Jan 30 1879.

James T. Tonkins, ae 28y, school teacher,
s/o James & Lucy Tonkins; Sarah J. Johnson,
ae 18y, d/o Henry & Mary Johnson; Jan 30
1879 by Rev. Wm. Thomas.

George Patterson, ae 25y, col'd, trucker,
of KIng and Queen Co VA, s/o Geo. Booker &
Mary Patterson; Catharine Roberson, ae 21y,
col'rd, d/o Soloman & Kitty Roberson; Feb 2
1879 by Rev. J. W. Booth.

Daniel Curtis, ae 21y, farmer, of Mathews
Co VA, s/o Frank & Harriet Curtis; Sally
Scott, ae 18y, col'rd, of King and Queen Co
VA, d/o Robert & Jane Scott; Feb 9 1879 by
Rev. Sam'l S. Harden.

James Jenkins, ae 18y, oysterman, s/o
Frederick & Frances Jenkins; Susan Jenkins,
ae 18y, d/o Winston & Anna Hogg Jenkins; Feb
9 1879 by Rev. W. S. Hawkins.

Henry T. Sears, ae 36y, farmer, s/o Beverly & Louisa Brooking Sears; Julia M. South,
ae 18y, d/o Hugh A. & Julia A. E. Bland
South; Feb 10 1879 by Rev. S. Harvey Johnson.

Albert H. Taylor, ae 28y, sailor, s/o
Geo. H. & Susan Dunston Taylor; Mary M.
Acra, ae 21y, d/o Jas. H. & Lilly Ann Roane
Acra; Feb 10 1879 by Rev. Geo. E. Booker.

James Washington Rowe, ae 19y, waterman,
s/o Jas. & Margaret Towe; Mary Ellen Robins,
ae 17y, d/o Joel & Mary Rowe Robins; Feb 13
1879 by Rev. W. S. Hawkins.

Americus Sibley, ae 25y, farmer, of Middlesex Co VA, s/o Stage Sibley & Fanny Buckner; Malinda Pearce, ae 25y, d/o Rob't B. &
Adaline South Pearce; Feb 19 1879 by Rev. M.
S. Colonna.

John Laws, ae 22y, col'rd, farmer, of
Lancaster Co VA, s/o James & Harriet Laws;
Sally Smith, ae 20y, col'rd, d/o Frank &
Catharine Smith; Feb 22 1879 by Rev. Sam'l
S. Harden.

Lawrence Whiting, ae 22y, col'rd, farmer,
s/o Isaac & Judy Whiting; Mary Frances
Jones, ae 16y, col'rd, d/o Alex & Martha
Jones; Feb 23 1878 by Rev. J. W. Booth.

Edward Owens, ae 27y, farmer, s/o Geo. &
Nancy Owens; Lizzie West, ae 26y, d/o Jas. &
Nancy West; Apr 10 1879 by Rev. W. S.
Hawkins.

Albert Green, ae 25y, widower, col'rd, of King and Queen Co Va, farmer, s/o Marlo & Sarah Green; Lucy Jackson, ae 24y, col'rd, d/o Fanny Jackson; Mar 4 1879 by Rev. E. W. Page.

William Chapman, ae 22y, col'rd, farmer, s/o Lewis & Sarah Chapman; Eliza Burwell, ae 22y, col'rd, d/o Major & Margie Burwell; Mar 8 1879 by Rev. E. W. Page.

Albert Lee, ae 21y, farmer, of James City Co VA, s/o Rich'd & Louisa Lee; Isabella Lemon, ae 21y, d/o Littleton & Matilda Lemon; Mar 15 1879 by Rev. J. W. Booth.

James Addison Crew, ae 33y, oyster, s/o John & Mary Jane Dunston Crew; Martha Easter, ae 27y, widow, d/o John Darnell; Mar 16 1879 by Rev. Wm. E. Wiatt.

John W. Holmes, ae 22y, col'rd, oyster, s/o Chas. & Lena Holmes; Rebecca Taylor, ae 21y, col'rd, d/o John & Lucinda Taylor; Mar 20 1879 by Rev. J. W. Booth.

William Brown, ae 28y, sailor, s/o John & Bethesda Winder Brown; Martha E. Thomas, ae 19y, d/o Jos. & Martha Smith Thomas; Mar 20 1879 by Rev. W. S. Hawkins.

John Morriss, ae 24y, col'rd, lumber business, s/o Harrison & Courtney Morriss; Evelina Phillips, ae 18y, d/o John & Lucy Ann Phillips; Mar 22 1879 by Rev. J. W. Booth.

William Ellis, ae 21y, col'rd, oyster, s/o Wm. & adaline Ellis; Octavia Williams, ae 21y, col'rd, d/o Simon & Katy Williams; Mar 21 1879 by Rev. Sam'l S. Harden.

George E. Miller, ae 21y, col'rd, farmer, s/o John Ellis & Betsy Miller; Julia Lewis, ae 21y, col'rd, d/o Matt & Susan Lewis; Mar 30 1879 by Rev. E. W. Page.

Peter Bird, ae 29y, col'rd, fireman at saw mill, of Caroline Co VA, s/o Thos. Gains & Susanna Bird; Maria Evans, ae 21y, col'rd, d/o John & Betsy Evans; Apr 5 1879 by Rev. Sam'l S. Harden.

Emanuel Claiborne, ae 25y, col'rd, lumber
cutter, s/o Dan'l & Polly Claiborne; Hester
Banks, ae 21y, col'rd, d/o Peter & Ellen
Banks; Apr 12 1879 by Rev. J. W. Booth.

Alexander D. Pointer, ae 26y, farmer, s/o
Soloman D. & Sarah Pointer; Louisa V. Moore,
ae 21y, d/o Rich'rd T. & Ellen F. Dutton
Pointer; Apr 17 1879 by Rev. Geo. E. Booker.

Morgan Treat, ae 22y, merchant, of Janes-
ville WISC, lived West Point VA, s/o David
S. & Eliza A. Morgan Treat; Sue E. Roane, ae
22y, d/o Warner P. & Frances A. Bland Roane;
Apr 22 1879 by Rev. Geo. E. Booker.

Mathew Tabb, ae 24y, col'rd, farmer, s/o
Willis & Betsy Tabb; Elleanora Carter, ae
21y, col'rd, d/o Anthony & Lucy Ann Carter;
Apr 29 1879 by Rev. J. W. Booth.

W. Tyler Seawell, ae 24y, clerk, s/o Watt
W. & Jane R. Seawell; India C. Edwards, ae
24y, of Norfolk City VA, d/o John A. & Fannie C. Murray Edwards; Apr 30 1879 by Rev.
Alex Y. Hundley.

Jesse G. Crouch, ae 29y, carpenter, of
Walton Co GA, lived Richmond VA, s/o John &
Martha E. Carter Crouch; Ida M. Kerns, ae
21y, of Lancaster CO PA, lived Gloucester Co
VA, d/o Maris V. & Emma J. Lefevre Kerns;
May 1 1879 by Rev. Wm. E. Wiatt.

Joshua Moore, ae 38y, widower, farmer, of
Goochland Co VA, s/o Bob & Jane Moore; Eliza
Page, ae 25y, col'rd, d/o Roche Page; May 3
1879 by Rev. E. W. Page.

George Booth Field, ae 24y, farmer, s/o
Wm. S. & Clara W. Jones; Laura Campbell
Wiatt, ae 18y, d/o Wm. E. & Charlotte S.
Coleman Wiatt; May 7 1879 by Rev. E. W. Page.

William E. Belvin, ae 21y, farmer, s/o
John & Susan Tillage Belvin; Margaret Dansen,
ae 34y, d/o ___ & Hetty Jenkins Dansen; May
8 1879 by Rev. W. S. Hawkins.

Dr. John C. Wise, ae 30y, surgeon U. S.
Navy, of Accomack Co VA, s/o John C. & Anne
Finney Wise; Agnes T. Brooks, ae 20y, of
Culpepper Co VA, d/o John Lewis & Maria
Louise Ashley Brooks; May 8 1879 by Rev.
Alex Y. Hundley.

Samuel Driver, ae 62y, widower, farmer, col'rd, s/o Wm. & Milly Driver; Tulip Hall, ae 60y, widow, of Mathews Co VA, d/o Bob & Patty Jackspon; May 11 1879 by Rev. Sam'l S. Harden.

Joseph H. Thomas, ae 25y, fisherman, s/o Washington & Eliabeth Thomas; Lucy Davis Hogg, ae 16y, d/o Stephen & Nancy Ann Robins Hogg; May 22 1879 by Rev. W. S. Hawkins.

Cornelius Ward, ae 24y, col'rd, oyster and farm, s/o Jas. & Scilla Ward; Leah Frances Cooke, ae 23y, d/o Rob't & Rachel Cooke; May 29 1879 by Rev. Wm. Thomas.

Aaron Nelson, ae 26y, col'rd, farmer, of Middlesex Co VA, s/o Warner & Peggy Nelson; Roberta Jones, ae 20y, col'rd, d/o Ellen Jones; June 5 1879 by Rev. J. W. Booth.

John Seaman, ae 25y, col'rd, farmer, s/o John & Ann Seaman; Caroline Cooke, ae 21y, col'rd, parents unk; June 8 1879 by Rev. Sam'l S. Harden.

Samuel Wyatt Tinsley, ae 27y, saw mill and Lumber business, of Hanover Co VA, s/o Sam'l H. & Sarah K. Davis Tinsley; Carrie Martin Shackelford, ae 21y, d/o Geo. E. & Martha C. Martin Shackelford; June 11 1879 by Rev. Geo. E. Booker.

Edward Y. Massey, ae 66y 9d, farmer, of King and Queen Co VA, s/o Peyton & Almira Drummond Massey; Mary Eliza Wolfe, ae 45y, widow, d/o Jas. & Nancy Chapman Dutton; June 12 1879 by Rev. Geo. E. Booker.

George Washington Mahoney, ae 21y, farm, of Portsmouth VA, s/o Jesse & Lucy Hogg Mahoney; Sarah Elizabeth Coleman, ae 24y, d/o Davy & Ann Minor Coleman; June 17 1879 by Rev. Wm. E. Wiatt.

Henry J. Coleman, ae 24y, farmer, s/o Davy & Ann Minor Coleman; Georgia Alexander, ae 22y, of King and Queen Co VA, d/o Wm. & Mary Thompson Alexander; June 17 1879 by Rev. Wm. E. Wiatt.

Armistead W. Green, ae 22y, col'rd, oysterman, of King and Queen Co VA, s/o Armistead W. & Matilda Ann Green; Lucy V. Foster, ae 16, col'rd, d/o Harry & Dolly; June 19 1879 by Rev. C. A. Green.

Lee Harris, ae 19y, col'rd, farmer, s/o
John Perrin & Lilly Harris; Mary Lee Lane,
ae 21y, col'rd, of Mathews Co VA, d/o Mary
Lane; June 19 1879 by Rev. Z. T. Whiting.

Thomas C. Douglas, ae 26y, farmer, s/o
John L. & Anna L. Rilee Douglas; Georgianna
Lamberth, ae 25y, d/o A. C. & Sarah Lyall
Lamberth; June 22 1879 by Rev. Geo. E.
Booker.

James Robins, ae 24y, farmer, s/o John &
Caroline Howard Robins; Alex Robins, ae 22y,
d/o Wm. & Lizzie Badger Robins; June 26 1879
by Rev. W. S. Hawkins.

Robert Belvin, ae 24y, farmer, s/o Jas. &
Rebecca Heywood Belvin; Mary Jane Heywood,
ae 22y, d/o Levi & Jane Diggs Heywood; June
26 1879 by Rev. W. S. Hawkins.

James Edward Sheppard, ae 21y, farmer,
s/o John & Elizabeth Griffin Sheppard; Indianna Lewis, ae 19y, d/o John T. & Mary Howlett Lewis; July 5 1879 by Rev. Geo. E.
Booker.

Samuel Turner, ae 22y, col'rd, farmer,
s/o Jas. & Mary Susan Turner; Tamer Harrod,
ae 18y, col'rd, d/o John & Lydia Harrod;
July 17 1879 by Rev. Sam'l S. Harden.

William Andrew Lee, ae 23y, farmer, of
Hartford Co MD, s/o Andrew & Elizabeth Jones
Lee; Mary Ann Brown, ae 18y, d/o Jas. H. &
Elizabeth Kinningham Brown; July 27 1879 by
Rev. Wm. E. Wiatt.

John Belvin, ae 22y, oysterman, s/o Jas.
& Rebecca Heywood Belvin; Margaret Jenkins,
ae 21y, d/o Machen & Dicey Jenkins; July 30
1879 by Rev. W. S. Hawkins.

Coleman Heywood, ae 26y, fisherman, s/o
Wm. & Eliza Deal Heywood; Ellen Hogg, ae
22y, d/o Thos. & Betsy Hogg; July 31 1879 by
Rev. W. S. Hawkins.

Lemuel Driver, ae 50y, col'rd, farmer,
s/o Sam & Sally Driver; Frances Easter, ae
23y, col'rd, d/o Frances Easter; Aug 6 1879
by Rev. John Wm. Booth.

Thomas West, ae 21y, farmer, s/o Christopher & Winey Smith West; Lizzie Smith, ae
27y, d/o Mike & Eliza Smith; Aug 7 1879 by
Rev. W. S. Hawkins.

Jack Scott, ae 22y, col'rd, farm and oyster, s/o Jack & Eliza Scott; Ellen Wyatt, ae 18y, col'rd, d/o John & Louisa Wyatt; Aug 10 1879 by Rev. E. W. Page.

Lewis Brown, ae 22y, col'rd, teamster, s/o Wm. & Amanda Brown; Hester Phillips, ae 21y, col'rd, d/o John & Lucy Ann Phillips; Sept 6 1879 by Rev. E. W. Page.

John Risby, ae 50y, col'rd, farmer, of Fredericksburg VA, s/o John & Katy Risby; Mary Burwell, ae 30y, widow, col'rd, d/o Chas. & Martha Spurlock; Sept 7 1879 by Rev. E. W. Page.

James Braxton, ae 23y, sailor, of King William Co VA, s/o Sam'l & Mary Ann Braxton; Rachel Smith, ae 26y, col'rd, d/o Emanuel & Caroline Smith; Sept 21 1879 by Rev. W. S. Hawkins.

William V. Holmes, ae 25y, col'rd, farm, s/o Walker & Judy Holmes; Amy Harwood, ae 19y, d/o Wm. & Arena Harwood; Sept 28 1879 by Rev. J. W. Booth.

William Robinson, ae 28y, col'rd, water-man, s/o Lewis & Nancy Robinson; Willie Ann Freeman, ae 29y, col'rd, of King and Queen Co VA, d/o Mack & Margaret Freeman; Oct 2 1879 by Rev. Geo. E. Booker.

Marcellus West, ae 21y, oysterman, s/o Frank & Fanny Smith West; Missouri Jarvis, ae 21y, of Mathews Co VA, d/o Wm. M. & Rach-el Hudgin Jarvis; Oct 2 1879 by Rev. W. S. Hawkins.

Lewis Lemon, col'rd, widower, farmer, s/o Reuben & Lena Lemon; Lavinia Gardner, col'rd, widow. d/o Geo. & Peggy Carter; Oct 9 1879 by Rev. Geo. E. Booker.

Henry Roane, ae 23y, col'rd, farmer, s/o Margaret; Nancy Driver, ae 21y, col'rd. d/o Sam & Nancy Driver; Oct 19 1879 by Rev. John Wm. Booth.

Albert Gardner, ae 24y, col'rd, farmer, s/o Albert & Aggy Gardner; Jenny Laws, ae 23y, col'rd, d/o Patsy; Oct 12 1879 by Rev. Sam'l S. HArden.

Miles Cary, ae 32y, col'rd, widower, oys-terman, s/o Miles & Polly Cary; Rachel Mont-ague, ae 24y, col'rd, d/o Soloman & Sarah Montague; Oct 19 1879 by Rev. E. W. Page.

James Cooke, ae 20y, col'rd, farmer, s/o
Augustine & Mary; Mary E. Booth, ae 20y,
col'rd, d/o Lucy Booth; Oct 23 1879 by Rev.
John Wm. Booth.

William Whittaker, ae 22y, col'rd, of
King and Queen Co VA, oysterman, s/o Jas. &
Lucy Whittaker; Dianna Kellis, ae 22y,
col'rd, of York Co VA, d/o Dianna Kellis;
Oct 30 1879 by Rev. W. S. Hawkins.

Julius Maloney Cooke, ae 21y, col'rd,
farmer, s/o Julius & Becky Cooke; Mary F.
Lewis, ae 20y, col'rd, d/o Matt & Susan
Lewis; Nov 3 1879 by Rev. John W. Booth.

John Hill, ae 29y, col'rd, farmer, of
Havre de Grace MD, Eastern Shore MD, s/o Wm.
& Adaline Hill; Betsy Taylor, ae 30y, widow,
d/o Wm. & Milly Payne; Nov 3 1879 by Rev. E.
W. Page.

John W. Hall, ae 27y, merchant, s/o John
F. & Elizabeth C. Spaulding Hall; Annie T.
Clements, ae 18y, d/o E. T. & E. V. Harwood
Clements; Nov 13 1879 by Rev. Nov 13 1879 by
Rev. Wm. E. Wiatt.

Charles Taylor, ae 25y, col'rd hand at
saw mill, of Middlesex Co VA, s/o Martha
Martha Ellis; Mary Fisher, ae 23y, col'rd,
of Middlesex Co VA, d/o Cordelia Smith; Nov
13 1879 by Rev. John W. Booth.

Soloman Foxwell, ae 40y, widower, oyster,
s/o Soloman & Nancy Foxwell; Frances Hutch-
erson, ae 28y, widow, d/o Alex & Mary Gibson;
Nov 16 1879 by Rev. Wm. E. Waitt.

Franklin R. Gwynn, ae 22y, farmer, s/o
Rob't H. & Bettie Booker Gwynn; Helen L.
Acra, ae 22y, d/o Wm. J. & Julia E. Booker
Acra; Nov 20 1879 by Rev. Wm. E. Wiatt.

Gilbert Foster, ae 21y, col'rd, oyster,
s/o Dolly Foster; Delphia Ransone, ae 18y,
col'rd, d/o Sam & Delphia Ransone; Nov 20
1879 by Rev. W. S. Hawkins.

Lewis Ruffins, ae 70y, widower, farmer,
of Essex Co VA, s/o Ruffin & Rose Ruffins;
Nelly Taylor, ae 30y, col'rd, Parents unk;
Nov 23 1879 by Rev. John W. Booth.

Simon Wright, ae 23y, col'rd, sailor, s/o
Stephen & Susan Wright; Nannie Johnston, ae
20y, d/o Rich'rd & Sally Johnston; Nov 30
1879 by Rev. E. W. Page.

James Gregory, ae 29y, col'rd, farmer, of
Richmond City VA, s/o John & Milly Gregory;
Areana Dennis; ae 25y, col'rd, d/o Areana
Gracy Dennis; Nov 30 1879 by Rev. Sam'l S.
Harden.

Thomas Williams, ae 22y, oysterman, s/o
Thos. & Lizzie Dunn Williams; Caroline Jen-
kins, ae 17y, d/o Geo. W. & Susan Howard
Jenkins; Dec 16 1879 by Rev. W. S. Hawkins.

Charles Dudley, ae 23y, oyster, s/o Thos.
& Susan Foxwell Dudley; Virginia Lemons, ae
17y, d/o Wm. & Elizabeth Pointer Lemons; Dec
17 1879 by Rev. Wm. E. Wiatt.

Stephen Fleming, ae 22y, col'rd, waterman,
s/o Harry & Nancy Fleming; Caroline Smith,
ae 21y, col/rd, d/o Emanuel & Caroline Smith;
Dec 18 1879 by Rev. Wm. Thomas.

Allen Hogg, ae 25y, widower, fisherman,
s/o Warner & Susan West Hogg; Matilda Hogg,
ae 25y, d/o Jas. & Nancy Belvin Hogg; Nov 30
1879 by Rev. W. S. Hawkins.

Robert B. Johnston, ae 25y, merchant, of
Middlesex Co Va, s/o John L. & Louisa Bland
Johnston; Verna L. Shackelford, ae 18y, d/o
Franklin & Parke F. Clements Shackelford; Dec
25 1879 by Rev. Geo. E. Booker.

Smiley Oliver, ae 21y, sailor, s/o Ryland
& Fanny Seawell Oliver; Louisa Goalder, ae
21y, of Warwick Co VA, d/o Sam'l & Jenny
Goalder; Dec 25 1879 by Rev. Wm. E. Wiatt.

Levi Hogg, ae 22y, fishing, s/o Thos. &
Betsy Hogg; Levifer Jane Jenkins, ae 21y,
d/o Jinks & Jane Jenkins; Dec 25 1879 by Rev.
W. S. Hawkins.

Addison Cooke, ae 44y, col'rd, farmer,
s/o Billy & Judy Cooke; Silvy Scott, ae 43y,
col'rd, d/o Godfrey & Molly Lewis; Dec 30
1879 by Rev. Geo. E. Booker.

Fielding Patterson, ae 23y, waterman,
col'rd, Chas. & Charlotte Patterson; Frances
Frayger, ae 20y, col'rd, d/o Julius & Patsy
Frayger; Dec 24 1879 by Rev. Sam'l S. Harden.

Gibson C. Bright, ae 28y, col'rd, bricklayer, s/o Sally Bright; Mary Susan Drummond,
ae 18y, col'rd, d/o Braxton & Sarah F. Drummond; Dec 25 1879 by Rev. John Wm. Booth.

Cary Washington, ae 24y, col'rd, farmer, s/o Geo. & Susan Washington; Cora Ann Hall, ae 19y, col'rd, d/o John & Martha Ann Hall; Dec 28 1879 by Rev. John Wm. Booth.

John Rich'rd Walker, ae 44y, widower, farmer, s/o Wm. & Nancy White Walker; Elizabeth Howlett, ae 44y, widow, of Middlesex Co VA, d/o Robert & Sarah Walden; Dec 30 1879 by Rev. Wm. E. Wiatt.

Robert Jones, ae 24y, col'rd, woodcutter, of New Kent Co VA, s/o Peyton & Judy Jones; Sarah Washington, ae 19y, col'rd, d/o Henry & Dinah Washington; Dec 30 1879 by Rev. John Wm. Booth.

Henry Smith, ae 21y, col'rd, farmer, s/o Bob & Courtney Smith; Caroline Taylor, ae 24y, col'rd, d/o Paul & Betsy Tay;or; Jan 1 1880 by Rev. E. W. Page.

William Scott, ae 21y, col'rd, laborer, s/o Jane Thornton; Lucy Frances Ross, ae 21y, col'rd, d/o Peter & Frances Ross; Jan 3 1880 by Rev. John Wm. Booth.

William H. Smith, ae 30y, col'rd, farmer, s/o Emanuel & Caroline Smith; Sarah Jones, ae 21y, col'rd, d/o Armistead & Hannah Jones; Jan 4 1880 by Rev. Wm. Thomas.

George Gregory, ae 23y, col'rd, farmer, s/o Geo. & Rainny Gregory; Margaret Moody, ae 21y, col'rd, d/o Phill & Nancy Moody; Jan 15 1880 by Rev. E. W. Page.

John T. Williams, ae 27y, merchant, s/o Edw'rd & Martha Brown Williams; Annis E. Haywood, ae 21y, d/o Wm. & Eliza Deal Haywood; Jan 15 1880 by Rev. W. S. Hawkins.

Zacharius Rowe, ae 23y, farmer, s/o Leroy & Julia Ann West Rowe; Mary Louisa Padgett, ae 23y, widow, d/o Wm. & Dolly Marchant Drisgall; Jan 18 1880 by Rev. W. S. Hawkins.

Charles Mathew Graves, ae 23y, farmer, s/o Jas. C. & Susan Davis Graves; Laura Virginia Bryan, ae 19y, of Queen Ann's Co MD, d/o Rich'rd H. & Catharine Birch Bryan; Jan 22 1880 by Rev. Wm. E. Wiatt.

Stephen D. Hogg, ae 20y, oysterman, s/o John R. & Sarah Foxwell Hogg; Mary R. Oliver, ae 18y, d/o Ryland & Fanny Seawell Oliver; Jan 22 1880 by Rev. Wm. E. Wiatt.

Robert Franklin West, ae 23y, oysterman, s/o Rob'rt & Sally Ann West; Indianna Haywood, ae 21y, of Warwick Co VA, d/o Rob't & Mary Ann Shackelford Haywood; Jan 25 1880 by Rev. W. S. Hawkins.

Joseph Willis, ae 27y, col'rd, working in timber, of Somerset Co MD, s/o Frank & Lucy Willis; Mary Mack, ae 21y, col'rd, d/o Alice Smith; Jan 27 1880 by Rev. Sam'l S. Harden.

William C. Trevillian, ae 36y, widower, farmer, s/o Augustine S. & Emily Mitchell Trevillian; Mary E. Bristow, ae 19y, d/o Wm. & Frances Pearce Bristow; Jan 28 1880 by Rev. Geo. E. Booker.

Joseph Washington, ae 26y, col'rd, farm, s/o Geo. & Susan Washington; Rosetta Washington, ae 18y, col'rd, of King and Queen Co VA, d/o Henry & Dianna Washington; Jan 28 1880 by Rev. John W. Booth.

Christopher West, ae 30y, widower, farm, s/o Christopher & Fanny Brown West; Susan West, ae 25y, d/o Jas. & Nancy Heywood West; Feb 3 1880 by Rev. W. S. Hawkins.

William H. Cary, ae 24y, col'rd, oyster, s/o Miles & Polly Cary; Pedora Pane, ae 21y, col'rd, d/o Wm. & Carolina Pedora; Feb 5 1880 by Rev. E. W. Page.

Beverly F. Groom, ae 27y, farmer, of King and Queen Co VA, s/o Beverly & Sarah South Groom; Alice Bew, ae 17y, of King and Queen Co VA, d/o John Henry & Mary J. Carlton Bew; Feb 18 1880 by Rev. M. S. Collona.

John William Belvin, ae 30y, fish & oyster, s/o John & Harriet Haywood Belvin; Sarah Missouri Brown, ae 16y, d/o John & Elizabeth Howard Brown; Feb 19 1880 by Rev. W. S. Hawkins.

Alonza West, ae 22y, oyster, s/o John & Sarah A. Robins West; Mary Catharine Williams, ae 21y, d/o Edw'rd & Martha A. Brown Williams; Feb 19, 1880 by Rev. Geo. E. Booker.

Emanuel Lockley, ae 27y, col'rd, oyster, s/o Rob't Wilson & Fanny Lockley; Ida Belle Booth, ae 25y, col'rd, d/o Ransone Evans & Lucy Booth; Feb 22 1880 by Rev. John Wm. Booth.

John Hern, ae 30y, col'rd, farmer, s/o
John & Susan Hern; Scinthy Thornton, ae 21y,
col'rd, d/o John & Milly Thornton; Feb 21
1880 by Rev. Sam'l S. Harden.

Walter C. Hogg, ae 20y, fisherman, s/o
Stephen & Nancy Robins Hogg; Sarah E. Shack-
elford, ae 22y, d/o Wm. & Mary Ann Thomas
Shackelford; Feb 24 1880 by Rev. W. S.
Hawkins.

Thomas Billups, ae 21y, col'rd, farmer,
s/o Thos. & Milly Billups; Mary Eliza Lee,
ae 21y, col'rd, d/o Lucy Briggerson; Feb 28
1880 by Rev. Sam'l S. Harden.

John Wm. Dixon, ae 21y, col'd, oysterman,
s/o Wm. & Betsy Dixon; Gabrielle Collins, ae
21y, col'rd, d/o John & Fanny Collins; Feb
29 1880 by Rev. Z. T. Whiting.

Andrew C. Robinson, ae 34y, widower,
house carpenter, of Middlesex Co VA, s/o
John H. & Sarah Ann Long Robinson; Rosa A.
Hibble, ae 22y, d/o Chas. W. & Mary M.
Hibble; Mar 10 1880 by Rev. Wm. E. Wiatt.

Lewis Bentley, ae 21y, col'rd, laborer,
s/i Dan'l & Isabella Bentley; Harriet Jones,
ae 20y, col'rd, d/o Wm. & Mary Jones; Mar 30
1880 by Rev. Wm. E. Wiatt.

John Hayes, ae 23y, col'rd, of Mathews Co
VA, sailor, s/o Robert & Betsy Hayes; Cuetta
Gardner, ae 21y, col'rd, d/o Wm. & Harriet
Gardner; Apr 4 1880 by Rev. Sam'l S. Harden.

George Howard, ae 25y, col'rd, laborer,
s/o Minoy & Eliza; Mary Eliza Hudgin, ae 22y,
col'rd, parents unk; Apr 5 1880 by Rev. John
Wm. Booth.

James Reed, ae 21y, col'rd, farmer, s/o
Henry & Susan Reed; Nancy Jackson, ae 15y,
col'rd, d/o John & Cordelia Jackson; Apr 6
1880 by Rev. R. Berkley.

Davy Robinson, ae 25y, col'rd, farmer,
s/o Davy & Betty Robinson; Frances Pryor, ae
21y, col'rd, d/o Dick & Fanny Pryor; Apr 8
1880 by Rev. R. Berkley.

Thomas Baytop, ae 70y, widower, col'rd,
hamper maker, s/o Frank & Liddy ; Hester
Berry, ae 40y, widow, d/o Rob'rt & Lucy
Booker; Apr 15 1880 by Rev. John W. Booth.

James Green, ae 23y, col'rd, oyster, s/o
John & Maria Green; Mary Almand, ae 18y,
col'rd, d/o Judy Ann Almand; Apt 9 1880 by
Rev. E. W. Page.

James T. Gray, ae 34y, widower, farm, of
Somerset Co MD, s/o Major Johnson Gray &
Margaret E. Furman; Louisa V. Pratt, ae 17y,
of MD, d/o Benj. & Elizabeth A. Pratt; Apr
11 1880 by Rev. Geo. E. Booker.

Robert Dillard, ae 21y, col'rd, steam
boat hand, of Lunchburg VA, s/o Wm. & Louisa
Dillard; Mary Rilee, ae 18y, col'rd, d/o Wm.
& Lucy Rilee; Apr 8 1880 by E. W. Page.

John Lewis Johnston, ae 57y, widower,
farm, s/o Godfrey & Molly Johnston; Polly
Dixon, ae 24y, col'rd, d/o Rich'd Evans &
Ailsy; Apr 15 1880 by Rev. Sam'l S. Harden.

Peter Daniel, ae 39y, widower, farm, s/o
John & Betsy White; Catharine Rowe, ae 26y,
d/o Leroy & Julia Ann West Rowe; Apr 20 1880
by Rev. W. S. Hawkins.

William T. Burke, ae 46y, widower, farm,
s/o Jeremiah & Sarah Blasingame Burke; Ann
Howlett, ae 30y, d/o Isaac & Ann Kemp Howlett; Apr 21 1880 by Rev. Wm. E. Wiatt.

Cecil Wray Sinclair, ae 23y, farm, of
Elizabeth City Co VA, s/o Fayette & M. E.
Allen Sinclair; Margaret B. Sinclair, ae 22y,
d/o Robert M. & M. Roena Baytop Sinclair;
Apr 27 1880 by Rev. Alex Y. Hundley.

William Bonnywell, ae 22y, waterman, s/o
Burwell & ___ Sparrow Bonnywell; Nannie
Brown, ae 19y, d/o Geo. & Nancy West Brown;
Apr 29 1880 by Rev. W. S. Hawkins.

Edward Jackson, ae 24y, col'rd, farm, s/o
Martha Jackson, Lucy Jane Hill, ae 16y,
col'rd, d/o Geo. & Georgianna Hill; May 13
1880 by Rev. Geo. E. Booker.

Coleman Thomas, ae 25y, fisherman, s/o
Jas. & Martha Smith Thomas; Maria F. Temple-
man, ae 18y, d/o Jackson & Maria F. Minor
Templeman; May 13 1880 by Rev. W. S. Hawkins.

Lewis C. Hall, ae 20y, farm, s/o Lewis O.
& Martha Enos Hall; Ella Minor, ae 19y, d/o
Wm. T. & Fanny Enos Minor; May 16 1880 by
Rev. W. S. Hawkins.

Jackson Seawell, ae 21y, col'rd, laborer, parents unk; Tishie Ann Foster, ae 18y, col'rd, d/o Dolly Foster; May 16 1880 by Rev. Wm. Thomas.

John H. Miller, ae 59y, widower, carpenter, s/o Jas. & Rosa Hunley Miller; Mary I. Cooke, ae 50y, widow, of Mathews Co VA, ˑˑˑ parents unk; May 16 1880 by Rev. R. A. Fox.

Major Hughes, Jr, ae 20y, col'rd, farmer, s/o Major Hughes; Fanny Ellen Johnston, ae 18y, col'rd, d/o John & Leziah Johnston; May 16 1880 by Rev. Sam'l S. Harden.

Charles E. Dutton, ae 31y, farm, s/o Edward C. & Rebecca Chapman Dutton; Mary Alice Forrest, ae 18y, of Mathews Co VA, d/o Jos. P. & Julia Forrest; May 16 1880 by Rev. Geo. E. Booker.

George Jackson, ae 21y, col'rd, oyster, s/o Phill & Judy; Jane Lee, ae 20y, col'rd, d/o Elijah & Eliza; May 20 1880 by Rev. Z. T. Whiting.

Albert Whiting, ae 22y, col'rd, oyster, s/o Wm. & Hester Hobday; Mary Pane, ae 21y, col'rd, d/o Robert & Jeannetta Pane; May 20 1880 by Rev. Z. T. Whiting.

George Stubbs, ae 22y, col'rd, farm, s/o Lorenzo & Polly Stubbs; Mary Tabb, ae 19y, col'rd, d/o Maria Griffin; May 27 1880 by Rev. Z. T. Whiting.

Luke Burwell, ae 23y, col'rd, oyster, s/o Edmund & Sally Ann Burwell; Paulina Allmand, ae 28y, col'rd, d/o Sam & Minerva Allmand; June 3 1880 by Rev. W. S. Hawkins.

William L. Johnston, ae 25y, mariner, s/o John R. & Catharine Graves Johnston; Sarah C. Robins, ae 17y, d/o Jas. R. & Ann Rowe Robins; June 8 1880 by Rev. Geo. E. Booker.

Thomas Pressy, ae 25y, col'rd, sailor, of York Co VA, s/o Philip & Frances Pressy; Fanny Curtis, ae 20y, d/o Rob't & Jane Franus; June 7 1880 by Rev. Sam'l S. Harden.

Benjamin F. Oliver, ae 35y, widower, oysterman, s/o Garett & D. Mildred Brown Oliver; Elvira D. Riley, ae 19y, d/o John M. & Caroline Foster Riley; June 13 1880 by Rev. Wm. E. Wiatt.

Thomas A. J. Oliver, ae 46y, farmer, s/o
Morgan D. & D. Mildred Brown Oliver; Elizabeth L. Tiley, ae 17y, d/o John M. & Caroline V. Foster Riley; June 13 1880 by Rev.
Wm. E. Wiatt.

John Lemon Jr, ae 22y, col'rd, sailor, s/o
John & Sally Lemon; Harriet Shorter, ae 19y,
d/o Wm. & Mary Ellen Shorter; June 19 1880
by Rev. Sam'l S. Harden.

William Curdley, ae 23y, col'rd, waterman, s/o Winchester & Nancy Curdley; Margaret Smith, ae 21y, col'rd, d/o Sye & Mary
Smith; June 19 1880 by Rev. E. W. Page.

Frank Shackelford, ae 23y, col'rd, farm,
s/o Isaac & Betsy Shackelford; Adelaide Davenport, ae 22y, col'rd, of King and Queen Co
VA, d/o Peter & Patsy; June 27 1880 by Rev.
J. B. Whiting.

Nathaniel B. Leigh, ae 25y, farm, lived
Mathews Co VA, s/o Wm. P. R. & Fanny Stubblefield Leigh; Roberta E. Rayfield, ae 26y,
widow, d/o Philip Mason & Amanda Bland; July
6 1880 by Rev. Geo. E. Booker.

David Miles, ae 39y, widower, col'rd, of
King and Queen Co VA, lived Gloucester Co
VA, s/o Sylvanus & Rebecca Miles; Mary Jane
Tabb, ae 26y, col'rd, d/o Mary Tabb; July 8
1880 by Rev. E. W. Page.

John Burwell, ae 42y, widower, col'rd,
waterman, s/o Phill & Sally Burwell; Rachel
Fox, ae 21y, col'rd, d/o Jas. & Sarah Fox;
July 24 1880 by Rev. Sam'l S. Harden.

Henry Hunley, ae 25y, col'rd, farmer, s/o
Frederick & Chrissy Hunley; Mary Eliza Lewis,
ae 18y, col'rd, d/o Ben & Abby Lewis; July
29 1880 by Rev. Sam'l S. Harden.

Joel Thomas, ae 49y, fisherman, s/o Jesse
& Nancy Williams Thomas; Frances Ann Williams, ae 25y, d/o Wm. & Malvina Hobday Williams; Aug 8 1880 by Rev. Geo. E. Booker.

Philip M. Sours, ae 37y, of Jersey City
N. J, s/o Peter & Mary M. M. Sours; Alice A.
Coates, ae 21y, d/o Cornelius & Averilla
Horseley Coats; Aug 12 1880 by Rev. Wm. E.
Wiatt.

Joel A. H. Dobson, ae 28y, sailor, s/o
Wm. & Margaret M. Hayes Dobson; Mary Etta
Wolthall, ae 24y, widow, of Williamsburg VA,
d/o Ryland & Mary Tillage Davis; Aug 25 1880
by Rev. W. S. Hawkins.

Lemuel J. Carmines, ae 23y, oyster, s/o
Dan'l L. & Susan F. Dunn Carmines; Mary P.
White, ae 17y, d/o John H. & Elizabeth Oli-
ver White; Aug 29 1880 by Rev. W. S. Hawkins.

John Hubbard, ae 21y, col'rd, farm, s/o
Billy & Nancy Hubbard; Amanda Smith, ae 21y,
col'rd, d/o Phill & Betty Smith; Aug 29 1880
by Rev. John Wm. Booth.

Jacob Warden, ae 26y, widower, col'rd,
farm, of Williamsburg VA, s/o Jacob & Fanny
Warden; Easter Williams, ae 21y, col'rd, d/o
Dan'l & Susan Williams; Sept 2 1880 by Rev.
Z. T. Whiting.

Robert Bonnywell, ae 23y, oyster, s/o
Burwell & Emily Sparrow Bonnywell; Alice
Quillins, ae 23y, of Portsmouth VA, d/o
Thos. & Milly Quillins; Sept 5 1880 by Rev.
W. S. Hawkins.

Wallace Braxton, ae 26y, col'rd, laborer,
s/o Nancy Braxton; Eliza Ellen Perrin, ae
22y, col'rd, d/o Edy Gordon; Sept 12 1880 by
Rev. Sam'l S. Harden.

James Lawrence white, ae 26y, farm, s/o
John Henry & Virginia M. Gressitt White;
Susan M. Purcell, ae 22y, d/o John & Susan
Brown Purcell; Sept 19 1880 by Rev. S. G.
Thrift.

Benjamin F. Howlett, ae 20y, farm, s/o
Benj. F. & Virginia Kemp Howlett; Nannie
Howlett, ae 18y, d/o Thos. J. & Maria White
Howlett; Sept 19 1880 by Rev. S. G. Thrift.

Martin Smith, ae 23y, oyster, s/o Taylor
& Jenny West Smith; Mary Jane Smith, ae 27y,
d/o Anthony & Charlotte West Smith; Sept 29
1880 by Rev. W. S. Hawkins.

Richard F. Blake, ae 28y, farmer, of Mid-
dlesex Co VA, s/o John L. & Margaret L.
Blake; Martha B. Glenn, ae 40y, d/o Mathew &
Bettie Glenn; Oct 17 1880 by Rev. M. S.
Colonna.

Charles Lewis Jones, ae 22y, col'rd, sailor, s/o Chas. & Sally Jones; Jennie Burwell, ae 24y, col'rd, d/o Wm. & Amy Burwell; Oct 10 1880 by Rev. Sam'l S. Harden.

Alfred B. Davis, ae 34y, teacher and attorney at law, s/o A. B. & Maria Pryor Davis; Lena Huntington Fitzhugh, ae 20y, d/o P. H. & Mary S. Christian Fitzhugh; Oct 13 1880 by Rev. Wm. E. Wiatt.

William Burwell, ae 45y, col'rd, farmer, s/o Lucy; Nancy Jones, ae 21y, col'rd, d/o Armistead & Hannah Jones; Oct 18 1880 by Rev. Wm. Thomas.

Charles Cooke, ae 22y, col'rd, oyster, s/o Chas. & Rachel Cooke; Emma Carter, ae 22y, col'rd, d/o Edward & Harriet Carter; Oct 9 1880 by Rev. W. S. Hawkins.

Granville S. Healy, ae 28y, widower, of Middlesex Co VA, farmer, s/o Rob't & Betty Boyd Healy; Mary A. Taliaferro, ae 23y, d/o Thos. B. & Mary M. Sinclair Taliaferro; Oct 21 1880 by Rev. Alex Y. Hundley.

Charles Henry Jones, ae 27y, col'rd, oysterman, s/o Bob & Rosetta Jones; Maria Bluford, ae 19y, col'rd, d/o Cary & Nancy Bluford; Oct 21 1880 by Rev. John Wm. Booth.

John Whiting, ae 26y, col'rd, oysterman, s/o Lewis & Betsy Whiting; Mary Catharine Brooks, ae 18y, col'rd, d/o Joseph & Ann Brooks; Oct 21 1880 by Rev. E.W. Page.

Frank Roane, ae 22y, col'rd, farmer, s/o Rachel Roane, of King and Queen Co VA, Margaret Hundley, ae 18y, of King and Queen Co VA, d/o Walker & Maria; Oct 23 1880 by Rev. John Wm. Booth.

Guy Brooks, ae 22y, col'rd, oysterman, s/o Joseph & Lilly Brooks; Sarah Whiting, ae 18y, col'rd, d/o Lewis & Betty Whiting; Nov 4 1880 by Rev. Z. T. Whiting.

George Thornton, ae 27y, widower, col'rd, oysterman, s/o Frank & Peggy Thornton; Isabella Jackson, ae 17, col'rd, d/o Sam & Betsy Jackson; Nov 4 1880 by Rev. Z. T. Whiting.

Joseph Jordan, ae 23y, oysterman, s/o Wm. & Maria J. Oliver Jordan; Mary Susan Belvin, ae 21y, d/o John & Susan Tillage Belvin; Nov 18 1880 by Rev. W. S. Hawkins.

Charles T. Jenkins, ae 27y, bookkeeper,
of Baltimore City MD, s/o Geo. Taylor &
Elizabeth Barroll Taylor; Emily M. Dimmock,
ae 20y, of Baltimore City MD, d/o Chas. H. &
Emily Moale Dimmock; Nov 17 1880 by Rev.
Alex Y. Hundley.

George W. Shackelford, ae 23y, boatsman,
s/o Geo. W. & Elizabeth Birch Shackelford;
Frances Ann Thomas, ae 20y, d/o Joel & Indianna Rowe Thomas; Nov 21 1880 by Rev. W.
S. Hawkins.

Ben Hall, ae 30y, col'rd, farm, s/o Ben
Hall & Fanny Scott; Synthia Bright, ae 22y,
col'rd, d/o Sam & Nancy Bright; Nov 24 1880
by Rev. Sam'l S. Harden.

Frank Paine, ae 24y, col'rd, oyster, s/o
Wm. & Caroline Paine; Mary Eliza Hall, ae
17y, col'rd, d/o John & Eliza Hall; Nov 26
1880 by Rev. Z. T. Whiting.

Coleman Fields, ae 23y, col'rd, oyster,
s/o Lucy Fields; Lucy Yates, ae 18y, col'rd,
d/o Gabriel & Victoria; Nov 29 1880 by Rev.
Sam'l S. Harden.

Robert M. Sinclair, ae 31y, merchant, of
Elizabeth City Co VA, s/o John & Mary C.
Thurston Sinclair; Cora A. Banks, ae 21y,
d/o Thos. W. & Eugenia Baytop Banks; Dec 1
1880 by Rev. Alex Y. Hundley.

Richard J. Horseley, ae 19y, farm, s/o
Allen H. & Elizabeth Horseley; Dora E. Walk-
er, ae 21y, d/o Elijah & Pinky Thrift Walker;
Dec 1 1880 by Rev. Geo. E. Booker.

William Brown, ae 26y, fish & Farm, s/o
Rob't & Mary Smith Brown; Mildred Jenkins,
ae 26y, d/o Wm. & Milly Green; Dec 5 1880 by
Rev. W. S. Hawkins.

Wm. F. Midget, ae 22y, col'rd, oyster, of
Portsmouth VA, s/o Lewis & Elizabeth Midget;
Sarah E. Jones, ae 21y, col'rd, d/o Adaline;
Dec 5 1880 by Rev. John Wm. Booth.

Joseph B. Cluverius, ae 25y, farm, s/o
Jas. W. & Mary Hobday Cluverius; Maria H.
Thrift, ae 25y, d/o Benja. P. & Catharine
Cluverius Thrift; Dec 7 1880 by Rev. Geo.
E. Booker.

John Mackey Blue, ae 24y, col'rd, oyst
s/o Tim & Margaret Blue; Lucy Ann Hawkins
ae 21y, col'rd, d/o Thos. & Mary Hawkins;
Dec 11 1880 by Rev. R. A. Fox.

Edward Whiting, ae 22y, col'rd, oyster
s/o Frances; Fanny Herns, ae 25y, col'rd,
d/o John & Susan Herns; Dec 12 1880 by Re
Sam'l S. Harden.

Charles Pannell, ae 40y, widower, col'
farmer, of King William Co VA, s.o Edmund
Milly; Jane Smith, ae 40y, col'rd, d/o Da
& Mary Jane; Dec 12 1880 by Rev. Sam'l S.
Harden.

Cary Oliver, ae 25y, oyster, s/o Washi
ton J. H. & Sarah Dunston Oliver; Mary V.
Cruser, ae 21y, d/o Jas. M. & Ann Ellen
White Cruser; Dec 19 1880 by Rev. Wm. E.
Wiatt.

Frederick W. Pitt, ae 22y, merchant, s
Rich'd G. & Maria J. Cluverius Pitt; Anni
Thrift, ae 21y, d/o Benj. P. & Sarah Thri
Dec 22 1880 by Rev. Geo. E. Booker.

Albert L. Pitt, ae 24y, merchant, s/o
Rich'd G. & Maria J. Cluverius Pitt; Sara
F. Minor, ae 21y, d/o John W. & Frances A
Mouring Minor; Dec 22 1880 by Rev. W. S.
Hawkins.

Thomas Lowry Sinclair, ae 26y, farmer,
Elizabeth City Co VA, s/o Jefferson & Mar
F. Lowry Sinclair; Louisa B. Browne, ae 2
d/o Junius B. & Emily Browne (now Roane),
Dec 23 1880 by Rev. Geo. E. Booker.

Daniel Robinson, ae 44y, widower, col'
farmer, s/o Cuffer & Becky Robinson; Mary
Smith, ae 38y, col'rd, widow, of King and
Queen Co VA, d/o Phill & Betsy; Dec 23 18
by Rev. E. W. Page.

James Washington, ae 21y, col'rd, oyst
s/o Harry & Phoeby Washington; Susan (Sar
Curtley, ae 19y, col'rd, d/o Winchester &
Nancy Curtley; Dec 25 1880 by Rev. E. W.
Page.

John Davenport, ae 22y, col'rd, oyster
s/o Geo. & Elmira Davenport; Lizzie King,
21y, col'rd, d/o Rob't & Sar

Thomas Ryland Seawell, ae 21y, farm
Benj. & Mary Oliver Seawell; Emma Miss
Hogg, ae 21y, d/o Wm. & Sarah Fosque H
Dec 26 1880 by Rev. W. S. Hawkins.

Benjamin Branch, ae 26y, col'rd, fa
Northampton Co N. C, s/o Benj. & Marth
Branch; Sarah Ann Cook, ae 18y, col'rd
Jesse & Sarah Cook; Dec 26 1880 by Rev
S. Hawkins.

William Cully, ae 25y, widower, col
sailor, s/o Jack & Joan Cully; Elizabe
Cook, ae 22y, col'rd, d/o Sarah France
Wilson; Dec 26 1880 by Rev. John W. Bo

James T. Davenport, ae 30y, col'rd,
s/o Thos. & Mary Ann Davenport; Eleano
Lockley, ae 22y, col'rd, of King and Q
Co VA, d/o Jas. & Mary Lockley; Dec 26
by Rev. John W. Booth.

Ross W. Cottee, ae 21y, oysterman,
J. & Catharine Adams Cottee; Ursilla W
ae 19y, d/o John W. & Sarah A. Robins
Dec 28 1880 by Rev. Geo. Ed. Booker.

William F. Lewis, ae 24y, farmer, o
hews Co VA, s/o Jas. T. & Columbia Tho
Lewis; Virginia S. German, ae 18y, d/o
Lethia Bridges German; Dec 28 1880 by
R. A. Fox.

John A. Harwood, ae 37y, farm, s/o
& Emma Enos Harwood; Annie E. Lawson,
d/o John W. & E. N. J. Mann Lawson; De
1880 by Rev. Geo. E. Booker.

James Albert Williams, ae 28y, oyst
of Mathews Co VA, s/o Albert & Belina
Williams; Sallie S. Cooke, ae 24y, d/o
cis W. & Catharine Chapman Cooke; Dec
1880 by Rev. Wm. E. Wiatt.

Richard B. Rowe, ae 29y, school tea
s/o John L. & Lucy S. Stevens Rowe; Lu
Stubblefield, ae 24, d/o Simon W. & Lu
Leavitt Stubblefield; Dec 28 1880 by R
Geo. E. Booker.

Madison Richeson, ae 57y, widower,
carpenter, s/o Leonard & Lucy Richeson
Elizabeth Kemp, ae 36y, widow, d/o Pet

Lewis Linebough, ae 22y, col'rd, farm,
s/o John & Lilly Linebough; Margaret Dung
ae 21y, col'rd, d/o Rob't & Mary Jane
Dungee; Dec 28 1880 by Rev. Sam'l S. Hard

William Burwell, ae 25y, col'rd, farm,
s/o Sye & Rachel; Gilly Ann Whiting, ae 1
col'rd, d/o Davy & Georgianna Whiting; De
30 1880 by Rev. J. W. Booth.

George W. Jordan, ae 29y, oyster, s/o
Willoughby & Maria Oliver Jordan; Ellen
Elizabeth Newton, ae 21y, of York Co VA,
Jas. & Catharine E. Holloway Newton; Dec
1880 by Rev. W. S. Hawkins.

John Henry Anderson, ae 21y, col'rd,
waterman, s/o Geo. & Dianna Anderson;
Rebecca Carter, ae 16y, col'rd, d/o Jas.
Eliza Carter; Jan 1 1881 by Rev. Sam'l S.
Harden.

William H. Duerick, ae 28y, oyster, of
Port Jefferson Long Island N. Y, s/o Nels
& Laura Bennett Duerick; Mary Sarah C.
Lewis, ae 16y, d/o Washington & Mary E.
Wallace Lewis; Jan 1 1881 by Rev. W. S.
Hawkins.

Benjamin Carter, ae 23y, col'rd, farm,
s/o Sam & Louisa Carter; Lucy Thornton, ae
22y, col'rd, d/o Frank & Peggy Thornton;
6 1881 by Rev. Z. T. Whiting.

Robert Allen, ae 24y, col'rd, oyster,
Emily Green; Mary Carter, ae 18y, col'rd,
d/o Mary Ann Thornton; Jan 9 1881 by Rev.
T. Whiting.

Silas Chandler, ae 50y, widow, farm, o
York Co VA, s/o Jas. C. & Eliza A. White
Chandler, lived Middlesex Co VA; Mary C.
Gayle, ae 38y, d/o Zelotes & Eliza White
Gayle; Jan 11 1881 by Rev. Geo. E. Booker

James Chapman, ae 24y, col'rd, oyster,
s/o Godfrey & nancy Chapman; Rebecca Cook
ae 24y, widow, d/o Henry & Mary Lemon; Ja
13 1881 by Rev. John Wm. Booth.

Joshua Hill, ae 24y, col'rd, oyster, s
Geo. & Anna Hill; Mary Frances Catlett, ae
21y, col'rd, d/o Chas. & Frances Catlett;

John F. Hatch, ae 25y, farmer, of Ma
Co VA, s/o N. A. & Emily S. Thompson Ha
Susan E. Brown, ae 21y, d/o Smith W. &
E. Garrett Brown; Jan 16 1881 by Rev. R
Fox.

Joseph Billups, ae 28y, col'rd, farm
s/o John & Maria Billups; Blanch Colema
22y, col'rd, of Richmond VA, d/o Mary W
lace; Jan 16 1881 by Elder R. Lattimore

Tabb Harris, ae 22y, col'rd, laborer
Wm. & Mary Cary Harris; Lucy Ann Lomax,
23y, col'rd, d/o John & Susan Lomax; Ja
1881 by Rev. John Wm. Booth.

Simon Patterson, ae 21y, col'rd, oys
s/o Chas. & Charlotte Patterson; Eleano
Whitaker, ae 19y, col'rd, d/o Jas. & Lu
Ann Whitaker; Jan 25 1881 by Rev. W. S.
Hawkins.

John M. Sutton, ae 23y, oyster, of K
and Queen Co VA, s/o R. A. & Rosa B. Fa
holt Sutton; Lou Carrie Carson, ae 21y,
New Kent Co VA, d/o Cornelius & Sarah C
Jan 26 1881 by Rev. W. D. Vaden in Rich
VIRGINIA.

Allen Hogg Jr, ae 22y, oyster, s/o J
Julia Dunston Hogg; Lucy Wilburn, ae 17
Jesse & Mary Davis Wilburn; Jan 27 1881
Rev. W. S. Hawkins.

William Sidney Heath, ae 27y, clerk,
Petersburg VA, s/o Seth & Martha Heath;
Lizzie Weaver, ae 28y, of Lancaster Co
d/o Christian & Rebecca Weaver; Jan 27
by Rev. D. Watson Werin.

Wm. Henry Cook, ae 25y, col'rd, oyst
s/o Frank & Polly Cook; Mary Kelly, ae
col'rd, d/o Uriah & Becky Kelly; Jan 30
by Rev. John William Booth.

Joel H. Thomas, ae 22y, fisherman, s
Joel & Indianna E. Rowe Thomas; Mildred
Shackelford, ae 22y, d/o Wm. & Mary Ann
Thomas Shackelford; Jan 18 1881 by Rev.
S. Hawkins.

Thomas Baytop. ae 26y, col'rd, oyste
s/o Chas. & Hetty Baytop; Nancy Boram.

William Meggs, ae 22y, col'rd, farm, s
Mary Meggs; Charlotte Thomas, ae 21y, col
d/o Alex & Eliza Thomas; Feb 9 1881 by Re
John Wm. Booth.

Robert Cooke, ae 30y, col'rd, oyster,
Fanny Jackson; Annie Cooke, ae 21y, d/o
Becky Dabney; Feb 10 1881 by Rev. John Wm
Booth.

Robert Johnson, ae 26y, col'rd, farm,
Middlesex Co VA, s/o Spencer & Judy; Mary
Harris, ae 34y, col'rd, d/o Wm. H. & Dian
Feb 10 1881 by Rev. John Wm. Booth.

George Jackson, ae 43y, col'rd, widowe
farm, of New Kent Co VA, s/o Billy & Jenn
Jackson; Charlotte Cook, ae 38y, col'rd,
widow, d/o Essex & Nancy Muse; Feb 10 188
by Rev. John Wm. Booth.

James Franklin Duncan, ae 25y, commiss
merchant, of St. Louis MISSOURI, s/o Jas.
Mary F. Franklin Duncan; Lucy Tabb Dabney
ae 26y, d/o Jas. K. & Sarah E. Tabb Dabne
Feb 16 1881 by Rev. Walter H. Robertson,
Licenticete Presbyterian Church.

Charles Henry Black, ae 23y, col'rd, o
Mathews Co VA, s/o Rob't & Jane Black; Su
an Hall, ae 22y, col'rd, d/o John & Martha
Hall; Feb 17 1881 by Rev. John Wm. Booth.

Willis Lewis, ae 23y, col'rd, saw mill
hand, s/oJas. & Franky Lewis; Harriet Sha
elford, ae 22y, d/o Isaac & Betsy Shackelford; Feb 19 1881 by Rev. S. S. Harden.

Alexander Diggs, ae 22y, fishing, s/o
John & Betsy Williams Diggs; Virginia Lee
Templeman, ae 18y, d/o Wm. H. & Mildred R
ins Templeman; Feb 27 1881 by Rev. W. S.
Hawkins.

James Whitaker, ae 23y, col'rd, farmer
s/o Jas. & Lucy Ann Whitaker; Rebecca Gre
ae 21y, col'rd, d/o Chas. & Maria Green;
3 1881 by Rev. R. A. Fox.

Thomas Cully, ae 23y, col'rd, oyster, a
Jack & Joan Cully; Maria Stubbs, ae 20y,
col'rd, d/o Adam & Catharine Stubbs; Mar
1881 by Rev. Geo. E. Booker.

Book 1: 1880's

Leroy Edwards, ae 21y, farm, s/o Dur
Lucy Ann Cauthorn Edwards; Frances Ann
Ware, ae 21y of King & Queen Co Va, d/c
& Catharine Walden Ware; Mar 8 1881 by
Geo. E. Booker.

Samuel Bird, ae 24y, col'rd, laborer
David Bird; Mary E. Smith, ae 17y, col'
d/o Hester Ann Segar; Mar 19 1881 by Re
John Wm. Booth.

Madison F. Howlett, ae 40y, clerk in
store, s/o Nicholas & Sarah Mason Howle
Martha E. Croswell, ae 20y, d/o Rich'd
Annie T. Seawell Croswell; Mar 13 1881
Rev. W. S. Hawkins.

George Roberson, ae 22y, col'rd, far
Norfolk Co VA, s/o Wilson & Malvina Rob
Ellen Lewis, ae 23y, col'rd, d/o John &
Lewis; Mar 24 1881 by Rev. W. S. Hawkin

William H. Harris, ae 58y, col'd, wi
ditcher, s/o Johnson & Easter Harris; S
Thornton, ae 27y, col'rd, d/o Paul & Ke
Thornton; Mar 26 1881 by Rev. John W. B

John Henry Fleming, ae 20y, farmer,
Jas. & Elizabeth Fleming; Lucy Field, a
widow, col'rd, d/o Davy & ___ Garrett;
27 1881 by Rev. Wm. Thomas.

Daniel Claiborne, ae 22y, col'rd, fa
s/o Dan'l & Polly Claiborne; Catharine
Bird, ae 21y, col'rd, d/o Davy & Hannah
Mar 27 1881 by Rev. John Wm. Booth.

Sye Carter, ae 65y, widower, col'd,
s/o Jacob & Mary Carter; Parthenia Lewi
29y, col'rd, d/o Lewis & Nancy Lemon; A
1881 by Rev. John Wm. Booth.

Richard Harris, ae 33y, col'rd, wido
farm, s/o Wm. H. & Dianna Harris; Eliza
Peterson, ae 35y, widow, col'rd, d/o --
Tamer Burwell; Apr 10 1881 by Rev. John
Booth.

John J. Clements, ae 24y, farm, of M
sex Co VA, s/o John W. & Hester Clarke
ments; Hester R. Walden, ae 24y, d/o Ro
Sarah Moore Walden; Apr 17 1881 by Rev.
S. Thrift.

Charles H. Post, ae 26y, waterman, of
York City N. Y, s/o Chas. M. & Kate M. G:
fin Post; Otelia E. Fary, ae 22y, d/o Wm
& Rosa Soles Fary; Apr 21 1881 by Rev. M
Colonna.

James C. Fleming, ae 28y, farmer, s/o
T. & Mary J. Williams Fleming; Loulie F.
Hayes, ae 20y, of Mecade Co KY, d/o Wm. '
Athalia F. Hogg Hayes; May 5 1881 by Rev
Geo. E. Booker.

Samuel Hall, ae 49y, col;rd, farm, s/
Edwin & Judy Hall; Catharine Taliaferro,
40y, widow, col'rd, d/o Henry & Hannah H:
rison; May 11 1881 by Rev. Z. T. Whiting

John T. Goode, ae 24y, farm, s/o John
& Mary C. Groom Goode; Maggie D. Clare, :
20y, d/o John D. Clare; May 5 1881 by Re\
M. C. Colonna in King and Queen Co VA.

Walter Buck, ae 33y, oyster, s/o Fran
& Lucretia J. Cochere Buck; Jane Rebecca
Seawell, ae 18y, d/o Wat W. & Jane Rebec
Seawell; May 25 1881 by Rev. Wm. E. Wiat

Henry Jackson, ae 34y, col'rd, widowe:
farm, s/o Isaac & Letty Jackson; Ella Jol
son, ae 23y, col'rd, d/o Martha Johnson;
25 1881 by Rev. Z. T. Whiting.

Reuben Sparks, ae 19y, col'rd, oyster
s/o Wm. & Gracy Ann Sparks; Frances Robi:
ae 21y, col'rd, d/o John W. & Silvy Robi:
May 28 1881 by Rev. Sam'l S. Harden.

Smith Redman, ae 21y, col'rd, cord wo
cutter, s/o Orange & Frances Redman; Hen:
etta Wilson, ae 21y, col'rd, of Middlese:
VA, d/o Betty Wilson; May 29 1881 by Rev
David Coulling.

Alexander T. Wiatt, ae 41y, surveyor
Gloucester Co VA, s/o Wm. G. & Louisa C.
Stubbs Wiatt; Maude R. Sinclair, ae 22y,
Rob't & Rowena M. Baytop Sinclair; May 3:
1881 by Rev. Wm. E. Wiatt.

Americus V. Rilee, ae 26y, farmer, s/
Pascal D. & Mary Ann Walker Rilee; Corac
Ann Dunston, ae 27y, divorced, d/o John :
Elizabeth Booker Walker; June 5 1881 by

Randall Hammons, ae 24y, col'rd, oys
s/o Abram & Rhoda Hammons; Polly Stokes
21y, col'rd, d/o Simon & Mary Stokes; J
20 1881 by Rev. Sam'l S. Harden.

Thomas M. Lowny, ae 30y, merchant, o
Hanover Co VA, s/o Albert & Priscilla W
kins Lowny; Hattie W. Bayse, ae 24y, d/
Lizzie Johnston Bayse; July 29 1881 by
Geo. E. Booker.

John Walker, ae 67y, widower, fish a
oyster, s/o Rob't & Nancy Ann Allmond W
er; Rebecca West, ae 30y, d/o Ambrose &
nah Green West; July 14 1881 by Rev. W.
Hawkins.

William Chaney, ae 45y, widower, col
laborer, s/o Thos. & Elsy Chaney; Betsy
well, ae 16y, col'rd, d/o Davy & Eliza
Burwell; July 28 1881 by Rev. John W. E

Simon Walker, ae 23y, col'rd, oyster
Simon & Emiline Lockley Walker; Polly S
ae 22y, col'rd, d/o Lorenzo & Polly Stu
Aug 7 1881 by Rev. E. W. Page.

James C. Willis, ae 24y, farm, s/o J
R. & Mary E. Harwood Willis; Ida Bell D
ae 19y, d/o Edw'd C. & Sarah A. Kemp Du
Aug 7 1881 by Rev. S. S. Thrift.

Samuel T. Richardson, ae 21y, marine
Baltimore City MD, s/o Caleb & Mary Haw
Richardson; Cassie Jane Brown, ae 21y,
Lewis & Catharine Fields Brown; Aug 10
by Rev. R. A. Fox.

James Seawell, ae 30y, widower, boat
builder and House carpenter, s/o Benj.
Mary Oliver Seawell; Ann Elizabeth Ambr
ae 21y, d/o Henry & Margaret Callis Amb
Aug 11 1881 by Rev. W. S. Hawkins.

Robert Lee Haven, ae 19y, farm, s/o
& Eliza Ann Hogg Haven; Ann Jane Owens;
25y, d/o Geo. & Ann Dugans Owens; Aug 9
by Rev. W. S. Hawkins.

George W. Deal, ae 27y, widower, cle
Court House, of Mathews Co VA, s/o Wm.
Mary C. Eddins Deal; Nannie B. Miller,
18y, d/o Rob't D. & Mary C. T

Augustine Dixon, ae 25y, col'rd, farm
Jim & Mary; Lina James, ae 25y, widow, c
d/o Armistead & Sally; Jan 6 1881 by Rev
S. Hawkins.

James Chapman, ae 23y, farm, s/o Chas
Polly Chapman; Martha Ellen Banks, ae 18
of King and Queen Co VA, d/o Washington
Nancy Banks; June 7 1881 by Rev. John W.
Booth.

J. Frank Soles, ae 23y, farm, s/o Wm.
Lucy Fary Soles; Nannie B. Haynes, ae 22
d/o Geo. & Milly Edwards Haynes; June 9
by Rev. M. S. Colonna.

James Allmand, ae 22y, col'rd, waterm
s/o Ned & Judy Allmand; Maria Walden, ae
d/o Caroline Stanley; June 16 1881 by Re
Z. T. Whiting.

William Lewis, ae 24y, col'rd, carpen
s/o Abraham & Martha Lewis; Hester Goldm
ae 18y, d/o Jack & Roberta Goldman; June
1881 by Rev. Sam!l S. Harden.

Monroe Allen, ae 22y, col'rd, oyster
Farm, s/o Emily Green; Henrietta Tabb, a
17y, d/o John & Fanny Tabb; June 23 1881
Rev. W. S. Hawkins.

Benjamin Jenkins, ae 22y, fishing, s/
Bailey & Mary E. West Jenkins; Ann West,
17y, d/o Jas. West & Nancy Haywood; June
1881 by Rev. W. S. Hawkins.

Alex Davenport, ae 26y, col'rd, divor
farmer, of King and Queen Co VA, s/o Tho
Patsy Davenport; Mary Chapman, ae 16y, c
d/o Davy & roas Chapman; June 30 1881 by
E. W. Page.

Henry Brooks, ae 27y, widower, col'rd
teamster, s/o Betsy Ruffner; Susan Smith
25y, col'rd, d/o Wallace & Harriet Smith
July 4 1881 by Elder R. Latimore.

John Walker, ae 55y, widower, millwri
s/o John W. & Nancy Bane Walker; Annie C
Ambrose, ae 31y, d/o Wm. & Julia A. Duns
Ambrose; July 5 1881 by Rev. Geo. E. Boo

James Brown, ae 20y, fish and Oyster,

Book 1: 1880's

Jerry Corbin, ae 22y, col'rd, oyster
York Co Va, s/o Lewis & Mary Eliza Corb
Maria Ellis, ae 21y, d/o Wm. J. & Adal
Ellis; Sept 5 1881 by Rev. Z. T. Whitin

Reuben Whiting, ae 28y, col'rd, oys
s/o Dick & Liddia Ann Whiting; Grace Ho
ae 30y, col'rd, d/o Chas. & Judy Howard
Sept 11 1881 by Rev. John Wm. Booth.

William Banks, ae 26y, col'rd, farm
Washington & Joicy Banks; Sally Jackson
28y, col'rd, d/o John & Laura Jackson;
18 1881 by Rev. E. W. Page.

William J. Simpson, ae 23y, farmer,
Norfolk Co VA, s/o J. A. & Sarah J. Her
Simpson; Mildred T. Coleman, ae 21y, d/
F. & Mildred Philpotts Coleman; Sept 2
by Rev. Geo. E. Booker.

Philip Spencer, ae 23y, col'rd, labo
s/o John & Rose Spencer; Robinette V. J
ae 19y, col'rd, d/o Chas & Viney Jones;
25 1881 by Rev. Sam'l S. Harden.

Samuel Banks, ae 68y, widower, farm
Adam & Jenny Banks; Eliza Jones, ae 45y
widow, col'rd, d/o Robin & Mary Banks;
1881 by Rev. Sam'l S. Harden.

Beverly Louden, ae 54y, widower, col
farmer, s/o Rich'd & Fanny Louden; Lucy
ter, ae 35y, col'rd, parents unk; Oct
1881 by Rev. Robert Berkeley.

George T. Wright, ae 24y, boatsman,
Benj. & Mary Smith Wright; Laura Ann Gr
ae 16y, d/o Jas. & Margaret Lyle Green;
27 1881 by Rev. W. S. Hawkins.

Miles Carter, ae 40y, widower, col'r
waterman, s/o Geo. & Jenny Carter; Moll
Hills, ae 23y, col'rd, d/o Bob & Betsy
Oct 27 1881 by Rev. E. W. Page.

William S. Brustar, ae 25y, sea capt
Baltimore City MD, s/o Henry & Mary Ann
Brown; Annie C. Smith, ae 20y, d/o Jas.
Ann C. Curfman Smith; Oct 27 1881 by Re
Geo. E. Booker.

William West, ae 18y, fish and Oyste
s/o Jas. & Nancy Haywood West; Lizzie M

Robert Hughes, ae 22y, col'rd, oysterma
s/o Jas. & Betty Hughes; Mary Billups, ae
27y, col'rd, of Mathews Co VA, d/o Susan
Billups; Nov 26 1881 by Rev. W. S. Hawkins

William L. Dunston, ae 21y, carpenter,
s/o Edmund & Betty Nuttall Dunston; Georgi
anna Palmer, ae 21y, d/o Powatan S. & Mary
Dutton Palmer; Nov 24 1881 by Rev. R. A. F

Landon J. Miller, ae 25y, oyster and fa
of Middlesex Co VA, s/o Christopher & Elle
er Walker Miller; Mary L. Hibble, ae 19y,
d/o Chas. W. & Mary E. Hibble; Dec 4 1881
Rev. S. S. Thrift.

Charles Willis,m ae 22y, col'rd, oyster
of Mathews Co VA, s/o Farner & Delia Willi
Harriet Mathias, ae 21y, col'rd, d/o Rich
& Hannah Mathias; Dec 11 1881 by Rev. Sam
S. Harden.

George W. Walker, ae 22y, farm, s/o Geo
& Emily Mason Walker; Sarah J. Horseley, a
18y, d/o Allen & Lizzie Horseley Horseley
Dec 14 1881 by Rev. H. C. Cheatham.

James Henry kemp, ae 21y, farm, s/o Tho
& Emily Seawell Kemp; Julia Ann South, ae
18y, d/o Thos. & Mira A. Edwards South; De
20 1881 by Rev. R. A. Fox.

Julius B. Roane, ae 26y, farm, of Middl
sex Co VA, s/o Wm. P. & Mary S. Bland Roan
Harriet E. Coleman, ae 26y, d/o John F. &
Mildred Philpotts Roane; Dec 21 1881 by Re
H. C. Cheatham.

Robert J. Shackelford, ae 22y, farm, s/
Franklin & Parke F. Clements Shackelford;
Addie E. Harwood, ae 21y, d/o Horatio W. &
Delia Leigh Harwood; Dec 21 1881 by Rev. F
C. Cheatham.

George Washington, ae 22y, col'rd, farm
s/o Mary Hill; Ethlyn Yates, ae 17y, col'r
d/o Bob & Mary Yates, (now Fields), Dec 22
1881 by Rev. John Wm. Booth.

Robert C. Booker, ae 23y, farm, s/o C.
C. & Frances A. Dutton Booker; Adalaide A.
Willett. ae 17y, d/o Jesse T. & Sarah A.
Cobb Willett; Dec 28 1881 by Rev. W. S. H

John Rusley Davenport, ae 23y, col'r
farmer, s/o Thos. & Mary Davenport; Mar
Ellen Johnson, ae 18y, col'rd, d/o Wise
Lucy Ann Johnson; Dec 28 1881 by Rev. J
W. Booth.

Thomas S. King, ae 29y, fish, s/o Th
Susan Cox King; Alice Robbins, ae 16y,
John & Caroline Howard Robbins; Dec 25
by Rev. W. S. Hawkins.

Joseph C. Lewis, ae 22y, oyster, s/o
J. & Lucy Ann Tillage Lewis; Mary Ann H
ae 18y, d/o Thos. R. & Henrietta Savage
ris; Dec 25 1881 by Rev. W. S. Hawkins.

William Whiting, ae 27y, col'rd, oys
s/o Lawrence & Louisa Whiting; Susan Pa
21y, col'rd, d/o Wm. & Lucy Page; Dec 2
1881 by Rev. E. W. Page.

Baylor Wormley, ae 43y, col'rd, farm
King and Queen Co VA, s/o Ralph & Katy
ley; Dec 25 1881 by Rev. E. W. Page.

George R. Hayes, ae 27y, teacher of
lic school, of Meade Co KY, s/o Wm. Hay
Fanny Hogg; Fanny S. Minor, ae 22y, d/o
W. & Sarah J. Mouring Minor; Dec 27 188
Rev. W. S. Hawkins.

Major Hughes, ae 47y, widower, col'r
farm, s/o Dick & Sulla Hughes; Elizabet
Hall, ae 28y, col'rd, divorced. d/o Bob
Fanny Hall; Dec 29 1881 by Rev. Sam'l S
Harden.

Thomas Lockley, ae 21y, farm, of Kin
Queen Co VA; Kate Montague, ae 21y, d/o
& Ellen Montague; Dec 29 1881 by Rev. H
Cheatham.

Richard H. Roane, ae 29y, farm, of K
and Queen Co VA, s/o Jas. & Valinda Cla
Roane; Margaret Hudson, ae 19y, of Seaf
DELAWARE, lived Gloucester, d/o C. W. &
Kennon Hudson; Jan 4 1882 by Rev. H. C.
Cheatham.

Henry Hudgin, ae 22y, col'rd, waterm
s/o John & Rose Hudgin; Mary Agnes Evan
21y, col'rd, d/o John & Scilla Ward; Ja
1882 by Rev. R. A. Fox.

Lewis Wright, ae 35y, widower, farmer,
York Co VA, Adaline Ellis, ae 40y, d/o Fr
& Judy Ellis; Jan 11 1882 by Rev. Z. Tayl
Whiting.

James Smith, ae 37y, widower, col'rd,
Hannah Smith; Catharine Morriss, ae 26y,
col'rd, d/o Jas. & Keziah Morriss; Jan 12
1882 by Rev. John Wm. Booth.

James West, ae 26y, sailor, s/o Frank
Frances Smith West; Belle Marshall, ae 21
d/o Geo. W. & Jane Marshall; Jan 15 1882
Rev. W. S. Hawkins.

William S. Seawell, ae 32y, farmer, s/
Wat W. & Jane R. Seawell; Frances West, a
24y, d/o Frank & Frances Smith West; Jan
1882 by Rev. W. S. Hawkins.

Gabriel Carter, ae 40y, widower, col'r
oyster, s/o Jas. & Judy Carter; Indianna
Dixon, ae 26y, col'rd, d/o Wm. & Betsy Di
Jan 22 1882 by Rev. E. W. Page.

Emanuel Moody, ae 35y, col'rd, woodcut
s/o Emanuel & Susan Moody; Lucy Carter, a
23y, col'rd, d/o Sam'l & Louisa Carter; J
22 1882 by Rev. E. W. Page.

James P. Johnson, ae 27y, col'rd, oyst
s/o Achilles & Sally Johnson; Malvena Lew
ae 23y, col'rd. d/o Lucy Ann Lewis; Jan 2
1882 by Rev. John Wm. Booth.

James Goldman, ae 42y, col'rd, waterma
s/o Willis & Sally Goldman; Amelia Ann Co
ae 19y, col'rd, d/o John & Margaret Ann C
Jan 22 1882 by Rev. Wm. Thomas.

John R. Sears, ae 33y, farm, s/o Jas.
& Arena F. Dutton Sears; Harriet A. Booke
ae 22y, d/o Chas. E. C. & Frances A. Dutt
Booker; Jan 25 1882 by Rev. R. A. Fox.

Eli Robins, ae 22y, sailor, s/o John &
Caroline Howard Robins; Indianna Bonnywel
ae 21y, d/o Geo. & Nancy Robins Bonnywell
Jan 26 1882 by Rev. W. S. Hawkins.

Peter Wellington Cooke, ae 28y, col'rd
farm, s/o Jas. & Elizabeth Cooke; Eliza J
Hobday, ae 22y, d/o John & Nancy Hobday;
31 1882 by Rev. Wm. Thomas.

Book 1: 1880's

Virgil P. Weaver, ae 40y, widower, i
of Selma ALABAMA, s/o Philip J. & Ann I
Gardner Weaver; Elizabeth P. Yeatman, a
27y, of Rockbridge VA, d/o A. A. & Jose
P. Gilmore Yeatman; Feb 2 1882 by Rev.
Hundley.

John T. Willis, ae 24y, sailor, of Y
Co VA, s/o John B. Mills & Margaret W.
gomery; Mary L. Allmand, ae 20y, d/o Ti
M. Allmand & Mary F. M. Puller; Feb 2 1
by Rev. Wm. E. Wiatt.

George W. Shackelford, ae 45y, widow
waterman, s/o Benj. & Tabitha Speed Sha
ford; Julia Frances Croswell, ae 28y, d
Houlder & Mary Minor Croswell; Feb 2 18
Rev. W. S. Hawkins.

Coleman Robins, ae 23y, fish and oys
s/o Joel & Mary Rowe Robins; Fanny Hall
17y, d/o John D. & Susan Brown Hall; Fe
1882 by Rev. W. S. Hawkins.

Charles Scott, ae 36y, col'd, blacks
s/o Franky Lewis; Catharine Thornton, a
widow, col'rd, of Mathews Co VA, d/o Jo
Harriet Burwell; Feb 4 1882 by Rev. E.
Page.

Philip Palmer, ae 21y, col'rd, farm,
Philip & Rebecca Palmer; Maria Jones, a
21y, d/o Gabriel & Lucy Jones; Feb 5 18
Rev. John Wm. Booth.

Richard C. Bridges, ae 34y, saw mill
s/o Rich'd M. & Caroline Clarke Bridges
Theodosia Fletcher, ae 23y, d/o Caleb M
Martha A. Purcell Fletcher; Feb 5 1882
Rev. H. C. Cheatham.

Samuel D. Pointer, ae 21y, farm, s/o
T. & Mary F. Dixon Pointer; Anna E. Min
ae 17y, d/o Thos J. & Joanna Enos Minor
9 1882 by Rev. Wm. E. Wiatt.

Horace W. Jones, ae 31y, druggist, c
Petersburg VA, s/o Walter F. & Fanny E.
Wellford Jones; Ella Waller, ae 29y, d/
Wm. J. & Martha C. Field Waller; Feb 9
by Rev. Wm. B. Lee.

Charles Larimore, ae 21y, col'rd, ti

Charles Williams, ae 26y, oyster, s/o
Sam'l & Mary Robins Williams; Mary Louisa
Hogg, ae 17y, d/o Mary Hogg; Mar 1 1882
Rev. W. S. Hawkins.

Guy Tyler, ae 24y, col'rd, oyster, s/o
Lewis & Milly Tyler; Sarah Allmond, ae 2
col'rd, d/o Jas. & Paulina Allmond; Mar
1882 by Rev. W. S. Hawkins.

Joseph Roberson, ae 35y, col'rd, oyste
of King and Queen Co VA, s/o Davy & Maria
Roberson; Nancy Lacy, ae 22y, col'rd, d/o
Squire & Margaret Lacy; Mar 2 1882 by Re
J. M. Campbell.

Henry Washington, ae 21y, col'd, labo
of Smyth Co VA, s/o Channy Hundley; Susa
Todd, ae 21y, col'rd, d/o Aaron & Jenny
Mar 19 1882 by Elder R. Latimore.

Albert Johnson, ae 21y, col'rd, farm,
Soloman & Lucy Lewis; Margaret S. Fleming
19y, col'rd, d/o Jas. & Lizzie Fleming; M
19 1882 by Rev. W. S. Hawkins.

Walter F. Jackmon, ae 20y, col'rd, fa
s/o Edw'd & Sarah Jackmon; Mary Ellen Br
tow, ae 19y, col'rd, d/o Wm. & Ann E. Br
tow; Mar 22 1882 by Rev. John Wm. Booth.

George W. Darnell, ae 21y 8m, farm, s
Wm. W. & Mary A. Dunston Darnell; Althea
Goode, ae 20y 8m, d/o Washington & France
E. Groom Goode; Mar 16 1882 by Rev. D. G
Butts.

Edward W. Clarke, ae 23y, col'rd, s/o
& Violet Clarke; Rosa Braxton, ae 18y, co
d/o Carter & Matilda Braxton; Mar 23 188
Rev. E. W. Page.

William T. Robins, ae 24y 8m, oyster,
Jefferson & Catharine Ransone Robins; Fra
ces Coats, ae 16y 4m, d/o John & Margaret
West Coats; Mar 29 1882 by Rev. W. S.
Hawkins.

Sterling Rowe Jr, ae 35y, oyster deal
s/o Sterling & Frances Ann Belvin Rowe;
Alice Acra, ae 18y, d/o John & Emily Nut
Acra; Mar 30 1882 by Rev. W. S. Hawkins.

George Corbin, ae 24y, col'rd, farm,
Wm. & Hannah Corbin; Sarah Wallace, ae 2

Andrew J. Cottee, ae 45y, widower, o
s/o Catharine Cottee; Virginia West, ae
marriage license shows 28y, d/o Howard
Nancy Green West; Apr 1 1882 by Rev. A.
Hundley.

William H. Harwood, ae 31y, farm, s/
A. & Eugenia E. Lewis Harwood; Catharin
Smith, ae 19y, d/o Geo. W. & Catharine
Hughes Smith; Apr 4 1882 by Rev. H. C.
Cheatham.

Charles E. Thomas, ae 23y, attorney
law, of Anne Arundell Co MD, s/o Henry
Elleanor Linthicum Harwood; Annie F. Ro
ae 21y, of New York City N. Y, d/o Walt
Susan Franklin Ross; Apr 20 1882 by Rev
Walter H. Robertson, minister Presbyter
Church.

Frank Reed, ae 30y, col'rd, farm, s/
Frank & Fanny Reed; Mary Eliza Whiting,
25y, col'rd, d/o John & Maria Whiting;
1882 by Rev. John William Booth.

Jack Hodges, ae 25y, col'rd, farm, s
Courtney Hodges; Martha Ann Whiting, ae
col'rd, d/o Frank & Mary Whiting; Apr 2
1882 by Rev. John Wm. Booth.

Charles Pannell, ae 45y, widower, co
farm, of Middlesex Co VA, s/o Edmund &
Pannell; Patsy Gregory, ae 29y, col'rd,
Henry & Sarah Gregory; May 30 1881 by R
E. W. Page.

Esau Claiborne, ae 21y, col'rd, labo
s/o Dan'l & Polly Claiborne; Frances Ra
dall, ae 21y, col'rd, d/o Beverly & Mil
Randall; May 6 1882 by Rev. John W. Boo

John Allen Blake, ae 36y, widower, 1
getter, of Middlesex Co VA, s/o Berkele
& Susan A. Blake; Lizzie Dudley, ae 21y
Benj. & Sarah Dudley; May 18 1882 by Re
G. C. Butts.

William Roane, ae 22y, col'rd, labor
s/o Richmond & Lucy Roane; Martha Smith
21y, col'rd, d/o Alice Smith; May 20 18
Elder R. Latimore.

Henry Washington, ae 21y, col'rd, to

William Joseph Paine, ae 21y, col'rd,
borer, s/o Wm. Paine Jr. & Caroline Paine
Betty Smith, ae 21y, col'rd, d/o Benj. &
Martha Smith; May 21 1882 by Rev. Z. T.
Whiting.

John Wesley Whiting, ae 23y, col'rd,
boatman, s/o Thos. & Easter Jenkins; Indi
na Hall, ae 20y, col'rd, d/o Thos. & Grac
Hall; May 28 1882 by Rev. John Wm. Booth.

James Morris, ae 25y, col'rd, boating,
s/o Addison & Frances Ann Morris; Viney M
Dixon, ae 15y, col'rd, d/o Wm. & Betsy Di
May 28 1882 by Rev. E. W. Page.

Joseph H. Bonnywell, ae 31y, oyster an
farm, s/o Geo. W. & Nancy Robins Bonnywel
Indianna Rowe, ae 23y, d/o Lucy Rowe & Ju
Ann West; May 29 1882 by Rev. W. S. Hawki

James Robert Kemp, ae 25y, farm, s/o
Peter D. & Sarah Hall Kemp; Mary Catharin
Hall, ae 18y, d/o Lewis O. & Martha Enos
Hall; June 1 1882 by Rev. H. C. Cheatham.

Thomas Gardner, ae 21y, col'rd, oyster
s/o Dan'l & Charlotte Gardner; Julia Robe
son, ae 21y, col'rd, d/o John & Channy Ro
berson; June 3 1882 by Rev. Sam'l S. Hard

Jacob Hyde, ae 48y, widower, oyster, o
Brooklyn N. Y, s/o David & Mary Quinby Hy
Charlotte E. Nuttall, ae 36y, widow, of
Queen Anne Co MD, d/o Wm. Birch & Carry
Howard June 4 1882 by Rev. W. S. Hawkins.

James Mitchell, ae 62y, widower, schoo
master, of King and Queen Co VA, s/o Wm.
Jackson & Alice Roane, (name changed to
Mitchell); Mary E. Fitzhugh, ae 40y, d/o
Patrick H. & Mary E. Christain Fitzhugh;
June 1 1882 by Rev. R. A. Fox.

Charles B. Rowe, ae 22y, fishing, s/o
Achilles & Emily Thomas Rowe; Mary Jane
Shackelford, ae 20y, d/o Wm. S. & Mary An
Thomas Shackelford; June 1 1882 by Rev. W
S. Hawkins.

John B. Lawson, ae 31y, farm, of King
Queen Co VA, s/o R. B. & Nancy Bland Laws
Lucy T. Minor, ae 22y, d/o John W. & Sara

James Washington Ware, ae 26y, col'r
farm, s/o Martha Davis; Fanny Whiting,
21y, col'rd, d/o Tom & Esther Whiting;
8 1882 by Rev. John Wm. Booth;

Thomas N. Smith, ae 34y, boat builde
s/o Thos. & Eliza Jenkins Smith; Pinky
elford, ae 17y, d/o Archer & Nancy West
Shackelford; June 22 1882 by Rev. W. S.
Hawkins.

Thomas G. West, ae 60y, widower, whe
wright, s/o Henry & Lucy Lewis West; El
beth F. Sheppard, ae 53y, widow, d/o He
Griffin, mother unk; June 15 1882 by Re
C. Cheatham.

Elijah Tyler, ae 24y, col'rd, oyster
farm, s/o Jas. & Nancy Tyler; Louisa Cr
well, ae 21y, col'rd, d/o Aaron & Matil
Cromwell; June 13 1882 by Rev. Sam'l S.
Harden.

Daniel Cosby, ae 22y, col'rd, waterm
s/o Dan'l & Rhody Cosby; Lucy Gardner,
21y, col'rd, d/o Harriet Cosby; June 29
by Rev. Sam'l S. Harden.

Edward Reed, ae 22y, widower, col'd,
s/o Chas. & Delphy Reed; Margaret Lemon
22y, col'rd, d/o John Wiatt & Mary Lemo
July 2 1882 by Rev. J. W. Booth.

John Bright, ae 24y, col'rd, sailor,
Billy & Susan Bright; Fanny Smith, ae 1
col'rd, d/o Jas. & Mary Smith; July 2 1
by Rev. Z. T. Whiting.

William Jenkins, ae 30y, fish, s/o W
Nancy Jenkins; Mary Frances Smith, ae 3
d/o John & Eliza Belvin Smith; July 5 1
by Rev. W. S. Hawkins.

James Kemp, ae 50y, widower, col'rd,
carpenter, of King and Queen Co VA,
lives Middlesex Co VA, s/o Jas. & Rache
Kemp; Martha Tabb, ae 35y, of King and
Co VA, widow, d/o Jas. & Susan Cary; Ju
1882 by Rev. J. W. Booth.

William Thornton, ae 26y, farmer, s/
John A. B. & Elizabeth Hayes Thornton;
mie Smith, ae 26y, d/o Wm. & Jane Freem

John Hughes, ae 24y, merchant, s/o Thos.
H. & Esther J. Hayes Hughes; Minnie Thornton,
ae 24y, d/o John A. B. & Elizabeth Hayes
Thornton; July 20 1882 by Rev. W. S. Hawkins.

Eli Conway, ae 41y, widower, waterman, of
Baltimore City MD, s/o John & Celestine Con-
way; Sarah West, ae 25y, d/o Christopher &
Viney Smith West; July 26 1882 by Rev. W. S.
Hawkins.

Edwin H. Cluverius, ae 22y, blacksmith,
s/o J. W. & Mary E. Hobday Cluverius; Carrie
S. Dobson, ae 24y, d/o John T. & Sally Cluverius Dobson; July 26 1882 by Rev. W. S.
Hawkins.

Robert Banks, ae 27y, col'rd, oyster, s/o
Wm. & Gracy Banks; Nancy Griffin, ae 18y,
col'rd, d/o Phill & Judy; Aug 6 1882 by Rev.
E. W. Page.

Joel Thomas Teagle, ae 27y, farm, s/o
John & Martha Hall Teagle; Susanna Jordan,
ae 19y, d/o Willoughby & Maria Oliver Jordan; Aug 13 1882 by Rev. H. C. Cheatham.

Philip Henry Williams, ae 25y, farm, s/o
Edmund & Rebecca Guthrie Williams; Sallie C.
Heywood, ae 23y, d/o Wm. & Virginia Hobday
Heywood; Aug 17 1882 by Rev. W. S. Hawkins.

Thomas Brown, ae 22y, col'rd, laborer, of
Mathews Co VA, s/o Reed & Dinah Brown; Eliza
Deadman, ae 30y, col'rd, d/o Joe & Annie
Deadman; Aug 19 1882 by Rev. Wm. E. Wiatt.

Joseph C. Daniel, ae 24y, col'rd, oyster,
of Lawrence Co GEORGIA, s/o How'd & Susan
Daniel; Adaline Payne, ae 20y, col'rd, d/o
Wm. Payne Jr. & Caroline; Aug 24 1882 by Rev.
W. S. Hawkins.

Alfred Smith, ae 44y, widower, col'rd,
waterman, s/o Joe & Mary Smith; Molly Cary,
ae 44y, widow, col'rd, d/o Ned & Mary Montague; Sept 5 1882 by Rev. E. W. Page.

David C. Jenkins, ae 31y, s/o David &
Susan Dunford Jenkins; Laura E. Tillage, ae
18y, d/o Joseph & Georgianna Belvin Tillage;
Sept 10 1882 by Rev. H. C. Cheatham.

George Burwell, ae 22y, col'rd, oyster,
s/o Edmund & Sarah A. Burwell; Julia Ann
Patterson, ae 17y, col'rd, d/o Major Burwell
& Elizabeth Patterson; Sept 11 1882 by Rev.
W. S. Hawkins.

Samuel Holt, ae 48y, widower, coachmaker, of Charles City Co VA, s/o John T. & Anna A. Hill Holt; Fannie Moore, ae 27y, d/o Rich'd T. & Ellen Dutton Moore; Sept 19 1882 by Rev. Walter H. Robertson.

William Evans, ae 36y, col'rd, oysterman, s/o John & Betsy Evans; Ellen Grevius, ae 27y, of Mathews Co VA, d/o Philip P. & Susan Grevius; Sept 21 1882 by Rev. Sam'l S. Harden.

Thomas E. Brown, ae 24y, farm, s/o Jas. H. & Ann Kinningham Brown; Sarah E. Oliver, ae 19y, d/o Washington J. & Sarah E. Dunston Oliver; Sept 21 1882 by Rev. W. S. Hawkins.

Peter B. Hughes, ae 42y, widower, farmer, s/o Wm. & Susan F. Stubblefield Hughes; Mary S. Rowe, ae 40y, widow, d/o Wm. T. & Susan Leavitt Mouring; Sept 28 1882 by Rev. W. S. Hawkins.

Andrew T. Whiting, ae 21y, col'rd, water-man, s/o Thos. & Milly Whiting; Rosetta Washington, ae 21y, col'd, d/o Warner & Jane Washington; Oct 1 1882 by Rev. Sam'l S. Harden.

Stephen Wright, ae 21y, col'rd, oyster, s/o Stephen & Susan Wright; Louisa King:1, ae 19y, col'rd, d/o Lydia Cosby; Oct 15 1882 by Rev. W. S. Hawkins.

William Clarke, ae 55y, widower, col'rd, farm, s/o Geo. & Milly Clarke; Fanny Robin-son, ae 48y, widow, col'rd, of King and Queen Co VA, parents unk; Oct 15 1882 by Rev. E. W. Page.

Felix Braxton, ae 23y, col'rd, oyster, s/o Carter & Matilda Braxton; Alice Holmes, ae 19y, col'rd, d/o Currell Holmes & Sally Johnston; Oct 25 1882 by Rev. W. S. Hawkins.

John C. Martin, ae 22y, farm, s/o Wm. H. & Mildred Kemp Martin; Columbia R. Lamberth, ae 22y, d/o A. C. & Sarah Lial Lamberth; Nov 1 1882 by Rev. H. C. Cheatham.

Walter Stokes, ae 28y, col'rd, oysterman, s/o Washington & Amsy Stokes; Emma Jane Cary, ae 21y, col'rd, d/o Lucy Cary; Nov 9 1882 by Rev. Z. Taylor Whiting.

A. Prosser Prince, ae 23y, lumber getter,
of Middlesex Co VA, s/o Rich'd R. & Catharine
Bridges Prince; Mary E. Bristow, ae 21y, d/o
Wm. L. & Elizabeth Bristow; Nov 9 1882 by
Rev. John M. Campbell.

Augustine P. Oliver, ae 49y, farm, s/o
Wm. & Catharine Bew Oliver; Mary J. Wilburn,
ae 36y, of Nansemond Co VA, d/o Jesse &
Martha Hogg Wilburn; Nov 9 1882 by Rev. W.
S. Hawkins.

Robert Lockley, ae 43y, widower, col'rd,
farm, s/o Dan'l & Milly Lockley; Fanny Whiting, ae 23y, col'rd, d/o Rich'd & Lilly Ann
Whiting; Nov 8 1882 by Rev. John Wm. Booth.

Levi Belvin, ae 26y, fish, s/o James &
Rebecca Haywood Belvin; Lucinthia D. Deal,
ae 17y, d/o John Wm. & Alice Blunt Deal; Nov
15 1882 by Rev. W. S. Hawkins.

Chas. Washington, ae 24y, widower, col'd,
coach cleaner, of King and Queen Co VA, s/o
Henry & Dianna Washington; Virginia Lewis,
ae 21y, col'rd, d/o Dennis & Cuetta Lewis;
Nov 23 1882 by Rev. Z. T. Whiting.

Soloman M. Kemp, ae 25, carriage maker,
s/o Geo. T. & Indianna Pointer Kemp; Maria
H. Robins, ae 29y, d/o A. W. & Elizabeth
P. Todd Robins; Nov 29 1882 by Rev. Wm. E.
Wiatt.

William Bailey, ae 32y, widower, col'rd,
oysterman, of York Co Va, s/o Tom & Milly
Bailey; Julia Thruston, ae 21y, col'rd, d/o
Joe & Elsy Thruston; Nov 30 1882 by Rev. W.
S. Hawkins.

William Griffin, ae 24y, col'rd, farm,
s/o Baylor & Sarah Griffin; Margaret Wormley,
ae 19y, col'rd, d/o Susan Scott; Dec 20,
1882 by Rev. Sam'l S. Harden.

William W. Lamberth, ae 34y, farm, s/o
John & Mildred Walker Lamberth; Lucy Iva
Chapman, ae 17y, d/o Sam'l B. & Harriet B.
Davies Chapman; Dec 20 1882 by Rev. James C.
Martin.

Thomas Gardner, ae 22y, col'rd, oyster,
s/o Bayley & Eliza Gardner; Margaret Steadman, ae 15y col'rd, d/o Sam & Tamer Steadman;
Dec 24 1882 by Rev. Sam'l S. Harden.

Jasper Hall, ae 24y, col'rd, oyster, s/o
John & Eliza Hall; Sarah Dudley, ae 17y,
col'rd, d/o Lewis & Nancy Dudley; Dec 24 1882
by Rev. W. S. Hawkins.

Charles Noggin, ae 21y, col'rd, farm, of
Mathews Co VA, s/o Bob & Liny Noggin; Peggy
Scott, ae 20y, col'rd, d/o Nelson & Jane
Scott; Dec 24 1882 by Rev. Sam'l S. Harden.

Thomas Bluford, ae 22y, col'rd, farm, of
King and Queen Co VA, s/o Billy & Hannah
Bluford; Mary Susan Moody, ae 21y, col'rd,
d/o Banks & Susan Moody; Dec 25 1882 by Rev.
John W. Booth.

Harristen W. Dutton, ae 24y, farm, s/o
Edward C. & Sarah A. Kemp Dutton; Nannie
Acra, ae 21y, d/o Wm. J. & Julia C. Booker
Acra; Dec 25 1882 by Rev. R. A. Fox.

Benjamin F. Sears, ae 25y, farm, of Mid-
dlesex Co VA, s/o Henry L. & Mira A. Edwards
Sears; Mary E. Acra, ae 17y, d/o Wm. J. &
Julia C. Booker Acra; Dec 25 1882 by Rev. R.
A. Fox.

James M. Williams, ae 35y, farm, s/o Edmund & Margaret Seabourn Williams; Fannie G.
Peatross, ae 27y, of Caroline Co Va, d/o
Rich'd W. & Fannie Grey Peatross; Dec 27
1882 by Rev. W. S. Hawkins.

William Henry Harrison, ae 23y, col'rd,
farm, s/o John & Jenny Harrison; Kitty Lancaster, ae 20y, col'rd, d/o Chas. & Pinky
Lancaster; Dec 28 1882 by Rev. E. W. Page.

John Robins, ae 23y, oyster, s/o John &
Caroline Howard Robins; Mary A. Rowe, ae
21y, d/o Achilles & Emily Nuttall Rowe; Dec
28 1882 by Rev. W. S. Hawkins.

Ceasar Smith, ae 21y, col'rd, sailor, s/o
Emanuel & Caroline Smith; Martha Ransome, ae
18y, col'rd, d/o Sam & Delpha Ransome; Jan 7
1883 by Rev. Wm. Thomas.

Edward Jackman, ae 45y, widower, col'rd,
farm, s/o Rob't Wilson & Mary Jackman; Arena
Bell, ae 20y, col'rd, d/o Mary Bell; Jan 15
1883 by Rev. John W. Booth.

Addison M. Wiatt, ae 26y, farm, s/o Wm.
E. & Charlotte L. Coleman Wiatt; Julia Belle
Shingerland, ae 23y, of Ortonville MICH, d/o
Storm & Charlotte Bingham Slingerland; Jan
17 1883 by Rev. Wm. E. Wiatt.

Wm. Shackelford, ae 48y, widower, farmer, s/o Geo. & Elizabeth Moore Shackelford; Bettie Lee King, ae 20y, d/o Thos. & Elizabeth Hall King; Jan 21 1883 by Rev. W. S. Hawkins.

Thomas Burwell, ae 22y, col'rd, sailor, s/o Wm. & Amy Burwell; Laura Jones Whiting, ae 22y, col'rd, d/o Lewis & Betsy Whiting; Jan 25 1883 by Rev. A. Y. Hundley.

Alexander P. Sears, ae 21y, farmer, s/o Beverly & Louisa Brooking Sears; Lelia C. South, ae 16y, d/o John L. & Harriet Rilee South; Jan 31 1883 by Rev. D. G. C. Butts.

John Bristow, ae 30y, widower, col'rd, farm, s/o Billy & Caty Bristow; Matilda West, ae 23y, col'rd, d/o Landon & Catharine West; Feb 1 1883 by Rev. Sam'l S. Harden.

George Taliaferro, ae 68y, widower, wood cutter, of King and Queen Co VA, s/o Edmund & Betsy Taliaferro; Matilda Booker, ae 36y, widow, d/o Spencer & Mary Reed; Feb 3 1883 by Rev. J. W. Booth.

Philip Smith, ae 22y, col'rd, oyster, s/o Till & Mary Smith; Sarah Smith, ae 21y, col'rd, d/o Alfred & Frances Smith; Feb 15 1883 by Rev. Jas. C. Martin.

Robert Lee Deal, ae 20y, fish and oyster, s/o John & Betty Brown Deal; Betty Robins, ae 22y, d/o John & Caroline Howard Robins; Feb 15 1883 by Rev. W. S. Hawkins.

Joseph Brown, ae 44y, widower, mechanic, s/o Thos. & Mildred Liairt Brown; Vianna Hogg, ae 28y, d/o Geo. A. & Rachel King Hogg; Feb 18 1883 by Rev. W. S. Hawkins.

Randall Cooke, ae 26y, col'rd, farm, s/o Peyton & Frances Ann Cooke; Lucy C. Davenport, ae 20y, col'rd, d/o Tom & Patsy Davenport; Feb 22 1883 by Rev. John W. Booth.

Charles O. Deal, ae 25y, merchant, of James City Co VA, s/o Wm. & Mary C. Eddens Deal; Lucy A. Davis, ae 25y, col'rd, d/o Wm. K. & Sarah E. Deal Davis; Feb 22 1883 by Rev. Samuel S. Harden.

Charles H. Philips, ae 22y, col'd, oyster, s/o Washington & Mary Ellen Philips; Sarah Scott, ae 20y, d/o Johnson & Rebecca Scott; Feb 25 1883 by Rev. Sam'l S. Harden.

Oliver B. Haynes, ae 22y 10y, farm, of
New London CONN, s/o Jas. Henry & Mary A.
Kinght Haynes; Mollie F. Proctor, ae 18y,
d/o Henry S. & Elizabeth Massey Proctor; Feb
28 1883 by Rev. Jas. E. Gates, Virginia
Conference.

Robert Hill, ae 54y, col'rd, farm, of
King and Queen Co VA, s/o Rob't & Jenny Hill;
Margaret Jane Cooke, ae 21y, col'rd, d/o
Reuben & Eliza Cooke; Mar 8 1883 by Rev.
John Wm. Booth.

Silas L. Hall, ae 21y, farm, s/o Lewis O.
& Martha A. Enos Hall; Sallie C. Dutton, ae
19y, d/o Edw'd C. & Sarah A. Kemp Dutton;
Mar 13 1883 by Rev. Jas. C. Martin.

George Frank Shackelford, ae 24y, col'rd,
farm, s/o Geo. & Courtney Shackelford; Lou
Coleman, ae 19y, col'rd, d/o Ann Smith; Mar
21 1883 by Rev. John W. Booth.

Benjamin F. Patterson, ae 21y, col'rd,
oyster, s/o Chas. & Charlotte Patterson;
Martha Ellen McCra, ae 21y, col'rd, d/o
Ellen McCra; Mar 22 1883 by Rev. Wm. Thomas.

Robert B. Pearce Jr, ae 23y, farm, s/o
Rob't B. & Adaline South Pearce; Josephine
Haynes, ae 24y, d/o Wm. & Fannie Padgett
Haynes; Mar 22 1883 by Rev. Jas. C. Martin.

Frank New Newcomb, ae 22, farm, s/o Rob't
& Almira F. Andrews Newcomb; Mary A. Enos,
ae 22y, d/o Sam'l P. & Ann Eliza Atkins Enos;
Mar 28 1883 by Rev. Jas. C. Martin.

William H. H. Redding, ae 35y, widower,
carpenter, of Hunterden Co N. J, s/o Chas. &
Jane Rainbow Redding; Lizzie Parks, ae 21y,
divorced, of King and Queen Co VA, d/o Albert
Davis & Elizabeth W. Burton; Mar 29 1883 by
Rev. W. S. Hawkins.

Warner Washington Jr, ae 21y, col'rd,
farm, s/o Warner & Jane Washington; Alice
Hicks, ae 21y, col'rd, d/o Jas. & Margaret
Hardin; Mar 29 1883 by Rev. Sam'l S. Harden,

Edward Fields, ae 25y, widower, col'rd,
teamster, s/o Humphrey & Matilda Fields;
Sarah Chapman, ae 19y, col'rd, d/o Rob't &
Sally Hill Chapman; Apr 1 1883 by Rev. E. W.
Page.

William Bundy, ae 25y, col'rd, farm, of
King and Queen Co VA, s/o Washington & Mary
Bundy; Tarnro Taliaferro, ae 26y, col'rd, of
King and Queen Co Va, d/o Sam & Easter Lou-
don; Apr 4 1883 by Rev. E. W. Page.

Henry Banks, ae 22y, col'rd, farm, s/o
Frank & Mary Ann Banks; Maria Lancasteer, ae
23y, col'rd, d/o Isaac & Frances Lancaster;
Apr 17 1883 by Rev. John W. Booth.

Delaware Hibble, ae 22y, farm, s/o Chas.
W. & Mary E. Hibble; Lelia V. Booker, ae 18y,
d/o Lewis T. & Lucy F. Fary Booker; Apr 19
1883 by Rev. Jas. C. Martin.

Frederick Smith, ae 23y, col'rd, saw mill
hand, of Mathews Co VA, s/o Foster & Jenny
Smith; Blanch Gardner, ae 21y, col'rd, d/o
Bailey & Eliza Gardner; Apr 19 1883 by Rev.
Sam'l S. Harden.

John H. Travers, ae 34y, widower, col'rd,
oyster, s/o Ned & Keziah Travers; Laura
Smith, d/o Wm. & Elizabeth Smith; Apr 21
1883 by Rev. Sam'l S. Harden.

Coleman White, ae 24y, col'rd, waterman,
s/o Claiborne & Caroline White; Indianna Anderson, ae 21y, col'rd, d/o Geo. & Dianna
Anderson; Apr 22 1883 by Rev. Sam'l S.
Harden.

Daniel Jones, ae 26y, col'rd, farm, s/o
Dan'l & Mary Jones; Celia Lee, ae 21y, col'd,
d/o Celia & Louisa Lee; Apr 22 1883 by Rev.
J. W. Booth.

Joseph T. Robins, ae 21y, fish, s/o Jos.
F. & Rebecca Ash Robins; Sarah Acra, ae 20y,
d/o John & Emily Nuttall Acra; May 10 1883
by Rev. W. S. Hawkins.

James Smith, ae 22y, carpenter, s/o Thos.
& Eliza Jenkins Smith; Lucy Jenkins, ae 16y,
d/o Frederick & Fanny Haywood Jenkins; May
15 1883 by Rev. W. S. Hawkins.

John Tabb, ae 36y, widower, teacher, of
Alexandria VA, s/o John Prosser & Rebecca
Lloyd Tabb; Mary Shepard James, ae 21y, of
Richmond City VA, d/o Joseph S. & Martha T.
Curtis James; May 15 1883 by Rev. A. Y.
Hundley.

James Park Corbin, ae 21y, col'rd, sailor,
s/o Geo. & Julia Corbin; Alice Morris, ae
21y, col'rd, d/o Chany Scott; May 20 1883 by
Rev. G. R. Scott.

Thomas Bradley, ae 43y, oyster and fish,
of Dorchester Co MD, s/o Elsberry & Elizabeth Bradley; Mildred Owens, ae 45y, widow,
d/o Christopher West; May 23 1883 by Rev. W.
S. Hawkins.

Alexander W. Gordon, ae 40y, widower,
col'rd, s/o Beverly & Betsy Gordon; Judy
Taliaferro, ae 25y, col'rd of King and Queen
Co VA. d/o Cellus & Jane Taliaferro; May 23
1883 by Rev. Z. T. Whiting.

Monroe Montague, ae 24y, col'rd, oyster,
s/o Soloman & Sarah Montague; Lucy Smith, ae
22y, col'rd, d/o Andrew & Pinky Smith; May
27 1883 by Rev. E. W. Page.

Octavius J. Harcum, ae 40y, widower,
farm, of Northumberland Co VA, s/o Cuthbert
& Ellen A. Burgess Harcum; Mary Susan Stubbs,
ae 26y, d/o W. W. & Mary Eastwood Stubbs;
May 29 1883 by Rev. Jas. C. Martin.

John W. Stubblefield, ae 26y, farm, s/o
Wm. A. & Sarah A. Fary Stubblefield; Lucy
Catharine Padgett, ae 24y, d/o John & Maria
Elliott Padgett; June 5 1883 by Rev. Jas. C.
Martin.

James C. Booker, ae 43y, col'rd, farmer,
s/o Harry & Dianna Booker; Sally Fox, ae 35y,
col'rd, widow, d/o Frank & Gracy; June 7
1883 by Rev. Z. Taylor Whiting.

Edwin Roper Eastwood, ae 25y, merchant,
s/o Alex G. & Virginia Wright Eastwood;
Fanny Archer Johnston, ae 24y, s/o John L. &
Louisa Bland Johnston; June 12 1883 by Rev.
Jas. C. Martin.

Sam Richerson, ae 37y, col'rd, widower,
farm, s/o Samuel & Louisa Richerson; Georgianna Cooke, ae 22y, col'rd, d/o Sarah & Frances Wilson; June 16 1883 by Rev. J. W. Booth.

Albert John Henry Reed, ae 25y, col'rd,
oyster, of King William Co VA, s/o Jas. &
Kitty Reed; Caroline Hall, ae 20y, col'rd,
d/o John & Martha Hall; June 24 1883 by Rev.
E. W. Page.

John Green, ae 22y, fisherman, s/o John &
Anna West Green; Nannie Jenkins, ae 16y, d/o
Jas. & Frances Jenkins; June 13 1883 by Rev.
W. S. Hawkins.

Bailey Jenkins, ae 23y, fisherman, s/o
Bailey & Emily West Jenkins; Susan Ann Green,
ae 17y, d/o Simon & Susan Oliver; June 17
1883 by Rev. W. S. Hawkins.

Benjamin Jenkins, ae 24y, farm, s/o Bailey & Emily West Jenkins; Josephine Bonnywell, ae 24y, d/o Wm. & Susan Jenkins Bonnywell; June 24 1883 by Rev. W. S. Hawkins.

Robert Goodchild, ae 75y, col'rd, s/o
Peter & Milly Goodchild; Rebecca King, ae
75y, col'rd, d/o Martha King; July 2 1883 by
Rev. R. Latimore. He was a basket maker.

Alexander King, ae 28y, col'rd, steam
mill hand, widower, s/o Buck & Violet King;
Nora Coles, ae 15y, col'rd, d/o Warner &
Charity Coles; July 3 1883 by Rev. J. W.
Booth.

Shuley Bayley, ae 29y, col'rd, farmer, of
Chesterfield Co VA, s/o Armistead & Joanna
Bailey; Sarah Lemon, ae 20y, col'rd, d/o
Emily Lemon; July 3 1883 by Rev. J. W. Booth.

Levi Brooks, ae 28y, col'rd, oysterman,
of York Co VA, s/o Dick & Henrietta Brooks;
Sarah Green, ae 20y, col'rd, d/o John &
Maria Green; July 8 1883 by Rev. E. W. Page.

Cornelius Braxton, ae 25y, oysterman, s/o
Frank & Viney; Martha Brown Gregory, ae 20y,
d/o Bob & Catharine Gregory; July 8 1883 by
Rev. J. W. Booth.

John W. Pierce, ae 23y, farm, lived Middlesex Co VA, s/o John M. & Julia Stubblefield Pierce; Hattie E. Regensburg, ae 21y,
d/o Sam'l A. & Rosa Fary Regensburg; July 17
1883 by Rev. WM. E. Wiatt.

William Meggs, ae 23y, col'rd, widower,
farm, s/o Mary Meggs; Maria L. Coles, ae
18y, col'rd, d/o Warner & Charity Coles;
July 31 1883 By Rev. J. W. Booth.

Levi Powell Oliver, ae 24y, oyster, s/o
Washington J. H. & Sarah Catharine Dunston
Oliver; Ann Catharine Brown; ae 19y, d/o Jas.
H. & Ann E. Kinningham; Aug 7 1883 by Rev.
F. H. Hall.

William Diggs, ae 53y, col'rd, widower,
well digger, of Mathews Co VA, s/o Betsy
Meggs; Peggy Fields, ae 53y, widow, col'rd,
d/o Peggy Dennis; Aug 11 1883 by Rev. Sam'l
S. Harden.

Lawson A. Carter, ae 30y, oyster, lived
Mathews Co VA, s/o Jas. T. & Eleanor Fit-
chett Carter; Martha H. Bristow, ae 33y, d/o
John & Harriet Chapman; Aug 22 1883 by Rev.
R. A. Fox.

James Gwynn, ae 30y, col'rd, farmer, s/o
Phill & Susan Gwynn; Harriet Waller, ae 30y,
col'rd, d/o Tom & Sarah Wyatt; Aug 26 1883
by Elder Latimore.

Thomas Lockley, ae 22y, col'rd, widower,
farm, s/o Rich'd & Lucy Ann Lockley; Maria
Philips, ae 19y, col'rd, d/o John & Lucy Ann
Philips; Sept 2 1883 by Rev. J. W. Booth.

Ceasar Jackson, ae 22y, col'rd, oysterman,
s/o Ceasar & Mary Jackson; Mat Ross, ae 23y,
col'rd, d/o Geo. & Mary Ross; Sept 8 1883 by
Rev. E. W. Page.

James cary, ae 40y, col'rd, widower,
brick layer, s/o Miles & Polly Cary; Rebecca
Gordon, ae 29y, widow, col'rd, d/o Albert &
Lucy Field; Sept 10 1883 by Rev. David
Coulling.

James Leigh, ae 46y, widower, printing
business, lived Baltimore MD, s/o Caleb &
Elizabeth Davis Leigh; Bettie E. Rowe, ae
31y, d/o Wm. H. & Virginia Stubblefield
Rowe; Sept 11 1883 by Rev. Jas. C. Martin.

Marlo Cooke, ae 40y, col'rd, farmer, s/o
Marlo & Sally Cooke; Sally Carter, ae 35y,
col'rd, d/o Edw'd & Malvina Carter; Sept 16
1883 by Rev. J. W. Booth.

William P. Brushwood, ae 28y, fisherman,
s/o Jas. & Elvira Southern Brushwood; Mary
Willett, ae 20y, d/o Jesse T. & Sarah A.
Cobb Willett; Sept 19 1883 by Rev. Wm. E.
Wiatt, Baptist minister.

Daniel Johnson, ae 24y, col'rd, farm hand,
s/o Phill & Sally Johnson; Annie Boyd, ae
24y, col'rd, d/o Major & Mary Boyd; Sept 18
1883 by Rev. David Coulling.

Richard Harris, ae 33y, col'rd, widower, farm, s/o Wm. & Dianna Harris; Lucy Smith, ae 20y, col'rd, d/o Rich'd & Julia Smith; Sept 22 1883 by Rev. J. W. Booth.

Peter Smith, ae 23y, col'rd, farm, of Mathews Co VA, s/o Lewis & Harriet Smith; Polly Laws, ae 25y, col'rd, of Lancaster Co PA, d/o Jas. & Harriet Laws; Sept 29 1883 by Rev. David Coulling.

Isaac Worthington Booker, ae 22y, col'rd, laborer, s/o Isaac & Mary Booker; Mary Ann F. Tibbs, ae 19y, col'rd, d/o Bob & Eliza Tibbs; Sept 30 1883 by Rev. J. W. Booth.

Samuel Collins, ae 28y, farm, of Somerset Co MD, lived Mathews Co VA, s/o Jonathan J. & Mary M. Hitch Collins; Anna J. Chapman, ae 20y, d/o A. C. & Courtney A. Blake Chapman; Oct 4 1883 by Rev. Jas. C. Martin.

Jackson Burwell, ae 60u, col'rd, widower, farm, s/o Thos. & Katy Burwell; Betsy Evans, ae 35y, col'rd, d/o Cain & Polly Evans; Oct 7 1883 by Rev. Wm. Thomas.

Walter Stokes, ae 21y, col'rd, oysterman, s/o Billy & Jane Duval; Alice White, ae 23y, col'rd, d/o John & Mary White; Oct 13 1883 by Rev. E. W. Page.

Elias Clarke, ae 24y, oyster, s/o Wm. & Violet Clarke; Margaret Jane Hobday, ae 17y, d/o Wm. & Hester Hobday; Oct 25 1883 by Rev. Z. Taylor Whiting.

John A. Willis, ae 24y, col'rd, carpenter, s/o John & Margaret Willis; Lilly Wood, ae 18y, col'rd, d/o Moses & Susan Wood; Oct 28 1883 by Rev. R. A. Fox.

Robert C. Heywood, ae 30y, farm, s/o Levi & Martha J. Diggs Heywood; Alice Ann Belote, ae 26y, d/o John & Frances Coates Belote; Nov 13 1883 by Rev. Wm. E. Wiatt.

Cornelius Albert Lancaster, ae 23y, col'd, farm, s/o Isaac & Frances Lancaster; Maria Lizzie Whiting, ae 18y, col'rd, d/o Martin & Matilda Whiting; Nov 18 1883 by Rev. John W. Booth.

Joel Robins, ae 50y, widower, farm. s/o Jesse & Mary Rowe Robins; Ellen Belote, ae 23y, d/o John & Frances Coats Belote; Nov 29 1883 by Rev. F. H. Hall.

Robert Smith, ae 22y, col'rd, farm, s/o Wm. & Elizabeth Smith; Lizzie Page Milton, ae 21y, col'rd, d/o Hiram & Lucy Milton; Dec 2 1883 by Rev. J. W. Booth.

P. Hersey Mason, ae 26y, farm, s/o Philip & Amanda Bland Mason; Sarah Catharine Pratt, ae 23y, of MD, d/o Benj. & ___ Leager Pratt; Dec 2 1883 by Rev. R. A. Fox.

Thomas Grevius, ae 27y, col'rd, oyster, of Mathews Co VA, s/o Philip & Susan Grevius; Phillis Jones, ae 22y, col'rd, d/o Judy Jones; Dec 2 1883 by Rev. Walter H. Robertson, minister Presbyterian Church.

Charles Heywood, ae 25y, fisherman, s/o Wm. & Eliza F. Deal Heywood; Elizabeth E. Jenkins, ae 16y, d/o Bayley & Emma West Jenkins; Dec 9 1883 by Rev. F. H. Hall.

Lawrence Lockley, ae 31y, col'rd, oyster, of Middlesex Co VA, s/o Dan'l & Milly Lockley; Aline Frances Banks, ae 22y, col'rd, d/o Frank & Mary Ann Banks; Dec 13 1883 by Rev. J. W. Booth.

Benjamin Robinson, ae 40y, col'd, widower, farm, of King and Queen Co VA, s/o Isaac & Betsy Robinson; Frances Cary, ae 26y, col'rd, of King and Queen Co Va, d/o Jas. & ___ Cary; Dec 16 1883 by Rev. H. Hill.

Robert Stubbs, ae 25y, col'rd, oysterman, s/o Adam & Catharine Stubbs; Mary Smith, ae 24y, col'rd, d/o Albert & Frances Smith; Dec 19 1883 by Rev. J. W. Booth.

Thomas Fox Jr, ae 24y, col'rd, oysterman, s/o Cambridge & Phillis Fox; Patsy Carter, ae 18y, col'rd, d/o Albert & Becky Carter; Dec 20 1883 by Rev. E. W. Page.

John Allmond, ae 23y, col'rd, oyster, s/o Julia Ann Allmond; Lucy Ann Taliaferro, ae 21y, col'rd, d/o John & Jenny Taliaferro; Dec 20 1883 by Rev. E. W. Page.

Thomas R. Lawson, ae 33y, saw mill business, s/o Jas. W. & Mary J. Lawson; Indie C. Darnell, ae 16y, d/o E. T. & Sarah C. Rilee Darnell; Dec 23 1883 by Rev. Jas. C. Martin.

James A. Booth, ae 22y, col'rd, farm, s/o Rob't & Ellen Booth; Sarah Smith, ae 20y, col'rd, d/o Andrew & Pinky Smith; Dec 25 1883 by Rev. E. W. Page.

James Green, ae 24y, col'rd, widower, oyster, s/o John & Maria Green; Mollie Carter, ae 18y, col'rd, d/o: Rob't Henry & Charlotte Carter; Dec 25 1883 by Rev. E. W. Page.

Sam Carter, ae 50y, widower, col'rd, farm, s/o Henry & Grace Carter; Hannah Washington, ae 40y, widow, col'rd, d/o Henry & Sarah Gregory; Dec 25 1883 by Rev. E. W. Page.

William H. Vaughn, ae 40y, widower, farm, s/o Wm. & Ann Cluverius Vaughn; Addie Mann, ae 30y, of King and Queen Co Va, d/o Thos. & Sarah Spencer Mann; Dec 25 1883 by Rev. David Coulling.

Alexander W. Moore, ae 28y, farm, s/o Zacheus & Elizabeth Pippin Moore; Mary Susan Lewis, ae 26y, d/o John T. & Mary Eliza Howlett Lewis; Dec 25 1883 by Rev. Jas. C. Martin.

James E. Huybert, ae 21y, farm, of Norfolk Co Va, s/o Jas. & Georgianna Jordan Huybert; Margaret C. Young, ae 21y, of deep Creek Norfolk Co Va. d/o ___ Young & Rosa A. unk; Dec 25 1883 by Rev. Jas. C. Martin.

Sam Jones, ae 22y, col'rd, oysterman, s/o Bob & Rosetta Jones; Nelly Burwell, ae 19y, col'rd, d/o Cain & Matilda Burwell; Dec 25 1883 by Rev. J. W. Booth.

James Deal, ae 22y, oyster, s/o John & Elizabeth Brown Deal; Missouri Bonnywell, ae 21y, d/o Geo. & Nancy Robins Bonnywell; Dec 26 1883 by Rev. Wm. E. Wiatt.

William L. Howard, ae 26y, farmer, s/o Henry A. & Martha A. Curry Howard; Fanny L. Rowe, ae 23y, d/o Wm. H. & Virginia L. Stubblefield Rowe; Dec 26 1883 by Rev. Jasmes C. Martin.

Lenius Bland, ae 24y, oyster, s/o Zachariah & Delilah E. Didlake Bland; Mary Ellen Padgett, ae 22y, d/o John & Maria Elliott Padgett; Dec 27 1883 by Rev. David Coulling.

Robert Robinson, ae 22y, col'rd, oyster, of Middlesex Co Va, s/o Corbin & Ceroray Robinson; Lou Seddon Dixon, ae 16y, col'rd, d/o Wm. H. & Betsy Dixon; Dec 27 1883 by Rev. F. H. Hall.

John Franklin Thomas, ae 17y, merchant,
s/o Joseph Thomas Sr, & Martha Smith; Ida E.
Thomas, ae 17y, d/o Jas. W. & Mary Jane Walker Thomas; Dec 23 1883 by Rev. Jas. C.
Martin.

William Hudgins, ae 21y, col'rd, oyster,
s/o John & Rose Hudgins; Jane Steadman, ae
19y, col'rd, d/o Sam & Tamer Steadman; Dec 30
1883 by Rev. Walter H. Robertson.

Isaac Cooke, ae 23y, col'rd, widower,
farm, s/o Peyton & Frances Ann Cooke; Elizabeth Davenport, ae 21y, col'rd, d/o Thos. &
Mary Ann Davenport; Dec 25 1883 by Rev. J.
W. Booth.

John Luther Thomas, ae 22y, oyster, s/o
John W. & Mary Jane Walker Thomas; Eudora
Belle Lewis, ae 23y, d/o Washington & ---
Wallace Lewis; Dec 27 1883 by Rev. Jas. C.
Martin.

William Rilee, ae 23y, col'rd, oysterman,
s/o Wm. & Fanny Rilee; Rebecca Braxton, ae
21y, col'rd, of New Kent Co VA, d/o Dick &
Maria Braxton; Dec 27 1883 by Rev. John Wm.
Booth.

John William Driver, ae 25y, col'rd, farm,
s/o Addison & Elizabeth Driver; Mary Ann
Ashley, ae 20y, col'rd, d/o Geo. & Susan
Ashley; Dec 27 1883 by Rev. John W. Booth.

Benjamin Franklin Williams, ae 22y; Nannie Virginia Deal, ae 16y.

Alfred Smith, ae 23y, col'rd, wagon, of
Middlesex Co VA, s/o Kingston & Maria Smith;
Janny Chapman, ae 18y, col'rd, d/o Sally
Jones; Jan 3 1884 by Rev. John W. Booth.

Thomas C. Walker, ae 27y, sailor, s/o
Thos. & Martha A. Hogg Walker; Mary Smit, ae
18y, d/o Jas. & Lizzie West Smith; Jan 3
1884 by Rev. F. H. Hall.

James Monroe Bolden, ae 23y, col'rd, s/o
Jas. & Polly Bolden; Lizzie Taliaferro, ae
21y, col'rd, d/o Moses & Catharine Taliaferro; Jan 3 1884 by Rev. F. H. Hall.

William Monroe, ae 30y, col'rd, divorced,
oyster, s/o Jas. & Betsy Monroe; Nannie E.
Smith, ae 18y, col'rd, of Norfolk VA, d/o
Edw'd & Julia Frances Smith; Jan 3 1884 by
Rev. Walter E. Robertson.

John Peterson Teagle, ae 26y, farm, s/o John A. & Martha J. Hall Teagle; Sarah A. L. Robins, ae 21y, d/o John W. & Mary Ann Moore Robins; Jan 6 1884 by Rev. Jas. C. Martin.

John Burwell, ae 21y, col'rd, oysterman, s/o Wm. & Abby Burwell; Louisa Johnson, ae 17y, col'rd, d/o Henry & Mary Johnson; Jan 6 1884 by Rev. F. H. Hall.

George Ransone, ae 32y, col'rd, widower, oyster, s/o Geo. & Frances Ransone; Mary Jones, ae 22y, col'rd, d/o Sam & Nelly Jones; Jan 3 1884 by Rev. Jas. C. Martin.

Thomas West, ae 26y, col'rd, sailor, s/o Thos. & Hannah West; Martha Ellen Curtis, ae 16y, col'rd, d/o Jas. & Susan Curtis; Jan 13 1884 by Rev. John Wm. Booth.

Joseph West, ae 26y, oyster, s/o David & Susan Sparrow West; Hattie Bailey, ae 16y, d/o Ward & Martha A. Bailey; Jan 15 1884 by Rev. F. H. Hall.

Edward German, ae 28y, farm, s/o Wm. & Leatha Bridges German; Martha Pratt, ae 18y, of Talbot Co MD, d/o Benj. & Elizabeth Ann Leager Pratt; Jan 17 1884 by Rev. R. A. Fox.

Edmund Godwin, ae 35y, col'rd, farm, of Northampton Co VA, s/o Isaac & Kate Godwin; Eliza King, ae 40y, col'rd, widow, parents unk; Jan 17 1884 by Rev. J. W. Booth.

Jack Rowe, ae 23y, col'rd, oyster, s/o Fayette & Mary Frances Philips; Susan Whiting, ae 22y, col'rd, d/o Isaac & Judy Whiting; Jan 20 1884 by Rev. J. W. Booth.

Walter L. Deal, ae 29y, capt. of vessell, s/o John & Elizabeth Brown Deal; Ida F. Williams, ae 26y, d/o Sam'l & Polly Robins Williams; Jan 24 1884 by Rev. Wm. E. Wiatt.

Joseph Deal, ae 39y, merchant, s/o John & Elizabeth Brown Deal; Lucretia Williams, ae 22y, d/o Sam'l & Polly Robins Williams; Jan 24 1884 by Rev. Wm. E. Wiatt.

Alpheus Weaver, ae 22y, farm, of Lancaster Co PA, s/o Christian & Rebecca Brewbaker Weaver; Mary A. Williams, ae 24y, d/o C. A. & Victoria Williams; Jan 22 1884 by Rev. F. H. Hall.

Philip Rank, ae 56y, widower, carpenter,
s/o Philip & Rachel Patten Rank; Mary F.
Goode, ae 39y, d/o John S. & Mary Lewis
Goode; Jan 23 1884 by Rev. Wm. B. Lee.

John T. South, ae 21y, farm, s/o John S.
& Harriet Rilee South; Eliza Jane Bristow,
ae 22y, d/o Henry & Elizabeth Lawson Bristow;
Mar 2 1884 by Rev. D. G. C. Butts.

Christian K. Weaver, ae 27y, wharfinger,
of Lancaster Co PA, s/o Christian & Rebecca
Brubaker Weaver; Ellen A. Smith, ae 23y, d/o
Wm. & Jane Freeman Smith; Mar 11 1884 by Rev.
James C. Martin.

James T. Hall, ae 44y, farm, s/o John &
Fanny Thornton Hall; Louisa Hudgins, ae 28y,
widow, d/o Wm. Shackelford & ___ Proctor;
Mar 14 1884 by Rev. David Coulling.

Edward Carter, ae 23y, col'rd, sailor, of
Middlesex Co VA, s/o Geo. & Hannah Carter;
Laura E. Waters, ae 18y, col'rd, of Somerset
Co MD, d/o Sam & Caroline Waters; Mar 13
1884 by Rev. E. W. Page.

Gregory Scott, ae 24y, col'rd, oyster,
s/o Jack & Eliza Scott; Sarah Montague, ae
21y, col'rd, d/o Soloman & ___ Montague; Mar
16 1884 by Rev. E. W. Page.

Samuel L. Riley, ae 24y, sailor, s/o John
M. & Caroline V. Foster Riley; Lucy O. Flem-
ing, ae 22y, d/o Jas. W. & Mildred Hobday
Fleming; Mar 23 1884 by Rev. F. H. Hall.

Frank Olvis, ae 21y, col'rd, farm, s/o
Cary & Louisa Olvis; Mary Wallace, ae 16y,
col'rd, d/o Geo. & Betty Wallace; Apr 8 1884
by Rev. Jas. C. Martin.

Henry W. Templeman, ae 28y, fisherman,
s/o Wm. & Mildred Robins Templeman; Lucy Lee
Lewis, ae 18y, d/o Washington & Mary E. Wallace Lewis; Apr 8 1884 by Rev. Jas. C.
Martin.

Joseph Scott, ae 22y, col'rd, farm, s/o
Nelson & Jane Scott; Ann Thomas Burwell, ae
19y, col'rd, d/o John & Eliza Burwell; Apr
15 1884 by Elder Latimore.

James West, ae 22y, fish and Oyster, s/o
Christopher & Viney Smith West; Julia Smith,
ae 28y, d/o Thos. & Eliza Jenkins Smith; Apr
24 1884 by Rev. F. H. Hall.

James Smith, ae 40y, col'rd, widower, farm, s/o Hannah Smith; Martha Seawell, ae 34y, widow, d/o Robin & Maria Curtis; Apr 27 1884 by Rev. J. W. Booth.

Washington Smith, ae 40y, col'rd, widower, s/o Jane Smith; Mary Hill, ae 20y, col'rd, d/o Major & Sally Hill; May 8 1884 by Rev. E. W. Page.

Richard Turner, ae 24y, col'rd, oyster, s/o Henry & Rosena Turner; Polly Ann Atkins, ae 21y, col'rd, d/o John & Hannah Atkins; May 8 1884 by Rev. Z. Taylor Whiting.

Arthur Shackelford, ae 24y, col'rd, farm, s/o Wm. & Martha Shackelford; Rosa Leigh, ae 21y, col'rd, d/o Julius & Rebecca Cook; May 15 1884 by Rev. James C. Martin.

Walter L. Chapman, ae 21y, s/o Sam'l B. & H. B. Davis Chapman; Rosa Otelia Lamberth, ae 21y, d/o A. C. & Sarah Liall Lamberth; May 22 1884 by Rev. Jas. C. Martin.

Andrew Armistead, ae 40y, widower, farm, s/o John & Caroline Armistead; Georgianna Mathias, ae 25y, widow, d/o Werter & Delphia Smith; May 25 1884 by Rev. G. R. Scott.

William F. Hogg, ae 23y, fishing, s/o Andrew & Rebecca Howard Hogg; Mary S. Heywood, ae 17y, d/o John & Eliza Hogg Heywood; Jan 31 1884 by Rev. Wm. E. Wiatt.

John R. Baytop, ae 25y, col'rd, bricklayer, s/o Harry & Mildred Baytop; Henrietta Drummond, ae 24y, col'rd, d/o Braxton & Sarah Ann Drummond; Jan 31 1884 by Rev. J. W. Booth.

Charles Drummond, ae 23y, col'rd, laborer, s/o Alfred Lemon & Areana Driver; Sarah Frances King, ae 33y, col'rd, d/o Elizabeth King; Feb 3 1884 by Rev. J. W. Booth.

Henry Clayton, ae 21y, col'rd, farm, s/o Rob't & Mary Clayton; Sally Ann Jones, ae 18y, of Danville VA, d/o Dock Stewart & Polly Turpin; Feb 5 1884 by Rev. John W. Booth.

Henry S. Nuttall, ae 21y, sailor, s/o Wm. & Emily A. Haynes Nuttall; Sarah C. Smith, ae 17y, d/o Jas. L. & Ann Curfman Smith; Feb 5 1884 by Rev. Wm. E. Wiatt.

Frank Lemon, ae 23y, col'rd, laborer, s/o
Henry & Betsy Lemon; Fanny T. Burwell, ae
20y, col'rd, d/o John & Lucy Lee Burwell;
Feb 7 1884 by Rev. John Wm. Booth.

Nelson Scott, ae 40y, col'rd, widower,
farm, of Northampton Co VA, s/o Abram & Fanny Nelson; Ellen Bamks, ae 40y, col'rd,
widow, d/o John & Ann Matilda Philips; Feb
10 1884 by Rev. J. W. Booth.

Warner Burwell, ae 26y, col'rd, waterman,
s/o Kender & Easter Burwell; Mary Frances
Wallace, ae 21y, col'rd, d/o Poldore & Mary
Wallace; Feb 17 1884 by Elder Latimore.

Charles Diggs, ae 21y, col'rd, laborer, of
Mathews Co VA, s/o Wm. & Rendy Diggs; Nelly
Roane, ae 21y, col'rd, d/o Richmond & Lucy
Roane; Feb 17 1884 by Rev. David Coulling.

John R. Ware, ae 27y, farm, of King and
Queen Co VA, s/o Jas. & Catharine Walden
Ware; Sarah Bristow, ae 22y, d/o Peter W. &
Lucy Ann Soles Bristow; feb 20 1884 by Rev.
WM. E. Wiatt.

John Taylor, ae 66y, col'rd, widower,
farm, s/o Peter & Lucy Taylor; Catharine
Gregory, ae 45y, widow, d/o Sally Moody; Feb
21 1884 by Rev. J. W. Booth.

William Shackelford, ae 23y, waterman,
s/o Jas. & Ellarsanna Walker Shackelford;
Hester Jenkins, ae 16y, d/o Jas. & Anna Hogg
Jenkins; Feb 24 1884 by rev. F. H. Hall.

Oliver Page, ae 21y, col'rd, sailor, s/o
John & Sarah Page; Tulip Harrison, ae 19y,
col'rd, d/o Elijah & Betty Harrison; Feb 26
1884 by Rev. Wm. B. Lee.

John West, ae 22y, oyster, s/o Frank &
Fanny Smith West; Lucy Coates, ae 19y, d/o
John R. & Margaret West Coates; Feb 27 1884
by Rev. F. H. Hall.

Peter Leigh, ae 43y, col'rd, widower,
laborer, of King and Queen Co VA, s.o Lewis
& Polly Leigh; Lucy Reed, ae 22y, of King
and Queen Co VA, d/o Joe & Nancy Reed; Feb
27 1884 by Rev. H. Hill.

Albert Dudley, ae 23y, col'rd, farm, s/o
Oliver & Hannah Dudley; Sarah Jones, ae 22y,
col'rd, d/o Gabriel & Lucy Jones; Feb 28
1884 by Rev. John Wm. Booth.

James Wood, ae 21y, col'rd, oyster, s/o
Moses & Susan Wood; Eliza Norton, ae 18y,
col'rd, d/o Harry & Rebecca Norton; May 25
1884 by Rev. R. A. Fox.

Christopher Casey, ae 22y, col'rd, sailor,
s/o Jas. Henry & Mary Casey; Ida Belle Slaughter, ae 23y, col'rd, d/o Wm. & Susan Slaughter; May 25 1884 by Rev. J. W. Booth.

Walker French, ae 22y, col'rd, waterman,
s/o Peter & Eliza French; Louisa Ann Cooke,
ae 17y, col'rd, d/o Lorenzo & Martha Ellen
Cooke; May 25 1884 by Rev. J. W. Booth.

Frederick Whiting, ae 33y, col'rd, farm,
s/o Dick & Lyddie Ann Whiting; Mary Eliza
Cully, ae 19y, col'rd, d/o Jack & Joan Cully;
May 27 1884 by Rev. E. W. Page.

Thomas C. McLelland, ae 22y, harness
maker, of King and Queen Co VA, s/o Thos. M.
& Bettie Saunders McLelland; Carrie L. Roane,
ae 21y, d/o Sam'l F. & Lucy F. Roane; May 29
1884 by Rev. James C. Martin.

Joseph Tillage, ae 23y, boatman, s/o Jos.
& Georgianna Belvin Tillage; Elizabeth Har-
ris, ae 15y, d/o Thos. R. & Henrietta Savage
Harris; June 4 1884 by Rev. Jas. C. Martin.

Thomas Bridges, ae 23y, merchant, s/o
John A. & Florida Stubblefield Bridges; Bar-
tow Hughes, ae 21y, d/o Dr. Thos. J. & Sarah
Hughes; June 5 1884 by Rev. Jas. C. Martin.

William Jenkins, ae 21y, fisherman, s/o
Frederick & Fanny Haywood Jenkins; Mildred
Green, ae 17y, d/o Geo. W. & Martha West
Green; June 8 1884 by Rev. F. H. Hall.

Benjamin Allen Hogg, ae 35y, widower,
oyster, s/o Washington & Elizabeth Boswell
Hogg; Roxanna Carmine, ae 19y, d/o Dan'l &
Susan F. Dunn Carmine; June 10 1884 by Rev.
F. H. Hall.

John Carr, ae 23y, waterman, s/o John &
Mary belote Carr; Ellen West, ae 16y, d/o
John & Susan Sparrow West; July 20 1884 by
Rev. F. Hall.

George Bonnywell, ae 25y, farm, s/o Geo.
W. & Nancy Robins Bonnywell; Mary Lizzie
Butler, ae 25y, d/o Joe & Gracy Jenkins But-
ler; Aug 3 1884 by Rev. F. H. Hall.

Robert Mory, ae 26y, oyster, s/o John W.
& Elizabeth Hogg Mory; Lucy Catharine Ambrose, ae 23y, d/o Len & Emily Lawson Ambrose; Aug 4 1884 by Rev. James C. Martin.

Simon Walker, ae 25y, col'rd, widower,
s/o Simon & Emiline Walker; Maria Smith, ae
18y, col'rd, d/o Andrew & Pinky Smith; Aug
10 1884 by Rev. E. W. Page.

Benjamin King, ae 25y, col'rd, farm, s/o
Ben King & Maria Noggin; Sarah Reed, ae 23y,
col'rd, d/o Frank & Mary Reed; Aug 17 1884
by Rev. David Coulling.

Levi Belvin, ae 28y, fishing, s/o Jas. &
Anna R. Kellum Belvin; Ida Susan Jenkins, ae
17y, d/o John Wm. & Catharine West Jenkins;
July 31 1884 by Rev. S. S. Thrift.

William Kellum, ae 21y 9m, sailor, s/o
Wm. & Elizabeth Hogg Kellum; Sarah Hall, ae
19y, d/o G. W. & Eliza Smith Hall; Aug 26
1884 by Rev. F. H. Hall.

William Thomas Hill, ae 24y, col'rd, farm,
s/o Dan'l & Adaline Hill; Margaret Reade, ae
21y, col'rd, d/o Wm. & Phillis Reade; Sept 7
1884 by Rev. E. W. Page.

Doctor Garland, ae 30y, col'rd, widower,
of Milton S. C, s/o Rich'd & Rhoda Garland;
Ellen Burwell, ae 18y, col'rd, d/o Jackson &
Arena Burwell; Sept 7 1884 by Rev. Wm. E.
Wiatt.

William Carter, ae 22y, col'rd, oyster,
s/o Miles & Milly Carter; Sarah Goldman, ae
18y, col'rd, d/o Jack & Roberta Goldman;
Sept 11 1884 by Rev. E. W. Page.

James S. Robins, ae 23y, sailor, s/o Jas.
W. & Virginia A. Rowe Robins; Ida B. Brushwood, ae 23y, of King and Queen Co VA, d/o
Jas. W. & Elvira Southern Brushwood; Sept 14
1884 by Rev. R. A. Fox.

Robert Seawell, ae 22y, farm, s/o Miles &
Hannah Seawell; Milly Cooke, ae 20y, d/o
Washington & Fanny Cooke; Sept 14 1884 by
Rev. J. W. Booth.

Andrew J. Muse, ae 26y, col'rd, farm, s/o
Essex & Nancy Muse; Julia Ann Cooke, ae 19y,
col'rd, d/o Peter & Agnes Cooke; Sept 18
1884 by Rev. J. W. Booth.

Humphrey Jarvis, ae 49y, widower, col'rd, farm, of Mathews Co VA, s/o Humphrey & Polly Jarvis; Sarah Noggins, ae 26y, col'rd, d/o Bob & Scina Noggins; Sept 25 1884 by Elder Latimore.

Peter H. Thrift, ae 23y, merchant, s/o Wm. Jackson & Margaret Dutton Thrift; Cora Ann Rilee, ae 17y, d/o Thos. R. & Annie L. Dutton Rilee; Oct 2 1884 by Rev. S. S. Thrift.

Washington Robins, ae 50y, widower, carpenter, s/o Thos. & Elizabeth Rowe Robins; Signora Jarvis, ae 28y, d/o geo. R. C. & Jane Singleton JArvis; Oct 2 1884 by Rev. Wm. B. Lee.

Robert Yates, ae 44y, widower, farm, s/o Rob't & Rachel Yates; Hester Ellen Ransone, ae 30y, widow, d/o Sam & Delphy Ransone; Oct 5 1884 by Rev. Wm. Thomas, pastor of Morning Star Baptist Church.

William Jenkins, ae 21y, farmer, s/o Mitchell & Dicey Smith Jenkins; Nannie Shackelford, ae 18y, d/o Archie & Nancy West ?? Shackelford; Oct 12 1884 by Rev. Jas. C. Martin.

Henry W. Sibley, ae 30y, farm, of Middlesex Co VA, s/o Benj. B. & Elleanor Blake Sibley; Missouri F. Hibble, ae 16y, d/o Chas. W. & Mary E. Hibble; Oct 15 1884 by Rev. Wm. E. Wiatt.

Heber Moore, ae 25y, farm, s/o R. T. & Ellen Dutton Moore; Mary Lizzie Leigh, ae 23y, d/o John W. & Julia E. Hughes Leigh; Oct 22 1884 by Rev. Jas. C. Martin.

Thomas Griffin, ae 22y, col'rd, sailor, s/o John & Lena Griffin; Elsey Jane Whiting, ae 23y, col'rd, d/o John & Maria Whiting; Oct 23 1884 by Rev. J. W. Booth.

Leonard Schools, ae 50y, widower, farm, of Essex Co VA, s/o Rich'd B. D. & Lucy Cross Schools; Mary Frances Wood, ae 17y, d/o Lewis Tyler & Priscilla Bland Wood; Nov 2 1884 by Rev. D. G. C. Butts.

Powatan R. Stubblefield, ae 32y, farm, s/o Rob't A. & Virginia Robins Stubblefield; Gertrude Regensburg, ae 20y, d/o Sam'l A. & Rosa A. Soles Regensburg; Nov 11 1884 by Rev. Wm. E. Wiatt.

James T. Dudley, ae 23y, farm, s/o Benj.
& Sarah E. Grsssitt Dudley; Martha V. Graves,
ae 16y, d/o Jas. C. Graves, mother unk; Nov
12 1884 by Rev. F. H. Hall.

Miles Bright, ae 22y, col'rd, oyster, s/o
Billy & Lucy Bright; Louisa Anna Lewis, ae
18y, col'rd, d/o Henry & Harriet Lewis; Nov
20 1884 by Rev. E. W. Page.

Henry Smith, ae 25y, widower, col'rd,
farmhand, s/o Bob & Courtney Smith; Elizabeth Patterson, ae 25y, col'rd, d/o Rainny
Patterson; Nov 20 1884 by Rev. Wm. Thomas.

Frank L. Jarvis, ae 23y, farm, s/o Geo.
R. C. & Jane B. Singleton Jarvis; Ann T.
Brushwood, ae 21y, of King and Queen Co VA,
d/o Jas. & Elvira Sutton Brushwood; Nov 24
1884 by Rev. R. A. Fox.

William F. Marnix, ae 30y, carpenter, s/o
W. W. & Mary F. Pippin Marnix; Ella N.
Brushwood, ae 17y, d/o Isaiah W. & Jane Hob-
day Brushwood; Nov 25 1884 by Rev. Wm. E.
Wiatt.

George Yates Jr, ae 27y, col'rd, farm, of
Mathews Co VA, s/o Geo. & Alice Yates; Polly
Driver, ae 17y, col'rd, s/o Washington &
Margaret Driver; Nov 25 1884 by Rev. J. W.
Booth.

Albert Berry, ae 32y, widower, col'rd,
oyster, s/o John & Patsy Berry; Nancy Elizabeth Holmes, ae 16y, col'rd, d/o Walker &
Judy Holmes; Nov 27 1884 by Rev. John Wm.
Booth.

James Edgar Haney, ae 21y, col'rd, farm,
s/o Noah & Anna Haney; Matilda Page, ae 21y,
d/o Alex & Matilda PAge; Nov 27 1884 by Rev.
John Wm. Booth.

Joseph F. Robins, ae 21y, saw mill hand,
s/o Joseph & Susan Hurst Robins; Virginia S.
Teagle, ae 18y, d/o John A. & Martha J. Hall
Teagle; Nov 27 1884 by Rev. Jas. C. Martin.

James M. Carmines, ae 52y, widower, farm,
s/o Smith R. & Elizabeth Grant Carmines;
Emma F. Bray, ae 29y, d/o Thos. J. & Martha
Hogg Bray; Dec 9 1884 by Rev. F. H. Hall.

Pleasant T. Edwards, ae 28y, col'rd,
school teacher, s/o Thos. & Amelia Edwards;
of Amherst Co VA, Rachel Chapman, ae 22y,
col'rd, d/o Chas. & Milly Chapman; Dec 11
1884 by Rev. J. W. Booth.

John Pendleton, ae 21y, col'rd, farm, s/o
John & Judy Pendleton; Judy Tazewell, ae 21y,
of Fluvanna Co VA, d/o Davy & Becky Tazewell;
Dec 13 1884 by Rev. E. W.Page.

William Whiting, ae 29y, widower, col'rd,
brick layer, of Middlesex Co VA, s/o Sam &
Patsy Whiting; Susan Burwell,Rae 24y, widow,
col'rd, d/o Lucy London; Dec 24 1884 by Rev.
Robert Berkeley of Middlesex Co VA.

Thomas Walter Rowe, ae 21y, merchant, s/o
Thos. B. & Rosa E. Marchant Rowe; Cora Alice
Bland, ae 18y, d/o John R. & Margaret A.
Roane Bland; Dec 18 1884 by Rev. Jas. C.
Martin.

Benjamin F. Williams, ae 22y, fishing,
s/o Edw'd & Martha A. Brown Williams; Nannie
Virginia Deal, ae 16y, d/o Jas. T. & Susanna
West Deal; Dec 20 1884 by Rev. F. H. Hall.

Aaron Nelson, ae 22y, widower, col'rd,
carpenter, of Middlesex Co VA, s/o Warner &
Peggy Nelson; Frances Johnson, ae 22y, d/o
Wise & Lucy Ann Johnson; Dec 21 1884 by Rev.
J. W. Booth.

William Greene, ae 21y, col'rd, farm, s/o
Marlow & Sarah Green; Susan Lewis, ae 21y,
col'rd, d/o Mat & Rachel Lewis; Dec 21 1884
by Rev. J. W. Booth.

Wilmore Green, ae 23y, col'rd, oyster,
s/o John & Maria Green; Martha Ann Moody, ae
18y, col'rd, d/o Peter & Ann Maria Moody;
Dec 24 1884 by Rev. A. T. Gayle.

William H. Blake, ae 19y, farm, of Middle-
sex Co VA, s/o Wm. H. & Fanny Cauthorn Blake;
Susan Thrift, ae 28y, widow, d/o Chas. W. &
Mary E. Hibble; Dec 25 1884 by Rev. Wm. E.
Wiatt.

Jefferson Cooke, ae 35y, widower, col'rd,
oyster, s/o Billy & Tishie Cook; Mary Dabney,
ae 24y, widow, col'rd, d/o Wash & Mary Payne;
Dec 23 1884 by Rev. Jas. C. Martin.

John H. Pierce, ae 23y, merchant, s/o
John H. & Mary F. Gressitt Pierce; Eleanora
Trevilian, ae 19y, d/o R. C. & Orinda Cle-
ments Trevilian; Dec 25 1884 by Rev. Wm. E.
Wiatt.

Thomas Mack, ae 23y, col'rd, oyster, s/o
Wm. & Elsy Mack; Lucinda Dixon, ae 19y,
col'rd, d/o John Robinson & Lucinda Dixon;
Dec 25 1884 by Rev. A. T. Gayle.

Howard Howser, ae 25y, ornamental paint-
ing, of Baltimore MD, s/o Jacob R. & Martha
Glass Howser; Mackie Walker, ae 28y, d/o W.
G. & Elvira B. Glass Walker; Dec 25 1884 by
Rev. James C. Martin.

William H. Stubblefield, ae 24y, clerk, of
Northampton Co Va, lived Middlesex Co VA, s/o
Wm. B. & S. M. Hill Stubblefield; Emma J.
Leigh, ae 21y, d/o Rich'd D. & Julia A.
Bland Leigh; Dec 24 1884 by Rev. Wm. E.
Wiatt, Baptist minister.

Jefferson Carter, ae 21y, col'rd, oyster,
of Petersburg VA, s/o Geo. & Catharine Carter; Sarah Elizabeth Hill, ae 21y, col'rd,
d/o Rob't & Elizabeth Hill; Dec 25 1884 by
Rev. A. T. Gayle.

William D. Horseley, ae 20y, farm, s/o
Allen S. & Elizabeth Horseley; Mealie A.
Coats, ae 19y, d/o J. S. & Sarah Lawson
Coats; Dec 25 1884 by Rev. Wm. E. Wiatt.

Nathaniel Dixon, ae 25y, col'rd, farm, of
Mathews Co VA, s/o Gabe & Betty Dixon; Mar-
tha Thornton, ae 21y, col'rd, d/o Jas. Henry
& Caroline Thornton; Dec 25 1884 by Rev. J.
W. Booth.

Stappleton Tabb, ae 27y, col'rd, oyster,
s/o Dick & Maria Tabb; Caroline D. Drummond,
ae 16y, d/o Braxton & Sarah Drummond; Dec 28
1884 by Rev. E. W. Page.

William H. Purcell, ae 25y, farm, s/o
John & Susan Brown Purcell; Mary Elizabeth
Aherron, ae 28y, d/o Wm. F. & Frances Stub-
blefield Aherron; Dec 30 1884 by Rev. Jas.
C. Martin.

Joseph W. Howlett, ae 21y, sailor, of
Middlesex Co VA, s/o Jos. W. & Elizabeth
Massey Howlett; Lucy Lee Burke, ae 21y, d/o
Wm. T. & --- Marchant Burke; Dec 30 1884 by
Rev. James C. Martin.

Robert Tilmon, ae 24y, col'rd, oyster,
s/o Jeff & Maria Jane Tilmon; Gracie Ann
Brooks, ae 20y, col'rd, d/o Gilbert & Ann
Maria Brooks; Dec 30 1884 by Rev. E. W. Page.

Essex T. Jones, ae 27y, col'rd, farm, divorced, s/o Dan'l & Mary Jones; Eliza Rilee, ae 19y, col'rd, d/o Wm. & Lucy Rilee; Jan 3 1885 by Rev. Jas. C. Martin.

Atwood T. Groom, ae 21y, farm, s/o Albert & Mary Frances Groom; Mary S. Darnell, ae 18y, d/o W. W. Darnell and Wife; Jan 8 1885 by Rev. D. G. C. Butts.

Lemuel Callis, ae 22y, col'rd, of York Co VA, s/o Bill & Keziah Callis; Susan Elliott, ae 19y, col'rd, d/o Sam & Sarah Elliott; Jan 5 1885 by Rev. Walter H. Robertson.

Thomas Nelson, ae 25y, col'rd, oysterman, s/o Warner & Peggy Nelson; Ann W. Reade, ae 20y, col'rd, d/o John & Catharine Reade; Jan 8 1885 by Rev. J. W. Booth.

Richard Green, ae 30y, col'rd, widower, house servant, s/o Wm. & Margaret Green; Catharine Deadman, ae 26y, col'rd, parents unk; Jan 13 1885 by Rev. Wm. Thomas.

Pleasant Goldman, ae 22y, col'rd, sailor, s/o Benja. & Maria Goldman; Martha Ellen Anderson, ae 22y, col'rd, d/o Dianna Anderson; Jan 14 1885 by Rev. A. T. Gayle.

John E. Russell, ae 37y, sailor, of Salem N. Y, s/o John Russell; Lavinia D. Rilee, ae 21y, d/o Pascal D. & Mary Walker Rilee; Jan 14 1885 by Rev. James C. Martin.

Robert Lee West, ae 21y, fishing, s/o Wm. & Frances Jenkins West; Susannah West, ae 20y, d/o Cary & Virginia Cox West; Jan 30 1885 by Rev. Walter H. Robertson.

Philip Pollard, ae 50y, col'rd, widower, farm, s/o Rich'd & Crissy Pollard; Martha Braxton, ae 40y, col'rd, of King and Queen Co VA, d/o Geo. & Milly Braxton; Feb 5 1885 by Rev. E. W. Page.

William Cooke, ae 23y, col'rd, farm, s/o John & Gracie Cooke; Maria Johnson, ae 20y, col'rd, d/o Henry & Mary Johnson; Feb 5 1885 by Rev. Wm. Thomas.

John Lemon, ae 70y, col'rd, widower, farm, s/o Bob & Nancy Lemon; Mary Lowry, ae 50y, col'rd, widow, parents unk; Feb 7 1885 by Rev. Walter H. Robertson.

Willie H. Leigh, ae 20y, farm, s/o John
H. & Julia E. Hughes Leigh; Ella D. Phil-
potts, ae 20y, d/o Elkanah D. & Rosa A. Sale
Philpotts; Feb 18 1885 by Rev. Jas. C.
Martin.

George Booth, ae 22y, col'rd, oyster, s/o
Geo. & Margaret Booth; Sarah Eliza Davenport,
ae 21y, col'rd, d/o Thos. & Mary Ann Davenport; Feb 22 1885 by Rev. J. W. Booth.

James Stubbs, ae 21y, col'rd, oyster, s/o
Chas. & Margaret Stubbs; Mary Eliza Carter,
ae 20y, col'rd, d/o Gabriel & Ailcy Carter;
Feb 25 1885 by Rev. Z. Taylor Whiting.

Walter Berry, ae 24y, col'rd, oyster, s/o
Rob't & Lucinda Berry; Louisa Taylor, ae
23y, col'rd, d/o Phill & Polly Taylor; Mar 1
1885 by Rev. J. W. Booth.

Walter Thornton, ae 24y, col'rd, farm,
s/o Frank & Peggy Thornton; Mary Catharine
Brown, ae 21y, col'rd, of York Co VA, d/o
Humphrey & Mary Brown; Mar 1 1885 by Rev. Z.
Taylor Whiting.

David Whiting, ae 28y, col'rd, farm, s/o
Rich'd & Liddy Ann Whiting; Lizzie Cooke, ae
25y, col'rd, d/o Louisa Cooke; Mar 5 1885 by
Rev. E. W. Page.

Frederick Alfred Hoge, ae 26y, col'rd,
farm, s/o Jas. W. & Mahally Hoge; Martha A.
Rowe, ae 19y, d/o Jasper & Jane Frances Rowe;
Mar 5 1885 by Rev. Z. Taylor Whiting.

Elijah Hughky, ae 35y, col'rd, farm, s/o
Frank & Fanny Hughky; Mary Purcell, ae 38y,
col'rd, Parents unk; Mar 5 1885 by Rev. John
Wm. Booth.

John Mathias, ae 26y, col'rd, farm, s/o
Brittain & Nelly Mathias; Patsy Mathais, ae
24y, widow, col'rd, d/o Phillis; Mar 5 1885
by Rev. A. T. Gayle, pastor of Zion Poplar
Baptist Church.

Willis Allmand, ae 21y, col'rd, oyster,
s/o Paulina Burwell; Isabella Patterson, ae
16y, col'rd, d/o Betsy Smith; Mar 8 1885 by
Rev. Wm. Thomas.

Lewis O. Hall, ae 49y, widower, farm, s/o
Lewis & Catharine Newbill Hall; Henrietta
Ann Robins, ae 21y, d/o John W. & Mary Maria
Moore Robins; Mar 8 1885 by Rev. James C.
Martin.

William Thornton Smith, ae 24y, col'rd, widower, oyster, s/o Wm. & Isabella Smith; Moses Ann Davenport, ae 28y, col'rd, widow, d/o Moses & Nancy Rowe; Mar 15 1885 by Rev. J. W. Booth.

Henry Stokes, ae 24y, col'rd, oyster, s/o Simon & Mary Stokes; Betty Ann Pannell, ae 18y, col'rd, d/o Chas. & Martha Pannell; Mar 15 1885 by Rev. E. W. Page.

William F. Darnell, ae 26y, farm, s/o Wm. & Mary A. Dunston Darnell; Mary E. Mathews, ae 17y, d/o Thos. & Rosa A. Rilee Mathews; Apr 1 1885 by Rev. David Coulling.

John Morriss, ae 23y, col'rd, farm, s/o John & Betsy Morriss; Catharine Jones, ae 19y, col'rd, d/o Bob & Rosetta Jones; Mar 29 1885 by Rev. J. W. Booth.

John H. P. Seawell Jr, ae 28y, farm, s/o John H. & Mary H. Seawell; Senora C. Williams, d/o Wm. Hunter & Angelina Clements Williams; Apr 2 1885 by Rev. Wm. E. Wiatt.

Thomas Jenkins, ae 24y, oyster, s/o Jas. & Caroline West Jenkins; Arena Belle Hall, ae 17y, d/o Wm. A. & Susannah Howard Hall; Apr 2 1885 by Rev. F. H. Hall.

Benjamin Baylor, ae 40y, col'rd, widower, hewer, of Hampton VA, parents unk; Henrietta Cooke, ae 20y, col'rd, d/o Sally Cooke; Apr 9 1885 by Rev. James C. Martin.

Parker Whiting, ae 34y, col'rd, farm, s/o Henry & Lucy E. Whiting; Mary Emily Borum, ae 25y, col'rd, d/o Dan'l & Polly Borum; May 14 1885 by Rev. E. W. Page.

James H. Kemp, ae 28y, col'rd, oyster, of Middlesex Co VA, s/o Jas. & Dicey Kemp; Eliza Braxton, ae 21y, col'rd, d/o Geo. & Lucy Jane Braxton; May 14 1885 by Rev. Rob't Berkeley.

Marvin W. Stubbs, ae 24y, farm, s/o W. W. & Mary Eastwood Stubbs; Annie M. Trevilian, ae 24y, d/o R. C. & Orinda Clements Trevilian; May 14 1885 by Rev. Jas. C. Martin.

John Thomas Morris, aae 20y, col'rd, farm and waterman, s/o Jas. & Louisa Helen Morris; Geogianna Lancaster, ae 21y, col'rd, d/o Isaac & Frances Lancaster; May 21 1885 by Rev. E. W. Page.

Charles S. Kimball, ae 26y, farm, of Baltimore City MD, s/o Wm. P. & Mary A. Daughady Kimball; Annie M. Hibble, ae 17y, d/o Christian B. & Annie M. Enos Hibble; May 20 1885 by Rev. Jas. C. Martin.

Jordan Bright, ae 25y, col'rd, oyster, s/o Sam & Nancy Bright; Mary Eliza Wiatt, ae 25y, col'rd, d/o Peter & Ann Thomas Wiatt; May 28 1885 by Rev. A. T. Gayle, pastor of Zion Poplars Bapt. Church.

Addison Wake, ae 24y, col'rd, oyster, of Middlesex Co VA, s/o John & Catharine Wake; Julia Middleton, ae 21y, col'rd, d/o Hyram & Lucy Middleton; June 3 1885 by Rev. John W. Booth.

William Bolden, ae 25y, col'rd, oyster, s/o Jas. & Polly Bolden; Nancy Frazier, ae 21y, col'rd, d/o Ellen Frazier; June 7 1885 by Rev. F. H. Hall.

William Braxton, ae 34y, col'rd, widower, hewer of ties, s/o Tom & Mary Braxton; Jane Thornton, ae 25y, col'rd, d/o Paul Thornton, mother unk; June 7 1885 by Rev. J. W. Booth.

James Bolden, ae 29y, col'rd, farm, s/o Bob & Easter Bolden; Louisa Tonkins, ae 25y, col'rd, d/o Thos. & Carter Tonkins; June 11 1885 by Rev. J. W. Booth.

John W. Larkins, ae 30y, widower, waterman, s/o Geo. & Mary Seawell Larkin; Flora Gardiner, ae 18y, of Middlesex Co Va, d/o Jas. & Mary Fisher Gardiner; June 11 1885 by Rev. F. H. Hall.

George Allen Roach, ae 27y, waterman, of Charles City Co VA, s/o Sandy & Betty Irby Roach; Susannah Oliver, ae 22y, d/o Washington J. H. & Sarah Dunston Oliver; June 11 1885 by Rev. James C. Martin.

Edward Hughes, ae 27y, col'rd, farm, s/o Rob't & Amelia Hughes; Ann Marie Morriss, ae 20y, col'rd, d/o Addison & Frances Morriss; June 21 1885 by Rev. J. W. Booth.

Joseph Daniel, ae 26y, col'rd, widower, farm, of Lawrence Co GA, s/o Hard & Susan Daniel; Mary Louisa Payne, ae 20y, col'rd, d/o Wm. & Caroline Payne; June 21 1885 by Rev. E. W. Page.

Horace W. Jones, ae 34y, druggist, of
Petersburg VA, s/o Walter F. & Fannie E.
Wellford Jones; Fannie W. Nelson, ae 23y,
d/o Dr. W. W. & Sally B. Catlett Nelson;
June 23 1885 by Rev. Walter H. Robertson.

Robert Dennis, ae 21y, col'rd, cook, s/o
Geo. & Mary Ellen Dennis; Jane Jackson, ae
20y, col'rd, d/o Phill & Mary Jackson; June
25 1885 by Rev. A. T. Gayle.

Robert Thomas Braxton, ae 18y 10d, col'd,
farm hand, s/o Wm. & Ellen Braxton; Eudora
Baytop, ae 17y, col'rd, d/o Chas. & Violet
Baytop; June 25 1885 by Rev. J. W. Booth.

Frank Bright, ae 36y, col'rd, widower,
oyster, s/o Nat & Mary Bright; Margaret Howard, ae 21y, col'rd, d/o Adam & Mary Howard;
July 9 1885 by Rev. E. W. Page.

John A. Brown, ae 22y, boatman, of Ports-
mouth VA, s/o Thos. L. & Frances M. Hobday
Brown; Mattie E. Belvin, ae 19y, d/o Benj. &
Mary Hanley Belvin; July 9 1885 by Rev. Wm.
B. Lee.

Thomas Lewellyn, ae 28y, col'rd, oyster,
s/o Elsy Tyler; Alice Jackson, ae 30y, col'd;
parents unk; July 16 1885 by Rev. E. W. Page.

John Holmes, ae 23y, col'rd, farm, of
Surry Co VA, s/o Chas. & Patsy Holmes; Elizabeth Gregory, ae 35y, widow, col'rd, parents unk; July 23 1885 by Rev. A. T. Gayle.

William P. Caudle, ae 26y, widower, yard
master, of Fluvanna Co Va, s/o John & Lucy
A. Higgins Caudle; Jue L. Roane, ae 22y, d/o
Warner P. & Fannie Bland Roane; July 28 1885
by Rev. James C. Martin. He was yard master
in West Point VA.

Sterling Robinson, ae 39y, widower, farm,
s/o Cuffy & Becky Robinson; Fanny Carter, ae
32y, widow, col;rd, d/o Lewis & Peggy Gibbs;
July 30 1885 by Rev. E. W. Page.

Lewis Hamlet, ae 22y, col'rd, wagon
driver, of King and Queen Co VA, s/o Mike &
Mary Hamlet; Lucy Dennis, ae 18y, col'rd,
d/o John & Lilly Dennis; Aug 9 1885 by Rev.
J. W. Booth.

Thomas S. Lyall, ae 25y, farm, s/o Wm. &
Adaline Rilee Lyall; Lelia Maud Kemp, ae 22y,
d/o Overton & Emiline Fary Kemp; Aug 30 1885
by Rev. David Coulling.

John William Walker, ae 37y, divorced,
col'rd, farm, s/o Harry & Mary Walker; Isabella Walker, ae 35y, widow, col'rd, of
Fredericksburg VA, d/o Henry & Mary Coleman;
Aug 9 1885 by Rev. David Coulling.

John S. Wright, ae 32y, widower, blacksmith and Wheelwright, of New Kent Co VA,
s/o Wm. D. & Sarah N. Minor Wright; Everett
E. Williams, ae 25y, d/o Wm. Hunter & Angelina Clements Williams; Aug 12 1885 by Rev.
Wm. E. Wiatt.

James Williams, ae 22y, farm, s/o Edw'd &
Martha A. Brown Williams; Georgie V. Bonni-
ville, ae 19y, d/o Jas. & Emma Sparrow Bon-
niville; Sept 6 1885 by Rev. J. W. Taylor.

David F. Kirkpatrick, ae 24y, farm, of
Londondary IRELAND, s/o Rob't & Mary Ann
Forest Kirkpatrick; Virginia Alice Streagle,
ae 25y, d/o London & Lilly Ann Haynes
Streagle; Sept 17 1885 by Rev. Jas. C.
Martin.

George Franklin Shackelford, ae 26y,
farm, col'rd, s/o Geo. & Courtney Shackelford; Elva Wilson, ae 18y, col'rd, d/o Lovey
Wilson; Sept 23 1885 by Rev. J. W. Booth.

Frank Catlett, ae 30y, col'rd, farm, s/o
Jesse & Sally Catlett; Mary Lewis, ae 21y,
col'rd, d/o Rob't & Sally Lewis; Sept 27
1885 by Rev. Wm. B. Lee.

Peter Gordon, ae 22y, col'rd, sailor, s/o
Peter & Edith Gordon; Maria Wyatt, ae 21y,
d/o Joe & Sarah Wyatt; Sept 27 1885 by Rev.
A. T. Gayle.

Edward Shackelford, ae 20y, farm, s/o Wm.
& Mary Ann Thomas Shackelford; Loulie Rob-
bins, ae 17y, d/o John & Caroline Robbins
Robbins; Oct 1 1885 by Rev. J. W. Taylor.

Samuel V. Corbell, ae 42y, widower, lumber business, of Nansemond Co VA, s/o Henry
J. & Arabella Vaughn Corbell; Agnes C. Thruston, ae 32y, d/o Edw'd T. & Julia P. Cary
Thruston; Oct 13 1885 by Rev. Wm. B. Lee.

William W. Darnell, ae 50y, widower, farm,
s/o Isaac & Julia Bristow Darnell; Rosa Mathews, ae 38y, widow, d/o Robert Rilee & Mary
Lamberth; Oct 14 1885 by Rev. D. G. C. Butts.

Anthony Smith, ae 23y, oyster, s/o John & Nancy Smith; Emma Haywood, ae 23y, d/o Lucy Haywood; Mar 13 1885.

James C. Lemon, ae 23y, col'rd, school teacher, s/o Jas. & Elizabeth Lemon; Molly Tompkins, ae 22y, col'rd, d/o Thos. & Carter Tompkins; Oct 15 1885 by Rev. J. W. Booth.

William P. Hughes, ae 55y, widower, lumber inspector, of Baltimore MD, s/o Henry & Ann Angel Hughes; Frances Jane Stubbs, ae 37y, d/o Wm. W. & Lucy Eastwood Stubbs; Nov 5 1885 by Rev. Jas. C. Martin.

Thomas E. Fleming, ae 28y, farm, s/o Jas. T. & Mary J. Williams Fleming; Mira Lee Fletcher, ae 22y, d/o Cyrus T. & Mira A. Amory Fletcher; Nov 22 1885 by Rev. Wm. E. Wiatt.

Richard Whiting, ae 23y, col'rd, farm, s/o Martin & Matilda Whiting; Elenora Thornton, ae 17y, d/o Geo. & Frances Thornton; Nov 26 1885 by Rev. J. W. Booth.

George G. Washington, ae 23y, farm, s/o Henry & Lucy Washington; Hester Ann Phillips, ae 20y, col'rd, d/o Henry & Maria Phillips; Dec 2 1885 by Rev. J. W. Booth.

William T. Moore, ae 24y, miller, of King and Queen Co VA, s/o W. W. & Catharine Stevenson Moore; Laura Belle Graves, ae 16y, d/o Wm. G. & Sarah F. Dunston Graves; Dec 3 1885 by Rev. Wm. E. Wiatt.

Richard Amos Walker, ae 27y, farm, s/o Rich'd H. & Sarah C. Rilee Walker; Rosa E. Walker, ae 30y, d/o Geo. & Emily S. Mason Walker; Dec 6 1885 by Rev. Jas. C. Martin.

Randall Small, ae 23y, col'rd, farm, s/o Noey & Polente Small; Dinah Fleet, ae 34y, col'rd, d/o Mary Fleet; Dec 8 1885 by Rev. J. W. Booth.

Albert Schools, ae 42y, widower, laborer, of Essex Co VA, s/o Dawson & Lucy Schools; Barbara Rowe, ae 22y, widow, of King and Queen Co VA, d/o Rob't & Laura Gains; Dec 10 1885 by Rev. A. B. Warwick in Middlesex Co.

John C. Horseley, ae 25y, farm, s/o Allen & Elizabeth Horseley; Emma L. Forrest, ae 22y, of Mathews Co VA, d/o Joseph P. & Julia Forrest; Dec 10 1885 by Rev. Jas. C. Martin.

Edward Taylor, ae 30y, col'rd, farm and
oyster, of King and Queen Co VA, s/o Armistead & Rosa E. Taylor; Bettie Montague, ae
21y, d/o Chas. & Hester Montague; Dec 13 1855
by Rev. A. T. Gayle.

Roswell P. Grey, ae 30y, merchant, of
Mathews Co VA, s/o Nelson R. & Octavia Bil-
lups Grey; Elvira A. Jones, ae 19y, d/o Wm.
R. & Clara Bunch Jones; Dec 16 1855 by Rev.
Wm. E. Wiatt.

George W. Walker, ae 44y, farm, s/o Wm. &
Margaret Hibble Walker; Maria F. Rilee, ae
43y, widow, parents unk; Dec 17 1885 by Rev.
Wm. E. Wiatt.

Bartelot Todd Robins, ae 32y, merchant,
s/o Augustine W. & Elizabeth Todd Robins;
Mattie Mallory Sinclair, ae 25y, of York Co
VA, d/o Jefferson & Mary Frances Lowny Sinclair; Dec 15 1885 by Rev. Wm. B. Lee.

Henry Page, ae 50y, widower, farm, of
King and Queen Co VA, s/o Moses & Nancy Page;
Jane F. Montague, ae 26y, d/o Tillion &
Catharine Montague; Dec 18 1885 by Rev. A.
T. Gayle.

Simon Jones, ae 22y, col'rd, oyster, s/o
Alex & Martha Jones; Eliza Easter Booth, ae
21y, col'rd, d/o Geo. & Lucinda Booth; Dec
17 1885 by Rev. J. W. Booth.

Isaiah Whiting, ae 24y, col'rd, oyster,
s/o Frank & Daphney Whiting; Milly Jackson,
ae 18y col'rd, d/o John & Laura Jackson; Dec
20 1885 by Rev. E. W. Page.

John Williams, ae 24y, col'rd, oyster,
s/o Rich'd & Judy Williams; Anna Jane Reed,
ae 21y, col'rd, d/o Phillis Reed; Dec 23 1885
by Rev. J. W. Booth.

Daniel Page, ae 21y, col'rd, oyster, of
Yorktown VA, s/o Wm. & Lucy Page; Mary Jones,
ae 22y, widow, of Middlesex Co VA, parents
unk; Dec 24 1885 by Rev. A. T. Gayle.

Thomas Carter, ae 24y, col'rd, farm, s/o
s/o James & Harriet Carter; Catharine Patterson, ae 21y, col'rd, d/o Arena Patterson;
Dec 24 1885 by Rev. Wm. Thomas and Rev. R.
G. Griffin of Yorktown Va.

Peter J. Clarke, ae 27y, col'rd, oyster and farm, s/o Thos. & Mollie Clarke; Ida Carter, ae 18y, col'rd, d/o Rob't Henry & Pinky Carter; Dec 24 1885 by Rev. Z. Taylor Whiting.

William Wiatt, ae 24y, col'rd, farm, s/o Temple & Harriet Wiatt; Mary Major, ae 16y, col'rd, d/o Maria Major; Dec 24 1885 by Rev. J. W. Booth.

Robert Lee Briggs, ae 21y, school teacher, of Roanoke VA, lived Mathews Co VA, s/o Claiborne & Lucy Briggs; Emma Jane Davenport, ae 18y, d/o Alex & Roseller Davenport; Dec 24 1885 by Rev. J. W. Booth.

Essex Curtis, ae 24y, col'rd, oyster, s/o Scipio & Betsy Curtis; Adeline Stubbs, ae 20y, d/o Ann Stubbs; Dec 24 1885 by Rev. J. W. Booth.

Sumpter Hogg, ae 23y, fishing, s/o Stephen & Nancy Robins Hogg; Clever Ambrose, ae 18y, d/o Franklin & Sarah Hogg Ambrose; Dec 27 1885 by Rev. J. W. Taylor.

Oscar F. Hinman, ae 20y 9m 16d, oyster and sailor, of Accomack Co VA, s/o Sam & Mary Watson Hinman; Ellen F. Daniel, ae 16y, d/o Peter Daniel, mother unk; Dec 27 1885 by Rev. J. W. Taylor.

William H. Croswell, ae 28y, merchant, s/o Houlder & Mary Minor Croswell; Carrie Bryan, ae 22y, of MD, d/o Rich'd H. Bryan, mother unk; Dec 27 1885 by Rev. F. H. Hall.

Mike Smith, ae 25y, oyster, s/o Mike & Ann Eliza West Smith; Susan Hogg, ae 23y, d/o Ben & Georgianna Heywood Hogg; Dec 27 1885 by Rev. J. W. Taylor.

Arthur C. Walker, ae 28y, farm, s/o Geo. & Emily S. Mason Walker; Ella R. Darnell, ae 16y, d/o Edw'd T. & Sarah Rilee Darnell; Dec 27 1885 by Rev. Jas. C. Martin.

Joseph Willis, ae 24y, col'rd, carpenter, s/o John & Margaret Willis; Lucy Gordon , ae 21y, col'rd, d/o Mary Jane now Mary J. Brown; Dec 27 1885 by Rev. A. T. Gayle.

Samuel Billps, ae 24y, col'rd, oyster, of Mathews Co VA, d/o Dan'l & Lucky Billups; Louisianna Fox, ae 21y, col'rd, d/o Cambridge & Phillis Fox; Dec 20 1885 by Rev. E. W. Page.

David Jones, ae 22y, col'rd, oyster, s/o
Thos. & Jane Smith; Sally Phillips, ae 21y,
col'rd, widow, d/o Johnson & Rebecca Scott;
Dec 31 1885 by Rev. A. T. Gayle.

John Cully, ae 23y, col'rd, oyster, s/o
Jack & Joan Cully; Lizzie Morriss, ae 16y,
col'rd, d/o Geo. & Susan Morriss; Dec 31
1885 by Rev. John W. Booth.

George W. Foxwell, ae 18y 7m, oyster, s/o
Geo. & Fannie Seawell Foxwell; Ida B. Wal-
lace, ae 18y, d/o Rich'd & Elizabeth Jenkins
Wallace; Dec 31 1885 by Rev. J. W. Taylor.

Wallace W. Driver, ae 24y, col'rd, farm,
s/o Augustine & Frances Driver; Georgianna
Thornton, ae 20y, col'rd, d/o Geo. & Frances
Thornton; Jan 3 1886 by Rev. J. W. Booth.

Frederick Smith, ae 24y, col'rd, laborer,
s/o Jas. & Susan Smith; Rosa Baytop, ae 17y,
col'rd, d/o Rosa Baytop; Jan 3 1886 by Rev.
J. W. Booth.

Charles K. Pierce, ae 23y, farm, s/o John
M. & Julia F. Stubblefield Pierce; Cora Regensburg, ae 19y, of King and Queen Co VA,
d/o Sam'l A. & Rosa A. Soles Regensburg; Jan
5 1886 by Rev. Wm. E. Wiatt.

Lloyd L. Thomas, ae 25y, fish and oyster,
of Accomack Co VA, s/o Levi & Sarah Ann Thomas; Rachel Haywood, ae 24y, d/o Levi & Martha A. Haywood; Jan 6 1886 by Rev. Wm. E.
Wiatt.

Joseph T. Willis, ae 23y, farm, s/o John
R. & Mary E. Hall Willis; Lucy Agnes Acra,
ae 18y, d/o Jas. H. & Matilda Acra; Jan 13
1886 by Rev. Jas. C. Martin.

Currell Wiatt, ae 22y, col'rd, oyster, s/o
Tom & Mary Eliza Wiatt; Ellen Tabb, ae 20y,
col'rd, d/o Rich'd & Maria Tabb; Jan 1886 by
Rev. E. W. Page.

Jefferson Burwell, ae 22y, col'rd, farm,
s/o Braxton & Ellen Burwell; Cuetta Banks,
ae 18y, col'rd, d/o Jas. & Lucy Banks; Jan
20 1886 by Rev. John W. Booth.

Robert Lemon, ae 21y, col'rd, farm, s/o
Theodrick & Louisa Lemon; Bettie Cooke. ae
23y, col'rd, d/o Peter & Agnes Cooke; Jan
21 1886 by Rev. J. W. Booth.

William Dungey, ae 21y, col'rd, farm, s/o
Rob't & Mary Jane Dungey; Mary Kelly, ae
21y, col'rd, d/o Henry & Matilda Kelly; Jan
23 1886 by Rev. David Coulling.

Thomas Jones, ae 21y, col'rd, oyster, s/o
Parrot & Eliza Jones; Charlotte Travers, ae
18y, col'rd, d/o Sarah Travers; Jan 31 1886
by Rev. Wm. E. Wiatt.

Joshua G. Bray, ae 27y, farm, s/o Thos.
J. & Martha A. Hogg Bray; Fannie W. Hawkins,
ae 23y, d/o Wm. S. & Louisa Seawell Hawkins;
Feb 2 1886 by Rev. J. M. Taylor.

James Kinningham Horseley, ae 56y, widower, farm, s/o Jas. K. & Elizabeth Lawson
Horseley; Mildred Ison, ae 37y, widow, d/o
Henry W. & Valinda Bland Brooking; Feb 4
1886 by Rev. Wm. E. Wiatt.

Chester Christian, ae 37y, widower, col,
farm, of York Co VA, s/o Jordan & Jane
Christian; Mary Gains, ae 17y, col'rd, d/o
John & Mary Gains; Feb 13 1886 by Rev. John
W. Booth.

Eleazor Whiting, ae 24y, col'rd, oyster
and Farm, s/o Lewis & Elizabeth Whiting;
Isabella Burwell, ae 20y, col'rd, d/o Coleman & Eliza Burwell; Feb 14 1886 by Rev. E.
W. Page.

Washington Hogg, ae 40y, widower, oyster
and fish, s/o Rich'd & Milly West Hogg; Isabella Heywood, ae 20y, d/o Rob't & Mary
Shackelford Heywood; Feb 11 1886 by Rev.J.
W. Taylor.

William Randall, ae 40y, col'rd, widower,
oyster, s/o John & Jane Randall; Mary Risby,
ae 35y, widow, d/o Chas. & Martha Spurlock;
Feb 21 1886 by Rev. E. W. Page.

John E. Philips, ae 20y, sailor, s/o John
E. & Pinky Fletcher Philips; Georgia A.
Brown, ae 19y, d/o John A. & Mary Walker
Brown; Feb 21 1886 by Rev. J. W. Taylor.

Lewis W. Evans, ae 28y, col'rd, oyster
and sailing, s/o Cain & Polly Evans; Frances
Cooke, ae 24y, col'rd, d/o G. W. & Mary A.
Cooke; Feb 25 1886 by Rev. J. W. Taylor.

Richard Bird, ae 39y, col'rd, widower,
farm, of Middlesex Co VA, s/o Sam & Amy Bird;
Rosa Kemp, ae 17y, col'rd, d/o Geo. & Mary
Kemp; Feb 24 1886 by Rev. P. T. Edwards.

Henry Jones, ae 24y, col'rd, oyster, of
Middlesex Co Va, s/o Ned & Eliza Smith; Zula
Smith, ae 28y, widow, col'rd, d/o Betsy Grif-
fin; Feb 28 1886 by Rev. A. T. Gayle.

Peter Bedford, ae 25y, col'rd, ditcher,
of Prince Edward Co VA, s/o John & Jane Bedford; Lilly Watkins, ae 20y, of King and
Queen Co Va, d/o Bob & Eliza Watkins; Mar 2
1886 by Rev. P. T. Edwards.

Mahern Massey, ae 36y, farm, s/o Chas. A.
& Mary A. Haynes Massey; Isa Hudgins, ae 23y,
widow. d/o Rich'd L. Padget & Matilda Carney;
Mar 21 1886 by Rev. David Coulling.

Cyrus Jones, ae 21y, col'rd, farm, s/o
John & Julia Jones; Mary Ann Jones, ae 16y,
col'rd, d/o Sam & Sally Jones; Mar 25 1886
by Rev. J. W. Booth.

Andrew J. Anmack, ae 24y, fisherman, of
Unionville Long Island N. Y, s/o Andrew J. &
Louisa W. Morris Anmack; Mary A. Latham, ae
25y, of King and Queen Co VA, d/o Wm. T. &
Addie Shelton Latham; Mar 30 1886 by Rev.
James C. Martin.

John M. Shackelford, ae 23y, merchant, s/o
Wm. & Mary Ann Thomas Shackelford; Alice
Senora Hogg, ae 17y, d/o Andrew & Rebecca
Howard Hogg; Apr 8 1886 by Rev. J. W. Taylor.

Thomas West, ae 30y, fish and oyster, s/o
Howard & Nancy Green West; Ida West, ae 20y,
d/o Cary & Ellen King West; Mar 9 1886 by
Rev. Wm. B. Lee.

Samuel Chapman, ae 30y, col'rd, oyster,
s/o Godfrey & Nancy Chapman; Eleanora Hunley,
ae 20y, col'rd, of King and Queen Co Va, d/o
John & Betty Hunley; Apr 25 1886 by Rev. J.
W. Booth.

Thomas S. Leigh, ae 29y, farm, s/o Wm. P.
R. & Frances E. Stubblefield Leigh; Emma E.
Clayter, ae 23y, d/o Jas. R. & Rebecca A.
Adams Chapman; Apr 29 1886 by Rev. Jas. C.
Martin.

Thomas Allmond, ae 45y, col'rd, widower,
oyster, s/o Miles & courtney Allmond; Ella
Young, ae 19y, col'rd, d/o Joe & Adaline
Young; Apr 29 1886 by Rev. Z. Taylor Whiting.

William T. Sheppard, ae 22y, farm, s/o
John D. & Elizabeth Frances Griffin Sheppard;
Ann Elizabeth Wilkins, ae 19y, d/o Nathan A.
& Frances A. Moore Wilkins; May 20 1886 by
Rev. James C. Martin.

Walter Emmett Lee, ae 23y, col'rd, oyster,
s/o Elijah & Louisa Lee; Sarah Smith, ae 23y,
col'rd. d/o John & Clara Smith; May 23 1886
by Rev. J. W. Booth.

Joseph W. Mills, ae 20y 4m, oyster business, of York Co VA, s/o John B. & Margaret
Montgomery Mills; Virginia S. Dutton, ae 18y,
d/o M. Pendleton & Sarah Stubblefield Dutton;
May 27 1886 by Rev. Wm. E. Wiatt.

Henry C. Shackelford, ae 65y, widower,
farm, s/o Warner & Hannah Bunn Shackelford;
Frances Ann Wilkins, ae 35y, widow, d/o
Zacheus & Elizabeth Pippin Moore; June 1
1886 by Rev. Jas. C. Martin.

Thomas Gwynn, ae 30y, col'rd, farm, s/o
Phill & Rosanna Gwynn; Mary Jane Dudley, ae
30y, col'rd, d/o Mary Baytop; May 4 1886 by
Rev. A. T. Gayle.

Rosewell C. Smith, ae 25y, oyster dealer,
s/o Peter W. & Frances J. Rowe Smith; Mary
F. Thomas, ae 19y, d/o Jas. S. & Martha J.
Smith Thomas; June 3 1886 by Rev. J. W.
Taylor.

Daniel Lockley, ae 60y, widower, col'rd,
farm, s/o Harry & Gracy Lockley; Matilda
Whiting, ae 40y, widow, col'rd, d/o Ransone
& ___ Evans; June 8 1886 by Rev. J. W. Booth.

Anthony Cooper, ae 23y, col'rd, sailor,
s/o Martin & Mary Cooper; Loulie Driver, ae
20y, col'rd, d/o Washington & Margaret Driver; July 6 1886 by Rev. J. W. Booth.

William Taliaferro, ae 26y, col'rd, widow-
er, farm, s/o Wm. & Sarah Taliaferro; Annie
Lee, ae 20y, col'rd, of York Co VA, d/o
Elijah & Louisa Lee; July 8 1886 by Rev.
Jas. C. Martin.

James West Jr, ae 25y, fish and oyster,
s/o James Sr, & Nancy Haywood West; Virginia
West, ae 19y, d/o Christopher & Viney Smith
West; July 25 1885 by Rev J. W. Taylor.

Washington Thomas, ae 37y, fish and oyster, s/o Jas. & Martha Thomas; Clara A. Hogg, ae 19y, d/o Andrew H. & Rebecca Howard Hogg; July 22 1886 by Rev. J. W. Taylor.

Cue Willis, ae 23y, col'rd, carpenter, s/o John & Margaret Willis; Phoebe Cosby, ae 21y, col'rd, d/o Mary Jane Brown; Aug 29 1886 by Rev. Madison Lewis, pastor of Union Zion Baptist Church.

Seldon Smith, ae 21y, col'rd, farm, s/o Lucy Ann Kemp; Nancy Redman, ae 21y, col'rd, d/o Orange & Becky Redman; Sept 6 1886 by Rev. J. W. Booth.

William Diggs, ae 56y, col'rd, widower, farm, of Mathews Co VA, s/o Rich'd & Betsy Diggs; Mary Roane, ae 23y, col'rd, d/o Richmond & Lucy Roane; Sept 21 1886 by Rev. David Coulling.

James Reed, ae 21y, col'rd, oyster, of Middlesex Co VA, s/o Wm. & Martha Reed; Martha Clayton, ae 16y, col'rd, d/o Gilbert & Judy Clayton; Sept 30 1886 by Rev. P. T. Edwards.

Dr. John B. Braoddus, ae 35y, physician, of Caroline Co VA, s/o Rob't S. & Letitia E. Miller Broaddus; Mattie A. Jones, ae 21y, d/o Dr. Walker F. & Martha A. Baytop Jones; Oct 4 1886 by Rev. Jas. C. Martin.

Samuel Driver, ae 29y, widower, col'rd, farm, s/o Augustine & Frances Driver; Sarah Lemon, ae 20y, col'rd, d/o Thos. & Amanda Lemon; Oct 14 1886 by Rev. J. W. Booth.

Robin Jones, ae 65y, col'rd, widower, shoemaker, s/o Harry & Maria Jones; Maria Carter, ae 45y, col'rd, widow, d/o James Cooke & Lizzie Lockly; Oct 21 1886 by Rev. J. W. Booth.

William Tazewell, ae 30y, col'rd, widower, farm, s/o Winston & Patty Tazewell; Ellen Rowe, ae 24y, col'rd, d/o Mary Ellen Rowe; Oct 21 1886 by Rev. E. W. Page.

E. C. Fields, ae 25y, merchant, s/o E. T. & Margaret Fields; Alice L. Foxwell, ae 17y, d/o Geo. & Fannie Foxwell; Oct 24 1886 by Rev. F. H. Hall.

Julian Heywood, ae 24y, farm, of West Point
VA, s/o R. C. & Mary M. Cooke Heywood; Lucy
E. Daniel, ae 18y, d/o Peter Daniel; Nov 4
1886 by Rev. J. W. Taylor.

Wise Baytop, ae 26y, col'rd, sailor, of
Prince George Co VA, s/o Jacob & Caroline
Baytop; Lizzie Jackman, ae 25y, col'rd, d/o
Jeff Jackman, mother unk; Oct 20 1886 by
Rev. A. T. Gayle.

James F. Bew, ae 21y, carpenter, of King
and Queen Co VA, s/o Jas. M. & Jane F. Strat-
ton Bew; Eulalia M. Stubbs, ae 19y, of King
and Queen Co VA, d/o Jas. M. & Parthenia A.
Didlake Stubbs; Oct 20 1886 by Rev. George
Rives.

Franklin Heywood, ae 34y, fisherman, s/o
Wm. & Eliza Ann Heywood; Virginia Ann East,
ae 18y, of Northampton Co VA, d/o John T. &
Nancy W. East; Nov 10 1886 by Rev. J. W.
Taylor.

George Lewis, ae 23y, fisherman, of Mathews Co VA, s/o Wescomb & Martha Lewis; El-
dora West, ae 21y, d/o Cary & Virginia West;
Nov 14 1886 by Rev. Wm. B. Lee.

James H. Lockley, ae 45y, col'rd, widower,
farm, s/o Armistead & Sally Lockley; Frances
Baytop, ae 40y, widow,col'rd, d/o Betsy;
Nob 18 1886 by Rev. J. W. Booth.

John H. Travis, ae 39y, col'rd, widower,
oyster, s/o Edward & Kesiah Travis; Mary Ann
Kemp, ae 19y, col'rd, d/o Henry & Matilda
Kemp (now Taliaferro); Dec 19 1886 by Rev.
Madison Lewis.

Charles H. Fox, ae 29y, col'rd, oyster,
s/o Jesse & Sally Fox, (now Sally Young);
Sarah Jackman, ae 22y, col'rd, d/o Jeff &
Rose Jackman; Dec 23 1886 by Rev. A. T.
Gayle.

Joseph Smith, ae 23y, fisherman, s/o Thos.
& Eliza Smith; Elizabeth F. Jenkins, ae 16y,
d/o Frederick & Fanny Jenkins; Dec 23 1886
by Rev. J. W. Taylor.

John H. Palmer, ae 21y, farm, s/o P. &
Mary E. Dutton Palmer; Maria E. German, ae
17y, d/o Wm. & Sarah L. Bridges German; Dec
23 1886 by Rev. Wm. E. Wiatt.

James Columbus Wilson, ae 22y, col'rd,
sailor, s/o Rob't & Lucy Wilson; Susan Bristow, ae 19y, d/o Wm. & Ann Bristow; Dec 25
1886 by Rev. John W. Booth.

John T. Caffee, ae 44y, col'rd, oyster,
s/o John & Mary Caffee; Rebecca Kelly, ae
44y, col'rd, widow, of King and Queen Co VA,
d/o Betsy Morriss, father unk; June 8 1886
by Rev. Jas. C. Martin.

Gabriel Dixon, ae 48y, col'rd, widower,
factory hand, s/o Phill & Dolly Dixon; Susan
Monroe, ae 27y, col'rd, d/o Iverson & Grace;
June 11 1886 by Rev. J. W. Booth.

James Whiting, ae 26y, col'rd, teamster,
of King and Queen Co VA, s/o Hezekiah &
Charlotte Whiting; Jenny Taylor, ae 23y,
col'rd, d/o Patra & Milly Taylor; June 13
1886 by Rev. J. W. Booth.

Robert H. Gayle, ae 23y, col'rd, farm, of
York Co VA, s/o Robin & Keziah Gayle; Sarah
Jackson, ae 22y, col'rd, of York Co Va, d/o
Simon & Lucy Ann Jackson; June 13 1886 by
Rev. A. T. Gayle.

Charles Jones, ae 29y, farm, s/o Wm. W. &
S. Maria Pollard Jones; Lula C. Jones, ae
28y, d/o Walker F. & Martha A. Baytop Jones;
June 16 1886 by Rev. Wm. E. Wiatt.

Iverson Monroe, ae 62y, col'rd, widower,
farm, s/o Jas. & Rose Monroe; Susan ward, ae
55y, widow, col'rd, d/o Maria Hill, father
unk; June 17 1886 by Rev. J. W. Booth.

William Morriss, ae 24y, col'rd, oyster
and farm, s/o John & Catharine Morriss;
Julia Burwell, ae 21y, col'rd, d/o Beverly &
Maria Burwell; June 23 1886 by Rev. J. W.
Booth.

Joseph S. Fauntleroy, ae 25y, col'rd,
carpenter, of Hanover Co Va, s/o Noah &
Eliza Fauntleroy; Mary Ann Carter, ae 17y,
col'rd, d/o Edmund & Minnie Carter; June 24
1886 by Rev. E. W. Page.

James Henry Jarvis, ae 23y, col'rd, farm,
of Mathews Co VA, s/o Humphrey & Lucy Jarvis;
Charlotte Tabb, ae 23y, col'rd, widow, d/o
Henry & Frances Patterson; June 24 1886 by
Rev. J. W. Booth.

William Thomas Carter, ae 25y, col'rd, farm, s/o Jas. & Lucinda Carter; Caroline E. Driver, ae 27y, col'rd, widow, d/o Miles & Hannah Seawell; June 30 1886 by Rev. J. W. Booth.

William Shorter Jr, ae 22y, col'rd, farm, s/o Wm. & Mary Shorter; Lucy Ann Monroe, ae 22y, col'rd, d/o Jas. & Betsy Monroe; July 4 1886 by Rev. A. T. Gayle.

Gilbert Daniel, ae 23y, col'rd, oyster, of Alabama Co GA, s/o Hard & Susan Daniel; Eliza Ellen Whiting, ae 20y, col'rd, d/o Manny & Henrietta Whiting; July 4 1886 by Rev. E. W. Page.

Abraham Washington, ae 21y, col'rd, farm, of York Town VA, s/o Wm. & Mary washington; Adalaide Brown, ae 18y, col'rd, d/o Miland & Roberta Brown; Dec 25 1886 by Rev. John W. Booth.

Joshua Thornton, ae 22y, col'rd, oyster and farm, s/o Oliver & Milly Thornton; Hetty Morriss, ae 21y, col'rd, d/o Chas. & Henrietta Morriss; Dec 25 1886 by Rev. A. T. Gayle.

Henry Wright, ae 26y, col'rd, oyster, s/o Stephen & Susan Wright; Alice Whiting, ae 16y, col'rd, d/o Jeff & Sarah Williams Whiting; Dec 25 1886 by Rev. E. W. Page.

John Randall, ae 23y, col'rd, farm, s/o Oscar & Sarah Randall (now Wiatt); Frances Wiatt, ae 20y, col'rd, d/o Rob't & Mary Wiatt; Dec 26 1886 by Rev. A. T. Gayle.

William F. Wallace, ae 26y, waterman, s/o Wm. & Elizabeth Williams Wallace; Emma A. Williams, ae 19y, d/o W. S. & Carrie B. Williams; Dec 26 1886 by Rev. F. H. Hall.

Aaron Williams, ae 22y, col'rd, oyster, s/o Rich'd & Judy Williams; Judy F. Smith, ae 21y, col'rd, d/o John Wm. & Ann Smith; Dec 26 1886 by Rev. John W. Booth.

Jefferson W. Carter, ae 21y, col'rd, farm, s/o Jas. & Lucinda Carter; Eugenia Bright, ae 21y, col'rd, d/o Louisa Bright; Dec 28 1886 by Rev. Wm. E. Wiatt.

John Berry, ae 21y, col'rd, oyster, of York Co Va, s/o Bill & Louisa Berry; Elizabeth Jones, ae 21y, col'rd, d/o Gabriel & Lucy Jones; Dec 30 1886 by Rev. J. W. Booth.

John R. Brown, ae 44y, widower, farm, of
Middlesex Co VA, s/o Smith W. & Susan H.
Garrett Brown; Ruth Helen Marble, ae 24y, of
Caroline Co MD, d/o R. H. & Mary M. Williams
Marble; Dec 26 1886 by Rev. T. H. Campbell.

Charles B. Fleming, ae 33y, seafaring,
s/o Jas. W. & Mildred F. Hobday Fleming; Ida
B. Williams, ae 21y, d/o Wm. H. & Malvenia
Hobday Williams; Dec 26 1886 by Rev. J. W.
Taylor.

Charles Henry White, ae 35y, widower,
fish and öyster, of Mathews Co Va, s/o Wm. H.
& Harriet F. White; Loretta Jenkins, ae 24y,
widow, d/o Jos. Tillage & Anna; Dec 29 1886
by Rev. J. W. Taylor.

Edward Braxton, ae 30y, col'rd, oyster,
s/o Temple & Rebecca Braxton; Sarah Evans,
ae 25y, col'rd, d/o John & Betsy Evans; Jan
2 1887 by Rev. Madison Lewis.

Joseph Richardson, ae 22y, col'rd, farm,
s/o Adam & Milly Richardson; Lizzie Smith,
ae 19y, col'rd, d/o Tice & Judy Smith; Dec
30 1886 by Rev. John Wm. Booth.

Ambrose Scott, ae 22y, col'rd, farm, s/o
Sam & Winny Scott; Laura Laws, ae 21y,
col'rd, d/o Jas. & Mary Laws; Jan 2 1887 by
Rev. A. T. Gayle.

James C. Larkins. ae 23y, farm, s/o Geo.
& Maria Seawell Larkins; Virginia Lee Blake,
ae 17y, parents unk; Jan 5 1887 by Rev. F.
H. Hall.

Christopher West, ae 71y, widower, öyster,
s/o Wm. & Rebecca West; Annie Smith, ae 18y,
d/o John & Nancy Smith; Jan 6 1887 by Rev.
J. W. Taylor.

William Cooke, ae 37y, widower, col'rd,
shoemaker, s/o Peter & Agnes Cooke; Ruth
Anna Noggin, ae 17y, col'rd, d/o Rob't &
Maria Noggin; Jan 6 1887 by Rev. A. T.
Gayle.

William Robert Green, ae 31y, col'rd,
oyster, s/o John & Maria Green; Louisa Ellen
Whiting, ae 20y, d/o Martin & Matilda Whiting, (now Lockley); Jan 13 1887 by Rev. E.
W. Page.

Richard Hughes, ae 29y, col'rd, oyster, s/o Jas. & Betsy Hughes; Agnes Winston, ae 21y, col'rd, d/o Geo. & Mary Winston; Jan 12 1887 by Rev. Z. Taylor Whiting.

William Woodson Moody, ae 27y, salesman, of Middlesex Co VA, s/o Woodson C. & Lucy F. Lumpkin Moody; Lottie Virginia Moody, ae 21y, of Washington D. C, d/o Alex W. & Virginia Partello Moody; Jan 15 1887 by Rev. Wm. B. Lee, Rector of Ware Parrish.

Arthur Lewis, ae 24y, col'rd, oyster, s/o Abram & Mary Lewis; Mary F. Fleming, ae 19y, col'rd, d/o John & Lizzie Fleming; Jan 16. 1887 by Rev. Z. Taylor Fleming.

George Thornton, ae 35y, col'rd, farm, s/o Paul & Keziah Thornton; Frances Smith, ae 30y, col'rd, widow, d/o Thos. & Patsy Smith; Feb 6 1887 by Rev. John W. Booth.

Joshua Thomas Minor, ae 27y, merchant, s/o Chas. E. & Ellen S. Stubblefield Minor; Lucy Elizabeth Ransone, ae 27y, d/o Jas. & Ann Stubblefield Ransone; Feb 7 1887 by Rev. F. H. Hall.

Charles Richardson, ae 30y, col'rd,widower, farm, s/o Adam & Milly Richardson; Maria Jones, ae 22y, col'rd, d/o Molly Jones; Feb 9 1887 by Rev. J. W. Booth.

Major Boyd, ae 25y, col'rd, farm, s/o Major & Mary Boyd; Fanny Todd, ae 22y, c'ld, d/o Aaron & Jenny Todd; Feb 13 1887 by Rev. A. T. Gayle.

James T. Dudley, ae 28y, widower, miller, s/o Benja. & Sarah Gressitt Dudley; Ida E. Gressitt, ae 17y, d/o Wm. Gressitt, mother unk; Feb 15 1887 by Rev. F. H. Hall.

James T. Jenkins, ae 34y, oyster, s/o Edmund & Martha Walker Jenkins; Emily F. Shackelford, ae 16y, d/o John W. & Virginia F. Shackelford; Feb 13 1887 by Rev. T. H. Campbell.

John H. Robins, ae 32y, carpenter, s/o John W. & Mary M. Moore Robins; Mary C. Minor, ae 17y, d/o Wm. T. & Mary F. Enos Minor; Feb 20 1887 by Rev. Wm. E. Wiatt.

Peter Williams, ae 21y, col'rd, oyster, of Yorktown VA, s/o Simon & Katy Williams; Susan Banks, ae 21y, d/o Jas. & Edith Banks; Feb 20 1887 by Rev. Z. Taylor Whiting.

Richard Jefferson Purcell, ae 22y, oyster,
s/o John & Margaret Ann James Purcell;
Indianna Belvin, ae 21y, d/o Edward & Mary
Aherron Belvin; Feb 22 1887 by Rev. T. H.
Campbell.

Thomas Jefferson Wray, ae 28y, minister,
of Greenville Co VA, s/o B. A. & M. J. Parr
Wray; Nora C. Shackelford, ae 16y, d/o Alex
& M. Ann Martin Shackelford; Feb 23 1887 by
Rev. Geo. W. Wray, minister of the Gospel M.
E. Church.

John Washington, ae 33y, col'rd, widower,
wood cutter, s/o Geo. & Susan Washington;
Lizzie Ann Pendleton, ae 21y, col'rd, d/o
Geo. & Peggy Pendleton; Mar 3 1887 by Rev.
J. W. Booth.

Thomas R. Scott, ae 27y, col'rd, oyster,
of Manchester VA, s/o John W. & Martha Scott;
Mary Etta Dixon, ae 21y, col'rd, d/o Wm. &
Betsy Dixon; Mar 27 1887 by Rev, E. W. Page.

Thomas Edwin Freeman, ae 28y, house Carp-
enter, s/o Thos. E. & Martha F. Curry Free-
man; Henrietta Griffith, ae 32y, widow, of
Norfolk City VA, d/o Rob't & Lucy Chapman
Howard; Mar 30 1887 by Rev. Wm. B. Lee,
Rector of Ware Parrish.

Robert Ware, ae 22y, col'rd, farm, s/o
James Henry & Nancy Ware; Mary Louisa Hudgin,
ae 22y, col'rd, d/o John & Rosa Hudgin; Apr 3
1887 by Rev. Madison Lewis.

Anthony Smith, ae 27y, oyster, s/o John &
Ann West Smith; Emma Heywood, ae 26y, d/o __
& Lucy Heywood; Apr 3 1887 by Rev. Wm. S.
Campbell, pastor of Presbyterian Church.

John Valentine, ae 35y, col'rd, widower,
laborer, of N. C, lived Gloucester Co VA,
s/o Rosetta Valentine; Sarah Diggs, ae 22y,
col'rd, widow, of Mathews Co Va, lived Glo.
Co VA, d/o Wm. & Lorenda Diggs; Apr 18 1887
by Rev. A. T. Gayle.

Sydny Barnhill, ae 26y, col'rd, laborer,
of Charlotte N. C, s/o Ison & Fanny Barnhill;
Mary Lizzie Lee, ae 22y, col'rd, of Yorktown
VA, d/o Elijah & Lucy Lee; Apr 17 1887 by
Rev. Wm. B. Lee.

William T. Nelson, ae 26y, col'rd, laborer, of Norfolk City VA, s/o Wm. & Susan Nelson; Elizabeth Guthrie, ae 22y, col'rd, d/o Waltz & Rachel Guthrie, (Rachel Townsend), Apr 30 1887 by Rev. Z. Taylor Whiting.

John W. Hopkins, ae 33y, sailor, of Cambridge MD, s/o Wm. & Eliza Brooks Hopkins; Kate D. Elliott, ae 18y, d/o Pascal & Martha A. Ware Elliott; Apr 21 1887 by Rev. Wm. E. Wiatt.

Christopher Lancaster, ae 36y, col'rd, widower, farm, s/o Isaac & Polly Lancaster; Keziah Lancaster, ae 23y, col'rd, d/o Patsy Lancaster; May 8 1887 by Rev. J. W. Booth.

Robert L. Thomas, ae 24y, fishing, s/o Rob't F. & Jemima Hogg Thomas; Martha Ellen Williams, ae 20y, d/o Ed & Martha Brown Williams; May 31 1887 by Rev. J. W. Taylor.

Robert C. Powell, ae 50y, widower, waterman, of Mathews Co VA, s/o Lewis & Mary F. Powell; Annie C. Walker, ae 35y, widow, d/o Wm. & Julia A. Dunston Ambrose; May 26 1887 by Rev. Wm. S. Campbell.

Charles R. Bridges, ae 40y, widower, hotel keeper, s/o Wm. H. & Ann Maria Gibbs Bridges; Pocahontas Clements, ae 21y, d/o E. Thos. & E. V. Harwood Clements; June 20 1887 by Rev. Wm. S. Campbell.

Coleman, ae 26y, col'rd, oyster, s/o Edmund & Sally Ann Burwell; Pinky Kemp, ae 32y, col'rd, widow, d/o Jas. & Mary Dixon; June 8 1887 by Rev. A. T. Gayle.

William Lomax, ae 28y, col'rd, oyster, of S. C, s/o Amy Washington; Mollie Moore, ae 22y, col'rd, d/o Rich'd & Jane Moore; June 13 1887 by Rev. A. T. Gayle.

John J. Walker, ae 22y, col'rd, oyster, of York Co VA, s/o Simon & Eliza Walker; Margaret Hughes, ae 21y, col'rd, d/o Jas. & Betsy Hughes; June 12 1887 by Rev. Z. Taylor Whiting.

Cary Whiting, ae 21y, farm, s/o Edmund & Jane Whiting; Viney Jones, ae 25y, widow, d/o Jack & Gracy Peyton; June 19 1887 by Rev. Wm. B. Lee.

William N. Waller, ae 28y, commission merchant, of Norfolk City VA, s/o Mathew Page & Mary Tazewell Waller; Annie F. Duncan, ae 23y, of St. Louis MISSOURI, lived Glo. Co VA, d/o Jas. & Mary F. Franklin Duncan; June 22 1887 by Rev. Wm. B. Lee.

Philip Pryor, ae 27y, farm, s/o Philip & Jane Pryor; Lucy Jackson, ae 22y, of Middlesex Co VA, d/o Philip & Mary Jackson; June 28 1887 by Rev. P. T. Edwards.

Albert Lockley, ae 48y, col'rd, widower, mechanic, of KIng and Queen Co VA, parents unk; Mary Susan Belcher, ae 21y, col'rd, d/o Eliza Lockly, father unk; July 7 1887 by Rev. J. W. Booth.

Charles Howard, ae 23y, col'rd, farm, s/o Martha Howard, father unk; Martha A. Stokes, ae 19y, col'rd, d/o Wm. F. & Mary E. Stokes; July 14 1887 by Rev. Z. Taylor Whiting.

J. E. Teagle, ae 28y, farm, s/o John E. & Martha A. Teagle; Clara B. Walker, ae 25y, d/o Enoch W. & Elizabeth H. Walker; July 17 1887 by Rev. J. W. Taylor.

Calvin E. Booker, ae 20y, farm, of King and Queen Co VA, s/o John T. & Lucy A. Booker; Margaret T. Walker, ae 19y, d/o John M. & Mary E. Walker; Aug 4 1887 by Rev. S. T. Thrift.

William Dudley, ae 25y, farm, s/o Thos. & Susan Dudley; Victoria Billy Ransone, ae 16y, d/o Jas. E. & Joicy F. Ransone; Aug 29 1887 by Rev. F. H. Hall.

Julious L. Lawson, ae 31y, farm, s/o Jas. L. & Jane Lawson; Lelia Ann Walker, ae 20y, d/o Wm. S. & Rosa A. Walker; Sept 1 1887 by S. S. Thrift.

Peter Hogg, ae 28y, oyster, s/o Geo. & Rachel Hogg; Mary Susan Smith, ae 18y, d/o Sam'l & Mary E. Smith; Sept 4 1887 by Rev. J. W. Taylor.

James P. Ash, ae 42y, widower, farm, s/o Thos. & Lucy Ash; Lizzie W. Hughes, ae 32y, d/o Jasper C. & F. A. Hughes; Sept 6 1887 by Rev. Wm. B. Lee.

Leonard Schools, ae 54y, widower, farm, s/o Dawson & Lucy Schools; Lucy Frances Brown, ae 18y, d/o Thos. & Elizabeth Nuttall Brown; Sept 13 1887 by Rev. Wm. S. Campbell.

William S. Horseley, ae 24y, farm, s/o Jas. K. & Martha Horseley; Satira Ann Ison, ae 16y, d/o Wm. W. & Harriet Ison; Sept 22 1887 by Rev. T. H. Campbell.

Cary Smith, ae 23y, laborer, s/o Parker & Alice Smith; N. Harrison, ae 23y, d/o Jos. & Nancy Harrison; Sept 27 1887 by Rev. A. T. Gayle.

William Wiatt, ae 36y, oyster and farm, s/o John & Louisa Wiatt; Mary Boyd, ae 22y, d/o W. & Susan Boyd; Oct 4 1887 by Rev. E. W. Page.

Coleman Heywood, ae 33y, widower, farm, s/o Wm. & E. Heywood; Jennie Smith, ae 19y, d/o Henry & M. E. Smith; Oct 9 1887 by Rev. J. W. Taylor.

John Green, ae 26y, s/o John & Anna Green; Margaret Heywood, ae 22y, widow, d/o Wm. & E. Kellum; Oct 13 1887 by Rev. J. W. Taylor.

William Patterson, ae 39y, widower, oyster, Jas. & Keziah Patterson; Elizabeth Green, ae 32y, d/o John & Maria Green; Oct 6 1887 by Rev. A. T. Gayle.

William H. Booth, ae 58y, widower, farm, s/o Wm. & Rose Booth; Fanny Davis, ae 45y, widow, d/o W. & H. Taliaferro; Oct 5 1887 by Rev. John W. Booth.

A. T. Gayle, ae 36y, widower, minister of the gospel, s/o Robin & K. Gayle; Eudora Williams, ae 26y, widow, d/o L. & C. Williams; Oct 18 1887 by Rev. John W. Booth.

Lee Lawson, ae 23y, farm, of King and Queen Co VA, s/o R. B. & Nancy Lawson; H. F. Smither, ae 27y, d/o --- & Elizabeth Willis Smither; Oct 20 1887 by Rev. T. H. Campbell.

J. R. Lewis, ae 24y, farm, of Mathews Co VA, s/o Jas. S. & Columbia A. Lewis; Mary Richeson, ae 19y, d/o Fleming W. & Ellen Richeson; Oct 20 1887 by Rev. R. A. Fox.

Jefferson D. Callis, ae 26y, merchant, of Middlesex Co Va, s/o Jas. Henry & Mary Jane Callis; Etta Revel Dutton, ae 17y, d/o A. F. & Elizabeth Dutton; Nov 1 1887 by Rev. C. T. Comer.

Felix Braxton, ae 27y, widower, oyster, s/o Carter & Matilda Braxton; Verna Johnston, ae 21y, d/o Rich'd & Sallie Johnson; Nov 3 1887 by Rev. Z. T. Whiting.

James T. Grey, ae 42y, widower, farm, of
Md, s/o Major & Margaret Grey; Lela R. Rowe,
ae 30y, widow, d/o Wm. & Mary E. Massey; Nov
11 1887 by Rev. E. M. Peterson in Mathews
Co VA.

James Braxton, ae 42y, widower, farm, of
King and Queen Co VA, s/o Esau & Sarah Braxton; Lucy Middleton, ae 40y, widow, d/o
Dan'l Roy & Franky Baytop formerly Roy; Dec
4 1887 by Rev. Frank Page.

John L. Hogg, ae 27y, oyster, s/o Wm. &
Sarah A. Hogg; Lulie V. Hogg, ae 22y, d/o
Vincent & Martha A. Hogg; Dec 8 1887 by Rev.
F. H. Hall.

W. T. Croswell, ae 38y, oyster, s/o Isaac
& Elizabeth Croswell; Josephine Croswell, ae
18y, d/o R. R. & Lucy A. Croswell; Nov 9
1887 by Rev. J. W. Taylor.

Robert C. Walton, ae 26y, sailor, of King
and Queen Co VA, s/o John C. & Sarah Dunn
Walton; Lillie Ann Miller, ae 19y, d/o Wm.
S. & Virginia A. Dutton Miller; Dec 11 1887
by Rev. J. W. Taylor.

W. W. Ison , ae 45y, widower, farm, of
King and Queen Co VA, s/o Reuben & Nancy
Walden Ison; Georgianna A. Padgett, ae 27y,
widow, d/o Jas. K. & M. A. Hibble Horseley;
Dec 22 1887 by Rev. C. C. Westonbaker.

William Patterson, ae 39y, widower, oyster, s/o J. Patterson; Elizabeth Green, ae
32y, d/o K. Patterson; Oct 6 1887 by Rev. A.
T. Gayle.

Geo. J. Claytor, ae 30y, farm, s/o Jas.
T. & Rebecca Adams Claytor; Fannie Cecil
Chapman, ae 18y, d/o Sam'l B. & Harriet B.
Davis Chapman; Dec 22 1887 by Rev. C. C.
Westonbaker.

Chas. H. Muse, ae 26y, widower, merchant,
of Essex Co VA, s/o S. W. Y. & Sarah J.
Coats Muse; Kate E. Gregg, ae 28y, widow, of
Middlesex Co VA, d/o Loland & Mary J. Montague Fleet; Dec 30 1887 by Rev. F. H. Hall.

Richard H. Bryant, ae 47y, widower, farm,
of Queen Ann Co MD, s/o Henry & Lucinda
Brown Bryant; Lucretia S. Bray, ae 24y, d/o
Thos. J. & Martha A. Bray; Nov 24 1887 by
Rev. F. H. Hall.

Les Sturges, ae 21y, sailor, s/o Jas. &
Hester Sturges; Emiline Lockley, ae 22y, d/o
Albert & Hester Lockley; Dec 22 1887 by Rev.
John W. Booth.

James Taliaferro, ae 23y, farm, s/o Cel-
lar & J. Taliaferro; Sally Brown, ae 19y,
d/o Frank & Lucy Brown; Dec 25 1887 by Rev.
John W. Booth.

Frank Beasley, ae 45y, sailor, of New
York, s/o John & E. McSwan Beasley; Virginia
Huel, ae 21y, d/o Franklin J. & Sarah E.
Foster Huel; Dec 28 1887 by Rev. Wm. B. Lee.

Benjamin F. Leigh, ae 34y, farm, s/o Benj.
& Maria Seawell Leigh; E. F. Leigh, ae 21y,
d/o W. P. R. & Frances Stubblefield Leigh;
Dec 27 1887 by Rev. S. S. Thrift.

Henry Gayle, ae 32y, farm, s/o Wm. &
Rachel Roberson Gayle; Charlotte Stokes, ae
40y, widow, Burrows & Jenny Taliaferro; Dec
27 1887 by Rev. E. W. Page.

Jefferson Thornton, ae 40y, farm, s/o
Eliza Thornton, father unk; Lucy Washington,
ae 30y, d/o Sarah Washington, father unk;
Dec 28 1887 by Rev. John W. Booth.

Willie T. Kemp, ae 24y, blacksmith, of
King and Queen Co VA, s/o Thos. & Julia
Pointer Kemp; Mary E. Hall, ae 17y, d/o
Lewis O. & Martha Enos Hall; Dec 28 1887 by
Rev. C. C. Westonbaker.

Frank Reed, ae 29y, farm, of King and
Queen Co VA, s/o Wm. Reed & Philis Braxton;
Ann M. Perrin, ae 25y, d/o Sarah Perrin,
father unk; Dec 29 1887 by Rev. P. T.
Edwards.

William T. Glass, ae 50y, farm, of Mathews
Co VA, s/o Andrew & Sarah Bagby Glass; Mar-
garette A. Pointer, ae 28y, d/o Wm. S. &
Mary F. Dixon Pointer; Dec 29 1887 by Rev.
J. W. Taylor.

William Roberson, ae 23y, oyster, s/o
Lewis & Susan Booth Roberson; Lizzie Cooke,
ae 17y, d/o Willie Stubblefield & Susan
Cooke; Dec 29 1887 by Rev. Z. Taylor Whiting.

R. Lee Jenkins, ae 22y, oyster, s/o Frederick & Fanny Heywood Jenkins; Lucy Hogg, ae
18y, d/o Warner & Susan Hogg; Dec 25 1887 by
Rev. J. W. Taylor.

William C. Ashley, ae 26y, farm, s/o Geo.
& L. Simon Ashley; Mary Driver, ae 21y, d/o
Addison & Elizabeth Collins Driver; Dec 29
1887 by Rev. John W. Booth.

Roane Patterson, ae 23y, farm, s/o Henry
& Frances Patterson; Georgianna Washington,
ae 16y, d/o Geo. & Leah Washington; Dec 31
1887 by Rev. Frank Page.

William Scott, ae 22y, farm, s/o John &
Rebecca Scott; Flora Thomas, ae 25y, widow,
d/o Chas. & Isabella Cary; Sept 15 1887 By
Rev. A. T. Gayle.

Lewis Roberson, ae 75y, widower, farm, s/o
Harry & Amy Roberson; Dafney Whiting, ae 50y,
widow, d/o Harry & Mary Carter; Dec 8 1887
by Rev. Z. Taylor Whiting.

Malvin Figins, ae 35y, widower, farm, of
Buford N. C, s/o Warren & R. G. Figins; Cate
S. Jackson, ae 17y, d/o Wm. & Sarah Jackson;
Oct 23 1887 by Rev. A. T. Gayle.

Robert Booker, ae 63y, widower, farm, s/o
Rob't & Alice Booker; Virginia Pollard, ae
37y, widow, d/o Geo. & Lucy Braxton; Dec 13
1887 by Rev. P. T. Edwards.

Emmanuel Gordon, ae 33y, widower, farm,
s/o Chas. & Nancy Gordon; Susan Tilman, ae
20y, d/o Jeff & Maria Johnston Tilman; Dec
25 1887 by Rev. A. T. Gayle.

C. H. Wallace, ae 25y, farm and oyster,
s/o Wm. & Elizabeth Williams Wallace; Annie
B. Hogg, ae 21y, d/o Wm. & Sarah Hogg; Nov
24 1887 by Rev. F. H. Hall.

Philip Clayton, ae 24y, farm, s/o Rob't &
Nancy Clayton; Maria Curtis, ae 19y, d/o
Jas. & Susan Curtis; June 30 1887 by Rev. P.
T. Edwards.

Elias Kemp, ae 24y, oyster, s/o Henry &
Elizabeth Kemp; Maria C. Dudley, ae 18y, d/o
Lewis & Nancy Dudley; June 30 1887 by Rev.
Z. Taylor Whiting.

M. R. Booker, ae 31y, widower, miller,
lived Middlesex Co VA, s/o Lewis T. & Lucy
F. Booker; Emma J. Hibble, ae 18y, d/o Chas.
W. & Mary E. Hibble; Oct 16 1887.

Charles Roberson, ae 22y, sailor, of Mid-
dlesex Co VA, s/o Sam & M. Hoskins Roberson;
Sally Banks, ae 21y, d/o John & Susan Banks;
Jan 2 1888 by Rev. Maddison Lewis.

William J. Dutton, ae 23y, farm, s/o Wm.
T. & Martha A. Dutton; Sarah A. Booker, ae
23y, d/o Chas. E. & Frances A. Booker; Jan
11 1888 by Rev. Wm. S. Campbell.

J. Henry Hobday, ae 34y, mechanic, s/o J.
F. & Helen N. Hobday; Alice J. Smith, ae
18y, d/o John & Alice Anna Smith; Jan 3 1888
by Rev. J. W. Taylor.

John H. Smith, ae 23y, oyster, s/o Wm. &
Mary Ransone Smith; Lucy Belvin, ae 21y, d/o
Henry & G. Smith Belvin; Jan 12 1888 by Rev.
F. H. Hall.

Robert Hall, ae 25y, oyster, s/o John &
Susan Brown Hall; Solona J. Brown, ae 21y,
d/o Seymour & Sarah J. Hogg Brown; Jan 5
1888 by Rev. J. W. Taylor.

Robert Scott, ae 25y, farm, s/o Jack &
Eliza Page Scott; Elizabeth Dabney, ae 23y,
d/o Jas. Dabney & Dilcy Page; Jan 5 1888 by
Rev. E. W. Page.

John Banks, ae 24y, oyster, s/o John &
Susan Smith Banks; Venus Jones, ae 21y, d/o
Chas. & Vena Peyton; Jan 1 1888 by Rev. A.
T. Gayle.

Charles Spurlock, ae 44y, farm, s/o Chas.
& Martha Spurlock; Catharine Payne, ae 76y,
widow, parents unk; Jan 19 1888 by Rev. E.
W. Page.

Albert Wiatt, ae 41y, widower, farm, s/o
Adam & Sally Wiatt; Elton Page Howe, ae 20y,
of Middlesex Co VA, d/o John & Mary Kinningham; Jan 26 1888 by Rev. J. W. Booth.

Robert H. McGee, ae 27y, farm, s/o Wm. &
Mary McGee; Mary E. McKendree, ae 26y, of
Essex Co VA, d/o Thos. & Mary McKendree; Feb
8 1888 by Rev. C. C. Westonbaker.

Hezekiah Croswell, ae 26y, farm, s/o J/ &
Sarah Fleming Croswell; Lucy A. Fletcher, ae
21y, d/o C. T. & Maria A. Emory Fletcher;
Feb 9 1888 by Rev. Wm. B. Lee.

William Miller, ae 22y, oyster, s/o Jake
& Vina Miller, (Morris); Sarah Morris, ae
21y, d/o John & Elizabeth (Wallace); Feb 19
1888 by Rev. John W. Booth.

Elex Richardson, ae 23y, farm, s/o Adam &
Milly Burnley Richardson; Lena Ann Smith, ae
20y, d/o Jos. & Cella Burwell Smith; Feb 19
1888 by Rev. E. W. Page.

R. Lee Moore, ae 26y, mechanic, s/o
Rich'd T. & Frances E. Moore; Harion F. Dut-
ton, ae 17y, d/o Edw'd F. & Belle Dutton;
Feb 21 1888 by Rev. C. C. Westonbaker.

Kit Morris, ae 27, laborer, s/o Jas. &
Kasiah Langston Morris; Margaret E. Muse, ae
27y, d/o Essex & Nancy Booth Muse; Feb 23
1888 by Rev. J. W. Booth.

William C. Lemon, ae 38y, widower, oyster,
s/o Jas. & Elizabeth Lemon; Mary Reed, ae 33y,
d/o Fanny Reed, father unk; Feb 22 1888 by
Rev. J. W. Booth.

Charles W. Hogg, ae 32y, widowerer, oys-
ter, s/o John & Julia Dunston Hogg; Sarah E.
Shackelford, ae 21y, d/o John W. & C. F.
Shackelford; Feb 25 1888 by Rev. F. H. Hall.

Robert A. Driver, ae 24y, farm, s/o Addison & Elizabeth Driver; Virginia A. Driver,
ae 23y, d/o Wm. & Arena Driver; Mar 13 1888
by Rev. J. W. Booth.

James J. Sinclair, ae 33y, farm, s/o John
& Lucy H. Baytop Sinclair; India L. Sinclair,
d/o Jefferson & Fanny Lowry Sinclair; Mar
15 1888 by Rev. Wm. B. Lee.

William Johnson, ae 23y, farm, of York Co
VA, s/o Phill & Martha Johnson; Addaline
Corbin, ae 19y, d/o Geo. & Judy Corbin; Mar
18 1888 by Rev. Z. Taylor Whiting.

John Hammond, ae 30y, widower, oysterman,
s/o Abram & Rosa Hammond; Lucy Thomas, ae
28y, widow, d/o Phill & Judy Walker; Mar 18
1888 by Rev. E. W. Page.

William K. Kemp, ae 23y, farm, s/o Henry
& Elizabeth Kemp; Sarah C. Fox, ae 21y, of
Hampton VA, d/o Cambridge & Phillis Fox; Mar
28 1888 by Rev. E. W. Page.

James T. Smith, ae 36y, widower, boatman,
s/o Wm. & Elizabeth Thompson Smith; Georgia
A. Smith, ae 16y, d/o Jas. K. & Sarah A.
Morey Smith; Apr 30 1888 by Rev. F. H. Hall.

Robert Driver, ae 22y, laborer, s/o Wm. &
Rena Driver; Euwinia King, ae 18y, d/o Sarah
Drummond, father unk; Apr 5 1888 by Rev. John
W. Booth.

W. E. Lawson, ae 32y, farm, s/o John W. &
E. Mann Lawson; M. C. Cox, ae 25y, d/o Geo.
W. & Sarah F. Williams Cox; Apr 7 1888 by Rev.
W. S. Campbell.

Thos. E. Lamberth, ae 50y, widower, farm, s/o John & Mildred Walker Lamberth; Cecelia A. Roane, ae 28y, d/o Warner P. & Fanny Bland Roane; Apr 5 1888 by Rev. C. C. Westonbaker.

Jas. P. Chapman, ae 21y, farm, s/o Wesley & Margaret Chapman; Martha Deadman, ae 19y, d/o Jim & Frances Deadman; Apr 14 1888 by Rev. P. T. Edwards.

Jacob A. Baytop, ae 25y, farm, s/o Randall & Frances baytop; Sally Leigh, ae 22y, d/o John & Eliza Leigh; Apr 22 1888 by Rev. Frank Page.

Monroe B. Sibley, ae 27y, oyster, of Middlesex Co VA, s/o Dan'l B. & Sarah F. Miller Sibley; Bettie E. Sibley, ae 21y, of Middlesex Co VA, d/o Stage & Frances Buckner Sibley; May 6 1888 by Rev. R. A. Folkes.

Henry Jones, ae 30y, farm, s/o Louisa Jones, father unk; Patcy Carter, ae 35y, widow, d/o Lewis Lemon, mother unk; May 10 1888 by Rev. Frank Page.

Squire Lacy, ae 22y, farm, s/o Squire & Margarette Lacy; Emma Wormley, ae 21y, of King and Queen Co VA, d/o Henry & Letty Wormley; May 10 1888 by Rev. Wm. J. Corbin.

Geo. W. Shackelford, ae 24y, farm, lived Mathews Co VA, s/o Rich'd R. & Ellen Massey Shackelford; Lucy V. Figg, ae 15y, d/o John & T. Blake Figg; May 17 1888 by Rev. Chas. F. Comer.

Wm. Groom, ae 33y, widower, laborer, of Queen Ann Co MD, s/o Rich'd & Nancy Groom; Maria Fox, ae 31y, widow, d/o Simon & Mary Stokes; May 26 1888 by Rev. WM. B. Lee.

Archie H. Robins, ae 35y, miller, of Mathews Co VA, s/o Augustine W. & Elizabeth P. Todd Robins; Mattie M. Robins, ae 29y, widow, of Elizabeth City Co VA, d/o Jefferson Sinclair Sr, & Frances Lowry; May 30 1888 by Rev. Wm. B. Lee.

Ransone White, ae 21y, farm, s/o John R. & Julia A. Diggs White; Mary S. Brushwood, ae 19y, d/o Jas. & E. R. Brushwood; may 31 1888 by Rev. C. C. Westonbaker.

John Payne, ae 24y, oyster, s/o Wm. &
Caroline Payne; Eliza Grevius, ae 18y, d/o
Davy & Mary Ellen Grevius; June 17 1888 by
Rev. E. W. Page.

David Baldwin, ae 66y, widower, retired
banker, of Baltimore City MD, s/o Pierson &
Sophia Aldngde Baldwin; Rosa S. Cooksey, ae
45y, widow, of Baltimore MD, d/o Geo. R. &
Amelia Jackson; June 20 1888 by Rev. W. B.
Lee.

William H. Pryor, ae 23y, laborer, s/o
Phill & Jane Taylor Pryor; Emiline Cooke, a
25y, widow, d/o Peter & Frances Ross; June
1888 by Rev. P. T. Edwards.

Alexander Deadman, ae 24y, farm, s/o R.
Mary Gwynn Deadman; Emma Wiatt, ae 19y, d/o
Temple & Harriet Whiting Wiatt; June 24 188
by Rev. Frank Page.

James H. Kemp, ae 32y, widower, col'rd,
laborer, of Middlesex Co VA, s/o Jas. &
Dicie Deans Kemp; Elizabeth Alice Cooke, ae
21y, col'rd, d/o Jas. & Emiline Ross Cooke,
July 11 1888 by Rev. P. T. Edwards.

John Dabney Shackelford, ae 20y, farm, c
Hanover Co VA, s/o J. W. & Fanny E. Cooke
Shackelford; Mary Alice Lamberth, ae 20y,
d/o Thos. E. & Maria L. Bridges Lamberth;
July 26 1888 by Rev. C. C. Westonbaker.

Peyton C. Seawell, ae 35y, carpenter, s
Benja. & Mary Oliver Seawell; Ann Elizabet
Seawell, ae 28y, widow, d/o Henry & Margare
Ambrose; July 22 1888 by Rev. F. H. Hall.

Jefferson Burrell, ae 24y, col'd, widow
farm, s/o Braxton Burrell & Ellen Phillips
Mary Elizabeth Banks, ae 20y, col'rd, d/o
Jas. & Lucy Lewis Banks; July 27 1888 by
Rev. A. T. Gayle.

Wm. Slaughter, ae 23y, col'rd, oyster,
Wm. & Susan Robinson Slaughter; Mary Lanca
ter, ae 18y, col'rd, d/o Isaac & Frances
Carter; Aug 5 1888 by Rev. J. W. Booth.

James W. Ambrose, ae 21y, oyster, s/o
Leonard Ambrose; Essa Gardner, ae 21y, of
Middlesex Co VA, d/o Rob't Gardner; Aug 8
1888 by Rev. F. H. Hall.

John Hogg, ae 24y, farm, s/o Thos. &
Elizabeth Hogg; Lulie Hogg, ae 24y, d/o
Benja. & Georgia Hogg; Aug 16 1888 by Rev.
F. H. Hall.

James M. Acra, ae 28y, oyster, s/o John
H. & Emily Nuttall Acra; Ada J. Thomas, ae
20y, d/o Joel & Indianna E. Rowe Thomas; Aug
9 1888 by Rev. F. H. Hall.

John Henry Minor, ae 23y, farm, s/o John
W. & Frances A. Mouring MInor; Hattie V.
Acra, ae 18y, d/o John H. & Emily Nuttall
Acra; Aug 9 1888 by Rev. F. H. Hall.

Seymour Taliaferro, ae 23y, farm, s/o Ben
& Maria Taliaferro; Rosetta Booth, ae 15y,
d/o Wm. & Elizabeth Booth; Aug 23 1888 by
Rev. John W. Booth.

Walker King, ae 22y, oyster, s/o Wm. &
Martha West King; Louisa Anna Hall, ae 18y,
d/o Armstead & Kitty Hogg Hall; Aug 28 1888
by Rev. F. H. Hall.

James Johnson, ae 22y, laborer, of Baltimore MD, lived Mathews Co VA, s/o Wm. & Nina
Bowyer Johnson; Harriet Willis, ae 20y, d/o
Cue Willis & Penelopy Mathews Willis; Sept
3 1888 by Rev. E. W. Page.

Dannmore Wiatt, ae 40y, col'rd, widower,
mechanic, s/o Thos. & Sally Anderson Wiatt;
Ann T. Booth, ae 30y col'd, widow, d/o Geo.
Dinah Reed Anderson; Sept 30 1888 by Rev. A.
T. Gayle.

Alexander Ebb, ae 43y, col'rd, government
service, of Baltimore County MD, s/o Wm. &
Sally Admans Ebb; Elizabeth Franch, ae 24y,
col'rd, d/o Peter & Eliza Burwell Franch;
Sept 30 1888 by Rev. John W. Booth.

Alfred Smith, ae 54y, col'rd, widower,
oyster, s/o Joc. & Mary Smith; Clara Whiting,
ae 32 y, col'rd, d/o Isaac & Eliza Whiting;
Oct 7 1888 by Rev. J. W. Booth.

Charles Cooke, ae 21y, col'rd, widower,
oyster, s/o Chas. & Rachel Dabney Cooke;
Mary Carter, ae 22y, col'rd, d/o Sally Ransone, father unk; Oct 8 1888 by Rev. F. H.
Hall.

Corbin Whiting, ae 28y, col'rd, sailor,
of King and Queen Co VA, s/o E. & Jane Whiting; Alice Taylor, ae 25y, col'rd, parents
unk; Oct 18 1888 by Rev. E. W. Page.

Sylvester Jenkins, ae 30y, oyster, s/o Geo. & Susan Howell Jenkins; Lucy Jenkins, ae 30y, widow, d/o John W. & Matilda Trevilian Shackelford; Oct 12 1888 by Rev. F. H. Hall.

L. E. Sutton, ae 26y, farm, of Craven Co N. C, s/o Lemuel & Ester Walker Sutton; Mary E. Bristow, ae 16y, d/o John R. & Mary Chapman Bristow; Oct 18 1888 by Rev. Charles F. Comer.

James Jenkins, ae 28y, widower, oyster, s/o Frederick & Frances Heywood Jenkins; Martha E. West, ae 18y, d/o Christopher & Malvena Smith West; Oct 18 1888 by Rev. F. H. Hall.

W. P. Williams, ae 25y, merchant, s/o Wm. Hunter & Angelina Clements Williams; Roberta A. Hogg, ae 20y, d/o Jas. W. & Cornelia H. Hogg; Oct 16 1888 by Rev. F. H. Hall.

Isaac Garnett, ae 35y, widower, col'rd, farm, of Spotsylvania Co VA, s/o Julia Dickerson, father unk; Fanny Ellis, ae 22y, col'rd, d/o Cain & Fanny Ellis; Oct 18 1888 by Rev. E. W. Page.

Hesekiah Edwards, ae 22y, farm, of King and Queen Co VA, s/o Dunbar & Lucy Cauthorne Edwards; Lucy Goode, ae 18y, d/o John & Catharine Goode; Oct 22 1888 by Rev. S. S. Thrift.

Robert E. Wilson, ae 28y, clerk, of Richmond City VA, s/o Rob't B. & Pamily W. Ould Wilson; Minnie C. Coleman, ae 20y, d/o R. C. & Bella G. Anderson Coleman; Oct 24 1888 by Rev. E. P. Wilson.

James Berry, ae 28y, oyster, s/o Jas. & Mary Hogg Berry; Roselia Deal, ae 22y, d/o Francis & Catharine West Deal; Nov 7 1888 by Rev. W. B. Lee.

Augustine D. Riley, ae 22y, oyster, s/o J. M. & Caroline V. Foster Riley; Delina D. Brown, ae 17y, d/o S. Thomas & Maria Savage Brown; Nov 7 1888 by Rev. F. H. Hall.

Landon J. Miller, ae 32y, widower, oyster and farm, of Middlesex Co VA, s/o Christopher & Elenora Walker Miller; Emma J. Hibble, ae 18y, d/o Chas. & Mary E. Hibble; Nov 6 1888 by Rev. J. H. Dalby.

Thomas H. Jenkins, ae 65y, widower, boat-man, of York Co VA, s/o Henry & Catharine Jenkins; Caroline Williams, ae 26y, widow, d/o Geo. W. Jenkins, mother unk; Nov 9 1888 by Rev. R. A. Folkes.

Christopher Casey, ae 27y, col'rd, farm, s/o J. H. & Mary Casey; Henrietta Bailey, ae 29y, widow, d/o Sally Cooke, father unk; Nov 15 1888 by Rev. Reuben Berkeley.

Albert G. Eaves, ae 41y, widower, manu-facturer, of Birmingham ENGLAND, s/o Thos. & Martha Pickin Eaves, lived New Castle N. Y; Mary E. Harwood, ae 35y, d/o Thos. & Lucy E. Stubblefield Harwood; Nov 19 1888 by Rev. W. B. Lee.

Isaac Burwell, ae 23y, col'rd, oyster, of York Co VA, s/o David & Fanny Jackson Bur-well Jackson; Nancy P. Dudley, ae 18y, d/o Lewis & Nancy Dudley; Nov 29 1888 by Rev. E. E. Page.

Cecil Stubbs, ae 25y, col'rd, farm, s/o Ann Stubbs, father unk; Mary C. Braxton, ae 21y, col'rd, d/o Thos. & Elizabeth Braxton; Nov 5 1888 by Rev. John W. Booth.

Thomas Banks, ae 20y, col'rd, farm, s/o Peter & Ellen Burwell Banks; Mary E. Burwell, ae 19y, col'rd, d/o Addison & Mary Fox Bur-well; Dec 12 1888 by Rev. Frank Page.

Wm. H. Goldman, ae 29y, col'rd, widower, farm, of King and Queen Co VA, s/o Elijah Goldman & Cordelia Collins; Rosa L. Shackel-ford, ae 26y, col'rd, widow, parents unk; Dec 18 1888 by Rev. Wm. J. Corbin.

William King, ae 28y, col'rd, s/o Wm. & Betsy King; Fanny Scott, ae 21y, col'rd, d/o Nelson & Jennie Scott; Dec 20 1888 by Rev. Frank Page.

Thomas J. Blake. ae 24y, oyster, s/o Thos. B. & Rebecca Coleman Blake; Addie J. Jenkins, ae 22y, d/o Wm. J. & mary Brown Jenkins; Dec 25 1888 by Rev. R. A. Folkes.

William Henry Monroe, ae 21y, col'rd, s/o Henry & Maria Monroe; Charlotte Olvis, ae 21y, col'rd, d/o Cary & Louisa Olvis; Dec 25 1888 by Rev. C. C. Westonbaker.

Robert Dillard, ae 23y, widower, oyster, of Lynchburg VA, s/o Wm. & Louisa Dillard; Harriet Ann Bright, ae 21y, d/o Wm. & Susan Bright; Dec 25 1888 by Rev. Z. Taylor Whiting.

John Carter, ae 46y, widower, farmer, G. & Ann Carter; Amanda Rice, ae 38y, widow, d/o R. & Kitty Rice; Dec 20 1888 by Rev. A. T. Gayle.

Iverson Whiting, ae 26y, oyster, s/o Davy & Mary Whiting; Mary Chivis, ae 17y, d/o Washington & Susan Chivis; Dec 20 1888 by Rev. John W. Booth.

Thomas Banks, ae 33y, oyster, s/o Washington & Jane Burwell Banks; Easter Dennis, ae 21y, d/o Geo. E. & Mary E. Dennis; Dec 25 1888 by Rev. A. T. Gayle.

Augustine Davis, ae 35y, farm, s/o Henry & Caroline Davis; Frances Roberson, ae 23y, widow, d/o Rich'd & Fanny Pryor; Dec 27 1888 by Rev. P. T. Edwards.

James Hubbard, ae 21y, col'rd, mason, s/o Wm. & Nancy Hubbard; Mary Reade, ae 20y, d/o John & Catharine Reade; Dec 27 1888 by Rev. J. W. Booth.

W. D. Robins, ae 25y, sailor, s/o J. & Catharine Robins; Sarah West, ae 19y, d/o Chas. & Susan West; Jan 10 1889 by Rev. F. H. Hall.

Lawrence Williams, ae 20y, col'rd, oyster, s/o John & Mry Williams; Mattie Lee, ae 20y, col'rd, d/o Willie & Nettie Lee; Jan 10 1889 by Rev. E. W. Page.

Emanuel Chapman, ae 30y, widower, oyster, s/o Godfrey & Nancy Chapman; Dianna Howard, ae 26y, col'rd, d/o Adam & Mary Howard; Jan 16 1889 by Rev. J. W. Booth

R. E. Burton, ae 21y, farm, s/o Thos. & Rosa A. Burton; Sarah J. Sears, ae 20y, d/o Rich'd & Mary V. Sears; Jan 20 1889 by Rev. W. B. Lee.

Frank Page, ae 43y, widower, minister of the gospel, s/o Isaac & Susan Pryor Page; Martha Carter, ae 23y, col'rd, d/o Edw'd & Mary Howard Carter; jan 19 1889 by Rev. John W. Booth.

Rob't C. Johnson, ae 27y, col'rd, farm, s/o Thos. & Elizabeth Johnson; Ada W. Reed, ae 16y, col'd, of King and Queen Co VA, d/o Henry & Martha E. Taliaferro Reed; Jan 24 1889 by Rev. E. W. Page.

Lewis Brown, ae 22y, col'd, farm, s/o Joshua & Mary Jane Brown; Grace Brown, ae 23y, col'd, d/o Randall & Minnie Brown; Jan 27 1889 by Rev. Wm. B. Lee.

John Perrin, ae 27y, col'd, laborer, of York Co VA, s/o Wm. & Rebecca Perrin; Caroline Graham, ae 21y, col'd, d/o Wm. & Nancy Graham; Feb 3 1889 by Rev. A. T. Gayle.

Thos. W. Thrift, ae 23y, farm, s/o Wm. J. J. & M. F. Thrift; Mary C. Kemp, ae 18y, d/o D. J. & Emiline Fary Kemp; Feb 10 1889 by Rev. Wm. E. Wiatt.

Jas. H. Hogg, ae 24y, oyster, s/o Wm. & Sarah A. Fosque Hogg; Mary C. Dunston, ae 17y, d/o Thos. H. & Mary L. Cavars Dunston; Feb 7 1889 by Rev. F. H. Hall.

Henry Cooke, ae 25y, oyster, s/o Rob't & Rachel Cooke; Mary A. Catlett, ae 17y, d/o Geo. & Frances Tabb Catlett; Feb 15 1889 by Rev. E. W. Page.

Gana Burwell, ae 23y, farm, s/o Rich'd & Milly Claiborne Burwell; Maria Burwell, ae 22y, d/o Phillip & Sarah Burwell; Feb 17 1889 by Rev. Frank Page.

Sam'l Redman, ae 22y, sailor, s/o Geo. & Eliza Frances redman; Ann Maria Ward, d/o Simon & Mary F. Ward; Feb 7 1889 by Rev. J. W. Booth.

John Olvis, ae 21y, laborer, s/o Cary & Louisa Olvis; Rebecca Smith, ae 21y, d/o Jane Smith, father unk; Feb 10 1889 by Rev. J. W. Booth.

Jas. P. Kemp, ae 30y, farm, s/o O. S. & P. A. Christian Kemp; Julia B. Rowe, ae 20y, d/o Wm. H. & Virginia Dobson Rowe; Feb 19 1889 Rev. Wm. E. Wiatt.

J. W. Collier, ae 27y, oyster, s/o Thos. S. & Mary A. Woodland Collier; Clara J. Sterling, ae 18y, d/o Ross W. & Mary Waddle Sterling; Feb 28 1889 by Rev. W. B. Lee.

Charles T. Brown, ae 23y, oyster, s/o
Lewis T. & Frances Ann Brown; Callania Tillage, ae 18y, d/o Wm. & G. Tillage; Feb 26
1889 by Rev. F. H. Hall.

James F. Belvin, ae 23y, sailor, s/o John
& Susan Tillage Belvin; Lucy Garrett Davis,
ae 17y, d/o Albert & E. W. Davis; Feb 27
1889 by Rev. F. H. Hall.

Alfred Morris, ae 21y, oyster, s/o John &
Catharine Sturges Morris; Caroline M. Ber-
nard, ae 17y, d/o Alfred D. & Eliza Jones
Bernard; Feb 28 1889 by Rev. J. W. Booth.

Charles Patterson, ae 52y, widower, farm,
s/o Lewis & Kitty Patterson; Sarah E. Montague, ae 32y, widow, d/o Harry & Nancy Fle-
ing; Mar 7 1889 by Rev. A. T. Gayle.

John Henry Willett, ae 28y, oyster, s/o
Jessie T. & Sarah Ann Cobb Willett; Kate M.
Hogg, ae 19y, d/o Jas. W. & Cornelia Hogg;
Apr 16 1889 by Rev. F. H. Hall.

Walter E. Lee, ae 27y, widower, farm, s/o
Elijah & Louisa Lee; Jenny Jackson, ae 20y,
d/o Frank & Bettie Jackson; Apr 27 1889 by
Rev. Z. Taylor Whiting.

F. H. Hall, ae 41y, widower, minister of
the gospel, of Lancaster Co VA, s/o A. & C.
C. Crittenden Hall; Nannie Heywood, ae 23y,
d/o R. C. & M. M. Cooke Heywood; May 7 1889
by Rev. R. A. Folkes.

George Shackelford, ae 22y, merchant, s/o
Wm. & M. M. Thomas Shackelford; Rachel Brown,
ae 18y, d/o Seymour & Sarah Hogg Brown; May
16 1889 by Rev. R. A. Folkes.

E. F. Thomas, ae 24y, fisherman, s/o Jas.
& Mary J. Walker Thomas; Mary E. Lewis, aw
20y, d/o Washington & Emily Lewis; May 31
1889 by Rev. C. C. Westonbaker.

William Cooke, ae 24y, farm, s/o Rob't &
Rachael Billups Cooke; M. B. Catlett, ae 17y,
d/o Geo. & Frances Tabb Catlett; May 25 1889
by Rev. E. W. Page.

Joseph Belvin, ae 29y, farm, s/o Martha
Belvin, father unk; Martha E. Butler, ae
19y, d/o Thos. H. & Gracy; July 9 1889 by
Rev. F. H. Hall.

Miles Cary, ae 38y, widower, farm, s/o
Miles & Polly Cary; Agnes Whiting, ae 19y,
d/o T. J. & Sarah Whiting; July 4 1889 by
Rev. Z. Taylor Whiting.

Rufus Miles, ae 39y, farm, of Chrisfield
MD, s/o Jas. & Charity Miles; Nancy Banks,
ae 25y, widow, d/o Sam'l & Judy Rilee Griffin; June 9 1889 by Rev. E. W. Page.

John A. Taliaferro, ae 35y, merchant, s/o
John P. & E. W. Anderson Taliaferro; M. S.
Seawell, ae 29y, d/o M. B. & M. S. Atchison
Seawell; June 27 1889 by Rev. T. J. Mercer.

W. F. Worlds, ae 28y, farm, lived King
and Queen Co VA, s/o Jos. T. & M. C. Lewis
Worlds; Mattie A. Horseley, ae 18y, d/o Allen & Elizabeth Horseley; June 30 1889 by
Rev. C. C. Westonbaker.

Charles Ellis, ae 22y, farm, s/o Frank &
Johanna Ellis; Harriet Carter, ae 19y, d/o
Randal & Mary E. Carter; June 30 1889 by
Rev. E. W. Page.

Godfrey Burwell, ae 23y, sailor, s/o Geo.
& Emily Cooke Burwell; Mary Ann Morriss, ae
18y, d/o Phill & Polly Morriss; July 9 1889
by Rev. J. W. Booth.

Daniel Johnston, ae 28y, widower, farm,
s/o Phill & Sally Johnston; Margaret Grimes,
ae 24y, d/o Mary Billups, mother unk; July
21 1889 by Rev. W. B. Lee.

Fielding Lewis Taylor, ae 40y, attorney
at law, s/o Fielding Lewis & Elizabeth F.
Fauntleroy Taylor; Ellen Yeatman Deans, ae
35y, d/o Josiah L. & Mary Yeatman Deans;
July 31 1889 by Rev. W. B. Lee.

Robert C. Bristow, ae 26y, carriage maker,
of King and Queen Co VA, s/o Wm. B. & Frances
Pearce Bristow; Esther A. Trevilian, ae 19y,
d/o Wm. C. & Maria F. Adams Trevilian; July
31 1889 by Rev. C. C. Westonbaker.

William Wallace, ae 55y, widower, farm,
of MD, parents unk; Susie A. Roach, ae 26y,
widow, d/o W. J. H. & Sarah Dunston Oliver;
Aug 8 1889 by Rev. F. H. Hall.

Abraham W. Whiting, ae 23y, col'rd, oyster, of York Co VA, s/o Joshua & June Burwell Whiting; Martha A. Cooke, ae 21y, d/o
Peter & Agnes Jones Cooke; Aug 28 1889 by
Rev. J. W. Booth.

A. J. Hogg, ae 21y, farm, s/o Lewis &
Martha Hogg; Caroline Hogg, ae 21y, d/o Thos.
& Elizabeth Hogg; Sept 12 1889 by Rev. F. H.
Hall.

Stephen Stubblefield, ae 21y, farm, s/o
S. & Sarah Walden Stubblefield; Delia Smith,
ae 19y, farm, d/o John & Nancy Smith; Sept 8
1889 by Rev. F. H. Hall.

James Hogg, ae 25y, farm, s/o Thos. &
Elizabeth Hogg Hogg; Sarah Hogg, ae 18y, d/o
Jas. & Elizabeth Hall Hogg; Sept 10 1889 by
Rev. F. H. Hall.

Andrew J. Dabney, ae 35y, farm, s/o Jas.
& Lucy Dabney; Maria F. Booth, ae 23y, d/o
Geo. H. & Lucinda Richardson Booth; Sept 12
1889 by Rev. J. W. Booth.

Thomas C. Walker, ae 28y, lawyer, s/o
Thos. & Grace A. Walker; Annie A. Williams,
ae 24y, of SOUTH CAROLINA, d/o Andrew &
Amelia; Sept 9 1889 by Rev. Dan'l L. Furber.
Admitted to record upon a certificate of
marriage issued by Geo. B. Gurney, city
clerk of the city of Chelsea MASS.

J. Leland Butler, ae 24y, tobacconist, of
Richmond City VA, s/o S. W. & M. V. Butler;
Mattie C. MArtin, ae 24y, d/o W. H. & Mil-
dred Martin; Sept 25 1889 by Rev. C. C.
Westonbaker.

Charles King, ae 23y, laborer, s/o Buck &
Violet Baytop King; Nannie Cooke, ae 18y, d/o
Emily Cooke, father unk; Sept 26 1889 by
Rev. John W. Booth.

William P. Hinman, ae 50y, widower,
sailor, of Accomack Co VA, s/o Galyn & Catharine Andrews Hinman; Mattie E. Hall, ae
38y, widow, of Middlesex Co VA, d/o Hugh A.
& Julia A. South Hall; Oct 3 1889 by Rev. W.
E. Wiatt.

Horace Roberson, ae 23y, farm, of King
and Queen Co VA, s/o Benja. & Dina Robinson;
Arico Chapman, ae 28y, d/o Sarah Chapman,
father unk; Oct 6 1889 by Rev. A. T. Gayle.

William Lewis, ae 30y, widower, farm, s/o
Abram & Martha Lewis; Virginia Smith, ae 16y,
d/o Jos. & Catharine; Oct 9 1889 by Rev. E.
W. Page.

H. Hammy Bew, ae 22y, farm, of King and
Queen Co VA, s/o Hezekiah & Sarah E. Didlake
Bew; Julia Ison, ae 14y, d/o Jas. H. & Mil-
dred Brooking Ison; Oct 10 1889 by Rev. W.
E. Wiatt.

Albert Tabb, ae 35y, oyster, s/o Andrew &
Maria Washington Tabb; Courtney Grimes, ae
45y, widow, d/o Peyton Whiting & Jane Washington; Oct 13 1889 by Rev. E, W. Page.

Lucues L. Croswell, ae 25y, farm, s/o W.
H. & Mary A. Croswell; Ella S. Gardner, ae
22y, of Middlesex Co VA, d/o Lewis Gardner,
father unk; Oct 14 1889 by Rev. F. H. Hall.

Lemuel P. Rilee, ae 21y, farm, s/o Pascal
D. & Mary Ann Walker Rilee; Lucy F. Booker,
ae 25y, d/o Lewis F. & Lucy F. Fary Booker;
Oct 20 1889 by Rev. W. E. Wiatt.

George Ward, ae 41y, widower, oyster, of
Middlesex Co VA, s/o Wm. & Cordelia; Lizzie
Roberson, ae 30y, widow, d/o Abram Willis &
Nancy Ware; Oct 23 1889 by Rev. E. W. Page.

Charles Noggins, ae 35y, widower, farm,
s/o Rob't & Lena Noggins; Rosanna Todd, ae
30y, d/o Aaron & K. Thias Todd; Oct 24 1889
by Rev. A. T. Gayle.

Thornton Walker, ae 39y, widower, farm,
s/o Phil & Judy Walker, of Fluvanna Co VA;
Crissie Burwell, ae 23y, d/o Davy & Fanny
Burwell; Nov 6 1889 by Rev. E. W. Page.

Edward German, ae 35y, widower, farm, s/o
Wm. & Elizabeth Bridges German; Lillian A.
Kemp, ae 19y, d/o Gregory & Elizabeth A.
Wiatt Kemp; Nov 27 1889 by Rev. W. E. Wiatt.

Alfred W. Withers, ae 24y, gentleman, of
Binghamton N. Y, s/o Alfred D. & Annie G.
Franklin Withers; Katharine P. Vandergrift,
ae 24y, of Alexandria VA, d/o Henry A. &
Martha D. Page Vandergrift; Dec 11 1889 by
Rev. W. B. Lee.

John Lemon, ae 47y, farm, s/o Wade &
Emiline Lemon; Pinky Lemon, ae 48y, d/o Cue
& Fanny Lemon; Dec 1 1889 by Rev. John W.
Booth.

Jas. C. Leigh, ae 40y, farm, s/o Rich'd &
Polly Duval Leigh; Virginia Pointer, ae 30y,
widow, d/o --- Smith & E. Smither; Dec 1
1889 by Rev. W. O. Waggoner.

William Jenkins, ae 25y, widower, farm,
s/o M. & D. Jenkins; Alice Shackelford, ae
19y, d/o Archibald & Nancy Shackelford; Dec
11 1889 by Rev. R. A. Folkes.

Thomas S. Bew, ae 22y, mechanic, of King
and Queen Co VA, s/o M. & Jane F. Bew; Cor-
inna L. Pearce, ae 21y, d/o Jas. H. & Mary
T. Pearce; Dec 8 1889 by Rev. S. S. Thrift.

Willie Watson, ae 24y, waterman, s/o
Willie & Mary Purcell Watson; Roberta E.
Moody, ae 24y, d/o Geo. H. & Catharine Moody;
Dec 4 1889 by Rev. John W. Booth.

Richard B. Davis, ae 21y, oyster, of King
and Queen Co VA, s/o E. W. & Abest. Davis;
Belle Jenkins, ae 15y, d/o Thos. H. & Susan
V. Jenkins; Dec 11 1889 by Rev. F. H. Hall.

J. Wesley Deadman, ae 28y, oyster, s/o
Joe & Annie Deadman; Mary K. Jackson, ae 24y,
d/o John & Laura Jackson; Dec 15 1889 by
Rev. E. W. Page.

John Mathew Wallis, ae 36y, engineer, of
New Orleans LA, lived Baltimore MD, s/o John
S. & Louisa Mathew Wallis; Alice S. Meredith,
ae 17y, d/o T. J. & Julia D. Steven. Merdith;
Dec 18 1889 by Rev. Wm. B. Lee.

John H. Brown, ae 28y, oyster, s/o Jas.
H. & Mary F. Blake Brown; Norah S. West, ae
18y, d/o Benja. F. & Nannie West; Dec 19 1889
by Rev. W. E. Wiatt.

Joseph C. Clements, ae 20y, farm, of Middlesex Co VA, s/o John W. & Mary Clements;
Roberta Cooke, ae 18y, of Baltimord MD,
parents unk; Dec 29 1889 by Rev. R. A. Folks.

William C. Kemp, ae 33y, farm, s/o Wm. &
Nancy Kemp; Ellen J. Sears, ae 18y, d/o John
& Ellen Haynes Sears; Dec 22 1889 by Rev. W.
E. Wiatt.

A. W. Walker, ae 33y, farm, s/o W. G. &
Elvira B. Glass Walker; Ella J. Davis, ae
24y, d/o Jas. W. & Mary Freeman Davis; Dec
25 1889 by Rev. W. O. Waggoner.

George Washington Thomas, ae 23y, oyster,
s/o Rob't & Jemima Hogg Thomas; Mary M. Conway, ae 16y, d/o Eli & Mary Coats Conway;
Dec 26 1889 by Rev. R. A. Folks.

James Lucas, ae 21y, farm, of Mathews Co VA, s/o Rob't & Hester Lucas; Ida Gregory, ae 18y, d/o Rebecca Gregory, father unk; Dec 29 1889 by Rev. A. T. Gayle.

Charles Smith, ae 21y, farm, d/o Jas. O. & Mary A. Smith; Cordelia Ward, ae 20y, d/o Frances Ward, father unk; Jan 6 1890 by Rev. J. W. Booth.

John Diggs, ae 44y, widower, farm, s/o Eliza Washington, father unk; Amelia Carter, ae 34y widow, d/o Paul & Elizabeth Taylor; Dec 8 1889 by Rev. E. W. Page.

Lineus H. Miller, ae 24y, s/o Wm. S. & Virginia Miller; Carrie D. Moore, ae 19y, d/o Thos. R. & Lucy E.; Jan 7 1890 by Rev. W. E. Wiatt.

J. W. Hudgins, ae 21y, waterman, s/o Wm. & Elizabeth Hudgins; Captolia Regensburg, ae 19y, d/o S. A. & Rosa Regensburg; Jan 8 1890 by Rev. Wm. E. Wiatt.

John Jenkins, ae 20y, farm, s/o Jas. & Frances Jenkins; Pinky Green, ae 16y, d/o Jas. & Elizabeth Green; Jan 9 1890 by Rev. R. A. Folks.

John Davis, ae 25y, farm, s/o Thos. & Betsy Davis; Lucy Smith, ae 19y, d/o John & Lucy Smith; Jan 12 1890 by Rev. J. W. Booth.

Davy Armstead, ae 20y, farm, s/o Andrew & Georgianna Armstead; Elizabeth Page, ae 18y, d/o Temple & Hannah Page; Jan 15 1890 by Rev. E. W. Page.

C. T. Corr, ae 21y, farm, s/o J. E. P. & Mary Ellen Corr; Fanny B. Haynes, ae 18y, d/o Wm. A. & H. H. Haynes; Jan 22 1890 by Rev. W. E. Bullard.

Sylvester S. Buntung, ae 27y, farm, of Accomac Co VA, s/o S. C. & Mary Trader Bunting; Margaret C. Givler, ae 27y, d/o Peter B. & Nannie A. Givler; Jan 23 1890 by Rev. Wm. B. Lee.

James H. Griffin, ae 23y, oyster, s/o John & Lena Lemon Griffin; Lucy Ann Whiting, ae 25y, widow, of New Kent Co VA, d/o Wm. & Minerva Tyler Whiting; Jan 23 1890 by Rev. W. O. Waggoner.

Thomas B. Pierce, ae 32y, farm, lived
Middlesex Co VA, s/o John M. & J. F. Pierce;
Tesora Regensburg, ae 20y, of KIng and Queen
Co VA, d/o S. A. & Rosa A. Regensburg; Dec
25 1889 by Rev. W. E. Wiatt.

Aaron Deadman, ae 23, farm, s/o Moses &
Elizabeth; Elnora King, ae 17y, d/o Lucy
King, father unk; Dec 24 1889 by Rev. Frank
Page.

James Chapman, ae 22y, widower, farm, s/o
Wesley & Margaret Chapman; Emma Deadman, ae
17y, d/o Jas. & Frances Deadman; Dec 27 1889
by Rev. P. T. Edwards.

William Coats, ae 39y, widower, oyster,
s/o John & Mary E. Horseley Coats; Mary West,
ae 21y, d/o Chas. & Mary Susan Brown West;
Dec 25 1889 by Rev. F. H. Hall.

Thomas Hogg, ae 20y, farm, s/o Anderson &
Susan Hogg; Bettie E. Smith, ae 23y, d/o
Griffin & Elizabeth Smith; Dec 26 1889 by
Rev. Wm. B. Lee.

J. S. Philpotts, ae 54y, widower, farm,
of Portsmouth VA, s/o John & Ann Philpotts;
Mary E. Franklin, ae 37y, of Portsmouth VA,
d/o Thos. & Sarah Franklin; Dec 24 1889 by
Rev. W. O. Waggoner.

Wm. H. Purcell, ae 32y, widower, farm,
s/o John & Susan M. Hudgins Purcell; Elnora
Hudgins, ae 24y, d/o Dawson & Catharine Hudgins; Dec 25 1889 by Rev. W. E. Wiatt.

George W. Coats, ae 24y, lumberman, s/o
Cornelius & Avy Coats; Mary J. Trevilian, ae
21y, d/o R. & Arena Trevilian; Dec 29 1889
by Rev. W. E. Wiatt.

John C. Lockley, ae 24y, merchant, s/o
Jas. & Martha Lockley; Lucy P. Baytop, ae
16y, d/o Randal & Frances Baytop; Dec 31
1889 by Rev. Reuben Berkeley.

Thomas Guthrie, ae 22y, farm, s/o Essex
& Maria Guthrie; Sue Jones, ae 19y, d/o
Rob't & Mary E. Jones; Dec 25 1889 by Rev.
A. T. Gayle.

John Harrison, ae 23y, laborer, s/o Elijah & Betty Hall Harrison; Amanda F. Jefferson, ae 19y, d/o Thos. W. & Emily Jones Jefferson; Dec 26 1889 by Rev. A. T. Gayle.

S. B. Blake, ae 30y, boatsman, s/o T. B.
& Rebecca Coleman Blake; Fanny Jenkins, ae
21y, d/o Wm. H. & Mary Brown Jenkins; Jan 26
1890 by Rev. James Waggoner.

Lucius Hughes, ae 22y, oyster, s/o Jas. &
Betsy Hughes; Caroline Taliaferro, ae 21y,
d/o Martha Braxton, father unk; Jan 30 1890
by Rev. A. T. Gayle.

James H. Brown, ae 22y, oyster, s/o Thos.
S. & Betty Blake Brown; Mollie Haynes, ae
25y, widow, d/o Henry & Elizabeth Proctor
Haynes; Feb 2 1890 by Rev. R. A. Fox.

William H. Blake, ae 49y, widower, farm,
of Middlesex Co VA, s/o Wm. H. & Cordelia
Blake; Elizabeth Proctor, ae 49y, widow, d/o
Massie & Mary Hudgins Proctor; Feb 2 1890 by
Rev. R. A. Fox.

James Ross, ae 22y, s/o Peter & Frances
Ross, farm; Ellen Thornton, ae 18y, d/o Jane
Braxton; Feb 5 1890 by Rev. J. W. Booth.

Doctor Simcoe, ae 34y, merchant, s/o Thos.
& Matilda A. Simcoe; Alice V. Eastwood, ae
25y, d/o A. G. & Virginia Eastwood; Feb 5
1890 by Rev. W. E. Wiatt.

James S. Scott, ae 30y, farm, s/o Ben &
Minerva Scott; Veria Harriss, ae 21y, d/o
Maria Harriss; Feb 8 1890 by Rev. P. T.
Edwards.

Thomas Henry Jenkins, ae 40, widower,
oyster, s/o Thos. H. & Mary E. Jenkins; Emma
F. Harris, ae 37y, widow, d/o David & Susan
Dunford Jenkins Harris; Feb 9 1890 by Rev.
W. O. Waggoner.

Thos. Wright, ae 23y, oyster, s/o Stephen
& Susan Wright; Ann E. Ellis, ae 16y, d/o
Frank & Joanna Ellis; Feb 12 1890 by Rev. E.
W. Page.

William Henry Wiatt, ae 25y, waterman,
s/o Wm Wiatt & Martha Stokes; Pinky Ann
Green, ae 21y, d/o Wm. & Emily Green; Feb 18
1890 by Rev. E. W. Page.

George W. Briggs, ae 50y, widower, farm,
of CANADA, s/o Zackariah & Mary Briggs;
Elizabeth Smith, ae 28y, widow, d/o Benja.
Lewis & Martha Jenkins; Feb 24 1890 by Rev.
R. A. Folks.

Thomas R. Rolph, ae 21y, conductor, s/o
W. F. & Mary B. Bray Rolph; Lelia E. Hughes,
ae 20y, d/o Peter P. & Catharine A. M. Wallace Hughes; Feb 26 1890 by Rev. R. A. Folks.

Charles E. Nash, ae 22y, clerk, of Norfolk
VA, s/o Jas. E. & Ann M. Cuthrell Nash; El-
len Ruth White, ae 22y, d/o John R. & Julia
A. Diggs White; Feb 26 1890 by Rev. W. O.
Waggoner.

Frank Robinson, ae 23y, oyster, s/o Isaac
& Percilla Smith Robinson; Eliza L. Smith,
ae 21y, d/o Jas. O. & Mary Banks Smith; Feb
27 1890 by Rev. J. W. Booth.

Noah Thomas, ae 23y, farm, s/o Jos. &
Mary Thomas; Catharine Carter, ae 17y, d/o
Rob't & Pinkey Carter; Feb 27 1890 by Rev.
J. W. Booth.

Geo. Washington, ae 24y, farm, s/o Henry
& Martha Keley Washington; Martha S. Lemon,
ae 25y, d/o Lucy Bolden; Mar 10 1890 by Rev.
J. W. Booth.

Terry Hall, ae 23y, farm, s/o Lewis O. &
Martha Ann Enos Hall; Maggie C. Deal, ae
16y, d/o John A. & Louisianna Bonnywell Deal;
Mar 12 1890 by Rev. W. O. Waggoner.

William West, ae 24y, farm, s/o Christo-
pher & Urna West; Bettie Smith, ae 19y, s/o
Thos. & Betty Smith; Mar 20 1890 by Rev. R.
A. Folks.

Naverous Gregory, ae 23y, oyster, s/o
Jas. & Betsy Gregory; India Reed, ae 23y,
d/o Washington & Jane Reed; Mar 23 1890 by
Rev. A. T. Gayle.

Randy F. West, ae 30y, farm, s/o Symouth
& Margaret Curtes West; Louisianna Booker,
ae 22y, d/o Isaac & Mary Wyatt Booker; Mar
30 1890 by Rev. E. W. Page.

Charles Lewis, ae 23y, oyster, s/o Dennis
& Curetta Lewis; Maggie E. Smith, ae 17y,
d/o Jos. & Catharine Smith; Apr 16 1890 by
Rev. E. W. Page.

William Hill, ae 22y, oyster, s/o Rob't &
Betsy Hill; Laura A. Payne, ae 22y, d/o Wm.
& Caroline Payne; Apr 23 1890 by Rev. A. T.
Gayle.

James H. Thornton, ae 20y, farm, s/o
Isaac & Julia Thornton; Mary E. Jackman, ae
17y, d/o Alex & T. Jackman; Apr 23 1890 by
Rev. J. W. Booth.

George W. Lowry, ae 21y, sailor, s/o Hugh
A. & L. Rilee Lowry, of Kent Co MD; Lucy E.
Wood, ae 19y, d/o Lewis T. & C. Bland Wood;
Apr 22 1890 by Rev. W. E. Wiatt.

James Smith, ae 24y, oyster, s/o Humphrey
& Charlotte Smith; Missouri Whiting, ae 21y,
d/o Emanuel & Henrietta Whiting; May 19 1890
by Rev. E. W. Page.

John Turpin, ae 22y, sailor, of MD, s/o
Henry & Mary Turpin; Laura Jarvis, ae 17y,
d/o Humphrey Jarvis, Mother unk; May 19 1890
by Rev. Frank Page.

Joseph Henderson, ae 42y, farm, of Lan-
caster Co VA, s/o Ralph & Betty Henderson;
Betsy Harris, ae 35y, widow, parents unk;
May 29 1890 by Rev. Frank Page.

Frederick Willis, ae 21y, oyster, s/o Cue
& Margaret Burwell Willis; Sarah Griffin, ae
21y, d/o Sam'l & Judy Rilee Griffin; May 29
1890 by Rev. E. W. Page.

William A. Hogg, ae 22y, oyster, s/o Wm.
& Sarah A. Hogg; Ida S. Carmine, ae 20y, d/o
Dan'l S. & Susan F. Carmine; June 5 1890 by
Rev. F. H. Hall.

James T. Howlett, ae 29y, oyster, of Middlesex Co VA, s/o Jos. W. & Elizabeth Howlett; Nannie Padgett, ae 17y, d/o J. R. & M.
F. Padgett; June 4 1890 by Rev. F. H. Hall.

Abram Jackson, ae 25y, oyster, s/o Sam'l
& Elizabeth Jackson; Nancy Fleming, ae 18y,
d/o Jas. & Mary E. Fleming; June 5 1890 by
Rev. A. T. Gayle.

John Allmond , ae 37y, widower, oyster,
s/o Sam & Minerva Allmond; Harriet Whittaker,
ae 19y, d/o Jas. & Lucy Whittaker; June 5
1890 by Rev. F. H. Hall.

Joseph H.Smith, ae 22y, farm, s/o John W.
& Alice A. Smith; Etta B. Brown, ae 18y, d/o
Benja. A. & Ellen F. Brown; June 17 1890 by
Rev. R. A. Folks.
: W. Taylor Robins, ae 30y, clerk, s/o A.
W. & E. P. Robins; Sallie M. Seawell, ae
30y, d/o W. T. & S. V. Seawell; June 26 1890
by Rev. WM. B. Lee.

William N. Marshall, ae 32y, widower,
mechanic, of Mathews Co VA, s/o John & Sarah
Marshall; Julia Elizabeth Robins, ae 19y,
d/o Wm. H. & Mary J. Robins; June 19 1890
by Rev. Wm. E. Wiatt.

Albert B. Willis, ae 30y, farm, s/o John
R. & Mary E. Willis; Evangie L. Haynes, ae
20y, d/o Geo. H. & Lucy F. Haynes; June 25
1890 by Rev. J. H. Dalby.

Thomas J. Chapman, ae 38y, widower, farm,
s/o R. C. & Caroline Chapman; Lattie V.
Richardson, ae 18y, d/o Fleming & Ellen
Richardson; July 3 1890 by Rev. R. A. Fox.

George Kellum, ae 20y, laborer, s/o Wm. &
Betsy Kellum; Margaret S. Heywood, ae 21y,
d/o Joel & Sally Green Heywood; July 17 1890
by Rev. R. A. Folks.

James A. Eastwood, ae 30y, farm, s/o Alex
& Virginia Wright Eastwood; Mary E. Wolffe,
ae 17y, d/o Frederick H. & Sarah Thrift
Wolffe; July 17 1890 by Rev. W. O. Wagoner.

J. R. Johnston, ae 21y, faRM, s/o Thos. &
E. Johnston; Mary Lou Jones, ae 19y, d/o
Rob't & Rosettaa Jones; July 27 1890 by Rev.
John W. Booth.

Ransone Evans, ae 40y, widower, farm, s/o
Benja. & Maria Evans; Alice Holmes, ae 20y,
d/o Wm. & Charlotte Holmes; July 30 1890 by
Rev. John Wm. Booth.

Firne Lester, ae 22y, farm, of York Co VA,
s/o John & Sally Lester; Queen Victoria Green,
ae 16y, d/o Rich'd & Sarah V. Green; July 31
1890 by Rev. Wm. Thomas.

John W. Burrell, ae 27y, farm, s/o Beverly
& Maria Burwell; Elizabeth A. Lemon, ae 22y,
d/o John T. & Sarah E. Lemon; Aug 7 1890 by
Rev. A. T. Gayle.

Edward Robins, ae 23y, oyster, s/o J. &
Catharine Robins; Mary Susan Ransone, ae 17y,
d/o Jas. E. & Pinky Ransone; Aug 7 1890 by
Rev. F. H. Hall.

John T. Smith, ae 26y, oyster, s/o John W.
W. & Allice A. Rowe; Nannie F. Brown, ae
16y, d/o Benja. M. & Ellen Hogg Brown; Aug
14 1890 by Rev. R. A. Folks.

Bunyan S. Hammonds, ae 31y, painter, of
Lancaster Co VA, s/o Geo. T. & Lucy B. Ham-
monds; Lena Padgett, ae 23y, d/o John & Maria
F. Elliott Padgett; Aug 21 1890 by Rev. W.
O. Wagoner.

John H. Lewis, ae 43y, farmer, s/o Wm. J.
& Lucy A. Lewis; Lavinia Belvin, ae 26y, d/o
John & Susan Belvin; Sept 13 1890 by Rev. F.
H. Hall.

John Smith, ae 23y, engineer, of Mathews
Co VA, s/o Abram & Susan Smith; Malvenia
Willis, ae 18y, d/o Jos. & Mary Willis; Sept
7 1890 by Rev. A. T. Gayle.

J. R. Shackelford, ae 23y, oyster, s/o
John W. & Cornelia Nuttall Shackelford; Cor-
nelia R. Ambrose, ae 18y, d/o Franklin &
Sarah E. Hogg Ambrose; Sept 4 1890 by Rev.
W. E. Wiatt.

Edward J. Clements, ae 25y, coach maker,
s/o Eli T. & Virginia Howard Clements; Betty
H. Ware, ae 19y, of Essex Co VA, d/o Wm. S.
& Fanny B. Street Ware; Sept 16 1890 by Rev.
J. M. Frost.

Philip Spencer, ae 30y, widower, farm,
s/o John & Rose Spencer; Ellen Smith, ae 28y,
d/o Jos. & Percilla Barwell Smith; Sept 18
1890 by Rev. Z. Taylor Whiting.

Robert W. Liall, ae 24y, blacksmith, s/o
W. J. & Abline Rilee Liall; Ella W. Groom,
ae 23y, of King and Queen Co VA, d/o Rich'd
Virginia Lackins Groom; Sept 24 1890 by Rev.
W. O. Wagoner.

James Selden, ae 45y, widower, oyster,
s/o Jasper & Lucy Selden; Sarah Banks, ae
23y, d/o Chas. & Catharine Taylor Banks;
Sept 30 1890 by Rev. A. T. Gayle.

Henry Patterson, ae 59y, widower, farm,
s/o Lewis & Mary Patterson; Lucy Johnston,
ae 35y, widow, d/o Clayton & Judy Johnston;
Sept 28 1890 by Rev. W. J. Corbin.

John Green, ae 25y, oyster, s/o John &
Maria Green; Clara Whiting, ae 18y, d/o Mar-
tin & Matilda Whiting; Sept 30 1890 by Rev.
J. W. Booth.

George W. Smith, ae 24y, oyster, s/o Thos.
J. & E. Smith; Dora B. West, ae 22y, d/o G.
W. & Georgianna West; Oct 7 1890 by Rev. R.
A. Folks.

James A. Collins, ae 24y, laborer, of Mathews Co VA, s/o Jonathan J. & Mary Rickle Collins; Lulie M. Rilee, ae 16y, d/o Rich'd C. & Laura C. Massie Rilee; Oct 5 1890 by Rev. W. E. Wiatt.

Thomas Cooke, ae 21y, oyster, of Portsmouth VA, s/o Rich'd & Louisa Cooke; Fanny Jones, ae 22y, d/o Wm. H. & Catharine Jones; Oct 5 1890 by Rev. A. T. Gayle.

Charles H. Carmines, ae 30y, sailor, s/o Dan'l M. & Susan F. Dunn Carmines; Rosa Croswell, ae 23y, d/o Rich'd R. & Lucy Harris Croswell; Oct 9 1890 by Rev. F. H. Hall.

Wm. Wiatt, ae 48y, widower, carpenter, of Petersburg VA, s/o Wm. & Clory Noggins Wiatt; Frances Cooke, ae 35y, widow, of King and Queen Co VA, d/o Beverly Sparks; Oct 9 1890 by Rev. A. T. Gayle.

Frank Goldman, ae 23y, farm, of Middlesex Co VA, s/o Elijah & Jane Goldman; Mary J. Chapman, ae 22y, d/o Wesley & Margaret Chapman; Oct 23 1890 by Rev. P. T. Edwards.

John B. Seawell, ae 29y, widower, musician, s/o W. W. & Jane R. Seawell; Virginia A. Seawell, ae 37y, of SOUTH AMERICA, d/o Wm. H. & Mary A. Phillips Seawell; Oct 28 1890 by Rev. R. A. Folks.

Jackson Burwell, ae 50y, widower, farm, s/o Thos. Walker & Katy Kemp Burwell; Polly Deans, ae 23y, of King and Queen Co VA, d/o Jos. & Jane Deans; Oct 30 1890 by Rev. A. T. Gayle.

William Jenkins, ae 30y, widower, farm, s/o Mitchell Jenkins, mother unk; Annie Jenkins, ae 20y, d/o Wm. & Catharine Jenkins; Nov 12 1890 by Rev. R. A. Folks.

Lewis Stubbs, ae 38y, widower, oyster, s/o Adam & Catharine Stubbs; Frances Nelson, ae 26y, widow, d/o Wise & Lucy Johnson Nelson; Nov 4 1890 by Rev. J. W. Booth.

John Frank Soles, ae 35y, widower, farm, s/o Wm. H. & Lucy A. Soles; Mary E. Darnell, ae 21y, d/o Thos. & Rosa Mathews Darnell; Nov 9 1890 by Rev. J. H. Dalby.

John King, ae 26y, oyster, of Middlesex Co VA, s/o Lewis & Jane King; Mary E. Jackson, ae 17y, d/o R. W. & Eliza Jackson; Nov 13 1890 by Rev. J. W. Booth.

James A. Christopher, ae 25y, farm, s/o
Thos. & Annie E. Hart Christopher; Annie E.
Milby, ae 18y, d/o Wm. C. & Sallie Milby;
Nov 16 1890 by Rev. W. E. Wiatt.

Walter F. Shackelford, ae 37y, widower,
oyster, s/o John W. & Elizabeth West Shackelford; Elizabeth F. Fleming, ae 21y, d/o
Jos. C. & Alice Teagle Fleming; Aug 28 1890
by Rev. F. H. Hall.

Samuel B. Taylor, ae 44y, widower, farm,
s/o Jos. H. & Frances Street Taylor, of
Northumberland Co VA; Virginia A. Miller, ae
40y, widow, d/o Wm. I. & Mary Dutton Miller;
Nov 20 1890 by Rev. Wm. B. Lee.

Joshua L. Hogg, ae 20y, farm, s/o Jas. M.
& Susan N. Hogg; Alice Seawell, ae 20y, d/o
Jas. & Pinky Seawell; Dec 4 1890 by Rev. F.
H. Hall.

J. R. Purcell, ae 22y, farm, s/o Horace &
Ann Purcell; Florence V. Banks, ae 17y, d/o
Jas. & Hetty Banks; Dec 10 1890 by Rev. W.
E. Wiatt.

Joseph W. Smith, ae 23y, oyster, s/o Jos.
H. & Lucy A. Smith; Effie Lee Robins, ae 20y,
d/o Jos. F. & Rebecca O. Ash Robins; Dec 14
1890 by Rev. R. A. Folks.

C. H. Jones, ae 23y, engineer, of Hampton
VA, s/o Rich'd C. & Nancy Jones; Mary E.
Curtis, ae 22y, d/o Scipio & Elizabeth Curtis;
Sept 7 1890 by Rev. Z. Taylor Whiting.

Jackson Carter, ae 55y, widower, steward,
of Berkeley Co VA, parents unk; Bertie Nelson, ae 50y, widow, d/o Selden & Rosetta
Leigh; Dec 31 1890 by Rev. A. T. Gayle.

Lambert Scott, ae 24y, oyster, s/o Jack &
Eliza Scott; Mary E. Dabney, ae 22y, d/o
Russell & Lucy Dabney; Dec 27 1890 by Rev.
A. T. Gayle.

William A. Morgan, ae 23y, farm, of MD,
s/o W. F. & Fanny Prigg Morgan; Pauline R.
Morgan, ae 27y, of MD, d/o Thos. H. & Martha Morgan; Dec 31 1890 by Rev. Wm. B. Lee.

Christopher Casey, ae 29y, farm, s/o J.
H. & Mary Casey; Mattie Seawell, ae 18y, d/o
Miles H. & Martha Seawell; Dec 1 1890 by
Rev. A. T. Gayle.

Oscar H. Brownley, ae43y, widower, farm, of
MATHEWS Co VA, s/o Jas. R. & Mary F. Evans
Brownley; Mary F. Thrift, ae 22y, d/o T. W. &
Annie P. Rilee Thrift; Dec 17 1890 by Rev.
W. H. Gregory.

Addison T. Lewis, ae 40y, nurseryman, s/o
A. T. & Lucy C. Lewis; Cora D. Walker, ae 21y,
d/o Geo. & Emily F. Walker; Dec 31 1890 by
Rev. W. H. Gregory.

Thomas H. Dutton, ae 22y, farm, s/o P. H.
& Rebecca C. Dutton; Mary M. Walker, ae 18y,
d/o John M. & Mary E. Walker; Dec 24 1890 by
Rev. W. H. Gregory.

F. Williams, ae 26y, farm, s/o C. A. & V.
A. Williams; S. Blanche Rowe, ae 20y, d/o
Benja. & Dollie A. Rowe; Dec 25 1890 by Rev.
Ra. A. Folkes.

Muscoe Burwell, ae 23y, farm, s/o Henry &
Mary Cooke; Mary Jackson, ae 19y, d/o
Harriet Jackson, father unk; Dec 24 1890 by
Rev. J. W. Booth.

James Brown, ae 22y, oyster, s/o Jos. &
Elizabeth Howard Brown; Emma Lee Smith, ae
21y, d/o Jos. H. & Lucy A. Thomas Smith; Dec
25 1890 by Rev. R. A. Folkes.

Fillmore Ruark, ae 24y, widower, sailor,
of DORCHESTER Co MD, s/o T. H. & S. J. Ruark;
Ida Johnston, ae 19y, d/o T. E. & Julia
Johnston; Dec 24 1890 by Rev. W. E. Wiatt.

John F. Brown, ae 32y, oyster, s/o John &
Elizabeth Howard Brown; Susan R. Deal, ae
21y, d/o Jas. T. & Susan West Deal; Dec 25
1890 by Rev. R. A. Folkes.

William Lewis, ae 23y, farm, of MATHEWS Co
VA, s/o Matt & Susan Coles Lewis; Elnora Pol-
lard, ae 20y, d/o John & Elizabeth Guthrie
Pollard; Dec 25 1890 by Rev. Reuben Berkeley.

Charles H. Wood. ae 37y, sailor, of LAN_
CASTER Co VA, s/o Jane Wood, father unk; El-
nora Johnston, ae 17y, d/o Peter & Rosa J.
Johnston; Dec 25 1890 by Rev. F. H. Hall.

David Jones, ae 37y, widower, oyster, s/o
Dan'l & Mary Jones; Martha Jane Williams, ae
23y, d/o Geo. & Lydia Williams; Dec 16 1890
by Rev. Z. Taylor Whiting.

Samuel Osborne, ae 22y, farm, of KING AND QUEEN Co VA, s/o Jas. & Martha E. Jones Osborne; Victoria Jones, ae 21y, d/o Albert & Charlotte Roots Jones; Dec 27 1890 by Rev. Pleasant T. Edwards.

Thomas H. Dutton, ae 21y, farm, s/o T. H. & R. C. Dutton; Mary M. Walker, ae 18y, d/o John M. & Mary E. Walker; Dec 24 1890 by Rev. W. H. Gregory.

James Thruston, ae 23y, col'rd, oyster, s/o Jos. & Elsie Thruston; Lucy V. Spencer, ae 18y, col'rd, d/o Banks & James Spencer; Jan 4 1891 by Rev. E. W. Page.

A. H. Green, ae 47y, widower, col'rd, shoemaker, s/o Henry & Elizabeth Harris Green; Louisa Berry, ae 35y, widow, col'rd, d/o Phillip & Polly Morris; Jan 8 1891 by Rev. John W. Booth.

John Bluford, ae 23y, col'rd, farm, s/o Elizabeth Bluford, father unk; Emma Carter, ae 21y, col'rd, d/o John & Georgianna Carter; Jan 8 1891 by Rev.W. H. Gregory.

Benjamin F. Weaver, ae 27y, lumber dealer, of PENNSYLVANIA, s/o Christian & Rebecca Brubaker Weaver; Susie May Jennings, ae 19y, of NEW YORK STATE, d/o Chas. Jennings; Jan 14 1891 by Rev. W. H. Gregory.

Frank Whiting, ae 24y, col'rd, farm, s/o Edmund & Jane Whiting; Eva Seawell, ae 21y, col'rd, d/o Geo. & Lucy Seawell; Jan 15 1891 by Rev. Wm. B. Lee.

William Lee, ae 23y, col'rd, oyster, of YORK Co VA, s/o Elijah & Louisa Lee; Lucy Whiting, ae 21y, col'rd, d/o John & Maria Whiting; Jan 15 1891 by Rev. W. H. Gregory.

M. A. Kerns, ae 26y, farm, s/o M. V. & E. J. Kerns; Mary L. Shackelford, ae 22y, d/o Alex & Ann Martin Shackelford; Jan 15 1891 by Rev. W. H. Gregory.

Christopher C. Dixon, ae 32y, col'rd, farm, s/o Wm. & Elizabeth Dixon; Rosetta Taylor, ae 21y, col'rd, d/o Paul & Elizabeth Taylor; Jan 22 1891 by Rev, E. W. Page.

George A. Williams, ae 26y, col'rd, sailor, s/o of RICHMOND Co VA, s/o John & A. Williams; Emma Patterson, ae 22y, d/o Henry & Elyn King Patterson; Feb 8 1891 by Rev. Frank Page.

William Armstrong, ae 26y, col'rd, oyster, of PRINCE GEOGE Co VA, s/o Sam'l & Peggy Armstrong; Mary E. Harriss, ae 16y, col'rd, d/o Jas. & Mary Harriss; Jan 29 1891 by Rev. W. J. Corbin.

Simon Wright, ae 28y, widower, oyster, s/o Stephen & Susan Hern Wright; Sarah Ann Reed, ae 21y, of KING AND QUEEN Co VA, d/o Henry & Martha E. Taliaferro Reed; Jan 29 1891 by Rev. Z. T. Whiting.

Carter Jones, ae 55y, widower, col'rd, oyster, s/o Dan'l & Milly Jones; Phillis Graham, ae 40y, widow, col'rd, d/o Jas. & Lucy Norton; Feb 1 1891 by Rev. E. W. Page.

William Scott, ae 23y, col'rd, oyster, of FLUVANNA Co VA, s/o Jack & Eliza Scott; Frances Brown, ae 21y, col'rd, d/o Joshua & Mary Brown; Feb 8 1891 by Rev. E. W. Page.

James M. Moore, ae 23y, farm, of KING AND QUEEN Co VA, s/o W. T. & Catharine Moore; Lucy T. Horseley, ae 34y, widow, d/o John W. & Mary A. Horseley; Feb 11 1891 by Rev. W. E. Wiatt.

John Seymour, ae 30y, widower, col'rd, laborer, s/o John & Ann Seymour; Emily West, ae 24y, col'rd, d/o Lewis & Catharine West; Feb 12 1891 by Rev. Frank Page.

James D. Oliver, ae 23y, oyster, s/o Thos. & Sarah Wright Oliver; Emma Lee Harris, ae 19y, d/o Eleazer & Lizzie Williams Harris; Feb 15 1891 by Rev. F. H. Hall.

Decatur Hogg, ae 26y, oyster, s/o John & Julia Dunston Hogg; Effie E. Phillips, ae 17y, d/o John E. & Sarah E. Harris Phillips; Feb 19 1891 by Rev. F. H. Hall.

Calvin B. Gray, ae 39y, merchant, s/o Nelson R. & Octavia Gray; Flora Leigh Leavitt, ae 22y, d/o Franklin & Emma Pointer Leavitt; Feb 25 1891 by Rev. W. H. Gregory.

William A. Burwell, ae 24y, col'rd, oyster, s/o John & Ann M. Carter Burwell; Patsy A. Brooks, ae 22y, col'rd, d/o Jas. H. & Louisa Tazwell Brooks; Feb 26 1891 by Rev. E. W. Page.

Joseph Whiting, ae 23y, col'rd, farm, s/o Rob't & Clara Whiting, of MIDDLESEX Co VA, Sarah Carter, ae 21y, col'rd, d/o Edmond & Lucy Carter; Mar 5 1891 by Rev. R. Berkeley.

S. S. Oliver, ae 23y, smith, s/o Washington & Sarah Oliver; Cora L. Shelton, ae 17y,
d/o Geo. W. & Hester H. Shelton; Mar 12 1891
by Rev. F. H. Hall.

Peter Wiatt Jr, ae 28y, col'rd, oyster,
s/o Peter & Ann T. Wiatt; Courtney White, ae
21y, col'rd, d/o John K. & Mary S. White;
Mar 15 1891 by Rev. A. T. Gayle.

Charles A. Carleen, ae 29y, widower, oys-
ter, of MIddlesex Co VA, s/o Alex & Sarah E.
Blake Carleen; Mary E. Blake, ae 21y, d/o ¶
John & Louisa Bedley Blake; Mar 18 1891 by
Rev. W. B. Lee.

Chas. T. Caffee, ae 22y, col'rd, oyster,
s/o John T. & Rebecca Caffee; Dora Lemon, ae
22y, col'd, d/o Thos. Lemon & Amanda Easter;
Mar 19 1891 by Rev. E. W. Page.

William H. Brown, ae 18y, oyster, s/o
Tyler & Sarah West; Florida Coats, ae 18y,
d/o Wm. & Nannie West Coats; Mar 26 1891 by
Rev. F. H. Hall.

William Bluford, ae 26y, col'rd, farm,
Parents Unk; Rosa Travers, ae 26y, col'rd,
of York Co VA, d/o Carl & Judy Peyton Travers; Mar 29 1891 by Rev. E. W. Page.

John E. Lyndon, ae 22y, oyster, of LIVER_
POOL ENGLAND, s/o John E. & Catharine Lyn-
don; Bertie C. Croswell, ae 16y, d/o R. A. &
Georgianna Croswell; Apr 9 1891 by Rev. F.
H. Hall.

John W. Hobday, ae 33y, col'rd, farm, s/o
John W. & Nancy Hobday; Mary E. Cooke, ae
21y, col'rd, d/o Geo. W. & Mary A. Cooke;
Apr 16 1891 by Rev. John W. Corbin.

Uriah Rowe, ae 37y, oyster, s/o Livingston & Lucy Spencer Rowe; Georgianna King,
ae 26y, d/o Wm. & Martha West King; Apr 22
1891 by Rev. F. H. Hall.

James Foster, ae 23y, col'rd, oyster, of
Hampton City VA, s/o Frances Foster, father
unk; Sarah A. Washington, ae 20y, col'rd,
d/o Wm. & Mary Ransone Washington; Apr 23
1891 by Rev. Wm. Thomas.

Antney Carter, ae 27y, col'rd, oyster,
s/o Sam'l & Louisa Carter; Rebecca French,
ae 23y, col'rd, d/o Rob't & Eliza Burrell
French; Apr 21 1891 by Rev. E. W. Page.

Borges Braxton, are 35y, col'rd, oyster, s/o D. & Sarah Braxton; Fanny Washington, ae 21y, col'rd, d/o Henry & Mary Washington; Apr 30 1891 by Rev. Frank Page.

Cornelius Johnson, ae 22y, col'd, sailor, s/o Wm. & Mary Johnson; Ida Smith, ae 17y, col'rd, d/o Rachel Braxton, father unk; May 3 1891 by Rev. Wm. Thomas.

Thomas Hogg, ae 45y, widower, farm, s/o John & Julia Hogg; Anna C. Ambrose, ae 21y, d/o Lemuel & Emily Ambrose; May 6 1891 by Rev. F. H. Hall.

James Gayle, ae 21y, col'rd, oyster, s/o Wm. & Rachel Gayle; Rebecca Whittaker, ae 16y, col'rd, d/o Mary Whittaker, father unk; May 24 1891 by Rev. F. H. Hall.

James Robins, ae 52y, widower, of Mathews Co VA, s/o Wm. & Mary Johnson Robins; Eudora West, ae 21y, d/o Lewis & Hester Smith West; May 27 1891 by Rev. R. A. Folks.

G. F. Horseley, ae 21y, clerk, s/o Jas. K. & Martha Hibble Horseley; Mary W. Thruston, ae 24y, d/o John M. & Mary A. Thruston; May 27 1891 by Rev. W. E. Wiatt.

William West, ae 24y, widower, farm, s/o Jas. & Nancy West; Mary S. Bonnywell, ae 23y, d/o Wm. & Susan Bonnywell; May 21 1891 by Rev. F. H. Hall.

Ambrose West, ae 23y, sailor, s/o Chas. & Mary Brown West; Clemmie West, ae 17y, d/o Geo. & Mary Jarvis West; June 4 1891 by Rev. R. A. Folks.

Henry Chapman, ac 26y, col'rd oyster, of King and Queen Co VA, s/o Henry & Mary Henderson Chapman; Mary Fox, ae 21y, col'rd, d/o Pleasant & Sarah Tazewell Fox; June 7 1891 by Rev. Z. Taylor Whiting.

Moses Tyler, ae 21y, col'rd, farm, s/o Jas. & Eliza Tyler; Ellen Cooke, ae 19y, col'rd, d/o B. Cooke, mother unk; June 16 1891 by Rev. F. H. Hall.

Albert H. Williams, ae 27y, lumber man, s/o C. H. & V. A. Williams; Elizabeth L. Rowe, ae 20y, d/o Benja. D. & Dolly A. Minor Rowe; June 17 1891 by Rev. R. A. Folks.

William Brooks, ae 32y, widower, col'rd,
farm, s/o Frances A. Brooks, father unk;
Catharine Rowe, , ae 22y, col'rd, d/o Rob't
& Mary F. Rowe; June 24 1891 by Rev. John W.
Booth.

Frank Banks, ae 27y, col'rd, waterman,
s/o Peter & Ellen Banks; Eliza Cosby, ae
21y, col'rd, d/o Thos. & Sally Cosby; June
28 1891 by Rev. Frank Page.

Humphrey Washington, ae 33y, col'rd,
oyster, s/o Davy & Colenet Washington; Julia
F. A. Stokes, ae 24y, col'rd, d/o Wm. & Mary
E. Stokes; June 25 1891 by Rev. E. W. Page.

Earnest Noggins, ae 21y, col'rd, stewart,
s/o Rob't & Maria Noggins; Chaney Dennis, ae
21y, col'rd, d/o Lowny & Lukey Dennis; July
5 1891 by Rev. Wm. B. Lee.

Isaiah Whiting, ae 27y, col'rd, widower,
oyster, s/o Frank & D. Whiting; Catharine
Whiting, ae 26y, col'rd, d/o John & Daffney
Whiting; July 8 1891 by Rev. A. T. Gayle.

Davy Travers, ae 35y, col'rd, laborer, of
James City Co VA, s/o Matt & Dauphney Travers; Lucy Washington, ae 23y, col'rd,
parents unk; July 16 1891 by Rev. F. H.
Hall, Baptist minister.

John C. Riley, ae 22y, farm, s/o John M.
& Caroline Rilee Riley; Effie H. Williams,
ae 23y, d/o Wm. & Malvena Williams; July 26
1891 by Rev. F. H. Hall.

Noah F. Sterling, ae 20y, oyster, s/o
Geo. W. & Ellen Deal Sterling; Missouri
Coats, ae 18y, d/o John & Margaret West
Coats; Aug 2 1891 by Rev. F. H. Hall.

Robert Lee Deal, ae 27y, widower, mer-
chant, s/o John & Elizabeth Brown Deal;
Malinda Coats, ae 17y, d/o John & Margaret
West Coats; Aug 2 1891 by Rev. F. H. Hall.

James T. Jenkins, ae 38y, widower, oyster,
s/o Edmond & Martha Walker Jenkins; Sarah E.
Jenkins, ae 23y, d/o Wm. & Betsy Belvin Jenkins; Aug 4 1891 by Rev. R. A. Folks.

James Henry Cotes, ae 21y, col'rd, farm,
s/o Warner & Charity Cotes; Amelia Davenport,
ae 21y, col'rd, d/o Thos. & Mary Davenport;
Aug 13 1891 by Rev. Reuben Berkeley.

John Coals, ae 21y, col'rd, farm, s/o
John & Martha Coals; Judy Burrell, ae 21y,
col'rd, d/o Major & Martha Burrell; Aug 27
1891 by Rev. F. H. Hall.

James A. Johnson, ae 32y, col'rd, farm,
s/o Banja. & Hannah Johnson; Harriet Smith,
ae 19y, col'rd, d/o Jos. & Adaline Smith;
Sept 2 1891 by Rev. A. T. Gayle.

George E. Sibley, ae 32y, widower, oyster,
of Middlesex Co VA, s/o Dan'l B. & Sarah F.
Sibley; Mary E. Hibble, ae 17y, d/o Chas. W.
& Mary Hibble; Sept 7 1891 by Rev. W. F.
Robins.

Joseph Taliaferro, ae 22y, col'rd, shoe
maker, s/o C. & Jane Taliaferro; Julia Williams, ae 21y, col'rd, d/o John & Mary Williams; Sept 9 1891 by Rev. E. W. PAge.

John A. Marshall, ae 24y, col'rd, caterer,
s/o P. & C. Marshall; Julia Williams, ae 19y,
d/o Sally Willaims, father unk; Sept 9 1891
by Rev. Frank Page.

Henry Jackson, ae 21y, col'rd, farm, s/o
Jas. Southerlen & Ellen Perrin; Mary Robin-
son, ae 18y, col'rd, d/o Augustine & Clara
Robinson; Sept 12 1891 by Rev. A. T. Gayle.

John Luke Bray, ae 22y, minister, s/o
John R. & Sally G. Luke Bray; Pauline J.
Clements, ae 20y, d/o Rob't J. & Mary L.
Williams Clements; Sept 17 1891 by Rev. F.
H. Hall.

Jefferson L. Haynes, ae 25y, oyster, s/o
John W. & Mary F. Nuttall Haynes; Ida B.
Brown, ae 17y, d/o Jas. H. & Elizabeth Kil-
lingham Brown; Sept 23 1891 by Rev. F. H.
Hall.

David Mathews, ae 23y, col'rd, laborer,
s/o Rich'd C. & Jane Mathews; Martha Willis,
ae 19y, col'rd, d/o John & Margaret Peyton
Willis; Sept 24 1891 by Rev. E. W. Page.

George Washington, col'rd, widower, farm,
s/o Jerry Gregory & Winnie Banks; Lucy A.
King, ae 30y, col'rd, widow, d/o Dan'l &
Pinky Smith; Oct 1 1891 by Rev. Frank Page.

H. E. Taliaferro, ae 33y, merchant, s/o
John P. & Eleanora W. Anderson Taliaferro;
Fanny Perrin, ae 24y, d/o Wm. K. & Lucy W.
Jarvis Perrin; Oct 22 1891 by Rev. Wm. B.
Lee.

Sanco Ransone, ae 21y, col'rd, blacksmith, of Mathews Co VA, s/o Sanco & Gabriella Ransone; Martha A. Harris, ae 19y, col'rd, d/o Jas. & Mary E. Jackson Harris; Oct 29 1891 by Rev. W. J. Corbin.

W. W. Ambrose, ae 23y, oyster, s/o Frank & Sarah Ambrose; Lavinia A. Gibbs, ae 19y, d/o Wm. H. & Martha N. Gibbs; Nov 5 1891 by Rev. F. H. Hall.

Philip Jackson, ae 21y, col'rd, oyster, s/o Sam & Betsy Jackson; Eliza Jane Fleming, ae 18y, col'rd, d/o Jas. & Mary E. Fleming; Nov 3 1891 by Rev. F. H. Hall.

J. J. Long, ae 35y, sailor, of Spotsylvania Co VA, s/o John & Minerva Long; Missouri C. Thomas, ae 25y, d/o Joel & Indianna Thomas; Nov 4 1891 by Rev. R. A. Folkes.

James H. Harris, ae 23y, col'rd, farm, s/o Martha M. Harris, father unk; Eliza Curtis, ae 16y, col'rd, d/o Jas. & Susan Curtis; Nov 10 1891 by Rev. Frank Page.

T. J. Woodland, ae 42y, widower, farm and sailor, s/o John & Catharine Woodland; Magnolia Coles Roane, ae 21y, d/o L. M. & Masious Fary Roane; Nov 10 1891 by Rev. R. A. Folkes.

William Phillips, ae 22y, col'rd, laborer, of King and Queen Co VA, s/o John A. & Lucy A. Smith Phillips; Emma Wilson, ae 15y col'rd, d/o Jas. A. & Harriet Brown Wilson; Nov 12 1891 by Rev. Reuben Berkeley.

James T. Deal, ae 19y, oyster, s/o Jas. T & Susan West Deal; Laura F. Deal, ae 18y, d/o Geo. W. & Fanny Williams Deal; Nov 22 1891 by Rev. R. A. Folkes.

Charles H. Nelson, ae 24y, col'rd, oyster, s/o Roberta Lee Nelson, father unk; Emma L. Cooke, ae 22y, col'rd, d/o Anthony & Lucy E. Rowe Cooke; Nov 16 1891 by Rev. John W. Booth.

Parker Whiting, ae 40y, widower, col'rd, farm, s/o Henry & Lucy Whiting; Phillis Wright, ae 20y, col'rd, d/o Stephen & Susan Wright; Nov 22 1891 by Rev. E. W. PAge.

Monroe Page, ae 21y, oyster, s/o Wm. & Lucy P. Field Page; Rebecca Madison, ae 21y, col'rd, d/o Alexander & Maggie Clark Madison; Nov 26 1891 by Rev. E. W. Page.

Malvin Phagens, ae 38y, widower, farm, of
Beaufort Co N. C, S/o Warner Phagens, mother
unk; Matilda Webb, ae 35y, widow, d/o Chas.
& Isabella Cary; Dec 13 1891 by Rev. Wm. J.
Corbin.

William Lloyd Jenkins, ae 25y, oyster,
s/o Jas. & Caroline West Jenkins; Mary C.
Belvin, ae 24y, d/o David & Sallie West Belvin; Nov 26 1891 by Rev. R. A. Folks.

Frank Reed, ae 40y, widower, laborer,
col'rd, s/o Frank & Mary Reed; Mary Wiatt,
ae 45y, widow, col'rd, parents unk; Dec 12
1891 by Rev. A. T. Gayle.

John Allmond, ae 28y, col'rd, oyster, s/o
Judy Allmond, father unk; India Johnston, ae
21y, col'rd, Rich'd & Sally Johnston; Dec 16
1891 by Rev. E. W. Page.

Samuel Byrd, ae 30y, col'rd, widower,
farm, s/o Davy & Jane Richardson Byrd; Sarah
Hayes, ae 32y, col'rd, d/o Nancy Hayes,
father unk; Dec 17 1895 by Rev. Frank Page.

Joseph Deal, ae 46y, widower, merchant,
s/o John & Elizabeth Brown Deal; Elvira Williams, ae 31y, d/o Sam'l & Polly Robins Williams; Dec 23 1891 by Rev. Wm. B. Lee.

William Harris, ae 72y, widower, farm,
parents unk; Frances Deadman, ae 46y, widow,
d/o Paul & Eliza Thornton Deadman; Dec 24
1891 by Rev. Wm. J. Corbin.

Johnson Smith, ae 39y, col'rd, oyster,
s/o Andrew & Pinky Smith; Hester Belcher, ae
17y, col'rd, d/o Jas. & L. Belcher; Dec 24
1891 by Rev. E. W. Page.

Wm. V. Hogg, ae 30y, farm, s/o Vincent &
Martha E. Hogg; Sarah S. Marble, d/o Rob't
H. & Elizabeth J. Marble; Dec 27 1891 by
Rev. Wm. E. Wiatt.

Stephen H. Hogg, ae 28y, farm, s/o Vincent & Martha E. Hogg; Laura J. Marble, ae
18y, d/o Rob't H. & Elizabeth J. Marble; Dec
27 1891 by Rev. Wm. E. Wiatt.

James willis, ae 22y, col'rd, laborer,
s/o Cornelius Norton & Delia Willis; Marga-
rey Dixon, ae 21y, col'rd, d/o Wm. & Patsy
Dennis; Dec 27 1891 by Rev. Wm.B. Lee.

Thomas Walker, ae 21y, col'rd, farm, s/o Julia Walker, father unk; Margaret Gregory, ae 15y, col'rd, d/o Rob't & Catharine Gregory; Dec 29 1891 by Rev. E. W. Page.

W. C. Brown, ae 25y, sailor, s/o John T. & Elizabeth F. Howard Brown; Mary Ellen Williams, ae 21y, d/o E. A. & Sally E. Cox Willaims; Dec 29 1891 by Rev. R. A. Folks.

Benjamin F. Belvin, ae 27y, oyster, s/o John & Harriet Heywood Belvin; Caccie V. Robins, ae 18y, d/o John R. & Caroline Howard Robins; Dec 31 1891 by Rev. R. A. Folks.

S. S. Ward, ae 28y, col'rd, oyster, s/o John & Jane Ward; Jane Lee, ae 19y, col'rd, d/o Jasper & Maria Lee; Dec 30 1891 by Rev. E. W. PAge.

Henry Berry, ae 28y, oyster, s/o Jas. & Mary Hogg Berry; Valley Lee West; ae 20y, d/o Geo. & Lelia Jarvis West; Dec 30 1891 by Rev. R. A. Folks.

George H. Proctor, ae 31y, farm, s/o Henry S. & Elizabeth Proctor; Lucy Ann Edwards, ae 21y, d/o Dunbar & Lucy Cauthorn Edwards; Apr 9 1891 by Rev. W. H. Gregory.

W. T. Robins, ae 24y, farm, s/o Jas. W. & V. A. Robins; Eliza M. Brushwood, ae 21y, d/o Jas. & Eloisa R. Brushwood; July 5 1891 by Rev. W. H. Gregory.

Alfred C. Corson, ae 30y, sailor, of New Kent Co VA, s/o Cornelius & Sarah Dudley Corson; Mattie A. Claytor, ae 26y, d/o Jas. R. & Rebecca Adams Claytor; Aug 26 1891 by Rev. W. H. Gregory.

Alexander B. Thomas, ae 20y, oyster, s/o Jas. & Martha Smith Thomas; Susie E. Lewis, ae 19y, d/o Wash. & Mary E. Wallis Lewis; Oct 13 1891 by Rev. W. H. Gregory.

Henry A. Howard, ae 30y, merchant, s/o Henry A. & Martha Howard; Eugenia W. Leigh, ae 21y, d/o John H. & Martha Leigh; Nov 5 1891 by Rev. W. H. Gregory.

E. F. Garner, ae 24y, minister of the gospel, of Petersburg VA, s/o Merritt T. & Lucy Bond Garner; Mattie Lee Gayle, ae 21y, of Middlesex Co VA, d/o John & Virginia Brown Gayle; Dec 1 1891 by Rev. W. H. Gregory.

Charles H. Hughes, ae 30y, policeman,
lived Richmond VA, s/o John H. & Julia Leavitt Hughes; Mattie S. Ash, ae 18y, d/o Wm.
H. & Lucy S. Ash; Dec 9 1891 by Rev. W. H.
Gregory.

Nelson R. Gray, ae 33y, merchant, s/o N.
K. & Octavia Billups Gray; H. Lizzie Roane,
ae 21y, d/o Sam'l F. & Harriet Roane; Dec 15
1891 by Rev. W. H. Gregory.

Mandt Carlton, ae 21y, farm, of King and
Queen Co VA, s/o Wm. H. & Bettie Carlton;
Emma B. Horsley, ae 16y, d/o Allen & Lizzie
B. Horsley; Oct 17 1891 by Rev. W. H.
Gregory.

Leonius R. Rilee, ae 30y, farm, s/o
Pascal D. & Mary A. Rilee; Corinth Rilee, ae
18y, d/o Henry D. & Mary J. Rilee; Dec 23
1891 by Rev. W. H. Gregory.

Robert L. Shackelford, ae 23y, sailor, of
King and Queen Co VA, lived Mathews Co VA,
s/o Rich'd & Ellen Shackelford; Laura D.
Massey, ae 18y, d/o J.T. & S. J. Massey; Dec
24 1891 by Rev. W. H. Gregory.

James R. Cluverius, ae 37y, blacksmith,
s/o Jas. W. & Mary E. Hobday Cluverius;
Rebecca C. Smith, ae 25y, d/o Wm. & Sarah J.
Freeman Smith; Dec 30 1891 by Rev. W. H.
Gregory.

Julius J. Davenport, ae 22y, farm, s/o
Thos. & Mary F. Lockley Davenport; Nora Baytop, d/o Peter & Rebecca Whiting Baytop; Dec
23 1891 by Rev. John W. Booth.

John Henry Seawell, ae 23y, oyster, s/o
Miles & Martha Curtis Seawell; Hester Ann
Morriss, ae 18y, d/o Addison & Frances Mor-
riss; Dec 23 1891 by Rev. John W. Booth.

Peter Richerson, ae 22y, laborer, s/o
Adam & Mary Richerson; Ellen Driver, ae 18y,
d/o Len & C. Driver; Dec 25 1891 by Rev.
John W. Booth.

Isaiah Miles, ae 28y, laborer, s/o Davy
& Elizabeth Miles; Mary Jones, ae 27y, d/o
Adaline Robinson, father unk; Dec 24 1891 by
Rev. John W. Booth.

Jas. H. Hughes, ae 23y, oyster, s/o Major
& Catharine Robinson Hughes; Florence John-
son, ae 20y, d/o Wise & Lucy Ann Johnson;
Dec 31 1891 by Rev. John W. Booth.

Jefferson Robinson, ae 33y, oyster, s/o
Dan'l & Eve Robinson; Harriet Willis, ae,
24y, d/o Thos. & Winnie Jackson Willis; Dec
31 1891 by Rev. John W. Booth.

John T. Massey, ae 48y, widower, farm,
s/o C. C. & Mary Massey; Catharine Hall, ae
44y, widow, d/o John T. & Mary A. Pearce;
Jan 1 1892 by Rev. W. H. Gregory.

W. J. H. Oliver, ae 48y, widower, farm,
s/o Morgan & Mildred Oliver; Anna J. Rilee,
ae 33y, d/o P. D. & Mary A. Rilee; Jan 10
1892 by Rev. W. H. Gregory.

John W. Stokes, ae 22y, col'rd, sailor,
s/o Guest & Delia Ward Stokes; Sarah E.
Driver, ae 21y, col'rd, d/o Fanny Driver,
father unk; Jan 14 1892 by Rev. John W.
Booth.

Moses Cooke, ae 25y, col'rd, oyster, s/o
Anthony & Lucy E. Rowe, Cooke; Sarah Virginia
Lemon, ae 20y, col'rd, d/o John T. & Sarah
E. Lee Lemon; Jan 14 1892 by Rev. John W.
Booth.

John E. Minor, ae 29y, merchant, s/o
Chas. E. & Ellen S. Stubblefield Minor;
Martha A. Hawkins, ae 25y, d/o Thos. S. &
Louisa J. Seawell Hawkins; Jan 20 1892 by
Rev. F. H. Hall.

Sye Berry, ae 23y, col'rd, sailor, s/o
Edmund & Hester Banks Berry; Mary Dabney, ae
19y, col'rd, d/o Benja. & Martha Carter Dabney; Jan 21 1892 by Rev. W. H. Gregory.

J. J. Jenkins, ae 52y, widower, farm, s/o
Reed & Nancy Jenkins; Mary A. Jenkins, ae
27y, d/o Wm. & Elizabeth Belvin Jenkins; Jan
28 1892 by Rev. F. H. Hall.

S. Slingerland, ae 70y, farm, s/o Jas. S.
& Magdaline Luke Slingerland; J. A. Williams,
ae 33y, d/o W. H. & Angeline Fleming Williams; Feb 4 1892 by Rev. F. H. Hall.

Thomas Payne, ae 23y, col'rd, oyster, s/o
Peter & Martha Whiting Payne; Mollie Grimes,
ae 22y, col'rd, d/o John T. & Courtney Whiting Grimes; Feb 11 1892 by Rev. A. T. Gayle.

William F. Hogg, ae 22y, oyster, s/o
Washington & Emiline Heywood Hogg; Ada B.
Hall, ae 16y, d/o Wm. A. & Susie Howard Hall;
Mar 27 1892 by Rev. R. A. Folks.

James R. Davenport, ae 23y, farm, s/o A.
D. & Rosetta Whiting Davenport; Mary J. Kidd,
ae 18y, d/o John & Eliza Deadman Kidd; Mar
24 1892 by Rev. Reuben Berkeley.

Ceasor Robinson, ae 25y, laborer, of King
and Queen Co VA, s/o Ben & Dianna Williams
Robinson; Ida Reed, ae 21y, of King and
Queen Co Va, d/o Wm. & Faletia D. Braxton
Reed; Mar 19 1892 by Rev. W. J. Corbin.

Joshua Whiting, ae 25y, farm, s/o Aaron &
M. Whiting; Sally N. Scipio, ae 21y, d/o
Chas. & Frances Scipio; May 2 1892 by Rev.
Frank Page.

Lewis Dudley, ae 21y, farm, s/o Oliver &
Mary Dudley; Elsy Johnson, ae 20y, d/o Kel-
lis & Maria Johnson; May 15 1892 by Rev. Z.
Taylor Whiting.

Joseph H. Roberts, ae 22y, farm, s/o
Rich'd B. & Elizabeth Roberts; Lucy Edlar
Brown, ae 18y, d/o Thos. & Ellen Brown; May
19 1892 by Rev. R. A. Folks.

Jacob H. Acra, ae 24y, farm, s/o Jos. H.
& Matilda N. Dutton Acra; Virginia H. Booker,
ae 21y, d/o Poindexter & Maria Wormley Booker; May 18 1892 by Rev. Wm. E. Wiatt.

Charles C. Kelly, ae 23y, laborer, s/o
Eliza Kelly, father unk; Queen Victoria Taliaferro, ae 16y, d/o Ben & Maria Wormley Taliaferro; May 29 1892 by Rev. Reuben Berkeley.

John S. Heywood, ae 32y, oyster, s/o John
& Eliza Hogg Heywood; Mary Bonnywell, ae 23y,
d/o Jas. & Emma Sparrow Heywood; May 29 1892
by Rev. R. A. Folks.

Beverly Perrin, ae 24y, col'rd, oyster,
s/o Peter & Elizabeth Perrin; Mary Boston,
ae 21y, col'rd, d/o Stephen & Susan Boston;
June 19 1892 by Rev. Frank Page.

Robert L. Kellam, ae 21y, oyster, s/o Wm.
& Betty Kellam; Louisianna West, ae 17y, d/o
Ambrose & Betty E. Green West; June 23 1892
by Rev. R. A. Folks.

Robert E. Leigh, ae 27y, farm, s/o Rich'd
D. & Julia Bland Leigh; Ella Ison, ae 16y,
d/o Jas. A. & Mildred Brooking Ison; June 22
1892 by Rev. W. E. Wiatt.

Enoch D. Hatch, ae 32y, farm, of Mathews Co VA, s/o N. A. & Emily S. Thompson Hatch; Mary E. Cooke, ae 29y, d/o Mordecai & Sarah E. Powers Cooke; July 6 1892 by Rev. Wm. L. Maget.

J. Henry Ambrose, ae 24y, sailor; s/o Henry & Margaret Callis Ambrose; Rosetta B. Fleming, ae 21y, d/o Jos. C. & Catharine A. Teagle Fleming; July 7 1892 by Rev. F. H. Hall.

John Lomax, ae 24y, farm, s/o John & Susan Lomax; Jessie West, ae 23y, d/o Thos. & Hannah West; July 14 1892 by Rev. Frank Page.

Robert H. Taylor, ae 24y, farm, s/o Dorothy Taylor, father unk; Mollie Berry, ae 21y, d/o Edmund & Earsley Banks Berry; July 14 1892 by Rev. John W. Booth.

Joseph H. Jackson, ae 24y, clerk, s/o G. L. & Susan Jackson; Jane F. Miller, ae 24y, d/o Dolly Tatterson, father unk; Aug 16 1892 by Rev. Z. Taylor Whiting.

Robert Johnston, ae 22y, farm, s/o Phill & Sally Johnston; Elizabeth Carter, ae 21y, d/o Billie & Anna Carter; Auh 8 1892 by Rev. A. T. Gayle.

John Smith, ae 19y, farm, s/o Jas. Harrison & Lucy Smith; Lizzie Deans, ae 21y, d/o Wm. & Patsy Deans; Aug 25 1892 by Rev. Wm. B. Lee.

Charles L. Sinclair, ae 25y, farm, of Elizabeth Co VA, s/o L. & M. E. Allen Sinclair; Anna W. Sinclair, ae 25y, of Elizabeth City Co VA, d/o Jeff & Frances Lowry Sinclair; Sept 14 1892 by Rev. W. B. Lee.

John T. Hobday, ae 22y, farm, s/o Wm. & Hester Hobday; Matilda F. Dorsey, ae 21y, d/o Adam & Mary Clark Dorsey; Sept 5 1892 by Rev. E. W. Page.

William Hogg, ae 22y, oyster, s/o Anderson & Susan Hogg; Louisa Jenkins, ae 17y, d/o Jas. J. & Anna Jenkins; Sept 15 1892 by Rev. R. A. Folks.

Henry Sturges, ae 36y, widower, farm, s/o Rachael Sturges, father unk; Susan Black, ae 30y, widow, d/o John & martha Hall; Sept 18 1892 by Rev. J. W. Booth.

William Jackson, ae 60y, widower, farm,
of FLORIDA, s/o Henry & Mildred Jackson;
Mary Wallace, ae 50y, widow, parents unk;
Oct 9 1892 by Rev. A. T. Gayle.

Robert E. Williams, ae 35y, farm, s/o
Lewis & Caroline Williams; Emma Burrell, ae
30y, d/o Beverly & Emma Burrell; Oct 13 1892
by Rev. J. W. Booth.

William J. Anderton, ae 25y, oyster, s/o
Jas. T. & Sarah M. Elliott Anderton; Mary J.
Thomas, ae 21y, d/o John W. & Mary J. Walker
Thomas; Oct 11 1892 by Rev. F. H. Hall.

Lemuel Gayle, ae 24y, farm, of York Co
VA, s/o Robin & Kesiah Gayle; Elizabeth
Cooke, ae 21y, d/o Addison & Sylvia Cooke;
Oct 13 1892 by Rev. A. T. Gayle.

William Bright, ae 33y, oyster, s/o Wm. &
Lucy Carter Bright; Mary F. Tabb, ae 23y,
d/o John H. & Ellen Hern Tabb; Oct 13 1892
by Rev. Z. T. Whiting.

Isaac Burwell, ae 28y, oyster, s/o Minerva Burwell, father unk; Margaret Walker,
ae 23y, widow, d/o Jim Hughes & Elizabeth
Gibbs; Oct 13 1892 by Rev. E. W. Page.

Hunter P. Williams, ae 24y, farm, s/o W.
H. & Angelina Clements Williams; Tabitha E.
Shackelford, ae 18y, d/o Geo. W. & S. E. M.
Dews Shackelford; Oct 20 1892 by Rev. F. H.
Hall.

Abraham Lewis, ae 60y, widower, farm, s/o
Soloman & Betty Lewis; Henrietta Perrin, ae
48y, widow, d/o Watt Scott & Martha Bright;
Oct 29 1892 by Rev. E. W. Page.

John Patterson, ae 23y, oyster, s/o Coleman & Frankie Bush Patterson; Lucy A. Smith,
ae 20y, d/o Peggie Smith, father unk; Sept
30 1892 by Rev. A. T. Gayle.

James Lawson Davis, ae 33y, farm, of King
and Queen Co VA, s/o Albert & Willenna Burton Davis; Nancie E. Walker, ae 26y, d/o
Thos. E. & Martha A. Hogg Walker; Oct 27
1892 by Rev. F. H. Hall.

Simon Evans, ae 22y, farm, s/o Washington
& Harriet Dixon Evans; Florence Grimes, ae
19y, d/o John T. & Courtney Whiting; Nov 3
1892 by Rev. E. W. Page.

Oscar B. Rowe, ae 23y, oyster, s/o T. J. & Johanna Thomas Rowe; Lucy H. Acra, ae 19y, d/o John & Emily Nuttall Acra; Nov 3 1892 by Reb. R. A. Folks.

James T. Goldman, ae 25y, oyster, s/o Jack & Roberta Carter Goldman; Catharine Carter, ae 22y, d/o Maria Jones, father unk; Nov 6 1892 by Rev. A. T. Gayle.

James T. Banghan, ae 30y, sailor, s/o Jas. & Sarah Parker Banghan, of Calvert Co MD; Rebecca Gregory, ae 35y, d/o Jas. & Betsy Chavers Gregory; Nov 6 1892 by Rev. A. T. Gayle.

Harry L. Thornton, ae 28y, farm, s/o J. A. B. & Sarah E. Thornton; Virginia Lee Rowe, ae 21y, d/o B. A. & Cornelia Rowe; Nov 15 1892 by Rev. R. A. Folks.

Robert Johnston, ae 22y, farm, s/o Phill & Lucy Johnston; Elizabeth Carter, ae 21y, d/o Billie & Anna Carter; Aug 8 1892 by Rev. A. T. Gayle.

George Washington, ae 24y, farm, s/o Henry & C. Washington; Ada Lee Tabb, ae 19y, d/o John & Ellen Tabb; Nov 17 1892 by Rev. E. W. Page.

Thomas Harvey, ae 49y, widower, farm, s/o John & Fanny Harvey; Caroline White, ae 21y, d/o John & Patsy White; Nov 17 1892 by Rev. E. W. Page.

Seymour Taliaferro, ae 23y, widower, farm, s/o Ben & Maria Taliaferro; Amanda Reed, ae 26y, of King and Queen Co VA, d/o Henry & Martha Reed; Nov 17 1892 by Rev. Z. Taylor Whiting.

Edward C. Robins, ae 24y, oyster, s/o J. W. & Virginia A. Robins; Mary Ida Brown, ae 22y, d/o A. A. & H. F. Brown; Nov 23 1892 by Rev. Wm. E. Wiatt.

Charles Stubbs, ae 50y, widower, farm, s/o Lorenzo & Polly Stubbs; Phobe Travers, ae 21y, d/o Carl & Judy Travers; Nov 23 1892 by Rev. E. W. Page.

Ross W. Cutter, ae 32y, widower, farm, s/o A. J. & Catharine A. Coats Cutter; Georgia E. Coats, ae 21y, widow, d/o Geo. C. & Mary F. Coats; Dec 6 1892 by Rev. R. A. Folks.

Samuel Driver, ae 24y, farm, s/o Sam'l &
Sarah Driver; Julia Bristow, ae 22y, d/o Wm.
& Ann Bristow; Dec 14 1892 by Rev. John W.
Booth.

James H. Ward, ae 25y, oyster, s/o Wm. &
Julia Burwell Ward; Rose Ellen Deadman, ae
18y, d/o Pendleton & Mary Green Deadman; Dec
1 1892 by Rev. Frank Page.

Wallace Braxton, ae 35y, widower, farm,
s/o Thos. & Nancy Braxton; Eliza Hundley, ae
21y, d/o Jas. & Chaney Hundley; Dec 22 1892
by Rev. A. T. Gayle.

Thomas J. Clements, ae 21y, farm, of Middlesex Co VA, s/o John W. & Mary Sibley Clements; Fanny S. Brown, ae 20y, d/o H. W. &
Lucy J. Hatch Brown; Dec 22 1892 by Rev. J.
K. Faulkner.

Brooks Whiting, ae 26y, farm, s/o Lewis &
Elizabeth Brooks Whiting; Mary E. Gregory,
ae 23y, d/o Jerry & Maria Lumpkin Gregory;
Dec 22 1892 by Rev. J. W. Booth.

Daniel Whiting, ae 23y, oyster, s/o Martin & Matilda Evans Whiting; Emma Cooke, ae
21y, d/o Albert & Elnora Kemp Cooke; Dec 25
1892 by Rev. Reuben Berkeley.

John W. Harris, ae 22y, oyster, s/o Thos.
R. & Henrietta Savage Harris; Nettie M.
Walker, ae 18y, d/o John C. & Maggie McLane
Walker; Dec 25 1892 by Rev. W. C. Smith.

Richard Claiborne, ae 26y, laborer, s/o
Dan'l & Polly Wormley Claiborne; Emiline
Ward, ae 19y, d/o Wm. & Julia Burwell Ward;
Dec 25 1892 by Rev. W. J. Corbin,

Simon Williams, ae 24y, oyster, s/o Simon
& Katy Williams; Harriet Hammond, ae 22y,
d/o Abram & Rosetta Hammond; Dec 25 1892 by
Rev. E. W. Page.

W. W. Harriss, ae 21y, oyster, s/o W. W.
& E. F. Jenkins Harriss; Talena T. Jenkins,
ae 16y, d/o F. H. & E. F. Jenkins; Dec 25
1892 by Rev. R. A. Folks.

Hampton Stubbs, ae 27y, farm, s/o Adam &
Catharine Stubbs; Mary A. Stubbs, ae 23y,
d/o Harrison & Rilla Stubbs; Dec 25 1892 by
Rev. J. W. booth.

James Edward Cox, ae 24y, farm, s/o Geo.
W. & S. F. Williams Cox; Ellen E. Minor, ae
23y, d/o Edw'd & Ellen C. Stubblefield Minor;
Dec 25 1892 by Rev. R. A. Folks.

Edward Cosby, ae 21y, farm, s/o Thos. &
Elizabeth Cosby; Abbrie Smith, ae 21y, d/o
Jos. & Percella Smith; Dec 28 1892 by Rev.
E. W. Page.

Zackariah L. Riley, ae 21y, farm, s/o W.
Curtis & Mary Walters Riley; Cora E. Booker,
ae 21y, d/o C. E. C. & E. F. Dutton Booker;
Dec 28 1892 by Rev. W. E. Wiatt.

Willis J. Abrams, ae 25y, merchant, of
King and Queen Co VA, s/o Wm. K. & Ellen
Hendley Abrams; Eloise Duval, ae 25y, d/o J.
R. & Cordelia Pargo Duval; Dec 28 1892 by
Rev. J. Harvey Hundly.

Marcellus Williams, ae 34y, farm, s/o Sam
& Mary Robins Williams; Virginia A. Causey,
ae 21y, d/o J. R. & Mary A. Hains Causey;
Dec 29 1892 by Rev. W. B. Lee.

Robert Thornton, ae 21y, farm, s/o Thos.
& Margaret Yates Thornton; Susan dean, ae
21y, d/o Wm. & Patsy Dixon Dean; Sept 8 1892
by Rev. Wm. B. Lee.

Albert G. Parker, ae 23y, oyster, s/o Albert & Harriet Parker; Jane Bentley, ae 24y,
d/o David & Isabella Bentley; Jan 1 1893 by
Rev. E. W. Page.

James E. Carter, ae 26y, oyster, s/o John
& Sarah Dixon Carter; Lucy Ann Carter, ae
20y, widow, d/o Simon Williams & Sarah Jackson; Jan 1 1893 by Rev. A. T. Gayle.

George W. Jenkins, ae 27y, widower, fish-
erman, s/o Edward & Martha jenkins; Rebecca
Walker, ae 21y, widow, d/o (given names unk)
West; Jan 4 1893 by Rev. R. A. Folks.

Joseph Smith, ae 23y, oyster, s/o Ralph &
E. Smith; Sarah Pollard, ae 21y, widow, d/o
Eml & Susan Pollard; Jan 5 1893 by Rev. E. W.
Page.

John Spurlock, ae 27y, farm, s/o Mary
Spurlock, father unk; Mary Lockley, ae 21y,
widow, d/o Eml & M. Jones; Jan 5 1893 by
Rev. 5 1893 by Rev. Z. ṭaylor Whiting.

James Chapman, ae 37y, widower, laborer, s/o Wesley & Margaret Chapman; Nancie E. Major, ae 17y, d/o Alfred Major, mother unk; Jan 22 1893 by Rev. Wm. J. Corbin.

George Smith, ae 22y, farm, s/o Thos. & L. West Smith; Ann Rebecca Heywood, ae 22y, d/o Joseph & Sally Green Heywood; Jan 22 1893 by Rev. R. A. Folks.

James E. Teagle, ae 33y widower, farm, s/o John A. & Martha J. Hall Teagle; Edla M. Brown, ae 24y, d/o L. T. & Maria F. Savage Brown; Jan 18 1893 by Rev. R. A. Folks.

H. P. Webb, ae 26y, s/o Wm. & Anna Foxwell Webb; Sarah E. Croswell, ae 19y, d/o R. A. & Georgianna Robins Croswell; Jan 26 1893 by Rev. R. A. Folks.

Samuel Jackman, ae 27y, farm, s/o Edmund & Sarah Lemon Jackman; Mary F. Tyler, ae 21y, d/o Wm. & G. A. Tyler; Feb 5 1893 by Rev. J. W. Booth.

John Harriss, ae 23y, farm, s/o John & Mary E. Harriss; Isabella Seawell, ae 19y, d/o Chas. & Martha Seawell; Feb 7 1893 by Rev. John W. Booth.

Cary T. Oliver, ae 38y, widower, farm, s/o W. J. H. & Sarah Dunston Oliver; Callie Horsely, ae 19y, d/o Geo. & Lucy Sheppard Horsely; Feb 8 1893 by Rev. Wm. E. Wiatt.

Mathew Walker, ae 22y, oyster, s/o John & Caroline Walker; Lue Oliver, ae 30y, widow, d/o Smiley & Lou Oliver; Feb 26 1893 by Rev. R. A. Folks.

Walter Mende Allmond, ae 21y, merchant, s/o T. W. & Mary F. Puller Allmond; Alverta Eastwood, ae 25y, d/o A. G. & Virginia Wright Eastwood; Feb 27 1893 by Rev. W. E. Wiatt.

Baylor Cooly, ae 65y, widower, farm, s/o Edward & Easter Cooly; Ceybia Homes, ae 60y, widow, d/o Wm. Lemon & Nancy Goalman; Mar 5 1893 by Rev. Z. Taylor Whiting.

William Jenkins, ae 23y, sailor, s/o Wm. & Katie Jenkins; Mamie Jenkins, ae 17y, d/o Reed & Ellen Jenkins; Mar 7 1893 by Rev. R. A. Folks.

Walter W. Hudgins, ae 25y, farm, s/o John & Elizabeth Page Hudgins; Cora L. Robins, ae 16y, d/o Wm. & Mary J. Smith Robins; Mar 7 1893 by Rev. Wm. E. Wiatt.

John H. Jenkins, ae 36y, oyster, s/o Geo. W. & Susan Howard Jenkins; Georgianna Belvin, ae 21y, d/o Fred & M. J. Belvin; Mar 7 1893 by Rev. R. A. Folks.

Robert B. Walthall, ae 24y, oyster, of Richmond VA, s/o Rich'd E. & Anna A. Coleman Walthall; Mary A. Hogg, ae 23y, d/o Jas. K. & Mary C. Townsend Hogg; Mar 9 1893 by Rev. R. A. Folks.

William Crittenden, ae 22y, oyster, of Essex Co VA, s/o Lewis & Lucy Ann Burnette Crittenden; Mary Kemp, ae 18y, d/o Wm. & Lucy Kemp; Mar 16 1893 by Rev. W. J. Corbin.

Frank Jackson, ae 23y, oyster, s/o Ceasar & Martha Jackson; Virginia Hubbard, ae 21y, d/o Wm. & Nancy Clayton Hubbard; Mar 14 1893 by Rev. Reuben Berkeley.

Richard Sterling, ae 21y, sailor, s/o Geo. & Ellen Deal Sterling; Lizzie Deal, ae 21y, d/o John A. & Louisianna Bonnywell Deal; Mar 22 1893 by Rev. Wm. B. Lee.

Philip A. Didlake, ae 31y, oyster, s/o John R. & Frances W. Didlake; Cora A. Bland, ae 20y, d/o W. C. & Virginia Bland; Mar 22 1893 by Rev. Leroy S. Banks.

William Scott, ae 23y, farm, s/o Jas. & Lucy Jackson Scott; Louisa Harris, ae 16y, d/o Adam & Betsy Roy Harris; Apr 6 1893 by Rev. Frank Pâge.

James Bristow, ae 28y, laborer, s/o Wm. & Ann Dabney Bristow; Martha L. Robinson, ae 21y, d/o Isaac & Mary Byrd Robinson; Apr 6 1893 by Rev. John W. Booth.

Isaac Davis, ae 23y, oyster, of MD, s/o Leroy & Martha Davis; Mary Sue West, ae 23y, d/o John & Susan Sparrow West; Apr 13 1893 by Rev. R. A. Folks.

Willis Taylor, ae 26y, oyster, s/o Paul & Betsy Taylor; Henrietta Stokes, ae 24y, d/o Wm. & Mary E. Carter Stokes; Apr 13 1893 by Rev. E. W. Page.

R. G. Sibley, ae 31y, widower, ship
builder, of Norfolk City VA, s/o Wm. H. &
Mary E. Stevens Sibley; Mary C. Anderton, ae
19y, d/o Jas. T. & Margaret S. Elliott Anderton; Apr 13 1893 by Rev. John S. Wallace.

Robert T. Milby, ae 28y, farm, of King
and Queen Co VA, s/o Wm. A. & Catharine Williams Milby; Estelle Brook Lawson, ae 21y,
d/o WM. J. & Mary J. Coats Lawson; Apr 16
1893 by Rev. Wm. E. Wiatt.

J. W. Lindsey, ae 23y, farm, s/o R. F. &
Fanny Blasingham Lindsey; Fanny Rowe, ae
23y, d/o John F. & Martha A. Smith Rowe; Apr
20 1893 by Rev. R. A. Folks.

Benjamin Morey, ae 23y, oyster, s/o John
W. & Willer A. Harvie Morey; Mary A. Hogg,
ae 18y, d/o Peter & Rosa A. Oliver Hogg; Apr
20 1893 by Rev. R. A. Folks.

Alampra Phillips, ae 39y, of Richmond Co
VA, s/o John W. & Maria S. Fogg Phillips;
Jennie Gordon Cameron, ae 19y, of Philadel-
phis PA, d/o R. T. & Margery Gordon Cameron;
Apr 20 1893 by Rev. W. B. Lee. Mr. Cameron
was a merchant.

William Jarvis, ae 25y, farm, s/o Humphrey & Lucy Jones Jarvis; Rosa Jackson, ae
20y, d/o WM. & Sarah Jackson; Apr 23 1893 by
Rev. R. J. Hall.

Willie C. Clopton, ae 26y, farm, s/o
THos. J. & M. Cecelia Clopton; Ada S. Lewis,
ae 27y, of Brunswick Co VA, d/o D. & Elizabeth Fitzhugh Lewis; Apr 26 1893 by Rev. W.
B. Lee.

Albert Harriss, ae 35y, sailor, of
Charles City Co VA, s/o Archer & Nancy Har-
riss; Gracy Anderson, ae 24y, d/o Wm. &
Ellen Anderson; May 16 1893 by Rev. Z.
Taylor Whiting.

Willie Lemons, ae 21y, farm, s/o Lizzie
Pointer, father unk; Lou Emma Harriss, ae
18y, d/o Wesley & Emma Jenkins Harriss; May
17 1893 by Rev. R. A. Folks.

Willie Taylor, ae 26y, oyster, s/o Paul &
Betsy Taylor; Henrietta Stokes, ae 24y, d/o
Wm. T. & Mary E. Carter Stokes; Apr 13 1893
by Rev. E. W. Page.

Isreal Decker, ae 40y, oyster planter, of
Staten Island N. Y, s/o John & Anthion W.
Prior Decker; Lillie M. Lanfair, ae 21y, of
New Haven CONN, d/o John R. & Abbie D. Lan-
craft Lanfair; May 25 1893 by Rev. W. E.
Wiatt.

Charles H. Gwynn, ae 24y, farm, s/o Lewis
Taylor & Betty Furn Gwynn; Rebecca A. Dud-
ley, ae 21y, d/o Oliver & Mary J. Johnston
Dudley; May 21 1893 by Rev. Z. T. Whiting.

Charles Holmes, ae 22y, oyster, s/o Chas.
& Lena Holmes; Annie Johnston, ae 22y, d/o
Thos. & Betsy Johnston; June 4 1893 by Rev.
John W. Booth.

Thomas J. Belvin, ae 22y, oyster, s/o
Edmund & Mary Aherron Belvin; Eugenia M.
Shackelford, ae 18y, d/o John & C. Shackel-
ford; June 7 1893 by Rev. R. A. Folks.

James T. Belvin, ae 25y, farm, s/o Benja.
F. & Mary E. Hundley Belvin; Cora A. Walker,
ae 21y, d/o John & Maggie McLane Walker;
June 11 1893 by Rev. R. A. Folks.

J. W. Jarvis, ae 26y, farm, s/o G. R. C.
& Jane B. Singleton Jarvis; Rachel Pritchard,
ae 24y, d/o John J. & Mollie DocKorty Pritchard; June 14 1893 by Rev. Wm. B. Lee.

H. P. Sears, ae 32y, widower, sailor, s/o
Beverly & Louisa Sears; Annie M. Wilson, ae
18y, d/o Joel & Emily S. Wilson; June 14 1893
by Rev. Leroy L. Banks.

Raymond J. Bristow, ae 22y, sailor, s/o
Rob't & Elizabeth A. Mason Bristow; Maggie B.
Lewis, ae 18y, d/o Rob't & Elizabeth Gibbs
Lewis; Sept 27 1893 by Rev. W. H. Gregory.

George W. Horsely, ae 57y, widower, farm,
s/o Jas. K. & Elizabeth Horsley; Mildred A.
Hall, ae 40y, widow, parents unk; Jan 26
1893 by Rev. W. H. Gregory.

Jos. T. Willis, ae 30y, widower, sailor,
s/o John & Mary E. Hall Willis; Emily F.
Thrift, ae 18y, d/o H. L. & Mary F. Mason
Thrift; Feb 17 1893 by Rev. W. H. Gregory.

William R. Stubbs, ae 37y, farm, s/o W.
W. & Mary F. Eastwood Stubbs; Olivis J. Bland,
ae 40y, widow, of Mecklenburg Co VA, d/o J.
N. & E. J. Arundel Anderson ; Mar 8 1893 by
Rev. W. H. Gregory.

Peter H. Thrift, ae 37y, widower, farm,
s/o W. Jackson & Margaret Thrift; Mattie W.
Dutton, ae 17y, d/o Wm. C. & Maria Dutton;
Mar 16 1892 by Rev. W. H. Gregory.

Richard Jones, ae 31y, oyster, s/o Cye &
Fanny Evans Jones; Lavinia Thornton, ae 22y,
d/o Ellen Thornton, father unk; Apr 3 1893
by Rev. Reuben Berkeley.

James H. Kinnard, ae 22y, oyster, of Mid-
dlesex Co VA, s/o Wm. J. & Mary E. Alford
Kinnard; Nora F. Rowe, ae 25y, d/o Henry &
Ann M. Stubblefield Rowe; Apr 13 1892 by
Rev. W. H. Gregory.

Jefferson Cooke, ae 45y, widower, farm,
s/o Wm. & T. Taylor Cooke; Mary Cooke, ae
30y, widow, d/o Washington & Martha Johnston
Dabney; Apr 22 1892 by Rev. W. H. Gregory.

William C. Rasch, ae 27y, sailor, s/o H.
& Louisa Allen Rasch; Otelia M. Puller, ae
21y, of Keny Co MD, d/o John S. & Sarah A.
J. Soles Puller; Apr 25 1892 by Rev. W. H.
Gregory.

Clarence H. Kemp, ae 21y, farm, s/o Thos.
& J. D. Pointer Kemp; Elenora Hall, ae 20y,
d/o Lewis O. & Martha A. Enos Hall; May 25
1892 by Rev. W. H. Gregory.

Edward T. Tuttle, ae 29y, seaman, of New
Haven CONN, s/o Horace & Cornelia Lewis
Tuttle; Jessie Lee Jennings, ae 24y, of
Patchogue, d/o Chas. & Easter Baker Jennings;
July 12 1893 by Rev. W. H. Gregory.

James P. Palmer, ae 45y, widower, s/o
Philip & Rebecca Howard Palmer; Rosa H. Dud-
ley, ae 35y, widow, of Caroline Co VA, d/o
Wm. Holmes; June 18 1893 by Rev. John W.
Booth.

Charles R. Cooke, ae 29y, oyster, s/o
Geo. W. & Mary A. Tonkins Cooke; Maria Lee
Cooke, ae 24y, d/o Rich'rd & Louisianna Rowe
Cooke; June 18 1893 by Rev. A. T. Gayle.

William R. Walker, ae 26y, farm, of Acco-
mac Co VA, s/o John R. & Catharine Walden
Walker; Susan M. Wilkins, ae 22y, d/o Nathan
& Frances A. Moore Wilkins; June 22 1893 by
Rev. W. H. Gregory.

R. B. Wilson, ae 64y, widower, of Portsmouth VA, lived Richmond VA, contractor, s/o Nathaniel & Ann Portlock Wilson; Mary E. Coleman, ae 48y, d/o Jas. & Mary E. Medlicott Coleman; June 28 1893 by Rev. W. H. Gregory.

Wane E. Stubblefield, ae 37y, farm, s/o W. E. & Maria Seawell Stubblefield; Lillian R. Dutton, ae 22y, d/o Pen & Sarah E. Dutton; June 28 1893 by Rev. Wm. E. Wiatt.

W. S. Miller, ae 23y, blacksmith, s/o W. L. & V. A. Dutton Miller; Pauline Walker, ae 19y, d/o John M. & Mary E. Brooking Walker; July 4 1893 by Rev. W. H. Gregory.

William Nuttall, ae 19y, farm, s/o Edmund & Maria Soles Nuttall; Arametta Kemp, ae 22y, d/o O. J. & Emiline Fary Kemp; July 4 1893 by Rev. Charles A. Raymond V. D. M.

Vincent Jenkins, ae 21y, farm, s/o Reed & Ellen Jenkins; Mollie Shackelford, ae 22y, d/o John & Ella Shackelford; July 11 1893 by Rev. R. A. Folks.

Jefferson Slaughter, ae 31y, farm, s/o Wm. & Susan Robinson Slaughter; India Cooke, ae 22y, d/o Frank & Rebecca Lemon Cooke; Jan 1 1893 by Rev. John W. Booth.

Jasper Willis, ae 30y, farm, s/o Washington & Rachel Selden Willis; Mary L. Seawell, ae 20y, d/o H. W. & Eley Ward Seawell; Jan 1 1893 by Rev. John W. Booth.

George Smith, ae 27y, widower, farm, of Loudon Co VA, s/o Jesse & Mahala Smith; Adosia Ellis, ae 26y, d/o Cane & Mary Ellis; July 11 1893 by Rev. E. W. Page.

William Washington, ae 35y, widower, oyster, s/o Parker & Fanny Washington; Bertie Hubbard, ae 22y, d/o Wm. & Nancy Hubbard; July 16 1893 by Rev. John W. Booth.

Joseph Belvin, ae 33y, widower, farm, s/o Jas. & Martha Belvin; Nannie Butler, ae 23y, d/o Thos. & Gracy Butler; July 18 1893 by Rev. R. A. Folks.

George Holland, ae 40y, widower, farm, of Southampton Co VA, s/o Randol & Mary Johnston Holland; Caroline Perrin, ae 35y, widow, d/o Wm. & Nancy Menkins Graham; July 25 1893 by Rev. E. W. Page.

Benjamin Taliaferro, ae 48y, widower, of King and Queen Co VA, farm, s/o John & Tabby Taliaferro; Harriet Carter, ae 25y, d/o Edmund & Harriet Carter; July 27 1893 by Rev. E. W. Page.

John Hubbard, ae 29y, widower, bricklayer, s/o Wm. & Nancy Clayton Hubbard; Eleanora Seawell, ae 19y, d/o Henry & Elsie Ward Seawell; July 30 1893 by Rev. John W. Booth.

James Henry Ambrose, ae 27y, oyster, s/o Frank & Sarah E. Hogg Ambrose; Alexine F. Williams, ae 21y, d/o W. S. & C. B. Fosque Williams; Aug 6 1893 by Rev. R. A. Folks.

James M. Bonnywell, ae 60y, widower, of Accomac Co VA, oyster, s/o John & Sally Turlington Bonnywell; Ellen Anderson, ae 29y, widow, d/o Frank & Fanny Heywood Jenkins; Aug 9 1893 by Rev. R. A. Folks.

Annanias Wise, ae 25y, farm, s/o Henry & Mary Carter Wise; Cordelia Davis, ae 19y, d/o Jas. & Frances A. Booth Davis; Aug 9 1893 by Rev. Reuben Burke.

John W. Walker, ae 28y, oyster, s/o John W. & Cornelia E. Jordan Walker; Grace Rowe, ae 21y, d/o Jasper & Fanny Rowe; Aug 24 1893 by Rev. R. A. Folks.

Wm. H. Horsley, ae 52y, widower, farm, s/o John W. & Mary Rilee Horsley; Mary E. Soles, ae 18y, d/o John T. & Cordelia A. Soles Walker Soles; Aug 10 1893 by Rev. W. C. Smith.

James Henry Boykin, ae 36y, widower, watchman, of Isle of Wight Co VA, s/o Jacob & Demia Crocker Boyken; Mary D. Frayser, ae 21y, d/o Julius & Patsy Payne Frayser; Aug 15 1893 by Rev. E. W. Page.

William Bailey Barton, ae 21y, insurance agent, of Dallas TEXAS, s/o Jas. W. & Clara A. Young Barton; Ellen C. Thruston, ae 20y, d/o John W. & Mary A. Robins Thruston; Sept 6 1893 by Rev. Wm. E. Wiatt.

John T. Oliver, ae 23y, oyster, s/o Thos. & Sarah E. Wright Oliver; Lorena Smith, ae 17y, d/o Polk & Sarah Morey Smith; Sept 10 1893 by Rev. R. A. Folks.

Miles Cary, ae 24y, oyster, s/o Miles &
Frances Young Cary; Mary Burrell, ae 21y,
s/o Coleman & Eliza Burrell; Sept 21 1893 by
Rev. Z. T. Whiting.

Richard Billups, ae 24y, oyster, s/o Tom
& Milly Billups; Emily Patterson, ae 21y,
d/o Coleman & Frances Patterson; Sept 24
1893 by Rev. A. T. Gayle.

William Carter Walker, ae 29y, merchant,
s/o Thos. & Grace Hubbard Walker; Rose Ellen
Booth, ae 24y, d/o Rob't E. & Ellen Dixon
Booth; Sept 20 1893 by Rev. John W. Booth.

Zachariah Lewis, ae 79y, widower, farm,
of Middlesex Co VA, s/o Adam & Daffney
Lewis; Lucinda Perrin, ae 45y, d/o Billy &
Becky Perrin; Sept 14 1893 by Rev. E. W.
Page.

William T. Heywood, ae 23y, farm, s/o
Coleman & Mary M. Cooke Heywood; Marian F.
Williams, ae 19y, d/o W. Hunter & Angelina
Clements Williams; Sept 14 1893 by Rev. R.
A. Folks.

Thomas B. Paschall, ae 27y, deputy
sheriff, of Seavye Co KANSAS, s/o John D. &
Pattie Hicks Paschall; Helen M. Sinclair, ae
23y, d/o R. M. & Roena Baytop Sinclair; Oct
10 1893 by Rev. W. B. Lee.

John Green, ae 41y, widow, farm, s/o
Benja. & Emily Green; Elizabeth Ross, ae 21y,
d/o Peter & Frances Ross; Oct 8 1893 by Rev.
Frank Page.

Augustine Dixon, ae 34y, widower, oyster,
s/o Jas. & Mary Dixon; Milcy Stokes, ae 19y,
d/o Guy & Mary Todd Stokes; Oct 19 1893 by
Rev. Z. Taylor Whiting.

Peter Perrin, ae 40y, widower, farm, s/o
Beverly & Dinah Perrin; Jenny Todd, ae 50y,
widow, parents unk; Oct 22 1893 by Rev. A.
T. Gayle.

Charles Bentley, ae 21y, farm, of Mathews
Co VA, s/o Dan'l & Isabella Bentley; Phillis
Norton, ae 21y, d/o Peter & Elenora Norton;
Oct 29 1893 by Rev. Reuben Berkeley.

Parker Whiting, ae 42y, widower, oyster,
s/o Henry & Lucy Mackie Whiting; Nancy Carter, ae 37y, widow, d/o Burruss & Jennie
Taliaferro; Oct 12 1893 by Rev. E. W. Page.

W. H. White, ae 28y, oyster, s/o J. H. &
Elizabeth Oliver White; Alice Hogg, ae 22y,
d/o B. A. & Hettie Hogg; Nov 16 1893 by Rev.
R. A. Folks.

Joseph A. Phillips, ae 23y, waterman, s/o
John A. & Pinky Howard Phillips; Susan E.
Brown, ae 18y, d/o John A. & Mary Brown; Nov
5 1893 by Rev. R. N. Crooks.

Willie A. Regensburg, ae 29y, farm, of
King and Queen Co VA, s/o S. A. & Rosa A.
Fary Regensburg; Jennie Lawson, ae 21y, d/o
John C. & Fanny L. Wiatt Lawson; Nov 9 1893
by Rev. W. E. Wiatt.

Eddie Kemp, ae 22y, seaman, s/o Beverly
& Rosa Dunston Kemp; Victoria J. Rilee, ae
21y, d/o Henry & Mary J. Walker Rilee; Nov
15 1893 by Rev. WM. E. Wiatt.

Oscar Robinson, ae 28y, oyster, of
Mathews Co VA, s/o Wm. & Ann Robinson; Emma
Cooke, ae 32y, d/o Jane Cooke, father unk;
Nov 8 1893 by Rev. R. J. Hall.

Beverly Burwell, ae 75, farm, s/o Rob't &
Peggy Jones; Sarah Carter, ae 55y, d/o Jas.
& Ann Fox; Nov 12 1893 by Rev. Z. Taylor
Whiting.

Maxwell H. Acra, ae 24y, farm, s/o Wm. &
Julia C. Booker Acra; Ellen Tabitha Booker,
ae 21y, d/o Miles H. & Rosa A. Mason Booker;
Nov 8 1893 by Rev. W. H. Gregory.

John E. Ransone, ae 26y, merchant, of
Lancaster Co VA, s/o Jas. & Ann Stubblefield
Ransone; Susie Jasper Rowe, ae 19y, d/o Jas-
per & Mary S. Mouring Rowe; Nov 30 1893 by
Rev. R. A. Folks.

Henry H. Borum, ae 28y, oyster business,
of Ronaten CONN, lived Greenport Suffolk N.
Y, s/o Sam'l & Henrietta B. Bell Borum;
Jessie M. Monsell, ae 20y, of S. Norwalk
CONN, lived Gloucester Co VA, d/o Jas. M. &
Sarah E. Myers Monsell; Nov 30 1893 by Rev.
W. H. Gregory.

Archibald D. Rowe, ae 23y, oyster, s/o J.
Monroe & Mary Jane Willey Rowe; Ada A. West,
ae 21y, d/o Chas. C. & Susan A. Brown West;
Dec 6 1893 by Rev. R. A. Folks.

John W. West, ae 22y, oyster, s/o Wm. &
Sarah Brown West; Emma F. Belvin, ae 18y,
d/o John Perrin & Elizabeth West Belvin; Dec
6 1893 by Rev. R. A. Folks.

Alex A. Davenport, ae 21y, farm, s/o A.
D. & Rosetta Whiting Davenport; Julia Coles,
ae 21y, d/o Warren & Chanty Coles; Dec 21
1893 by Rev. Reuben Berkeley.

James T. Kellum, ae 22y, oyster, s/o Wm.
& Betsy Hogg Kellum; Ida Susan Jenkins, ae
20y, d/o Beverly & Mary E. West Jenkins; Dec
26 1893 by Rev. R. A. Folks.

John Reed, ae 21y, oyster, s/o Warner &
Sarah Guthrie Reed; Martha Lewis, ae 21y,
d/o Matt & Susan Coleman Lewis; Dec 21 1893
by Rev. John W. Booth.

R. H. Claiborne, ae 23y, farm, s/o Jas. &
Molly Claiborne; Julia Burrell, ae 18y, d/o
Phill & Sarah Burrell; Dec 23 1893 by Rev.
Frank Page.

Richard L. Edmund, ae 23y, farm, s/o Wm.
C. & Mary Haynes Edmund; Mary Maud Miller,
ae 19y, d/o Wm. F. & Virginia A. Miller; Nov
24 1893 by Rev. Wm. E. Wiatt.

Allen Jenkins, ae 22y, sailor, s/o Jos.
A. & Addie F. East Jenkins; Cornelia J.
Brown, ae 20y, d/o Jos. & Catharine Rowe
Brown; Dec 25 1895 by Rev. R. A. Folks.

Thomas J. Taylor, ae 21y, clerk, of King
and Queen Co VA, s/o Thos. J. & Sarah J.
Greggs Taylor; Mary A. Figg, ae 19y, d/o
John & Jaynie C. Blake Figg; Dec 25 1895 by
Rev. J. H. Burns.

E. H. Green, ae 24y, oyster, s/o John &
Anna West Green; Sarah Jenkins, ae 21y, d/o
Jas. & Anna Hogg Jenkins; Dec 26 1895 by
Rev. R. A. Folks.

Logan G. Miller, ae 37y, merchant, of
Portsmouth VA, s/o John & M. E. Brooks
Miller; Mary Lou Cooke, ae 30y, d/o Thos. S.
& Mary T. Geryor Cooke; Dec 27 1893 by Rev.
J. D. Hank.

James H. Waddell, ae 23y, clerk, s/o Wm.
& E. A. Williams Waddell; Maggie B. Robins,
ae 21y, d/o R. C. & Lelia Buford Robins; Dec
27 1893 by Rev. W. E. Wiatt.

John Green, ae 34y, widower, farmer, s/o
Lucy Jarvis, father unk; Alice Carter, ae
24y, d/o Lucy Moody, father unk; Dec 27 1893
by Rev. John W. Booth.

William F. Stubblefield, ae 38y, farm,
s/o W. E. & Marian Leavitt Stubblefield;
Zena Eastwood, ae 18y, d/o Wm. T. & Fanny
Bryan Eastwood; Dec 27 1893 by Rev. J. D.
Hank.

John S. Morriss, ae 20y, farm, s/o A. & F.
Morriss; Martha E. Cooke, ae 21y, d/o Albert
& E. Kemp; Dec 28 1893 by Rev. J. W. Booth.

Isaac Tibbs, ae 21y, farm, s/o R. & Eliza
Lewis Tibbs; Rachael Cooke, ae 21y, d/o Jas.
& Emiline Cooke; Dec 28 1893 by Rev. Frank
Page.

James Henry Scipio. ae 25y, farm, s/o
Chas. & Mary Berry Scipio; Sanna Middleton,
ae 21y, s/o Frankie Baytop, father unk; Dec
28 1893 by Rev. Frank Page.

Michael Driver, ae 28y, blacksmith, s/o
A. & Elizabeth Collins Driver; Mary S. Phillips, ae 24y, d/o Henry & Maria Hayes Phillips; Dec 28 1893 by Rev. John W. Booth.

John Iverson, ae 38y, widower, oyster, of
Caroline Co VA, s/o Wm. & Maria Rawlings
Iverson; Esther A. Hobday, ae 26y, d/o John &
Nancy Hobday; Dec 28 1893 by Rev. Wm. Thomas.

J. T. Owens, ae 25y, oyster, s/o B. C. &
M. E. A. Owens; Wnnie E. West, ae 21y, d/o
Geo. W. & Georgianna Jenkins West; Dec 28
1893 by Rev. R. A. Folks.

Peyton Page, ae 22y, farm, s/o Frank &
Frances Page; Mary Berry, ae 18y, d/o Nelson
Scott & Lucy Berry; Dec 31 1893 by Rev.
Frank Page.

John W. Kemp, ae 23y, farm, s/o John &
Matilda Taliaferro Kemp; Harriet Hudgins, ae
25y, d/o John & Rose Hudgins; Dec 17 1893 by
Rev. E. W. Page.

Wm. McCare, ae 28y, oyster, of Halifax Co
VA, s/o Essex & Emma McCare; Mary L. Whiting,
ae 24y, d/o Parker & Sarah Williams Whiting;
Dec 21 1893 by Rev. E. W. Page.

W. T. Wyatt, ae 19y, farm, s/o Wm. & A.
M. Smith Wyatt; Martha Robinson, ae 18y, d/o
Sterling & Julia Robinson; Dec 27 1893 by
Rev. E. W. Page.

Eddie Moody, ae 25y, oyster, s/o Peter &
Ann Colive Moody; Annie Williams, ae 26y, of
Fluvanna Co VA, d/o Julia Walker, father unk;
Dec 28 1893 by Rev. E. W. Page.

Christopher C. Wilkins, ae 24y, oyster,
s/o John & Mollie Howlett Wilkins; Rosa Lee
Jenkins, ae 21y, d/o Wm. A. & Elizabeth Belvin Jenkins; Jan 1 1894 by Rev. Paul Bradley.

William Robert Reed, ae 22y, laborer, s/o
Aaron Bush & Mary Reed; Marilla Stokes, ae
22y, d/o Guest & Delia Stokes; Jan 4 1894 by
Rev. J. W. Booth.

Elias Kemp, ae 27y, widower, oyster, s/o
Henry & Elizabeth Kemp; Fanny Montague, ae
22y, d/o Phill & Mary E. Montague; Jan 3
1894 by Rev. Z. Taylor Whiting.

Jefferson Sinclair, ae 22y, widower, farm,
of Elizabeth City Co VA, s/o Jefferson &
Frances Lowry Sinclair; Mary Graham Jones,
ae 33y, d/o Walker F. & Mary Agnes Baytop
Jones; Jan 9 1894 by Rev. J. D. Hank.

James Shipley Brown, ae 23y, oyster, s/o
L. T. & Maria F. Savage Brown; Catharine E.
Walker, ae 19y, d/o Enock W. & Elizabeth A.
Brown Walker; Jan 10 1894 by Rev. Paul Brad-
ley.

Willie W. Bright, ae 27y, street car
driver, of Currituck Co N. C, s/o Westley &
Sarah Powers Bright; Anna Florence Fleming,
ae 21y, d/o Jos. C. & Catharine A. Teagle
Fleming; Jan 14 1894 by Rev. Paul Bradley.
Mr. Bright lived in Norfolk VA.

William Henry Bryan, ae 24y, farm, of
Kent Co MD, s/o Rich'd H. & Mary O. Birch
Bryan; Barbara E. Erdman, ae 25y, of Balti-
more MD, d/o Chas. & Emma E. Reed Erdman;
Jan 15 1894 by Rev. J. D. Hank.

J. V. Bray, ae 40y, widower, mechanic, of
King and Queen Co VA, lived West Point VA,
s/o John & Mira Newcomb Bray; Emma J. Leigh,
ae 30y, widow, d/o Jas. R. & Rebecca E.
Adams Claytor; Jan 16 1894 by Rev. J. D.
Hank.

James W. George, ae 27y, merchant, of
Lancaster Co VA, lived Middlesex Co VA, s/o
Jas. M. & Margaret Sands George; Mary E.
Haynes, ae 18y, of King and Queen Co VA, d/o
Chas. E. & Virginia D. Milby Haynes; Jan 17
1894 by Rev. R. H. Younger.

Thomas P. Brothers, ae 38y, widower, of Pasquotank N. Y, merchant, s/o T. P. & Dicy Brothers; Elizabeth P. Chandler, ae 23y, d/o J. J. & Lucy Chandler; June 8 1894 by Rev. W. E. Wiatt.

George R. Jarvis, ae 38y, farm, s/o Geo. R. & M. R. Singleton Jarvis; Maggie V. C. Chandler, ae 21y, d/o J. J. & Lucy Chandler; Jan 18 1894 by Rev. W. E. Wiatt.

John F. Thomas, ae 25y, fisherman, s/o Rob't & Minerva Hogg Thomas; Nannie E. Thomas, ae 23y, d/o Wm. T. & Eliza Jane Thomas; Jan 21 1894 by Rev. R. A. Folks.

Daniel Ellis, ae 22y, oyster, s/o Frank & Johannah Ellis; Fanny Reed, ae 22y, of King and Queen Co VA, d/o Harry & Martha Taliaferro Reed; Jan 25 1894 by Rev. R. A. Folks.

Albert Kelly, ae 20y, farm, s/o John & Martha Kelly; Margaret Curtis, ae 20y, d/o Davy Carter & Georgianna Adams; Feb 4 1894 by Rev. J. W. Booth.

Harrison Stubbs, ae 46y, widower, farm, s/o Harrison & Clara Stubbs; Laura L. Booth, ae 39y, widow, d/o John Hall, mother unk; Feb 6 1894 by Rev. J. W. Booth.

Charles S. Hall, ae 24y, oyster, s/o Rich'd & Elizabeth Bridges Hall; Sarah Robins, ae 23y, d/o John & Caroline Howard Robins; Feb 11 1894 by Rev. R. A. Folks.

Charles E. Harper, ae 30y, farm, s/o Edward & Elizabeth Sheppard Harper; Ida R. Kemp, ae 21y, d/o L. M. & Harriet E. B. Dutton Kemp; Feb 18 1894 by Rev. J. D. Hanks.

Robert T. Claytor, ae 32y, farm, s/o Jas. R. & Rebecca Adams Claytor; Fanny E. Corson, ae 21y, d/o Cornelius & Sarah Dudley Corson; Feb 22 1894 by Rev. J. D. Hank.

William H. Hooks, ae 21y, farm, s/o Rob't & Julia Noggins Hooks; Lucy Cooke, ae 21y, d/o Abe & Fannet Cooke; Mar 1 1894 by Rev. Frank Page.

Edward H. Belvin, ae 27y, farm, s/o John & Harriet Heywood Belvin; Susan E. Hall, ae 21y, d/o Wm. & Susan Harwood Hall; Mar 10 1894 by Rev. R. A. Folks.

William H. Emerson, ae 33y, farm, of Talbot Co MD, s/o Aene & S. Wormley Emerson;
Sarah F. Hudgins, ae 18y, d/o John F. &
Louise H. Hall Hudgins (Shackelford, maiden
name); Mar 15 1894 by Rev. W. E. Wiatt.

George Corbin, ae 33y, widower, farm, s/o
Wm. & Hannah Corbin; Delcey Singleton, ae
27y, d/o Louisa Singleton, father unk; Mar
15 1894 by Rev. Z. Taylor Whiting.

Thomas Bright, ae 21y, farm, s/o Jos. &
Cinderilla Bright; Mary E. king, ae 21y, d/o
Kitty Whiting, father unk; Mar 21 1894 by
Rev. E. W. Page.

Joshua Driver, ae 24y, carpenter, s/o Add-
ison & Elizabeth Collier Driver; Virginia
Lemon, ae 21y, d/o Thos. & Amanda Easter
Lemon; Mar 28 1894 by Rev. John W. Booth.

John S. Singleton, ae 23y, oyster and
farm, s/o Wm. R. & Sarah F. Callis Singleton; Virginia S. Wyatt, ae 22y, d/o Hugh &
Betty Singleton Wyatt; Apr 1 1894 by Rev. W.
E. Wiatt.

John Washington, ae 43y, widower, farm,
s/o Geo. & Susan Washington; Louisa Morriss,
ae 43y, widow, d/o John & Martha Hall; Apr 4
1894 by Rev. John W. Booth.

John J. Brown, ae 24y, sailor, s/o Seymour
& Sarah J. Hogg Brown; Martha E. Thomas, ae
20y, d/o Washington & Harriet Thomas; Apr 19
1894 by Rev. R. A. Folks.

William H. Chapman, ae 27y, farm, s/o
Davy & Rosa Chapman; Alice Greene, ae 24y,
d/o Soloman & Fanny Williams Greene; Apr 19
1894 by Rev. John W. booth.

James F. Walker, ae 26y, teacher, s/o
Thos. & Grace Hubbard Walker; Rebecca A.
Jones, ae 24y, d/o Chas. H. & Agnes Curry
Jones; Apr 25 1894 by Rev. A. T. Gayle.

Jefferson D. Stubbs, ae 25y, farm, s/o
Jas. N. & Eliza Medlicott Stubbs; Emma E.
Coleman, ae 23y, d/o Rich'd C. & Bella G.
Anderson Coleman; Apr 25 1894 by Rev. J. D.
Hanks.

John R. Howlett, ae 21y, sailor, s/o W.
H. & E. Walden Howlett; Laura Wilkins, ae
21y, d/o Nathan & F. A. Moore Wilkins; May 6
1894 by Rev. J. D. Hank.

Alexander Davis, ae 56y, widower, laborer, s/o Joe & Sally Davis; Becky Dabney, ae 52y, widow, d/o Jos. & Mary Smith; May 10 1894 by Rev. John W. Booth.

Robert S. Kemp, ae 25y, farm, s/o Jas. & Lucy A. Carney Kemp; Lulie Hodges, ae 23y, d/o John L. & Eliza Hodges; May 17 1894 by Rev. Charles A. Raymond.

William H. Gibbs, ae 23y, sailor, s/o W. H. & Matilda N. Croswell; Florence F. Hogg, ae 19y, d/o Jas. R. & Mary C. Townsend Hogg; May 24 1894 by Rev. R. A. Folkes.

Alexander Hogg, ae 27y, fisherman, s/o Andrew & Rebecca Howard Hogg; Betty Heywood, ae 19y, d/o John & Eliza Hogg Heywood; May 27 1894 by Rev. Paul Bradley.

James Dabney, ae 25y, farm, s/o Jas. & Betty Dabney; Patty Roberson, ae 20y, d/o Sterling & Julia Monkins Roberson; May 31 1894 by Rev. Z. Taylor Whiting.

William Thomas Newton, ae 28y, oyster, s/o Thos. & Elizabeth Jenkins Newton; Maggie Mae Jenkins, ae 17y. d/o John & Lucy Shack-elford Jenkins; June 6 1894 by Rev. Paul Bradley.

Harry Turner, ae 27y, farm, s/o Henry & Roana Turner; Ida Griffin, ae 23y, d/o Cyrus & Maria Griffin; June 14 1894 by Rev. Z. Taylor Whiting.

Thomas F. Anderton, ae 28y, oyster, s/o Jas. T. & Sarah M. Elliott Anderton; Nora B. Rowe, ae 24y, d/o Edward C. & Mary S. Williams Rowe; June 21 1894 by Rev. R. A. Folks.

Robert T. Braxton, ae 24y, widower, farm, s/o Wm. & Ella Braxton; Missouri A. Burrell, ae 19y, d/o Wm. & Mary Burrell; July 2 1894 by Rev. John W. Booth.

James Jenkins, ae 22y, farm, s/o J. K. & Frances Jenkins; Alice Jenkins, ae 17y, d/o Warner & Frances West Jenkins; July 19 1894 by Rev. R. A. Folkes.

George W. Ross, ae 28y, farm, of Dorchester Co MD, s/o Harry & Mary Ross; Susie Small, ae 21y, d/o Randal & Dinah Small; Aug 1 1894 by Rev. Frank Page.

Decatur T. Hogg, ae 24y, farm, s/o Wm. & Sarah Foster Hogg; Nannie L. Thomas, ae 19y, d/o John W. & Josephine Thomas; Aug 2 1894 by Rev. R. A. Folkes.

John Mathias, ae 34y, widower, farm, s/o Britton & Molly Mathias; Lorena Carter, ae 25y, d/o Edward & Mary Carter; Aug 7 1894 by Rev. A. T. Gayle.

Charles R.Thomas, ae 35y, fisherman, s/o Jas. W. & Mary J. Walker Thomas; Georgianna A. Hogg, ae 25y, d/o Andrew & Rebecca Howard Hogg; Aug 9 1894 by Rev. R. A. Folks.

Robert Evans, ae 24y, farm, s/o Wash & Harriet Evans; Rosa Williams, ae 22y, d/o John & Mary Williams; July 5 1894 by Rev. E. W. Page.

Cornelius Smith, ae 21y, farm, of Lancaster Co VA, s/o Jas. & Sarah A. Griffith Smith; Charlotte Tazewell, ae 17y, d/o Wm. Tazewell & Sarah Carter; July 19 1894 by Rev. E. W. Page.

Prosser Johnson, ae 25y, farm, s/o Henry & Mary Johnson; Alice Thomas, ae 21y, d/o Moses & Mary Thomas; Aug 2 1894 by Rev. E. W. Page.

Charles E. Brooks, ae 26y, laborer, s/o Gilbert & Caroline Bright Brooks; Phoebe R. Washington, d/o Jolly & Martha Bright Washington; Sept 6 1894 by Rev. E. W. Page.

C. L. Palmer, ae 44y, widower, merchant, s/o Lewis & Martha Green Palmer; Bettie South, d/o John L. & Harriet South; Sept 13 1894 by Rev. W. E. Wiatt.

James H. Hall, ae 24y, oyster, s/o A. H. & Caroline Hogg Hall; Mary A. Smith, ae 18y, d/o Geo. W. & Mary Taylor Smith; Sept 16 1894 by Rev. R. A. Folks.

Corbin G. Waller, ae 24y, of Norfolk VA, s/o Matthew & Mary T. Waller; Fannie M. Byrd, ae 24y, d/o R. C. & Ann Garden Byrd; Sept 18 1894 by Rev. Wm. B. Lee.

Russell A. Stubblefield, ae 26y, farm, s/o W. E. & Minerva Leavitt Stubblefield; Minnie L. Dutton, ae 19y, d/o P. & Sarah A. Dutton; Sept 19 1894 by Rev. Wm. E. Wiatt.

Delaware Page, ae 24y, waterman, s/o Rich Page & Eliza Price; Mary Lewis, ae 27y, widow, d/o Jim & Lizzie Fleming; Sept 23 1894 by Rev. E. W. Page.

Alexander Banks, ae 27y, oyster, s/o Wm. & Catharine Taylor Banks; Mary Ransone, ae 27y, widow, d/o Rob't Lewis & Mary Howard; Sept 22 1894 by Rev. J. W. Booth.

Norwood Jones, ae 23y, machinist, of Elizabeth Co VA, s/o Wm. F. & Emily F. Lowery Jones; Emily E. Brown, ae 21y, d/o Junius B. & Emily Roane Brown; Sept 25 1894 by Rev. Wm. B. Lee.

Benja. F. Brown, ae 25y, oyster, s/o John A. & M. J. West Brown; Mollie A. Jenkins, ae 21y, d/o W. T. & Melvina West Jenkins; Sept 25 1894 by Rev. Wm. B. Lee.

Armistead Jones, ae 30y, laborer, s/o Isaac & Charlotte Thos. Jones; Emily Grevious, ae 24y, d/o Philip & Maria Perrin Grevious; Sept 26 1894 by Rev. E. W. Page.

Thaddeus Ernest Duval, ae 25y, clerk, s/o John R. & Laura C. Paguad Duval; Alice Synnor Tabb, ae 24y, d/o John Tabb & Judith Logan Coleman; Oct 10 1894 by Rev. Wm. B. Lee.

Thomas M. Goode, ae 23y, sailor, of Middlesex Co VA, s/o Rich'd & Drusilla Witch Goode; Rachel Whitaker, ae 21y, d/o Jas. & Lucy Stokes Whitaker; Oct 14 1894 by Rev. Z. Taylor Whiting.

Jerry P. Gregory, ae 30y, minister, of King and Queen Co VA, s/o Jerry M. & Maria Singleton Gregory; Nelly L. Evans, ae 24y, of Mathews Co VA, d/o Soloman Evans & Martha A. Lee; Oct 17 1894 by Rev. E. W. Page.

Charles West, ae 22y, oyster, s/o John & Mary S. Sparrow West; Courtney West, ae 21y, d/o Wm. & Sarah Brown West; Dec 11 1894 by Rev. A. N. Lambert.

Boswell Machen Roy, ae 23y, farm, s/o Churchill & Eliza Owens Roy; Lola Smith Haynes, ae 18y, d/o W. L. & Louisa Thomas Haynes; Dec 11 1894 by Rev. T. O. Edwards.

Claudious Humphrey, ae 39y, widower, farm, of Somerset Co MD, s/o W. E. & Jane Dashield Humphrey; Elizabeth B. Leavitt, ae 23y, d/o Franklin & Emiline Pointer Leavitt; Dec 4 1894 by Rev. J. D. Hank.

Thos. Jefferson Farinholt, ae 36y, farm, of New Kent Co VA, s/o Rob't A. & Martha Simcoe Farinholt; Elizabeth C. Duval, ae 33y, d/o John R. & Laura C. Pagurd duval; Nov 7 1894 by Rev. J. D. Hank.

Rob't C. Armstrong, ae 24y, farm, s/o Harry & Lucy Waller Armstrong; Hester Laramore, ae 19y, d/o John & Betty Armstead Laramore; Oct 23 1894 by Rev. A. T. Gayle.

Henry Ames Williams, ae 32y, bank cashier, of Albemarle co VA, s/o John Henry & Elizabeth Victoria Smith Williams; Elizabeth Maud Dimmock, ae 25y, d/o Chas. Henry & Elizabeth Lewis Selden Dimmock; Oct 24 1894 by Rev. Wm. B. Lee.

Simon Stokes, ae 40y, widower, oyster, s/o C. & Ann Stokes; Lizzie James, ae 22y, d/o Henry & Lona James; Nov 11 1894 by Rev. E. W. Page.

Samuel M. Hibble, ae 21y, farm, s/o Geo. W. & Martha H. Walker Hibble; Cora Taylor, ae 21y, d/o Wm. C. Taylor, mother unk; Dec 19 1894 by Rev. W. E. Wiatt.

Seth Johnston, ae 21y, oyster, s/o Wise & Lucy Johnston; Lizzie Davis, ae 17y, d/o Isaac & Fanny Taliaferro Davis; Dec 20 1894 by Rev. Reuben Berkeley.

Christopher Morris, ae 23y, widower, farm, s/o Jones & Kesiah Morriss; Elizabeth Cooke, ae 23y, widow, d/o Thos. & Mary Davenport; dec 20 1894 by Rev. Reuben Berkeley.

James Page, ae 70y, widower, carpenter, s/o Jas. Taliaferro, mother unk; Maria Green, ae 70y, widow, parents unk; Dec 20 1894 by Rev. E. W. Page.

William H. Evans, ae 23y, farm, s/o Jas. & Fanny Whiting; Julia Carter, ae 23t, d/o Andrew & Mary Carter; Dec 23 1894 by Rev. A. T. Gayle.

Iverson Whiting, ae 30y, widower, farm, s/o Davy & Mary Whiting; Mary A. cooke, ae 23y, d/o Anthony & Lucy E. cooke; Dec 23 1894 by Rev. John W. Booth.

Joseph Cooke, ae 45y, widower, farm, s/o Wm. & Tisha Cooke; Hester Selden, ae 40y, widow, d/o Walker & Judy Holmes; Dec 23 1894 by Rev. John W. Booth.

Stephen F. Whiting, ae 21y, farm, s/o John
& Mary Whiting; Lucy Graves, ae 21y, d/o Wm.
& Betty Graves; Dec 20 1894 by Rev. E. W.
Page.

John Walker, ae 48y, widower, farm, s/o
Henry & Mary Walker; Carrie Davis, ae 21y,
d/o Augustine & Julia Davis; Dec 23 1894 by
Rev. R. J. Hall.

William Bluford, ae 40y, widower, farm,
s/o Thos. & Martha Bluford; Sarah Kelly, ae
26y, d/o John & martha Kelly; Dec 25 1894 by
Rev. James H. Smith.

Carter E. Frazier, ae 26y, farm, s/o John
& Martha Frazier; Martha Tabb, ae 19y, d/o
Henry & Amanda Tabb; Dec 28 1894 by Rev. E.
W. Page.

Frank Harriss, ae 21y, farm, s/o Adam &
Elizabeth Harriss; Bettie Deadman, ae 18y,
d/o Pendleton & Mary Gwynn Deadman; Dec 25
1894 by Rev. J. H. Curtis.

Isaiah Wormley, ae 21y, farm, of KIng and
 Queen Co VA, s/o Edmond & Fannie A. Daven-
port Wormley; Alberta Davenport, ae 18y, d/o
Cornelius & Julanna Davenport; Dec 25 1894 by
Rev. John W. Booth.

William S. Brown, ae 28y, sailor, s/o
John & Elizabeth Carney Brown; Laura Bristow,
ae 19y, s/o Rich'd & Nannie Chapman Bristow;
Dec 26 1894 by Rev. R. A. Folkes.

Isaac K. Ward, ae 26y, miller, of Key West
N. J, s/o Isaac D. & Emma Forrest Ward; Nellie
Lee Rowe, ae 23y, d/o J. H. & Fanny C. Hall
Rowe; Dec 26 1894 by Rev. Geo. H. McFaden.

Fred Redmond, ae 38y, widower, farm, of
St. Mary's Co MD, s/o Thos. S. & Matilda
Redmond; Jane Brushwood, ae 40y, widow, d/o
Henry & Elizabeth Hobday; Dec 26 1894 by Rev.
Edgar A. Potts.

J. D. Ross, ae 26y, oyster, s/o Harrison &
Sarah Cooke Ross; Ida Thomas, ae 22y, d/o
Mary Thomas, father unk; Dec 26 1894 by Rev.
Z. Taylor Whiting.

Richard P. Cooke, ae 28y, oyster, s/o
John & Lucy Tonkins Cooke; Pinky Ann Dixon,
ae 21y, d/o John & Bunch Washington Dixon;
Dec 26 1894 by Rev. Z. Taylor Whiting.

Robert Whiting, ae 23y, waiter, s/o Edmund & Jane Whiting; Dinah Steadman, ae 18y, d/o Sam'l & Fanny Steadman; Dec 27 1894 by Rev. Wm. B. Lee.

L. H. Proctor, ae 28y, mechanic, s/o Thos. J. & Lucretia Fletcher Proctor; Laura E. Burke, ae 21y, d/o Jeff T. & Eliza F. Driscell Burke; Dec 27 1894 by Rev. Geo. H. McFaden.

Thomas Johnson, ae 25y, oyster, s/o Rich'd & Sally Moody Johnson; Alice Paine, ae 21y, d/o Rob't & Henrietta Bright Paine; Dec 27 1894 by Rev. E. W. PAge.

William James, ae 22y, oyster, s/o Henry & Barbara James; Sarah Cooke, ae 21y, d/o Rob't & Betsy Cooke; Dec 27 1894 by Rev. E. W. Page.

Albert Green, ae 24y, farm, s/o Wm. & Maria Green; Eliza Thomas, ae 35y, d/o Henry & Hester Thomas; July 7 1894 by Rev. E. W. Page.

Benjamin F. Lindsay, ae 22y, painter, s/o B. F. & Julia T. Blasingham Lindsay; Susie V. Williams, ae 18y, d/o E. A. & Dolly Williams; Jan 1 1895 by Rev. Wm. E. Wiatt.

Thomas H. Corbin, ae 38y, widower, col'rd, farm, s/o Fountain & Lucy Orrell Corbin; Matilda Thomas, ae 26y, col'rd, d/o Moses & Mary Thomas; Jan 3 1895 by Rev. Wm. Thomas.

Clyde Bunting Jr, ae 25y, farm, s/o S. C. & M. E. Trader Bunting; Lamie Corson, ae 24y, d/o Cornelius & Sarah E. Corson; Jan 9 1895 by Rev. J. E. Potts.

Edward W. Farinholt, ae 30y, merchant, of King and Queen Co VA, s/o Davy & Mary Edwards Farinholt; Virginia Farinholt, ae 21y, d/o John L. & Georgia Roane Farinholt; Jan 15 1895 by Rev. J. E. Potts.

Edward Payne, ae 24y, col'rd, oyster, s/o Rob't & Henrietta Bright Payne; Lizzie Harris, ae 19y, col'rd, d/o Major & Adelaide Washington Harris; Jan 14 1895 by Rev. E. W. Page.

Coleman Burrell, ae 40y, col'rd, widower, farm, s/o Major & Edith Burrell; Letitia Johnston, ae 21y, col'rd, d/o Soloman & Lucy Lewis; Jan 22 1895 by Rev. Z. T. Whiting.

George Johnson, ae 23y, col'rd, oyster,
s/o Wm. & Lucy A. Johnson; Mary Ann Morris,
ae 18y, col'rd, d/o Sarah Jane Scott, father
unk; Jan 24 1895 by Rev. John W. Booth.

Emanuel Jones, ae 28y, col'rd, oyster,
s/o Wm. & Mary Jones; Elnora Gregory, ae
28y, col'rd, d/o Jas. & Betsy Gregory; Jan 27
1895 by Rev. A. T. Gayle.

Harrison Foster, ae 22y, col'rd, laborer,
of Middlesex Co VA, s/o Wallace & Fanny
Braxton Foster; Ellen King, ae 19y, col'rd,
d/o Geo. & Elizabeth Dolavier King; Jan 27
1895 by Rev. Frank Page.

Frank Lewis, ae 47y, col'rd, widower, of
Mathews Co VA, s/o Jackson & Maria Brooks
Lewis; Julia Wood, ae 47y, col'rd. widow,
d/o Rev. & mary Robson; Feb 3 1895 by Rev.
A. T. Gayle.

Morgan Castlow, ae 27y, farm, of King and
Queen Co VA, s/o Wm. H, mother unk; Cassy
Soles, ae 22y, d/o John & Cordelia Walker
Soles; Feb 14 1895 by Rev. J. E. Potts.

Benjamin Scott, ae 21y, col'rd, oyster,
s/o Jas. & Lucy Jackson Scott; Susan Laws,
ae 19y, col'rd, d/o Cella Laws, father unk;
Feb 14 1895 by Rev. Wm. B. Lee.

Benjamin Hobday, ae 26y, col'rd, oyster,
s/o John & Nancy Ransone Hobday; Ida A.
Cooke, ae 25y, col'rd, d/o Barnaby & Esther
Smith Cooke; Feb 27 1895 by Rev. Wm. Thomas.

John T, Lemon, ae 50y, widower, col'rd,
farm, s/o Jas. & Patsy Lemon; C. Ellen
Shorter, ae 21y, col'rd, d/o Wm. & Mary E.
Morriss Shorter; Feb 28 1895 by Rev. John W.
Booth.

James Harriss, ae 43y, widower, col'rd,
farm, s/o Rebecca Harriss, father unk; Mary
Holmes, ae 25y, col'rd, d/o Chas. & Lena
Holmes; Mar 5 1895 by Rev. J. E. Potts.

William J. Ware Jr, ae 21y, clerk, s/o W.
S. & Fannie B. Street Ware, of Petersburg
VA; Susan Adelaide Minor, ae 21y, d/o Thos.
J. & Josie A. Minor; Mar 27 1895 by Rev. R.
A. Folkes.

Silas H. Teagle, ae 25y, farm, s/o John &
Martha Hall Teagle; Icenola Proctor, ae 24y,
d/o T. J. & Lucretia Fletcher Proctor; Apr 3
1895 by Rev. Geo. H. McFaden.

Charles Muse, ae 24y, col'rd, laborer, of Essex Co VA, s/o Alex & Julia Brokenborough Muse; Martha Wilson, ae 26y, col'rd, d/o Jas. & Lucy Simon Wilson; Mar 28 1895 by Rev. J. W. Booth.

James Robins, ae 52y, widower, farm, of Mathews Co VA, s/o Wm. & Mary Johnston Robins; Alice Rowe, ae 21y, d/o Levi & Julia A. West Rowe; Apr 4 1895 by Rev. Geo. H. McFaden.

Joseph T. Willis, ae 33y, widower, sailor, s/o John & Mary E. Hall Willis; Dorothy Thrift, ae 18y, d/o Hiram & Mary T. Mason Thrift; Apr 3 1895 by Rev. J. E. Potts.

Charles Pendleton, ae 24y, col'rd, oyster, s/o Chas. & Martha Pendleton; Margaret Gregory, ae 20y, col'rd, d/o Patsy Gregory, father unk; Apr 3 1895 by Rev. E. W. Page.

Alexander B. Singleton, ae 26y, farm, s/o Wm. R. & Sarah T. Callis Singleton; Nannie Jarvis, ae 25y, d/o Geo. R. C. & Jane B. Singleton Jarvis; Apr 11 1895 by Rev. Wm. E. Wiatt.

William Henry Boston, ae 21y, col'rd, farm, s/o Stephen & Susan Boston; Louisa Patterson, ae 21y, col'rd, d/o Wm. & Martha Patterson; Apr 21 1895 by Rev. Frank Page.

James Carter, ae 22y, col'rd, farm, s/o Gabriel & Eley Carter; Sarah B. Whiting, ae 21y, col'rd, d/o Thos. J. & Sarah Whiting; Apr 24 1895 by Rev. Z. Taylor Whiting.

Lewis Taylor, ae 24y, col'rd, oyster, s/o John & Ann Braxton Taylor; Lucy Smith, ae 19y, col'rd, d/o John & Clara Williams Smith; Apr 28 1895 by Rev. J. W. Booth.

Godfrey Cooke, ae 29y, col'rd, farm, s/o Frank & A. Seymour Cooke; Alice Walker, ae 22y, col'rd, d/o Thos. & Grace Walker; Apr 30 1895 by Rev. Wm. B. Lee.

Joshua Smith, ae 23y, col'rd, oyster, s/o Rachel Smith, father unk; Martha Hundley, ae 21y, col'rd, d/o Wm. & Mary Washington Hundley; May 2 1895 by Rev.Z. Taylor Booth.

Jos. W. Rilee, ae 18y, farm, s/o John M. & Caroline Foster Rilee; Colloman Brown, ae 24y, widow, d/o Wm. & Anna Tillage; May 12 1895 by Rev. G. H. McFaden.

Samuel Banks, ae 21y, col'rd, oyster, s/o
Wm. & Clara Banks; Silvy Jones, ae 21y,
col'rd, d/o Chas. & Susan Jones; May 11 1895
by Rev. A. T. Gayle.

James T. Sterling, ae 22y, oyster, s/o
Thos. & Mollie Waddell Sterling; Ida B.
Deal, ae 20y, d/o Geo. W. & Laura T. Wil-
liams Deal; May 15 1895 by Rev. A. N.
Lamberth.

John Lancaster, ae 21y, col'rd, farm, s/o
Peter & Easter Lancaster; Sarah Evans, ae
20y, d/o Ransone & Frances Baytop Evans; May
19 1895 by Rev. John W. Booth.

Henry L. Williams, ae 24y, col'rd, farm,
s/o Geo. & Sylvia A. tabb Williams; Emma
Jane Taylor, ae 24y, col'rd, d/o John H. &
Ann Braxton Taylor; May 19 1895 by Rev. Z.
Taylor Whiting.

John Armstead Rowe, ae 28y, farm, s/o
John F. & Martha T. Smith Rowe; Fanny E.
Seawell, ae 21y, d/o Watt W. & Janie R. Sea-
well; May 28 1895 by Rev. R. A. Folkes.

John W. H. Smith, ae 28y, col'rd, farm,
s/o Hester Gayle, father unk; Margaret
Smith, ae 28y, col'rd, d/o Isaac & Charlotte
Dillard; May 30 1895 by Rev. Jos. E. Potts.

Thomas Leonard Willett, ae 27y, farm, s/o
Jessie T. & Sarah Cobb Willett; Helen Aurelis
Williams, ae 19y, d/o Wm. Hunter & Angelina
Clements Williams; May 23 1895 by Rev. W. T.
Haynes.

J. S. Thornton, ae, 32y, farm, s/o J. A.
B. & Sarah E. Thornton; M. C. Richardson, ae
25y, d/o Theo & Susan Hayes Richardson; June
8 1895 by Rev. R. A. Folkes.

Benjamin Allston, ae 35y, col'rd, cook
and waiter, s/o John & M. Allston; Fanny
Stokes, ae 22y, col'rd, d/o Simon & Mary
Stokes; June 3 1895 by Rev. Wm. B. Lee.

Dunmore Wiatt, ae 50y, widower, col'rd.
carpenter, s/o Tom & Sally Wiatt; Martha A.
Whiting, ae 25y, col'rd, d/o Peter & Agnes
Cooke; June 6 1895 by Rev. J. W. Booth.

William C. Keys, ae 23y, oyster, s/o Wm.
& Fannie Massie Keyes; Lucy Jane Jenkins, ae
18y, d/o Wm. T. & Lorena West Jenkins; June
6 1895 by rev. R. A. Folkes.

Christopher Freeman, ae 22y, oyster; col'rd, Lelia Moody, ae 21y, col'rd; June 9 1895.

Alfred Major, ae 53y, widower, farm, of Halifax Co VA, s/o Jack & Dicy Major; Laura Lemon, ae 54y, widow, col'rd, d/o Geo. Carter, mother unk; June 10 1895 by Rev. J. E. Potts.

Robert F. gayle, ae 27y, col'rd, oyster, s/o Moses & Percilla Holmes Gayle; Harriet Lewis, ae 21y, col'rd, d/o Henry & Harriet Allmond Lewis; June 9 1895 by Rev. Z. Taylor Whiting.

Thomas E. Rowe, ae 23y, farm, s/o J. D. & Emma Robins Rowe; Blanche McLane, ae 19y, d/o Robert & Nannie Robins McLane; June 16 1895 by Rev. R. A. Folkes.

John Ellis, ae 21y, col'rd, farm, s/o Cain & Fanny Ellis; Fanny Cully, ae 21y, col'rd, d/o Jack & Joan Cully; Jan 13 1887 by Rev. John Wm. Booth.

INDEX

STUBBS (Continued)
  188 190 191 209 213 227
  228 232 234 240 258 273
  290 291 296 305 306
STURGES, 43 62 85 143 159
  250 261 288
SUITER, 120
SUMMERS, 77
SUMMERSON, 12 37
SUTTON, 187 223 257
SWANN, 31
TABB, 18 47 48 51 62 70 78
  81 92 95 105 107 120 148
  150 169 179 180 188 192
  201 208 225 235 241 260
  261 264 289 290 309 311
  315
TALBOT, 49
TALIAFERRO, 17 43 44 45 47
  54 58 61 80 92 96 100 104
  108 112 120 136 140 150
  153 160 182 190 206 208
  209 213 215 238 240 248
  250 256 260 262 268 277
  281 287 290 299 300 303
  305 310
TATTERSON, 288
TAYLER, 99
TAYLOR, 30 48 49 51 56 71
  81 99 105 111 127 134 158
  161 167 168 173 175 183
  219 227 231 233-241 243
  246-250 252 255 256 262
  266 272 274 276 288 294
  295 297 302 308 309 310
  314 315
TAZEWELL, 43 59 87 91 120
  131 140 151 224 239 247
  279 308
TAZWELL, 277
TEAGLE, 20 29 55 71 103 126
  202 216 223 247 274 288
  293 304 313
TEMPLE, 84 135
TEMPLEMAN, 67 122 147 178
  188 217
TERRELL, 71
THAIS, 160
THAWLEY, 54 84
THIAS, 53 70 160 264
THOMAS, 5 10 15 19 22 35 39
  40 44 49 64 75 81 92 98
  104 108 110 118 119 123-
  125 129 131-134 137 147
  149 151 159 163-168 170
  174 175 177 178-180 182

THOMAS (Continued)
  183 187-189 195 196 199
  205 207 212 215 222 223
  226 227 229 231 233 235
  238 239 246 251 253 256
  261 265 269 271 275 278
  279 282 284 289 290 303
  305 306 308 309 311-313
THOMPSON, 14 19 28 59 97
  109 170 185 187 253 288
THOMSON, 62
THORNTON, 13 33 45 47 51 54
  58 65 72 73 84 87 88 91 94
  95 97 99 109 110 118-121
  127 128 138 143 144 147
  151 156 158 162 175 177
  182 186 189 191 197 201
  202 217 225 227 229 232
  235 242 244 250 268 270
  283 290 292 297 315
THRIFT, 3 12 23 29 32 39 43
  45 87 102 113 134 181 183
  189 191 194 221 222 224
  247 250 257 260 265 271
  275 296 297 314
THROCKMORTON, 146
THRUSTON, 17 54 100 105 112
  204 231 276 279 299
THURSTON, 3 144 183
TIBBS, 156 212 303
TILEY, 180
TILLAGE, 122 150 157 169
  181 182 195 202 220 243
  261 314
TILLEDGE, 5 39
TILLEGE, 8
TILMAN, 85 251
TILMON, 85 225
TINSLEY, 144 170
TODD, 30 59 89 135 139 198
  204 233 244 254 264 300
TOMKINS, 131
TOMPKINS, 60 232
TONKINS, 124 167 229 297
  311
TOWE, 167
TOWILL, 21
TOWNS, 126
TOWNSEND, 40 152 294 307
TOWNSHEND, 22
TRADER, 266 312
TRAVERS, 129 208 236 278
  280 290
TRAVILLIAN, 8
TRAVIS, 138 240
TREAT, 169

www.ingramcontent.com/pod-product-compliance
Lightning Source LLC
Chambersburg PA
CBHW070551270326
41926CB00013B/2274